Crime and Justice in America

Crime and Justice in America
An Introduction to Criminal Justice

Joycelyn M. Pollock

Second Edition

AMSTERDAM • BOSTON • HEIDELBERG • LONDON
NEW YORK • OXFORD • PARIS • SAN DIEGO
SAN FRANCISCO • SINGAPORE • SYDNEY • TOKYO

Anderson Publishing is an imprint of Elsevier

ELSEVIER

Anderson Pulishing is an imprint of Elsevier
225 Wyman Street, Waltham, MA 02451, USA
Elsevier, The Boulevard, Langford Lane, Kidlington, Oxford, OX5 1GB, UK

Library of Congress Control Number: 2011901134

British Library Cataloguing-in-Publication Data
A catalogue record for this book is available from the British Library.

ISBN: 978-1-4377-3512-3

For information on all Anderson Publishing publications
visit our Web site at www.elsevierdirect.com

Printed in China

11 12 13 14 9 8 7 6 5 4 3 2 1

To Greg and Eric, as always . . .

Contents

Section 3   **The Law as Social Control**

Preface and Acknowledgments

Is there a need for yet another Introduction to Criminal Justice book? I think there is and I hope this book meets that need. This textbook has been developed in response to a perceived need for a shorter, less expensive, introductory text for instructors who desire an alternative to the comprehensive textbooks that are currently available. I have attempted to provide the "bare bones" of theory, law, and organizational descriptions without going into too much detail in any area. This second edition retains the same chapters and basic organization of the first edition.

The most unique characteristic of this text, I believe, is the "In the State of…" exercises that help the instructor adapt the text to a particular state. Too often, it seems, students become confused when textbook descriptions do not match their own state's criminal justice system. These exercises allow instructors to have students keep a notebook of these completed exercises so they can have a reference to understand the system in their own state.

Another characteristic of the book that sets it apart from some other textbooks is the inclusion of women and minorities in each chapter, rather than relegating relevant information to a single chapter. I believe this provides a more cohesive treatment of the subject of minorities and women in the criminal justice system and offers it in a way that is better utilized and understood than the single-chapter method.

I have also attempted to provide a unifying theme of due process throughout the book, and as it relates to each subsystem of the criminal justice system. Since law is the bedrock of the system, it has been given a more prominent emphasis here than perhaps in other textbooks. The concept of due process is especially relevant to current discussions concerning the war on terrorism; thus, I include a discussion of current issues in the final chapter. I have also discussed the goals and responsibilities of local law enforcement in the war on terrorism.

In this second edition, I have updated all statistics and provided two new heuristic elements: "Focus on Crime" boxes provide a "snapshot" of certain types of crimes to help students understand these specific crimes. Another addition is the "Breaking News" boxes, which have been provided to highlight current news events that are especially relevant to discussions of crime and justice.

I must thank Mickey Braswell for the idea and opportunity to create this book and appreciate the opportunity to improve it in a second edition. He provided the impetus and guidance for the development of the text and allowed me the opportunity to create it. He read and offered guidance on early drafts of the chapters and the book has benefited from his advice. I most sincerely thank him for his vision, insights, and guidance along the way. It has been a real honor to work and become friends with Mickey and Susan Braswell and everyone at Anderson over the years, and I am extremely grateful for the friendship and support that has come my way.

I want to thank the folks at Anderson/Elsevier for their assistance in the production of this book. Elisabeth Ebben has, as always, improved the book considerably with her ideas and skills. Sarah Binns at Elsevier has also been instrumental in shepherding the text to completion.

I want to also thank those individuals who have communicated with me regarding this text. Thanks to all of you who have emailed and/or spoken with me at conferences about the content. I encourage any instructor using this book to contact me with criticisms or suggestions for improvement. I welcome your contribution: jp12@txstate.edu.

The Criminal Justice System as Social Control

CHAPTER 1

Criminal Justice as Social Control

WHAT YOU NEED TO KNOW

- Television presents a highly artificial perspective of crime, criminals, and the criminal justice system.
- Common law is the compilation of early decisions by magistrates in England. Common law is the basis of the legal system in the United States.
- Felonies are usually serious crimes punishable by more than a year in prison and misdemeanors are less serious crimes punishable by up to a year in jail (in most states).
- Police power is the power to make laws. The federal government's ability to create law is limited to the enumerated powers as stated in Article I of the Constitution. All other police power resides in the states.
- The "flowchart" of the criminal justice system starts with arrest and ends with release. Certain basic steps are common to all states.
- Expenditures for the criminal justice system have been increasing even though crime has been on the decline since the mid-1990s.
- An ideology is a body of doctrines or beliefs that guide an individual or group. Two ideologies relevant to criminal justice issues are the crime control and due process ideologies.

CONTENTS

Blood, bloated corpses, high-speed chases, true-blue detectives, and evil criminals who revel in their wickedness are the images of crime on television. They are not reality. Criminal justice became one of the fastest-growing majors on college campuses in the 1980s and 1990s. When the *CSI* shows first appeared on television in 2000, a profession that had been arcane and "geeky" became a hot new occupational interest. Forensic investigation majors have now been created in many universities to tap the huge market of interested students, many of whom may not realize that crime scene analysts typically have science degrees and if you didn't enjoy your high school biology or chemistry class, it may not be the profession for you. The definition of **forensic science** is "science that serves the court"; in other words, *forensic* is an adjective that is used to describe something as being related to the legal system. Some of the applications of the term are shown in Box 1.1.

BOX 1.1 WHAT ARE FORENSICS?

Forensic is an adjective used to describe something as related to the legal system. A forensic pathologist is someone who conducts autopsies to determine cause of death; a forensic scientist uses scientific methods to answer questions about crime; a forensic handwriting analyst is called upon to testify in forgery or fraud cases, and so on. You might remember that your high school debate class also might have used the word *forensics*, which has a second meaning of "the art or study of debate." This is because the root of the word comes from the Latin word *forensis*, meaning "forum." Legal cases were tried in front of a forum of citizens who decided guilt or innocence based on the skill of the orator who defended the guilty, and thus the connection between the two uses of the word.

Before the *CSI* shows, the television series *Law and Order* introduced countless viewers to the criminal justice system via the perspective of the police and the prosecutors. Many viewers today know most of what they know about the criminal justice system through these and other television series. This is not necessarily a new trend. In earlier decades, *Adam 12*, a series about two LAPD officers, depicted them reciting the *Miranda* warning to arrestees almost every week. Before long, we all knew that: "You have the right to remain silent. If you give up that right, anything you say can and will be used against you in a court of law. You have the right to an attorney, and if you cannot afford one, one will be appointed for you." Viewers may not have known where the *Miranda* warnings came from, or when police needed to recite them, but they remembered the warning in the same way they did advertising jingles for chewing gum or coffee. Some officers ruefully admit that, in some ways, the most realistic police show was *Barney Miller*, a comedy/drama about New York City police detectives who dealt with a steady stream of strange and humorous victims and offenders, interspersed with mundane stories about the detectives' personal lives.

Reality television offers viewers a supposedly realistic glimpse of the criminal justice system. From the first show *Cops* to today's *48 Hours Mystery, American Justice, Dateline NBC,* and the *Forensic Files,* these programs present an edited version of reality. There is even a cable network called truTV (formerly Courtroom Television Network) devoted to crime and justice programs. What spurs our fascination for crime? Every decade of television has had its share of crime drama shows. Some of these are displayed in Box 1.2. In fact, crime dramas with either police officers or attorneys seem to be perennial favorites

BOX 1.2 TELEVISION CRIME DRAMAS

1960s: Perry Mason, N.Y.P.D., Dragnet, Mannix, Felony Squad, Scales of Justice, Burke's Law, For the People

1970s: Adam 12, CHIPs, Barney Miller, Baretta, Columbo, Hawaii Five-0, Mod Squad, Quincy, M.E., Starsky & Hutch, Streets of San Francisco, Police Woman, Serpico, The D.A., The Guardians, Sword of Justice, The Blue Knight, McMillan and Wife, Owen Marshall, Counselor at Law, The Rookies, Police Story, McCloud, S.W.A.T.

1980s: Cagney & Lacey, Hill Street Blues, Miami Vice, Night Court, In the Heat of the Night, L.A. Law, Matlock, McClain's Law, Police Squad, Crime Story, Houston Knights, Mancuso, FBI, True Blue

1990s: Law and Order, N.Y.P.D. Blue, Homicide: Life in the Streets, The Commish, Profiler, High Incident, Murder One, NY Undercover, The Practice, Against the Law, Broken Badges, Equal Justice, Scene of the Crime, Street Justice, Undercover, Bodies of Evidence, Third Watch, Cold Case Squad, The Detectives, Walker, Texas Ranger, JAG, The Wright Verdicts, The Thin Blue Line, The Sentinel, Public Morals, American Justice, Real Stories of the Highway Patrol, Swift Justice

2000s: Texas Justice, The Division, The District, CSI, Crossing Jordan, The Guardian, Law & Order/Criminal Intent, UC: Undercover, Anatomy of a Scene, Just Cause, NCIS, Without a Trace, CSI/Miami, The Shield, The Wire, Bones, Criminal Minds, Cold Case, Boston Legal, Prison Break, CSI/New York, The Closer, Numbers, Shark, Vanished, Justice, Conviction, In Justice, Saving Grace, The Mentalist

among scriptwriters, along with medical dramas. Perhaps these professions are chosen because they are more likely to provide gripping tales of life and death. It is difficult to squeeze nail-biting drama out of a television show about accountants or teachers, for instance.

It is important to remember, however, that these television shows, even the so-called reality shows, may color our perception of reality. For instance, when you ask someone what they think of when you say *crime*, they are probably going to say murder or rape or some violent crime; not a relatively low-dollar property crime, which, in reality, is the most common crime. If you ask who they think of when you say *criminal*, they may think of the murderer or "gangbanger" portrayed on a popular television show, rather than the legions of petty offenders who pass through our courts every day. These perceptions have the power to influence our decision making and opinions about real issues. For instance, when habitual felon or "three strikes" laws are debated, most people believe that they apply only to seriously violent offenders, the type that they see on television generally. In reality, such laws often apply to property offenders, drug offenders, and others of whom voters are not necessarily thinking when they support such laws.

Christopher Meloni portrays Detective Elliot Stabler and Mariska Hargitay portrays Detective Olivia Benson in *Law & Order: Special Victims Unit*. Photo: NBC/NBCU Photo Bank via AP Images

Lawyers and journalists have coined the term "*CSI effect*" to describe the effect this television show has had on criminal court trials and jury deliberation. What seems to be happening is that viewers confuse reality with television and expect that every criminal case should have the type of scientific evidence portrayed in the show. According to anecdotal reports, when prosecutors are unable to present DNA evidence, fingerprints from any type of material, findings from scent identifiers, and so on, jurors may acquit defendants, believing that if the evidence doesn't exist, the case must be weak. Defense attorneys also complain about the show's effect, arguing that jurors believe that scientific evidence is infallible and don't consider human error or bias or even technological weaknesses when such evidence is utilized by the prosecutor. Evidently, the show has even influenced criminals and some police say that criminals are more likely today to pour bleach around crime scenes in an attempt to destroy DNA and trace evidence [1]. In one study to determine if the *CSI* effect really exists, researchers surveyed 1,000 jurors about their viewing habits and expectations regarding evidence. About half of the respondents (46%) expected to see scientific evidence in every type of criminal case, 71% wanted to see fingerprint evidence in breaking and entering cases, and 73% wanted to see DNA evidence in rape cases. About 45% of the juror-respondents watched *Law and Order* and 42% watched *CSI*. Those who did so were also more likely to watch other justice-related television shows. Those who watched crime shows were more likely than those who did not to expect to see scientific evidence; however, if there was victim or witness testimony, the viewers were not less likely than nonviewers to convict. The researchers concluded that there was little evidence, at least from their research, to prove a pervasive *CSI* effect [2]. Other studies have found that lawyers believe there has been an effect on jurors and they have adjusted their trial tactics accordingly, placing more focus on scientific evidence. Interestingly, as the public has become aware of forensic science, the professional criminal justice community has become more skeptical. Forensic evidence has been implicated in more than a dozen wrongful convictions, and a growing number of crime labs have come under scrutiny for shoddy practices or clear bias. In 2010, the National Research Council issued a report titled *Strengthening Forensic Science* that was very critical of some crime labs and certain areas of forensic investigation, such as bite mark analysis [3].

THE FUNCTION OF SOCIAL CONTROL

What is the function of the criminal justice system? You probably said "to punish wrongdoers," and that is partially correct. The underlying function of the system, however, is social control. There are other institutions of society that socialize us and control our behavior. Schools, churches, and neighborhood associations are examples of other institutions of social control. However, sometimes those institutions are unsuccessful in controlling a person's behavior and, when that happens, the criminal justice system steps in.

Every society needs to control the actions of citizens when they threaten the social order. One of the most well-known concepts in philosophy and the sociology of law is the **social contract**. This concept comes out of the work of Thomas Hobbes (1588-1679), John Locke (1632-1704), and Jean-Jacques Rousseau (1712-1778) [4]. According to Hobbes, before civilization, man lived in a "war of all against all" and life was not very pleasant. A more peaceful existence for everyone could only come about if every person agreed to give up the liberty to aggress against others in return for society's protection against aggressors. Rousseau's "social contract" is the idea that citizens agree to abide by the law in return for the law's protection. Of course, it is not really the case that we all consciously agree to such a contract. Our agreement is implicit when we choose to accept the benefits of living within a society. Part of the idea of the social contract is that if we break the law, we have agreed to the consequences; specifically, prosecution and punishment.

The earliest tribal societies had leaders who mediated conflicts and handed down punishment. As society became more complex, layers of authority developed between the king/ruler and the populace, so that even as early as Hammurabi, "laws" were written down to be administered when offenses occurred. In Box 1.3, a few of Hammurabi's laws are presented. Gradually, rudimentary court systems were created, and then, eventually, law enforcement emerged as a public agency (as opposed to private protection paid for by those who could afford it). The emergence of law and law enforcement is a very interesting historical process, and one can see that it is part of the development of any society.

BOX 1.3   THE CODE OF HAMMURABI

Hammurabi was a ruler of Babylon. Hammurabi's reign (1975-1750 BCE) is noted for many things, but one of the greatest is his celebrated code of laws. It is not the earliest code of laws, but one of the most complete. It is also noteworthy in that this ruler made public the entire body of laws, arranged in orderly groups, so that the citizenry would know what was required of them. The code was carved upon a black stone monument, eight feet high, and clearly intended to be in public view. This noted stone was found in the year 1901, not in Babylon, but in a city in the Persian mountains. It consists of 282 laws. A few examples are offered below:

3. If any one bring an accusation of any crime before the elders, and does not prove what he has charged, he shall, if it be a capital offense charged, be put to death.

6. If any one steal the property of a temple or of the court, he shall be put to death, and also the one who receives the stolen thing from him shall be put to death.

8. If any one steal cattle or sheep, or an ass, or a pig or a goat, if it belong to a god or to the court, the thief shall pay 30-fold therefore; if they belonged to a freed man of the king he shall pay 10-fold; if the thief has nothing with which to pay he shall be put to death.

132. If the "finger is pointed" at a man's wife about another man, but she is not caught sleeping with the other man, she shall jump into the river for her husband.

195. If a son strike his father, his hands shall be hewn off.

196. If a man put out the eye of another man, his eye shall be put out.

199. If he put out the eye of a man's slave, or break the bone of a man's slave, he shall pay one-half of its value.

THE AMERICAN LEGAL SYSTEM

Our legal system comes from English **common law**. Starting around the 1500s, magistrates appointed by the kings and queens of England handed down decisions regarding both civil disputes and criminal offenses. Over time, these decisions were written down to be used as guidance when similar cases were brought before that magistrate or others. The common law was the compilation of all those decisions. In the 1700s, William Blackstone, a famous English jurist, undertook the mammoth effort of organizing and identifying the principles of law that derived from these decisions. Blackstone's *Law Commentaries* collected the common laws together in a single source for the first time.

After the American Revolution, the common law was still the pervading law of the land, but as states were created, many began to write their own **penal codes**, which are basically an organized list of laws of the state. You may have seen an Internet item that lists obscure and ridiculous old laws that supposedly still exist, such as no kissing in public or no shooting buffalos from a moving train. This is largely urban legend, because penal codes are periodically reviewed and rewritten by legislators, aided by the bar association of each state. On the other hand, it is an interesting exercise to become more familiar with the penal code of your own state and see some of the quirky, old, and/or ignored laws that do still exist.

The exercise provided on this page is the first of many in this book, designed to help you become more familiar with the criminal justice system of your state. One of the challenges in writing a criminal justice text is that the criminal justice system and the laws of each state are slightly different. Thus, in each chapter, there is an exercise designed to help you become more familiar with your state's criminal justice system. Today, the Internet is an invaluable tool to quickly and conveniently discover most of this information. An important thing to remember, however, is that Web sites can be created by anyone. When researching criminal justice issues, it is best to look for official sites, such as state attorneys-general sites, federal sites such as the Bureau of Justice Statistics, and university-sponsored sites. Of course, other sites can be used as well (such as the one identified in this exercise). However, be careful to double-check facts when using Web sites that are not affiliated with official sources.

EXERCISE: IN THE STATE OF...

1. Go to www.dumblaws.com.
2. Look up the "dumb laws" listed for your state.
3. Check the link provided to read the original law or, when the link is not provided, obtain a copy of your state penal code. This is often available over the Internet. Use the Google or Yahoo search engines to find a link to your state's penal code. Try to find the law mentioned.

Laws define the "do's and don'ts" of society. They can be broken down into felonies, misdemeanors, ordinances, and violations. **Felonies** are the most serious misbehaviors and are usually punishable by a year or more in prison. Most of the crimes you think of (murder, rape, assault) are felonies, although sometimes a crime might be either, such as larceny/theft, which may be a felony or a misdemeanor depending on the dollar amount of the theft. **Misdemeanors** are less serious (such as simple assault) and can be punished by up to a year in jail. It is possible that in your state misdemeanors must be committed in the presence of a police officer for them to be able to arrest the offender without an arrest warrant. In some states, when misdemeanors occur in the absence of police, a victim must go to the prosecutor's office and file a complaint. The prosecutor will ask a magistrate to sign an arrest warrant if he or she determines there is probable cause. States usually further subdivide felonies and misdemeanors into classes or levels indicating their seriousness.

State legislatures have the power to create criminal laws. They can also delegate this authority to local political bodies, such as counties and cities. City ordinances (i.e., skating on the sidewalk) are created by city councils or the local political entity, and are usually punishable by fines. City code violations (i.e., keeping livestock within city limits) are also created by local political bodies and punished by fines. The power these local political entities possess comes to them from the state and can be restricted and modified by state legislatures.

Law enforcement exists at the state and local levels to enforce these laws, although, as you are probably aware, police officers and prosecutors have a great deal of discretion. Just because a law is broken does not necessarily mean there will be an arrest or prosecution. Typically, a state will have a state law enforcement agency (highway patrol) that enforces the state's highway laws, but it can also be called in to help investigate local crime. There is usually a county-level law enforcement agency (county sheriff and deputies). Most of us are familiar with the city police officer, but there are also other types of law enforcement officers, depending on the state, such as constables, park or airport police departments, port authority police, transportation police, and university police departments. These specialized police forces must be created by the state legislature. Law enforcement agencies will be discussed more fully in Chapters 4 and 5.

There are also various layers of courts that prosecute the laws. City ordinances and code violations are typically heard in municipal courts, while misdemeanors and felonies are heard in county and state courts. Every state has a court structure that allows for appeals, and the highest appellate court in the state is often called the *state supreme court,* not to be confused with the United States Supreme Court, the highest court in the country. Court systems and court procedures will be discussed more fully in Chapters 8 and 9.

Each state also has a corrections system, although, typically, only prisons are state-level agencies. Jails and probation departments are usually funded and managed at the county level. Sentencing and corrections will be discussed more fully in Chapters 11 to 14.

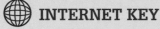 **INTERNET KEY**

To look at the U.S. federal criminal code, go to http://uscode.house.gov/.

The federal criminal justice system parallels the state systems. Federal laws are passed by Congress and can be found in the United States Code. You can purchase a "compact" version that is only 700 pages long!

One thing to remember is that Article I of the United States Constitution specifically enumerates the powers held by the federal government. All other powers are held by states. The Tenth Amendment to the United States Constitution made this division of power clear by stating: *The powers not delegated to the United States by the Constitution, nor prohibited by it to the States, are reserved to the States respectively, or to the people*. **Police power,** the authority to set and enforce most laws, lies with the states. The federal government's role in crime control has historically been strictly limited and must be derived from one of its other powers, that is, the power to protect the borders or regulate interstate commerce.

BREAKING NEWS.... ARIZONA, IMMIGRATION, AND FEDERAL LAW

In 2010, the state of Arizona passed a state law that created a firestorm of controversy and illustrates that the balance between state and federal powers is sometimes controversial. The new law requires law enforcement officers to check the papers of anyone they suspect of being an illegal alien. It also allows law enforcement to hold anyone arrested for any crime until their immigration status has been confirmed and makes it a state crime for noncitizens to be in Arizona without proper visa documents. The Department of Justice sued for and obtained an injunction against the Arizona law, which was granted by Judge Susan Bolton of the Federal District Court. She prohibited the law from taking effect until a full hearing, which should occur sometime in the fall of 2011 or spring of 2012. In granting the injunction, she held that Arizona usurped a federal power (immigration) and that the law could result in unjustified deprivations of liberty, that is, false arrest of citizens. The case will probably end up on the Supreme Court docket, and the Court will resolve the issue of whether or not states can address the problems of illegal immigration through their police power.

Source: *Archibold, R. Judge Blocks Arizona's Immigration Law. New York Times, July 28, 2010. Retrieved 9/5/2010 from http://www.nytimes.com/2010/07/29/us/29arizona.html.*

Despite the limitations created by the Constitution, we have a large number of federal laws that must be enforced by federal law enforcement agencies. We are most familiar with the Federal Bureau of Investigation (FBI), but other federal agencies, such as the border patrol, customs, post office inspectors, and treasury agents, also investigate and enforce federal criminal laws.

As you know, the Department of Homeland Security was created after the terrorist attacks of September 11, 2001. The purpose of creating this department was to streamline and create better communication among the many federal law enforcement agencies that are involved with protecting the country from terrorist acts. Box 1.4 shows how the various agencies are linked into a single large organization whose mission is to protect the country from terrorist threats.

INTERNET KEY

For information on the Department of Homeland Security, go to http://www. dhs.gov/.

It is important to note that federal laws and procedures have made a distinction between domestic crimes and international terrorism when allocating powers of investigation and prosecution to federal agencies.

BOX 1.4 DEPARTMENT OF HOMELAND SECURITY

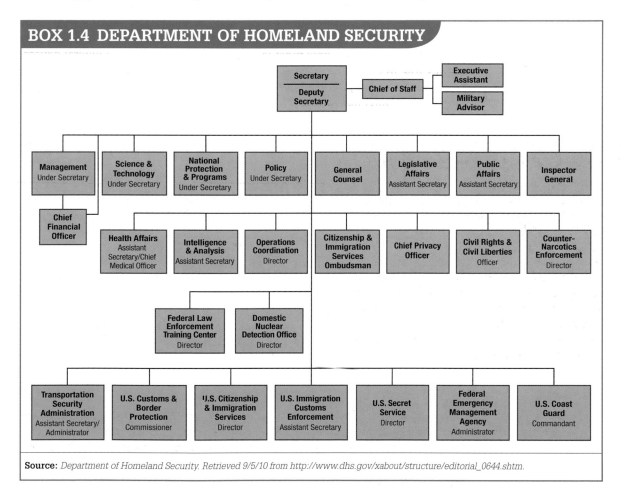

Source: *Department of Homeland Security. Retrieved 9/5/10 from http://www.dhs.gov/xabout/structure/editorial_0644.shtm.*

A passenger undergoes a pat-down search from a TSA officer, Wednesday, Nov. 24, 2010, at Seattle-Tacoma International Airport in Seattle. *AP Photo/Ted S. Warren*

Typically, federal agencies, such as the FBI and Central Intelligence Agency (CIA), have greater powers when investigating international offenders who are suspected of terrorism than when they are investigating "regular" crimes. Of course, there are often blurry lines between domestic crimes, such as bank robbery or smuggling drugs, and international terrorism. One of the most hotly contested elements of the USA PATRIOT Act was increased law enforcement powers in domestic investigations when there is reason to believe a connection to international terrorism exists. We will revisit in Chapter 15 the PATRIOT Act and law enforcement's role in protecting the nation from terrorism.

FLOWCHART OF THE SYSTEM

In Box 1.5, a rough flowchart of a felony offender's experience going through the criminal justice system is presented. An individual may exit the system through:

- Nonprosecution at any stage up to conviction
- Acquittal
- Successful completion of a pretrial diversion program
- Successful completion of probation
- Successful completion of parole
- Completion of jail or prison sentence

BOX 1.5 THE CRIMINAL JUSTICE SYSTEM

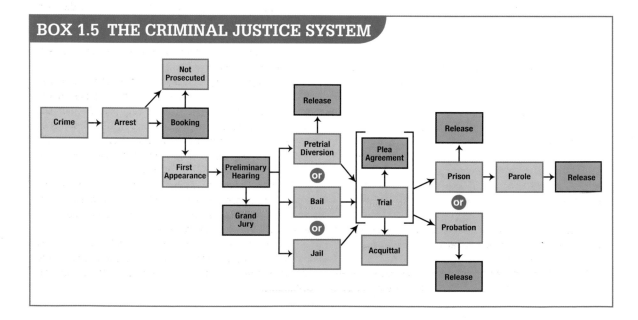

The criminal justice system is typically divided into three subsystems: police, courts, and corrections. The use of these three subsystems has become a standard way to describe the system. Police take center stage up to arrest; their role is to investigate crimes, arrest the suspect, and gather evidence. Courts are obviously involved in the process of adjudication, which determines guilt or innocence and sets the amount of punishment for the guilty. Corrections takes over after sentencing. Of course, real life doesn't have such simple categories. Police investigate offenders who are on probation or parole. Pretrial adjudication programs often use probation officers to supervise clients who haven't been found guilty. Probationers who violate the conditions of their probation may go back to court for a motion to revoke probation hearing. It is even possible for someone on parole to get a probation sentence.

Once an offender is arrested, with or without an arrest warrant, the individual has started his or her entry into the "system." In Box 1.6, the steps of the system

BOX 1.6 THE CRIMINAL JUSTICE PROCESS

Booking is basically an administrative entry into jail. The suspect's fingerprints are taken, officers take his or her property, issue jail clothing and, sometimes, the suspect undergoes some form of health screening before being placed in the jail population.

First Appearance is usually within the first 24 hours of arrest (and it must take place within a "reasonable" period after arrest). In this short hearing before a magistrate, the charges are read and the magistrate determines if there is sufficient probable cause for the arrest. The magistrate may also begin the process of determining if the suspect is indigent, in which case an attorney will be appointed.

Preliminary Hearing is basically to determine whether there is sufficient evidence to go forward with a trial. Often, the preliminary hearing is waived. In some states, the grand jury system completely takes the place of the preliminary hearing.

Grand Jury Hearing is with a jury appointed by the administrative judge of a jurisdiction. This group hears the evidence presented by a prosecutor to determine if there is probable cause to go forward to trial. If they agree that there is, they issue an indictment. Not all states use the grand jury system.

Arraignment is where the offender may plead guilt or innocence and, if indigent, have an attorney appointed if one has not been appointed yet.

Pretrial Diversion may occur at any time before trial and after charges have been filed. Typically, the suspect must admit guilt and agree to conditions that range from work and restitution programs to community service.

Plea Bargaining is an agreement between the defendant, represented by his or her attorney, and the prosecutor to plead guilty in exchange for a recommended sentence.

Pretrial Hearings are when judges decide procedural issues relevant to the trial, such as the admission of evidence or change of venue.

Trials may be "bench trials," which means that they are held only in front of a judge with no jury. If the defendant requests a jury trial, voir dire takes place before the jury is seated, which basically involves ensuring that jury members will be unbiased in their judgment.

Sentencing Hearing is a separate proceeding, although appointed attorneys are required to continue to represent the offender through the sentencing hearing (and first appeal). There may be some time between the trial and the sentencing hearing in order for a presentence report to be written. While some states allow juries to sentence, others release the jury and have the judge do the sentencing.

Prison/Probation is the basic sentencing decision in felony cases. Some states have strictly limited which crimes are eligible for a probation sentence; in other states, potentially any felon can be sentenced to probation.

Parole comes *after* a prison sentence, while probation is *instead* of a prison sentence (in most cases). They are very similar in that both involve supervised release into the community.

are described briefly. It is important to note that there are differences among the states in these steps. We will more carefully explore the various steps taken in the criminal justice flowchart in Chapter 9.

COSTS OF THE SYSTEM

The criminal justice system is an incredibly expensive operation. As Figure 1.1 shows, the costs of the system have been increasing exponentially for the last 30 years and now reach almost $70 billion just for state expenditures as compared to less than $11 billion in 1982. States spend more for criminal justice than they do for education or health and human services. In fiscal year 2006, federal, state, and local governments spent about $214 billion for police protection, corrections, and judicial and legal activities. It is estimated that criminal justice functions cost every person in the United States well over $600.00 per year [5].

What is interesting about the huge increase in expenditures for criminal justice functions is that in the decade of the 1990s through the early 2000s, we experienced a dramatic decline in all types of crime. As we shall see shortly, some crime rates have declined to 30-year lows. The declining crime pattern was experienced across the country, in cities as well as small towns. We will discuss the crime decline in more detail in Chapter 2.

FIGURE 1.1
Direct expenditure by criminal justice function, 1982-2006. **Source:** *Bureau of Justice Statistics, Justice Expenditure and Employment Extracts. Retrieved 9/5/2010 from http://bjs.ojp.usdoj.gov/ content/glance/exptyp.cfm.*

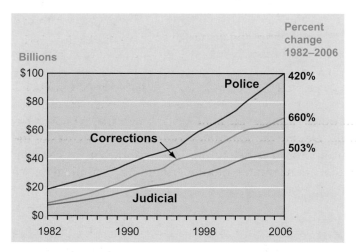

MISSION AND GOALS OF THE SYSTEM

The basic mission of the criminal justice system is to prevent victimization by preventing criminal behavior. Each of the subsystems has its own specific, but complementary, goals to achieve this general mission. The goals of *law enforcement* are to:

1. Prevent crime by patrol
2. Educate the public on crime prevention
3. Investigate crime and arrest those suspected of committing a crime

The goals of the *court system* are to:

1. Determine guilt or innocence through due process
2. Determine a just sentence

The goals of the *correctional system* are:

1. Punishment: we believe that criminals must be punished because they deserve it
2. Deterrence: we believe that what we do to offenders will make others decide not to commit crimes and will also discourage that offender from committing additional crimes
3. Rehabilitation: we believe that programs and what is done to the offender in the system may create some internal change that will make him or her become more law-abiding
4. Incapacitation: if nothing else, we believe that we should hold the offender in a manner that will prevent him or her from committing any additional crimes, at least for that period of time

The important thing to remember is that basically each of the subsystems has the same overriding goal of crime prevention, but it seeks to accomplish that goal in different ways. Most analyses and discussions of the criminal justice system utilize a **systems approach**, meaning that the various elements of police, courts, and corrections are viewed as working together as an integrated whole toward a single goal. In general, this is true, although the various subsystems sometimes have contradictory objectives. In fact, some police officers might say that the court system works "against" the police by letting offenders out as fast as police lock them up. Despite the sometimes contradictory objectives of the subsystems, a systems approach is helpful because it allows us to consider two major concepts that are relevant to our understanding of criminal justice agencies.

The first is the concept of open versus closed systems. An **open system** is one that is permeable and responsive to outside influences. The criminal justice system, for instance, can be described as a fairly open system because it must and does respond to outside influences such as public opinion, legislative changes in the law, executive prioritizing, and so on. A **closed system** is one that does not respond to outside influences and, though the criminal justice system itself is open, there may be examples of certain agencies in the system that are closed. Historically, prisons were fairly closed systems that were isolated from public scrutiny and fairly autonomous. This is no longer the case, however, and even prisons must respond to outside pressures from the public, prisoners' rights advocates, and the legislature.

The second concept is that of **homeostasis**—the idea that any system will adjust to changes by adapting in such a way as to maintain "business as usual." This is important and can arguably explain why we are spending just as much money (actually more!) after a decade-long drop in crime as we did during the years with the highest crime rates. Systems theory argues that there is a tendency for systems to maintain the status quo. In criminal justice, we might point to the fact that rarely do we ever close prisons despite reduced crime rates, and rarely do changes in the law dramatically affect the courtroom work group's decision-making procedures. In general, the system responds to outside pressures by minor adjustments or reinterpretations that tend to allow a continuation of "business as usual." We will discuss these concepts in more detail in later chapters.

IDEOLOGIES IN CRIME AND JUSTICE

An **ideology** is a body of doctrines or beliefs that guides an individual or group. It is a way of organizing knowledge, in that we interpret things we see and hear with reference to our existing belief systems. In fact we may even reject information that doesn't fit our existing ideology and only accept information that does. In 1968, Herbert Packer [6] described two models of law enforcement that are extremely helpful in understanding the issues and the decision-making that occur in reference to the entire criminal justice system, not just law enforcement. In fact, what he termed *models* could also be called ideologies. Packer called his two models *crime control* and *due process*.

In the **crime control ideology**, the basic belief is that controlling crime and punishing the criminal are more important than anything else, best expressed by a Supreme Court justice who argued that the criminal should not be set free because "the constable blundered." Some of the beliefs that are consistent with Herbert Packer's crime control ideology follow:

- Reducing crime is the most important function of law enforcement.
- The failure of law enforcement means the breakdown of order.
- The criminal process guarantees social freedom.
- Efficiency is a top priority.
- The emphasis is on speed and finality.
- There is a presumption of guilt, once the suspect is in the system.

The **due process ideology** supports controlling crime, but in this ideology, crime control is not the most important goal. The most important mission of the criminal justice system is the enforcement of law in a fair and just manner, as characterized by the comment: "It is better to let 10 guilty men go free than punish one innocent." Beliefs that are consistent with this ideology include:

- There is a possibility of error in the system.
- Prevention of mistakes is more important than efficiency.
- Protection of the process is as important as protection of innocents.
- The coercive power of the state is always subject to abuse.
- Every due process protection is there for a reason and should be strictly adhered to.

These basic ideologies are very pervasive in our thinking and opinions regarding criminal justice issues. You can see evidence of them in the television shows we discussed earlier, in politicians' statements, in television and radio talk show hosts' rantings, and in "letters to the editor" in the local newspaper. If one's ideology is purely "crime control," then some consistent beliefs would include:

- Criminals are the "enemy" and fundamentally different from "good" people.
- Police are the "army" that fights the enemy, using any means necessary to control, capture, and punish them.
- "Good" people accept and understand that the police are in a "war" and must be allowed deference in their decision making because they, not we, are the experts and only they "know the enemy."
- Due process protections, such as the *Miranda* warnings, exclusionary rule, and search warrants "hamstring" the police from doing their job.

On the other hand, if one has a dominant ideology of due process, then other beliefs are more consistent and might include:

- Criminals are not a distinct group; they also shop, pay taxes, have kids and parents, may be victims themselves, and often are one's next-door neighbor.
- Police have limited ability to affect crime rates one way or the other because crime is a complex social phenomenon and, in fact, the history of law enforcement originates in order maintenance, not crime control.
- Police, as "public servants," serve all people, and it is important to remember that suspects are not criminals until a court of law finds them so.
- The law is more important than catching criminals, so if police officers break the law to catch a criminal, then they become criminals themselves.
- Due process protections, such as the *Miranda* warnings, exclusionary rule and search warrants are an inherent element of the job of the police; therefore, when they ignore, subvert, or skirt these protections, they are not doing their job [7].

One's belief system influences how new information is received. For instance, the USA PATRIOT Act was lauded by those with a crime control ideology as a step in the right direction in that it allocated greater powers of search to law enforcement officers investigating terrorism. On the other hand, for some with a due process ideology, it was perceived as a direct attack on civil liberties and previous privacy protections enacted by Congress. One's ideology influences perceptions of acceptable crime control strategies. For instance, in a Gallup poll, only 47% of those who identified themselves as liberal approved of the practice of profiling airline passengers on the basis of their age, ethnicity, or gender, but 83% of those respondents who identified themselves as conservative approved of this type of profiling [8]. While the "liberal" and due process ideology are not exactly the same, the poll's results do show that ideology affects the way people view criminal justice issues. Interestingly, ideology in this sense does not seem to affect confidence in the criminal justice system. In another Gallup poll, there was very little difference between groups in their reported confidence in the criminal justice system with 71% of conservatives, 74% of moderates, and 73% of liberals expressing a great deal of confidence in the system [9].

Of course, most of us do not have pure ideologies and so you might think that you lie between these two, or, indeed, have a different overriding ideology entirely. The point of examining ideologies is simply that they sometimes obscure our understanding or acceptance of new information. There is a distinct possibility that your receptiveness to certain facts in this book, and every other book you read, is colored by your ideology. If, for instance, you don't believe something in this book is true, then you should explore the facts, either through the footnote provided, or your own research. The piece of information may be wrong, it may be out of date, or it may be that it simply doesn't fit your idea of the way things are, which is shaped by your ideology. For example, there is a widespread belief that immigrants and especially illegal aliens are responsible for a disproportionate share of crime. The Focus on Crime box explores this common perception using current research.

Of course the writers of textbooks (including this one) have their own ideologies; therefore, their presentation of facts may be influenced by their own ideology. The goal of every textbook writer is to present a balanced view of the facts; however, facts are sometimes more complicated than we think and, although we may strive for objectivity, it is not always easy to do. One of the most difficult things, for instance, in writing research papers is to seek out all the facts and write a balanced review of the research, rather than use only those facts that fit the conclusion that you want to reach. At the end of this book is a short guide to writing a research paper. While there are more detailed instructions available in other sources, this short discussion may help you to identify and narrow a topic and organize the material in a logical and cogent manner.

FOCUS ON CRIME: ILLEGAL ALIENS AND CRIME

Several national leaders have stated that illegal aliens are more likely to commit crime than legal residents. This association has been one of the reasons there is currently strong pressure to crack down on illegal immigration. An individual who comes across the border illegally or stays longer than his or her visa has already committed a federal crime, and thus is a criminal under our definition of crime. Whether they should be considered criminal is a political and philosophical question and outside the scope of our inquiry. Whether they are similar to other types of criminals is a legitimate criminological question. Whether these individuals are more likely than others to commit other types of crimes (such as drug crimes, burglary, or robbery) is the question that we will address here.

The idea that immigrants and especially illegal immigrants are more involved in crime than native-born individuals is an assumption that has emerged repeatedly in this nation's history. This position was buttressed by a 2007 report from the U.S. Department of Justice, Office of the Inspector General Report that sampled 100 cases out of 262,105 files of deportable aliens obtained from the National Crime Information Center (NCIC). They found that in 73 out of the 100 cases the individual had committed subsequent crimes after release and the average number of arrests was six. This finding obviously supports the view that illegal aliens are very likely to be recidivistic criminals; on the other hand, there was no explanation of how this sample of 100 was selected, only that it was not a random sample.

A more careful study of the recidivism of illegal versus nonillegal immigrants was conducted with releases from the Los Angeles County jail by Laura Hickman and Marika Suttorp. In this sample, the two groups were followed for a year to determine whether either group was more likely to recidivate. The authors found that even though 35% of the "nondeportable" immigrants and 43% of the deportable immigrants were rearrested in the year following release, once researchers controlled for other variables such as prior arrests, age, and drug involvement, the difference disappeared.

An even better measure of whether illegal immigrants are more likely to engage in crime is to compare crime rates of neighborhoods that have higher and lower concentrations of illegal immigrants or neighborhoods over time when there has been an increase in their number. In these studies, researchers such as Ramiro Martinez have found no differences between areas with high concentrations of illegal immigrants and areas with lower numbers of them. Studies have also found that first-generation immigrants have lower crime rates than their children and subsequent generations. Evaluating the available research does not lead to a conclusion that illegal immigrants are responsible for a disproportionate share of crime.

Sources: *R. Martinez, M. Lee, On Immigration and Crime, in G. LaFree, G. R. Bursik, J. Short, R. Taylor (Eds.), Criminal Justice, 2000: The Changing Nature of Crime, vol. 1, National Institute of Justice Criminal Justice, Washington, DC, 2000. R. Martinez, The impact of immigration policy on criminological research. Criminol. Publ. Policy 7 (1) (2008) 53-58. L. Hickman, M. Suttorp, Are deportable aliens a unique threat to public safety? Comparing the recidivism of deportable and nondeportable aliens, Criminol. Publ. Policy 7 (1) (2008): 59-82.*

CAREERS IN CRIMINAL JUSTICE

It is possible that you are reading this book because you are interested in a career in the field of criminal justice. One of the interesting features of the field is the wide variation in professions. Criminal justice encompasses drug counselors and border patrol agents, prison guards, and public defenders. You've probably heard that "you'll never get rich" in this field, and that is true. Table 1.1 shows low and high average salaries for certain selected professions associated with criminal justice.

Although there are no riches to be earned in this field, there are not that many professions that have such potential to change lives. Almost all the occupations and professions in this table (except for private security and private attorneys)

Position	Lowest $	Average $	Highest $
Police officer	30,000	51,400	79,600
Police chief		90,000-113,000	
Police sergeant		58,700-70,300	
FBI (GS 10-13)		53,900-105,000	
Private detective	23,500	41,700	76,600
Security guard	16,000	23,400	39,300
Correctional officer	25,000	38,300	64,000
Probation officer	29,400	45,900	78,000
Attorney	50,000	110,000 (wide variation)	
Judge	32,000	110,200	162,000
Drug counselor	21,700	37,200	61,000

Table 1.1 Annual Salaries

Source: *Bureau of Labor Statistics. Retrieved 9/5/2010 from http://www.bls.gov/oco/.*

are public servants. Public servants are individuals whose salary comes from the public purse; therefore, they have special duties to put the public's interest before their own. They have discretion and power over the lives of others, and therefore must be held to high standards of integrity and ethics. If public servants do not respect the law, then everyone is at risk and corruption inevitably follows. In the chapters that follow, we will examine in greater detail not only the offenders who pass through the criminal justice system, but also the women and men who are the agents of social control and the law.

CONCLUSION

In this chapter, we have learned some basic facts about the criminal justice system. Obviously, the television shows that portray the system do not present realistic views of what happens in real life. We should be concerned that sometimes false perceptions influence decisions, such as what is described in the *"CSI* effect."

Criminal justice is basically an institution of social control. The powers invested in system actors come from our Constitution, which places most "police powers" in the state. States pass laws, cities pass ordinances, and they are all enforced by law enforcement at the state and local level, although there is also a parallel federal system to enforce federal laws. The flowchart of the criminal justice system displays how an offender enters the system and how he or she can exit. We use systems theory to understand what we call the criminal justice system, but we must also recognize that the various subsystems may sometimes have contradictory objectives. Positions that are consistent with the ideologies of crime control or due process can be seen in the media. Ideologies are inevitable but they may prevent one from accepting facts that do not fit one's "view of the world." It is important to constantly challenge one's ideologies with facts as they develop. In the next chapter, we will further explore crime and how we measure it.

Review Questions

1. What is common law?
2. Define felonies, misdemeanors, and violations.
3. What is police power?
4. What specific powers were given to the federal government?
5. Name and describe each of the steps of the flowchart of criminal justice.
6. How much do we spend on criminal justice agencies?
7. What has been the pattern of crime in the last decade?
8. What is systems theory and what are open and closed systems?
9. Explain the concept of homeostasis.
10. What is an ideology? Explain the crime control and due process ideologies.

VOCABULARY

closed system does not respond to outside influences

common law English magistrates' decisions regarding both civil disputes and criminal offenses; eventually, they became a body of legal decisions that formed the basis of the American legal system

crime control ideology the basic belief that controlling crime and punishing the criminal is the most important goal of the criminal justice system

due process ideology the belief that the most important mission of the criminal justice system is the enforcement of law and protecting the rights of the individual

felonies the most serious misbehaviors, usually punishable by a year or more in prison

forensic science science that serves the court; in other words, *forensic* is an adjective that is used to describe something as being related to the legal system

homeostasis the idea that any system will adjust to changes by adapting in such a way as to maintain "business as usual"

ideology a body of doctrines or beliefs that guide an individual or group; it is a way of organizing knowledge in that we interpret things we see and hear in reference to our existing ideologies

misdemeanors less serious offenses (such as simple assault) that can be punished by up to a year in jail

open system one that is permeable and responsive to outside influences

penal codes an organized list of laws of the state

police power the authority to set and enforce laws

social contract a concept proposed by philosophers Hobbes, Locke, and Rousseau that explains that individuals give up the liberty to aggress against others in return for protection from being victimized themselves

systems approach a type of analysis utilizing the definitions and characteristics of a system

ENDNOTES

[1] R. Willing, CSI effect has juries wanting more evidence, USA Today, August 5 (2004) B1.

[2] D. Shelton, Y. Kim, G. Barak, A study of juror expectations and demands concerning scientific evidence: does the CSI effect exist? Vand. J. Ent. Technol. Law 9(2) (2006) 331–368.

[3] C. Cooley, The CSI effect: the true effect of crime scene television on the justice system, New Engl. Law Rev. 41 (2007) 471–501. Committee on Identifying the Needs of the Forensic Sciences Community, National Research Council. Strengthening Forensic Science in the United States: A Path Forward, National Academies Press, Washington, DC, 2009.

[4] See T. Hobbes, Leviathan, Penguin Classics, New York, 1651/1982. See also J. Rousseau, The Social Contract, Penguin Classics, New York, 1762/1968.

[5] Bureau of Justice Statistics. Retrieved 9/5/2010 from http://ojp.usdoj.gov/bjs/glance/exptyp.htm.

[6] H. Packer, The Limits of the Criminal Sanction, Stanford University Press, Stanford, CA, 1968.

[7] J. Pollock, Ethical Dilemmas and Decisions in Criminal Justice, fifth ed., ITP/Wadsworth, Belmont, CA, 2007, pp. 190–191.

[8] Gallup Poll, Table 2.0025.2010, Attitudes toward Profiling of Airline Passengers to Prevent Terrorism, 2010, Sourcebook of Criminal Justice Statistics Online. Retrieved 9/5/2010 from http://www.albany.edu/sourcebook/pdf/t200252010.pdf.

[9] Gallup Poll, Table 2.11.2009, Reported Confidence in the Criminal Justice System, 2010, Sourcebook of Criminal Justice Statistics Online. Retrieved 9/5/2010 from http://www.albany.edu/sourcebook/pdf/t2112009.pdf.

CHAPTER 2

Crime in Society

WHAT YOU NEED TO KNOW

- The majority of crime is low-dollar property crime.
- Crime is defined by our laws and the definition of crime can change.
- The two most important sources of crime data are the Uniform Crime Reports (UCR) and the National Crime Victimization Survey (NCVS).
- Crime has declined dramatically in the last 15 years, but this decline has leveled off. The three strongest correlates of crime are sex, age, and, for certain crimes, race.

CONTENTS

What is crime? This seems like an easy question, and it is, in a way. However, the answer is not necessarily murder, robbery, or rape. Those may be examples of crime, but the definition of **crime** is simply "those actions that are prohibited by law." The definition exemplifies one of the fundamental problems of criminology. If criminology is the study of why people commit crime, then one can see why such a study may be difficult if the definition of crime changes. For instance, in past years abortion was a crime, and now it is not (at least in the first 3 months of a pregnancy), but it might be again in the future. Gambling is usually illegal, unless it is buying a state lottery ticket or unless the state has legalized that specific form of gambling. So, how does one construct an explanation for why people commit such "crimes" when sometimes they are and sometimes they are not crimes at all?

What is deviance? Crime and deviance may be considered synonyms, but they are definitely not. **Deviance** can be defined as behaviors that are contrary to the norm. Deviance has a negative connotation, but it simply means that the behavior is unusually infrequent. Most crime is deviant. There are very few serial killers (thank goodness!) and even relatively few burglars compared to the total population. On the other hand, some "crime" is not deviant at all. Can you think of some? (Hint: How many people break speeding laws?) Because some crime is very deviant (serial murder) and some crime is very common (speeding), how does one construct a theory of crime? You might decide that theories might only explain violent crime; however, even simple assault is not really deviant. In fact, perhaps you have been a victim or a perpetrator of simple assault and never realized it. The definition of simple assault in one state follows:

(1) Intentionally, knowingly, or recklessly causes bodily injury to another, including the person's spouse,
(2) Intentionally or knowingly threatens another with imminent bodily injury, including the person's spouse, or
(3) Intentionally or knowingly causes physical contact with another when the person knows or should reasonably believe that the other will regard the contact as offensive or provocative [1]

So, if you pushed or even hugged someone who you knew would consider it to be provocative or offensive, you have committed simple assault. This is a Class A misdemeanor unless some other conditions are met; therefore, it is not a very "serious" crime. Most simple assaults are not brought to the attention of the criminal justice system. However, many other, more serious crimes are also never reported. This creates what is known as the **dark figure** of crime, which is crime that does not find its way into official numbers. Crimes such as domestic violence, acquaintance rape, and even theft, are more likely than other crimes to be part of this dark figure of crime.

Because the dark figure of crime is so high, it makes theorizing about who commits crime difficult. We do not know if the offenders who never come to the attention of authorities are similar to those who do. We do not know if these unknown offenders have similar motivations and patterns of criminal offending. Studies that are based only on known offenders may be faulty in that they are not able to base findings on all offenders—only those we know about.

DEFINING CRIMES

Crime is called a "constructed reality" because it is created by the definitions and perceptions of the observers, formal system actors (such as police), victims, and the actions of the perpetrator. Box 2.1 illustrates the sequence of decision making. Person A shoves Person B. Is it simple assault? It would be, only if Person A did it intentionally, believing it to be offensive to Person B. Is it a crime? It is, only if it meets the legal definition as provided above. Is it prosecutable? It might be, only if Person B reports it (unless a police

BOX 2.1 CONSTRUCTING A CRIME

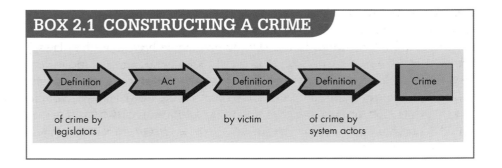

officer happened to be standing nearby). Will it be prosecuted? A variety of factors affect the decision to prosecute, including the wishes of the victim, the resources of the prosecutor's office, the nature of the evidence and, some say, perhaps the race and ethnicity of the offender and/or victim.

Definition of crime by legislators

Before we can punish any act as a crime, a law has to be created by legislation. As we learned in the last chapter, most of our laws come from common law; however, state and federal legislators are constantly fine-tuning our criminal codes and adding new laws or changing existing laws. Two examples of the dynamic nature of law-making are offered below.

In most states, carrying a weapon onto state property, such as a university, is a crime, unless one is a licensed peace officer on duty. Since the tragedy at Virginia Tech University in 2007, when Seung-Hui Cho killed 32 students and professors and wounded dozens more, many states considered legislation that would make it legal to carry concealed weapons onto college campuses. As of 2010, only Utah permits individuals with conceal and carry licenses to carry guns onto campuses. Measures to allow carrying guns in other states have been stalled or voted down by legislatures. Advocates are now attacking the bans in court, arguing that they are a constitutional infringement of the Second Amendment [2]. In the early 2000s, Enron, the giant energy company, failed and several of its top executives were convicted of a variety of crimes related to defrauding investors as to the true value of the company's stock. Other accounting scandals occurred in Tyco, Adelphia, and WorldCom. The wrongdoing cost investors billions of dollars and threatened the security markets. Congress, in response, passed the Sarbanes-Oxley Act, which held lawyers, auditors, and CEOs more responsible for the company's profit statements. Obviously, the new law did not avert the most recent Wall Street debacle; however, the cause of the stock market crash of 2007 evidently was not the same blatant fraud and manipulation of profit statements that occurred in the early 2000s. These examples illustrate the dynamic nature of law. Legal changes often occur in response to specific events. Both examples also illustrate that laws proposed in response to events are hotly debated. Proponents and opponents of both of these laws argued their positions and influenced what happened. The public has a great deal of influence in determining what to define as a crime, and the amount of punishment for certain crimes. The perceptions and response to domestic violence, drunk driving, and drug use have undergone dramatic change in the last 30 years. Drug laws, especially, have changed in response to public sentiment and legislative initiatives.

Definition of crime by victim

Before a crime can be counted by officials, it must be reported by the victim. Why might someone *not* report a crime to authorities? The most common reason is that they believe police can't do anything about it, but they might also interpret the event as a private matter and not a crime. Domestic violence victims sometimes do not want the involvement of the police even though they are obviously victims of assault.

Rape victims also may not report their own victimization, sometimes because they do not want formal intervention, but sometimes because they do not interpret the event as a crime. Studies have shown that female victims who are raped in "date-rape" scenarios by someone they know in circumstances where the lack of consent may be somewhat ambiguous sometimes do not define what occurred as a crime. If the victim does not perceive the event as a crime, or does not want formal system intervention, then the event is never reported to police and does not appear in our crime statistics [3]. In 2007, only 40% of all criminal victimizations were reported to police. Robberies with injury and auto theft were reported by 85% of victims, but only a quarter of some other types of crimes were reported to police [4].

INTERNET KEY

For more information about which types of victims report crimes, go to http://www.albany.edu/sourcebook/pdf/13332007.pdf.

Definition of crime by system actors

Police do not arrest in a large percentage of cases where an arrest is legally justified; perhaps in as many as half of all cases. Although arrests are usually made in serious felony cases, or in situations in which victims demand an arrest, even assaults may be dealt with informally rather than by initiating a formal report or arrest [5]. Understanding when and why police choose to make arrests is a necessary part of understanding crime statistics. We forget that crime reports are simply the crimes that victims choose to report, and arrest statistics represent only the cases in which police officers decide to make an arrest. Both are only a portion of the total number of criminal incidents.

One of the most important questions in the study of criminal justice is whether police enforce the law unfairly and are more likely to target minorities for formal system responses. There are many studies that explore the issue, but it is not an easy topic to analyze because it must involve the researcher being able to access information on each police-citizen interaction that might have resulted in an arrest to determine if certain factors, such as race, age, sex, or demeanor, affected the decision.

One of the reasons researchers use homicide, robbery, and burglary as indicators of crime is that they are less subject to the discretion of system actors. When these acts occur, it is more likely that everyone agrees that they are crimes, and system actors are more likely to begin formal processing. Other crimes, such as prostitution, show changes over time but it is likely that declines or increases in arrests have just as much to do with enforcement pattern changes as with changes in the frequency of prostitution. As we discussed earlier, even assault may be subject to individual definitions and interpretations of the offender, victim, and system actors; therefore, fluctuations in assault rates may be real differences in such behavior, or differences in perception and/or enforcement of the behavior that can be defined as assault.

VICTIM-HARMING CRIMES

It might be helpful to consider crime as either victim-harming or victimless. **Victim-harming crimes** are those where there is a specific victim who has been injured or suffered a loss. **Victimless crimes** are those where there is no direct victim. Thus, most drug laws are victimless crimes, as are gambling, underage drinking, and so on. These acts are prohibited because society has deemed them injurious to at least the perpetrator and, sometimes, others, but not in a direct way. Some might argue, in fact, that no crimes are truly victimless because such actions may harm, even if indirectly, family members or friends of the perpetrator.

Crimes such as assault, rape, robbery, burglary, larceny/theft, and others are victim-harming crimes. Even theft from large corporations or income tax evasion would be considered victim-harming because there is a loss that is suffered directly from the action. What about computer hacking? Simply breaking into a computer security system on a dare and not doing any damage could still be considered an injury because it requires the company to bolster its defenses; therefore, one might place computer hacking into the victim-harming category.

What about prostitution? (Victimless?) Teen prostitution? (Victim-harming?) Pornography? (Victimless?) Child pornography? (Victim-harming?). If you disagree, what are the elements of your argument as to why it should be the other category? What are some other crimes that are victimless crimes? What are some that are victim-harming? Drug-related crimes include simple possession, possession with intent to sell, and smuggling. Are some victim-harming

Dallas police arrest a young woman for prostitution as part of an intervention program in Dallas, Wednesday, November 4, 2009. Dallas is taking a new approach to the world's oldest profession. Rather than treat prostitutes as criminals, police are treating them as sex crime victims. And rather than locking them up, Dallas police are giving some the chance to get clean and get off the streets. *AP Photo/LM Otero*

and some victimless crimes? The reason we may want to distinguish victim-harming and victimless crimes is that if we want to understand what motivates people to commit a crime, then there might be dramatically different answers depending on the crime. One can see, for instance, that different explanations might be applied to why someone uses drugs or gambles, from why someone rapes or robs another. On the other hand, there are some criminologists who would argue that the same underlying reason could explain both victim-harming and victimless crimes [6].

Usually, crime is not glamorous or worthy of Hollywood scriptwriters' attention. Usually, crime is not committed by offenders who painstakingly plan their act and play cat-and-mouse games with determined detectives or by bloodthirsty supervillains or by engaging antiheroes. Mostly, crimes are mundane, committed by individuals who are not necessarily committed to a criminal lifestyle, and result in relatively modest losses to the victim. Even homicide is rarely as it is depicted on television. On television, homicide is often committed by strangers; in reality, many homicides occur between people who know each other and happen as a result of a dispute or an altercation. Serial killers populate the airwaves but are exceedingly rare in real life.

Before we can ask the question "Why do people commit crime?" we need to be aware of the characteristics of crime. In other words, we need to know the "who, what, and where" of crime. To understand crime patterns, we use a number of sources of crime data. These are not perfect and each has inherent weaknesses, but they are the source of everything we think we know about crime in this country.

SOURCES OF CRIME DATA

The two most common sources of crime data are the Uniform Crime Reports and the National Crime Victimization Survey. It is important to note that everything that we think we know about crime is derived primarily from these sources; thus, if there is some bias (inaccuracy) in the way they present the pattern of crime, then what we think we know is not necessarily accurate.

The Uniform Crime Reports

The most well-known and used source of crime statistics in this country is the **Uniform Crime Reports**. This collection of local crime reports and arrest data began in 1929 and is now produced by the Federal Bureau of Investigation.

The numbers come either directly from local law enforcement agencies or from a state agency that collects the data from local agencies and delivers it in a centralized format. About 98% of law enforcement agencies submit crime data to the FBI [7]:

The Uniform Crime Reports presents crime in terms of **rates** as well as raw numbers. A rate is the number of crimes divided by the population and then multiplied to display by a standard number. Using the following mathematical formula, one computes the number of crimes committed per every 100,000 people in the population.

$$\textbf{Rate} = \frac{\textbf{\# crimes known to police}}{\textbf{\# total population}} \times \textbf{100,000}$$

The advantage of a rate is that it allows us to compare patterns of crime in very different populations. For instance, with rates, we can compare the same city in two different periods, even if the city has grown. We can also compare two different cities, even if one is very large and the other very small. Knowing, for instance, the raw number of burglaries in New York City, Portland, Oregon, and Detroit, Michigan, tells us something, but it doesn't tell us the relative risk of victimization in these cities because they do not have the same populations. The only way to compare the crime of two different populations is to compute the rate of each city, then compare the rates. In 2008, the *numbers* of reported burglaries and the *rates* for these cities [8] looked like this:

City	Population	Number of Burglaries	Rate
New York City	8,345,075	19,867	238
Portland	553,023	4307	778
Austin	753,535	8586	1139
Washington, DC	591,833	3781	638

Who would have thought that there were more burglaries per 100,000 people in Portland, Austin, and Washington, D.C., than in New York? One might conclude that it was somehow connected with having a large population that made New York City's crime rate so low, but compare other big cities:

City	Population	Number of Burglaries	Rate
Houston	2,238,895	26,947	1203
Los Angeles	3,850,920	19,726	512

These cities also had higher crime rates than New York City. So, despite the stereotype of high crime in the Big Apple, these numbers indicate that maybe the city is not as unsafe as we might think. Interestingly, the New York Police Department has been accused of manipulating crime statistics by chronically undercounting or underclassifying crime reports [9]. The charges have not been substantiated; however, it is important to realize that crime statistics are only as accurate as the law enforcement agencies' accuracy in reporting.

EXERCISE: IN THE STATE OF…

1. Go to http://www.fbi.gov/ucr/cius2008/data/table_08.html.
2. Go to the tables that provide information on the crimes reported by state.
3. Find the rate per 100,000 for your state for the crimes of murder, rape, robbery, and burglary.
4. Find the rates for at least three states you would like to compare your state to and construct a table.
5. How do they compare?

It should also be noted, however, that the FBI cautions against anyone using these numbers to compare the crime risk between cities because there are so many variables that go into them, including recording practices, urban density, the department's reporting practices, and so on. If a city extends its limits out into the suburbs, the crime rate will be lower because crime occurs less often in suburban than in urban areas. Thus, New York's city limits may be drawn in such a way that it brings down the rate of burglary compared to other cities. Also, burglaries may not be recorded in the same manner or people may be less inclined to report them in New York City.

It is very important to have an accurate population base for rates to mean anything. If the population base is inaccurate, then so too will be the rate. If, for instance, the population base is out of date and the actual population has grown considerably, then the crimes (which inevitably would increase with a larger population) will be divided by an artificially small population indicating that the rate of crime in that locale (the amount of crime per person) is higher than what it actually is. In contrast, if the population used is inaccurate in the other direction and shows a much larger population than what actually exists (perhaps because people have been moving away from that area), and crimes are divided by this inaccurately high population, then the crime rate will appear to be lower than it actually is. Usually, the FBI uses the most recent census numbers for the area, but these numbers may be vulnerable to rapid fluctuations in population/ migration.

You can look at the crime rates for your state or even your city by going to the FBI Web site or by looking in a library for their yearly report, titled *Crime in the United States.* Crimes are reported by state and region, and by city-rural categories.

🌐 **INTERNET KEY**

Look for crime in your city by going to http://www.fbi.gov/ucr/cius2009/index.html.

These numbers are gathered from law enforcement agencies via a standard reporting form so that, for instance, larceny means the same thing in all states whether or not state laws differ in defining the dollar amount that would change larceny from a misdemeanor to a felony. Because these are standard definitions, they may or may not conform to the state's definition for that particular crime. Also, because of the index crime definitions, it is difficult to use this source to find out about certain crimes such as domestic violence or identity theft, because the reporting is not set up to identify them.

The UCR provides the total number of reported crimes for the eight index crimes: murder and non-negligent manslaughter, forcible rape, robbery, aggravated assault, burglary, larceny-theft, motor vehicle theft, and arson. Table 2.1 shows how violent crime reports have decreased over the years, and Table 2.2 shows property crimes.

The numbers of arrests are by no means a measure of crime, because they capture only the crimes in which a suspect was identified and a decision to arrest was made. It is interesting, however, that arrests also decreased during the period when we saw the large drop in reported crime. Arrest data are presented for 21 crime categories in Table 2.3. The table shows that arrests for most crimes have been decreasing over the last 15 years.

Table 2.1 Uniform Crime Reports—Violent Crime (Estimated Crimes, Rate per 100,000)

Crime	1986	1990	1994	1998	2004	2008
Violent crime	620.1	729.5	713.6	567.6	463.2	454.5
Murder	8.6	9.4	9.0	6.3	5.5	5.4
Rape	38.1	41.1	39.3	34.5	32.4	29.3
Robbery	226.0	256.3	237.8	165.5	136.7	145.3
Agg. assault	347.4	422.9	427.6	361.4	288.6	274.6

Source: *UCR, Table 1, Crime in the United States, By Volume and Rate, 1986-2008. Retrieved from www.fbi.gov/ucr/05cius/data/table/_.01/html. Crime in the United States, 2008, By Volume and Rate, 1989-2008. Retrieved from, www.fbi.gov/ucr/cius2008/data/table_01.html.*

Table 2.2 Uniform Crime Reports—Property Crime

Crime	1986	1990	1994	1998	2004	2008
Property crime	4881.8	5073.1	4660.2	4052.5	3514.1	3212.5
Burglary	1349.8	1232.2	1042.1	863.2	730.3	730.8
Larceny/theft	3022.1	3185.1	3026.9	2729.5	2362.3	2167.0
Motor vehicle theft	509.8	655.8	591.3	459.9	421.5	314.7

Source: *UCR, Table 1, Crime in the United States, By Volume and Rate, 1986-2005. Retrieved from www.fbi.gov/ucr/05cius/data/table/_.01/html. Crime in the United States, 2008, By Volume and Rate, 1989-2008. Retrieved from www.fbi.gov/ucr/cius2008/data/table_01.html.*

Many crimes go unsolved or are not cleared. Crimes are considered cleared when an arrest is made for an offense. The UCR reports the number of crimes cleared by arrest with a statistic called the **clearance rate**. The clearance rates vary greatly by crime. In 2004, murder and non-negligent homicide had the highest clearance rate (62.6%), while burglary had the lowest clearance rate (12.9%) [10]. In 2009, the clearance rate for murder and non-negligent homicide increased to 66.6%, while motor vehicle theft and burglary declined to 12.4% and 12.5%, respectively [11].

One of the most-often cited criticisms of the UCR is that it represents only reported crimes. If someone does not report a criminal victimization to the police, it does not get counted as a crime. Consequently, we note that there is a "dark" figure of crime that never appears in the UCR. The amount of unreported crime varies by the type of crime, but in general, it is estimated that about half of all crime does not appear in the UCR. This presents a distinct problem if one uses the UCR as a measure of crime. In fact, it is not a measure of crime, but only a measure of **reported** crime. Another problem is that crimes such as identity theft and cybercrimes are not easily identified in the traditional UCR. The Focus on Crime box on page 34 describes more fully the scope of these crimes, and it should be noted that our traditional sources of crime data do not track these crimes very well.

The FBI has also been collecting crime statistics in a different format. The National Incident-Based Reporting System (NIBRS) gathers much more detailed information about each criminal incident. While the UCR reporting format is hierarchical, meaning that only the most serious crime is counted, NIBRS requires information to be submitted on each crime within a criminal transaction. Instead of reporting crimes via the eight index offenses, NIBRS will display information on Group A offense categories (22) and Group B offenses (11). More information is obtained about each offense, including information about the victim and offender. NIBRS reports are not comparable to the UCR because the way crimes are counted is different. For instance, a robbery,

Table 2.3 Uniform Crime Report Arrests (Rate per 100,000)

Crime	1995	2000	2005	2009
Murder/non-negligent manslaughter	8.5	4.8	4.7	4.1
Forcible rape	13.5	9.8	8.6	7.0
Robbery	70.2	39.7	39.2	42.0
Aggravated assault	223.0	173.9	152.2	138.2
Burglary	148.8	104.0	101.2	98.1
Larceny/theft	592.7	429.5	392.6	442.3
Motor vehicle theft	75.9	54.2	49.7	26.8
Arson	7.6	5.9	5.5	4.0
Other assaults	496.5	471.4	440.2	432.3
Forgery and counterfeiting	46.8	39.1	40.0	28.1
Fraud	162.9	117.4	106.4	67.6
Embezzlement	5.9	6.9	6.5	5.9
Stolen property	65.1	43.2	45.6	34.6
Vandalism	118.5	101.3	94.8	88.8
Weapons	95.3	57.9	65.6	54.6
Prostitution	41.3	33.7	28.8	23.6
Sex offenses	36.8	33.6	27.2	25.2
Drug abuse violations	582.5	572.4	496.8	544.2
Gambling	8.0	4.0	2.2	3.4
Offenses against family and children	53.4	50.1	55.3	36.6
DUI	526.0	508.6	328.2	463.8
Liquor laws	221.6	239.3	128.4	186.6
Drunkenness	268.4	232.5	80.1	196.7
Disorderly conduct	285.9	231.5	293.3	216.1
Vagrancy	10.4	12.1	10.4	11.0
All other (except traffic)	1486.3	1324.2	933.2	1228.4
Curfew and loitering	58.5	58.0	86.1	37.4
Runaways	96.6	51.4	19.7	30.8

Source: *UCR, Table 30, Crime in the United States, 1995, 2000, 2005: Number and Rate of Arrests. Retrieved from http://www.fbi.gov/ucr/cius; http://www.fbi.gov/ucr/05cius/data/table_30.html, and http://www.fbi.gov/ucr/cius2009/data/table_30.html.*

rape, and murder would only be reported as a murder in the UCR, but as three separate crimes under NIBRS. Law enforcement agencies have been slow to adopt the NIBRS reporting procedures, most probably because it is much more detailed, requiring more effort to enter the data. There is also the concern that NIBRS will make it appear that there is an increase in crime because it would

FOCUS ON CRIME: IDENTITY THEFT AND COMPUTER CRIME

One of the problems with the UCR is that it does not give us much information about the crimes that many people are concerned with today—specifically, identity theft (including credit card theft), cybercrime, and other forms of white-collar crime. These crimes are not part of the index crimes, and they are submerged in arrest statistics under general crime categories such as forgery, fraud, embezzlement, or larceny-theft. NIBRS provides more information about such crimes because fraud is broken down into identity/credit card/ATM fraud, among other types of frauds, but still many forms of white-collar crime are reported as "all other offenses." NIBRS also includes a data entry for whether the offender used a computer in the crime; therefore, computer crime statistics will be more accessible as law enforcement agencies begin to report under NIBRS.

Identity theft is obtaining and using or attempting to use another person's identity (name, Social Security number, address) without the owner's permission and/or the unauthorized use of a credit card or a bank account. Identity theft is both a state and a federal crime. In addition, crimes utilizing identity theft may violate federal wire-fraud and credit card fraud laws. The Bureau of Justice Statistics, reporting on the National Crime Victim Survey of 2007, reports that such crime increased 23% from 2005 to 2007. Almost 8 million households had at least one member report being a victim of this type of crime. This compares to about 3 million households reporting burglary and about 600,000 reporting robbery and 200,000 reporting purse snatching. The most common type of identity theft is the unauthorized use of a credit card, followed by the unauthorized access of other accounts (bank or cellular phone account). The average loss was $1830. Clearly, modern thieves are much less likely to use a gun or burglary tools than a computer or stolen credit card. Cases of identity theft increased dramatically with the increasing use of computers. "Phishing" refers to false emails that appear to be from banks or other accounts that request the user to enter passwords and other private information. Generally, once an identity has been obtained, the offender can access and steal from bank accounts, use credit card numbers to make purchases, and/or set up credit in the victim's name and incur huge amounts of debt. Identity theft is difficult to investigate and many cases go unreported. Merchants and banks continue to improve their security devices to guard against identity

theft and computer crimes, including enhanced encryption and authentication techniques, but there is no doubt that it is one of the most pervasive crime problems in America today.

Computer crimes ("cybercrime") include crimes where the computer is used as a *tool* for crime (i.e., phishing) and crimes in which the computer is the *target* of the crime (hacking). The Internet Crime Complaint Center (www.ic3.gov) is a joint operation of the National White Collar Crime Center and the FBI. It received 336,655 complaints of Internet-related crime in 2009, a 22% increase from 2008. The most often reported Internet crime was fraud involving either fraudulent association with the FBI or nondelivery of merchandise. Also present were advance-fee fraud and identity theft. The total loss of all complaints was about $560 million. Because this represents only voluntary reporting, the numbers and types of crimes must be viewed with caution as nonrepresentative of total Internet-related crime. Some offenders target computers in order to obtain identities, either through hacking or simply by stealing workers' laptops that carry sensitive information. Another crime where the computer is the target is the intentional creation and/or spreading of viruses. Some of these individuals have no motive other than to wreak havoc on Internet users. Other offenders have more sinister motives, including disabling security systems of banks so that they can gain access, or testing governmental security. *Cyberterrorism* is a new word that portends a serious new threat because so much of modern society is inextricably connected to the use of computers, including our banking industry, energy distribution, transportation, and health-care administration, to name only a few essential services that depend on computers. Computer crimes include "hijacking" (malicious software that takes over a victim's computer without their knowledge), "sniffing" (monitoring data), "spamming" (frequent, unwanted advertisements), "spoofing" (getting access through fraud), and use of "spyware" (illegally installed software that collects information). Almost all computer users have been the direct victim of at least the minor types of cybercrime, but probably all of us are indirect victims in that businesses and government entities now must expend huge amounts of money to protect themselves from computer criminals and these costs are passed to the consumer in the form of higher prices for goods and services.

FOCUS ON CRIME: IDENTITY THEFT AND COMPUTER CRIME—CONT'D

Sources: Barnett, C. The Measurement of White-Collar Crime Using Uniform Crime Reporting (UCR) Data. Washington, DC: U.S. Department of Justice, Federal Bureau of Investigation, Criminal Justice Information Services Division, n.d. L. Langton, K. Baum, Identity Theft Reported by Households, 2007—Statistical Tables. Washington, DC: Bureau of Justice Statistics, 2010. Retrieved 9/15/2010 from http://bjs.ojp.usdoj.gov/content/pub/pdf/itrh07st .pdf. See also Sourcebook of Criminal Justice Statistics, Estimated Percent Distribution of Personal and Property Victimization. Retrieved 9/15/2010 from http://www .albany.edu/sourcebook/pdf/t3332007.pdf. Sourcebook of Criminal Justice Statistics, Household Experiencing Identity Theft. Retrieved 9/15/2010 from http://www. albany.edu/sourcebook/pdf/t300022007.pdf. Internet Crime Complaint Center, 2009 Internet Crime Report. Washington, DC: Bureau of Justice Assistance, Federal Bureau of Investigation, 2010.

report each separate criminal incident instead of use the hierarchical reporting system. In 2008, only 22% of the nation's population was represented by crime statistics reported under NIBRS [12].

Victimization studies

Another source of crime statistics comes from victimization surveys. The Bureau of Justice Statistics presents findings from the **National Crime Victimization Survey**. Begun in 1973 as the National Crime Survey, the U.S. Bureau of the Census has been interviewing household members in a nationally representative sample. In 1992-1993, the survey was redesigned and relabeled as the National Crime Victimization Survey. The redesign effort was intended to obtain more information about less serious crimes. The items in the survey capture more information than what is available through the UCR. For instance, one question asks the respondent whether the crime was reported to the police. This is the source for our information about how much crime goes unreported.

Questions cover information on the victim (i.e., age, sex, race, ethnicity, income, and educational level), and, if known, the offender (i.e., age, sex, race). It also reports findings on the victimization itself, including time and place and level of injury or loss. Findings from the National Crime Victimization Survey can be accessed most easily through the Bureau of Justice Statistics, an agency that also presents other forms of crime statistics.

These two sources of crime data may be compared, but it is important to note their differences. The NCVS excludes homicide, arson, commercial crimes, and crimes against children under age 12 (the UCR includes these crimes). The NCVS also does not include any information on victimless crimes such as drug crimes, gambling, or prostitution. The UCR only collects arrest data on simple assault and sexual assaults other than rape, not reported crimes. Further, the NCVS calculates rates on the basis of 1000 *households,* while the UCR calculates rates based on 100,000 *persons.* Thus, it would be a mistake to treat findings from the two sources as comparable statistically. In general, the UCR gives us a broad picture of crime patterns (as reported to police) in the United States, while the NCVS gives us more information about the characteristics of victimizations and reporting trends by victims.

Because the NCVS is based on a random sample of the population and does not collect reports of all victimizations, it is subject to all the potential problems of sampling and survey weaknesses. If any principles of random sampling are violated, then the applicability to the general population is in doubt. The sample size of the NCVS has been decreasing over the years, and some observers have begun to worry that the smaller sample size has begun to affect the representativeness of the sample. However, it is important to note that the NCVS also showed a decline of reported crime victimization in the last decade; thus, the two sources of crime data were consistent in measuring a crime decline.

Self-report studies

Another source of crime data is simply to ask the offender. Self-report studies ask individuals to report the crimes they have committed. Obviously, there are problems inherent in such an approach, such as whether the individual is answering honestly or not. Self-reports are generally only obtained from targeted groups, specifically juveniles (who are still in school) and offenders (who are incarcerated). We do not administer self-report surveys door to door to samples of citizens. Self-report studies provide interesting information, but the findings must be considered in light of the characteristics of the sample. For instance, self-report studies of juveniles often use measures of behavior that stretch the definition of "crime" to the breaking point by including minor deviances, such as truancy and other forms of juvenile misbehavior. The definitions of wrongdoing are expanded in such studies because most students have not committed any criminal acts. Therefore, in order to get sufficient numbers for statistical analysis, the definition of "offender" is expanded. It should be kept in mind when reading these studies that these "offenders" are not necessarily who we think of as criminals.

Part of the reason that student self-report studies have difficulty obtaining sufficient numbers of offenders for statistical analysis when testing crime theories is that by the time they are administered in junior or senior years, many high-risk juveniles have already dropped out or are not in school the day the study is administered. Therefore, the young people most likely to have committed crimes are likely to be absent from the study, and the reports of criminal activity are likely to under-represent the true nature of juvenile crime.

Like school samples, prisoner samples are relatively easy to obtain, but non-representative. Prisoners do not represent all offenders (only those who are caught and sentenced to prison). They also may not admit or may exaggerate their criminal activities. In addition, these surveys are subject to the potential inaccuracies of all surveys in that respondents may forget or misremember when events occurred.

Self-report studies give us more information about the offenders' patterns of criminal activity—if we can trust the data. One of the uses of self-report studies is to see if official statistics accurately represent who commits crime. We have found from self-reports of juveniles, for instance, that many more juveniles have committed crimes than official arrests indicate. This raises the question, "When do system actors (police) utilize formal methods of social control versus informal?"

Cohort studies

One other source of crime data is **cohort study**, which follows a group of subjects over a long period. For instance, one cohort study followed all males born in Philadelphia in 1948 [13]. Another longitudinal study conducted by the Harvard Program on Human Development and Criminal Behavior collected data on a cohort sample [14]. Typically, the follow-up period extends throughout childhood and into adulthood. Proponents of longitudinal research argue that this method of data collection can illuminate how factors work at various times in one's life. Longitudinal research identifies those correlates of delinquency that emerge during the lifetime of the cohort members. For instance, Farrington et al. [15] identified the following as correlates of delinquency and crime:

> We know that the typical high-rate offender is a young male who began his aggressive or larcenous activities at an early age, well before the typical boy gets into serious trouble. We know that he comes from a troubled, discordant, low-income family in which one or both parents are likely to have criminal records themselves. We know that the boy has had trouble in school—he created problems for his teachers and does not do well in his studies. On leaving school, often by dropping out, he works at regular jobs only intermittently. Most employers regard him as a poor risk. He experiments with a variety of drugs—alcohol, marijuana, speed, heroin—and becomes a frequent user of whatever drug is most readily available, often switching back and forth among different ones [16].

Thus, individual differences, family influences, school influences, and peer influences were all identified as potential predictors of the onset of, continuation in, and desistance from crime.

PATTERNS OF CRIME

According to the Uniform Crime Reports and the National Crime Victimization Survey, crime has shown a steady overall decline since the early 1990s. In Figure 2.1, we see that there is much more property crime than violent crime, and that property crime has shown a more dramatic decline than violent crime. The long timeline in Figure 2.1 does not show enough detail to see that violent crime actually declined quite substantially from a high of 758 crimes per 100,000 in 1991 to a low of 429.4 in 2009. The violent crime rate in 2009 is about the same level of violent crime reported in 1973.

INTERNET KEY

For more information on crime patterns, go to http://bjs.ojp.usdoj.gov/.

The National Crime Victimization Survey also indicates that Americans have experienced a dramatically declining crime rate over the last decade. In Figure 2.2, victimization survey data shows that for violent crime and property crime, the decline is comparable to that recorded in the Uniform Crime Reports.

Comparing the United States to other countries

There is a widespread perception that the United States has more crime than similar Western countries such as the United Kingdom, France, or Canada. This is true only for violent crimes. Property crime rates in the

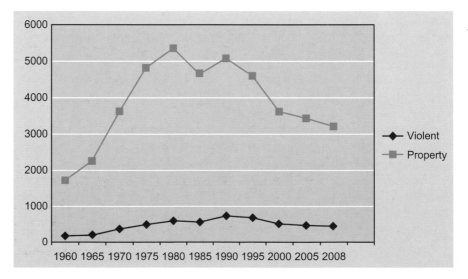

FIGURE 2.1
Uniform crime rate over time. **Source:** *Sourcebook of Criminal Justice Statistics, 2010, Table 3.106.2008. Retrieved 9/12/2010 from http.www. albany.edu/sourcebook/pdf/ t31062008.pdf.*

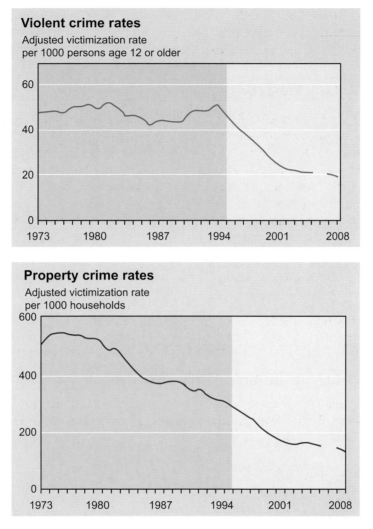

FIGURE 2.2
Victimization rates for violent and property crimes. **Source:** *Bureau of Justice Statistics, Property and Violent Crime Victimization.* *Retrieved 9/12/2010 from http://bjs.ojp.usdoj.gov/ content/glance/viort.cfm,* and *http://bjs.ojp.usdoj.gov/ content/glance/house2.cfm.*

United States are roughly comparable to those of other countries. It should be pointed out that comparing crimes cross-culturally is difficult because definitions and reporting practices that affect crime statistics vary. The United Nations Office of Drugs and Crime, however, has collected and makes available crime rates as reported by member nations in order to make some tentative comparisons. In the latest report available, about 120 countries are represented.

🌐 **INTERNET KEY**

For information on how the United States' crime rates compare to other countries, go to http://www.unodc.org/ unodc/en/data-ana-analysis/crimedata.html.

Homicide is perhaps the most consistently reported crime and offers the most reliable comparison. The homicide rate of the United States is about 5.2. In countries such as Norway (0.6), the rate is very low as compared to the United States and in others, such as Honduras (60.9), it is very high. Other crimes show great variability in the rates between countries, which probably has as much to do with reporting differences as differences in criminal behavior. On the other hand, we can be fairly confident that U.S. rates for such crimes as burglary and other property crimes are not too dissimilar from our "sister" countries such as Australia and the United Kingdom. Table 2.4 shows the rate of selected crimes in some countries.

Table 2.4 Selected Crime Rates from Selected Countries

Homicide		Russian Federation	172.5
USA	5.2	*Lowest*	
U.K.	1.6	Algeria	0.9
Canada	1.7	Liechtenstein	2.8
Australia	1.2	Sierra Leone	3.3
France	1.4	Japan	3.4
Highest		Albania	4.6
Honduras	60.9	**Burglary/breaking**	
Jamaica	59.5	**& entering**	
El Salvador	51.8	USA	713.0
Guatemala	45.2	UK	877.0
Lowest		Canada	630.0
Austria	0.5	Australia	1146.0
Norway	0.6	France	480.0
Hong Kong	0.6	*Highest*	
Algeria	0.6	Denmark	1715.0
Bahrain	0.8	New Zealand	1401.0
Robbery		Sweden	1024.0
USA	141.8	Chile	964.0
UK	105.9	Iceland	865.0
Canada	97.1	*Lowest*	
Australia	78.3	Azerbaijan	0.4
France	171.9	Mongolia	1.1
Highest		Mexico	2.6
Belgium	1836.8	Syria	3.4
Spain	1067.0	Egypt	5.6
Portugal	195.3		

Source: *United Nations Office of Drugs and Crime (2010), UNODC Crime and Criminal Justice Statistics. Retrieved 9/16/2010 from http://www.unodc.org/unodc/en/data-and-analysis/ crimedata.html.*

THE GREAT AMERICAN CRIME DECLINE

The biggest "story" in criminal justice in the last 20 years was the decline in crime experienced through the latter half of the 1990s. Although the decrease has leveled off in some locales in recent years, we experienced truly dramatic drops in all crime, including homicide and other violent crimes. Why? It could be due to any of the following factors:

- Aging birth cohort of baby boomers
- Stabilization of drug markets
- Higher incarceration rates
- Community policing
- "Zero tolerance" policing
- Home health care and pre- and post-natal health services
- Violence prevention programs in schools
- Increased numbers of abortions in the late 1970s and 1980s [17]

There is no consensus as to whether any of these factors, either alone or in combination, account for the dramatic decline of crime. One thing that hasn't happened as a result of the recorded decline, however, is any decline in the size of the criminal justice system. News reports indicated in September 2010 that crime had declined again from 2008 to 2009 (see the Breaking News box).

BREAKING NEWS: CRIME DECLINES AGAIN!

Newspapers reported across the country on September 13, 2010, that "the number of violent crimes in the United States declined for the third consecutive year" and that property crime declined for the seventh consecutive year. Actually, since they were reporting from an FBI press release announcing findings from the 2009 Uniform Crime Reports, they should have reported that *reports* of crime had declined. The news reports also didn't indicate that the decline between 2008 and 2009 is consistent with a decade-long decline in both violent and property crime. News reports indicated that murder and non-negligent manslaughter and robbery had the largest decreases among violent crimes and motor vehicle theft showed the largest decline in property crimes.

CORRELATES OF CRIME

These summary statistics of crime do not tell us much about who commits crime, when and where it is committed, or against whom. A **correlate** of crime is a factor that is associated statistically with the incidence of crime. In other words, it can be a predictor of crime. The three strongest predictors of crime seem to be sex, age, and race. We say "seem to be" because the information we have available is based on arrest statistics. We know who is arrested for crimes, and we assume that those arrested represent those who commit crimes, but we cannot be completely sure. For instance, the **chivalry theory** proposes the idea that women are less likely to be arrested than men in similar circumstances, and if arrested, are less likely to be tried and convicted. There has been a great deal of research testing whether or not this occurs, and the weight of evidence indicates that it occurred to some extent, for some women, for some crimes, in the past, but seems to be less likely to occur today [18].

Generally, we are fairly certain that women are much less likely to commit violent crime than men and somewhat less likely to commit most property crimes. In Table 2.5, we see that for almost all crime categories, the number of arrests of men exceeded that for women (even though women comprise a little more than half of the population). For some crimes, the differential was quite extreme (homicide and rape); for others, it was marginal (fraud) and in 2009 there were actually more arrests of women than men for embezzlement. Arrests of women show an increase in some crimes while men's arrests declined (robbery, burglary, other assaults). In some crime categories, both men's and women's arrests increased (drug violations). There are some changes that seem extreme; for instance, between 1996 and 2009, arrests of men for larceny-theft dropped by 143,547 (but showed little change at all between 2000 and 2009). Women's arrests have swung down and then up again. There were 310,666 arrests of women for larceny-theft in 1996; that number dropped

Table 2.5 Ten-Year Arrest Trends by Sex, 1996-2009

	Male		Female	
Offense	*1996*	*2009*	*1996*	*2009*
Total	6,773,900	6,174,287	1,845,799	2,087,303
Murder/manslaughter	8,572	6,437	992	756
Rape	18,512	12,469	233	148
Robbery	73,192	67,906	7,788	9,384
Aggravated assault	260,469	209,078	54,936	58,236
Burglary	195,124	159,017	25,674	29,764
Larceny/theft	595,297	451,750	310,666	354,854
Motor vehicle theft	86,405	38,987	13,913	8,486
Arson	9,972	6,432	1,628	1,300
Other assaults	597,763	592,155	158,366	211,334
Forgery/counterfeiting	45,250	31,152	26,853	18,840
Fraud	137,874	78,550	117,288	61,385
Embezzlement	5,545	5,743	4,607	6,013
Sex offenses	52,296	42,609	4,188	4,019
Drug abuse violations	688,006	806,669	142,678	189,039

Sources: *Crime in the United States, Table 33. Retrieved 05/21/2007 from http://www.fbi.gov/ ucr/05cius/data/table_33.html. Crime in the United States, 2009, Table 33. Retrieved 9/15/2010 from http://www.fbi.gov/ucr/cius2009/data/table_33.html.*

to 258,379 in 2000, increased to 270,765 in 2005, and then increased again to 354,854 in 2009. Because these are arrest figures, these changes could be the result of increased (or decreased) criminal acts or increased (or decreased) inclination to arrest by system actors.

There continues to be debate about whether women are increasing their participation in violent crimes (aggravated assault, robbery, homicide); however, most of the change in the ratio between men's and women's violent crime participation is due to the dramatic decline of men's crimes with the relatively modest decline of women's rather than any increase in women's violent crime. Why women's violent crime rates haven't declined as dramatically as men's seems obvious: women's rate of, for instance, aggravated assault (as measured by the NCS/NCVS) was between 2 and 4 per 1000 between 1973 and 1999 and then dropped to below 2 per 1000. Men's started much higher at about 23 per 1000 in 1973, dropping 67% to about 7 per 1000 in 2005 [19]. Although the women's assault rate dropped "only" 56% compared to the men's 67% decrease, it is unreasonable to assume that aggravated assault by women would ever be so close to 0. Similar numbers exist for other violent crime. Just as small base numbers make using percentage increase figures extremely suspect, the small base numbers also do not allow for much room for decreases because there will always be some commission of crime by women. The real question regarding gender and crime is why men's violent crime decreased so dramatically, not why women showed more modest decreases over the same period.

Another clear correlate of crime is age. Crime is typically committed by those between the ages of 18 and 25. Figure 2.3 illustrates this trend and shows how crime declines after age 30.

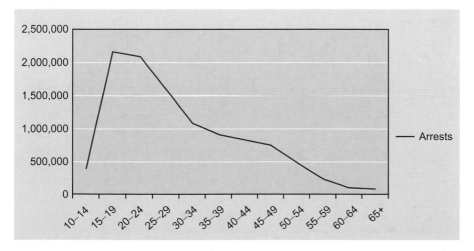

FIGURE 2.3
Age of arrests, 2005.
Source: *Crime in the United States, Table 38. Retrieved 9/15/2010 from http:// www.fbi.gov/ucr/09cius/ data/table_38.html.*

Table 2.6 Arrests by Race, 2009

	Percentage of Distribution		
Offense	***White***	***Black***	***Am Indian/Asian***
Total	69.1	28.3	3.6
Murder/manslaughter	48.7	49.3	2.0
Rape	65.1	32.5	2.4
Robbery	42.8	55.5	1.7
Aggravated assault	63.5	33.9	2.6
Burglary	66.5	31.7	1.8
Larceny/theft	68.1	29.0	2.8
Motor vehicle theft	61.1	36.3	2.6
Assaults	65.2	32.2	2.7
Forgery/counterfeiting	66.7	31.7	1.6
Fraud	67.0	31.2	1.7
Embezzlement	66.0	31.7	2.3
Sex offenses	73.5	23.8	2.7
Drug abuse violations	65.0	33.6	1.4

Source: *Crime in the United States, Table 43. Retrieved 5/21/2009 from http://www.fbi.gov/ucr/cius2009/data/table_43.html.*

Race, a third correlate of crime, is not as predictable. The correlation between race of the offender and crime varies depending on the type of crime. Unfortunately, the FBI statistics used to construct tables of those arrested does not include information on ethnicity; therefore, "whites" include both whites and nonblack Hispanic offenders. Table 2.6 shows that, considering their population percentage of about 13%, blacks are arrested at disproportionate rates, although for most crimes, not dramatically so. On the other hand, for some crimes, their arrest rates are highly disproportionate. Murder and robbery have very high rates of arrests for blacks and these two crimes are usually associated with black offenders in the public's mind. Although not displayed on the table, some of the more minor crimes have very high percentages of arrests for blacks as well. More than 40% of the arrests for vagrancy were of blacks and 68.6% of arrests for gambling in 2009 were of blacks [20]. Because it is highly doubtful that close to 70% of those who engage in illegal gambling are black, we must look at whether other factors affect the arrest decision.

PUBLIC ATTITUDES TOWARD CRIME AND CRIMINALS

Public concern about crime does not seem to bear much relationship to crime reports. Figure 2.4 shows that the percentage of Americans who fear walking alone at night is exactly the same as it was in 1965. On the other hand, about two-thirds of Americans frequently or occasionally worry about identity theft (66%) [21].

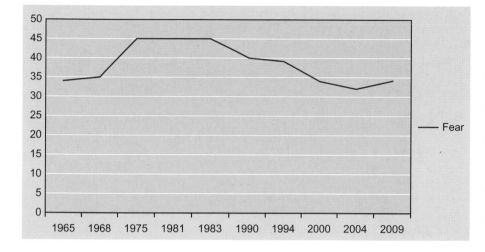

FIGURE 2.4
Public opinion toward crime and punishment. Fear walking alone at night within 1 mile from home (percent).
Source: *Sourcebook of Criminal Justice Statistics, Public's Views on Crime.* Retrieved 9/15/2010 from http://www.albany. edu/sourcebook/pdf/ t2372009.pdf.

The Gallup Poll indicates that the public has always favored social programs over more police and prisons. In 1989, 61% of the public favored social programs over law enforcement to address the crime problem, and in 2006, 65% of the public favored social programs [22]. However, the Gallup Poll also indicates that the public thinks courts don't deal harshly enough with offenders. In 2003, only 6% of respondents thought the criminal justice system was "too tough," but 65% thought it wasn't "tough enough." This is quite a bit less than the 83% who thought the courts were not tough enough in 1992 [23]. Other sources indicate that the public may be favorably inclined to community sanctions when they believe they are strictly managed. In one study, when asked about 25 crimes, only 27% of respondents chose prison as the appropriate sentence when offered a range of community alternatives [24].

The Sentencing Project, a private nonprofit policy body, offers statistical reports on sentencing practices and promotes alternatives to incarceration. This organization offers evidence that there are many myths that exist, such as the following:

1. **Crime is increasing.** The public is not generally aware of the official statistics that show crime has been declining for a decade. There is a widespread belief that crime continues to increase year after year, and this misperception fuels the desire for harsh punishment.
2. **Criminals are not being sentenced to prison or not sentenced harshly enough.** Although the public believes that imprisonment is given rarely, it is now the most frequent sentence handed down. The public is not aware that "truth in sentencing" statutes have drastically increased the

percentage of the sentence that an average criminal serves. For instance, Florida residents, when polled, believed that offenders only served about 40% of their sentence, but, in reality, offenders in Florida are required to serve 85% of their sentence.

3. **The public is in favor of three-strikes laws and harsh sentences.** When asked, respondents indicate their approval of three-strikes laws; however, when presented with case scenarios that realistically portray criminal defendants, they favor alternative sanctions. This is so even though such offender profiles would be the types of offenders who would be subject to three-strikes sentences. Thus, it appears that the public favors the concept of three strikes, but not necessarily how it is likely to be implemented.

4. **The public supports "tough on criminal" platforms of politicians.** Again, the concept is different from reality. Politicians may be surprised to learn that one study reported that policymakers estimated that only 12% of the public would be in support of alternative sanctions, but actually 66% of respondents indicated their support. Also, the majority of respondents favor social programs over police and prison responses to crime prevention [25].

CONCLUSION

In this chapter, we have discussed the reality of crime; however, we first note that it is a "constructed reality" created by the perceptions of the victim and system actors. Only a portion of all crimes find their way into official statistics. Even the Uniform Crime Reports, our most commonly utilized source for crime statistics, can only report those crimes that are reported to the police. The "dark figure" of crime is that which is unreported. We do not know whether these offenders are similar to or different from those who appear in official statistics.

In addition to the Uniform Crime Reports, we also have the National Crime Victimization Survey, which provides additional information. We know more about victims' injuries and who is likely to report criminal victimization to the police because of victimization surveys. However, the NCVS also has some weaknesses and is not strictly comparable to the UCR in how crime is reported.

The biggest news is that crime declined dramatically during the last part of the 1990s and early 2000s. It now appears that the most dramatic decline has slowed and, in some crime categories, and in some locales, the trend has reversed itself. We must be alert to new crime reports to determine if crime will continue to rise, decline again, or remain stable. The strongest correlates of crime are sex, age, and, to a much lesser degree, race. We know that most crime is committed by young men. Why this is so and what motivates individuals to commit crime is the subject of the next chapter.

Review Questions

1. Why is the definition of crime problematic for the study of criminal justice and criminology?
2. Why is the dark figure of crime problematic for the study of criminal justice and criminology?
3. What do we mean when we say crime is a "constructed reality"?
4. Describe and provide examples of victim-harming and victimless crimes.
5. Describe the Uniform Crime Reports and crime "rates."
6. What are the most commonly committed crimes? What are the most infrequently committed crimes?
7. What are clearance rates?
8. What has been the pattern of crime in the last 30 years?
9. Describe the three correlates of crime.
10. Describe public opinion concerning what should be done about crime.

VOCABULARY

chivalry theory proposes the idea that women are less likely to be arrested than men in similar circumstances and, if arrested, less likely to be tried and convicted

clearance rates the percentage of crime solved by arrests

cohort studies a group of subjects followed over a long period with data collected multiple times during the course of their lives

correlate (of crime) a factor that is associated statistically with the incidence of crime

crime actions that are prohibited by law

crime rate the number of crimes divided by the population and then multiplied to display by a standard number (usually 100,000)

dark figure of crime crime that does not find its way into official numbers

deviance behaviors that are contrary to the norm

National Crime Victimization Survey survey of a nationally representative sample about criminal victimization

Uniform Crime Reports collection of local crime reports and arrest data begun in 1929 and now produced by the Federal Bureau of Investigation

victim-harming crimes crimes that harm specific victims (either physically or financially)

victimless crimes crimes for which there is no direct victim

ENDNOTES

[1] Texas Penal Code. Retrieved 4/10/2007 from http://tlo2.tlc.state.tx.us/statutes/docs/PE/content/htm/pe.005.00.000022.00.htm#22.01.00.

[2] "South Carolina considers gun law," Fox News, retrieved 4/10/2007 from http://www.foxnews.com/story/10,2933,272974,00.html. W. Buchanan, Three years after Virginia Tech shooting, college gun bans prevail, Christian Science Monitor, April 16, 2010. Retrieved 9/12/2010 from www.csmonitor.com/USA/Education/2010/0416/Three-years-after-Virginia-Tech-Shooting-college-gun-bans-prevail.html.

[3] See H. Cleveland, M. Koss, J. Lyons, Rape tactics from the survivor's perspective, J. Interpers. Violence, 14(5) (1999) 532–548.

[4] Sourcebook of Criminal Justice Statistics Online, 2010. Retrieved 9/9/2010. Table at http://www.albany.edu/sourcebook/pdf/13332007.pdf.

[5] See C. Mendias, E. Kobe, Engagement of policing ideals and the relationship to the exercise of discretionary powers, Crim. Just. Behav. 33(1) (2006) 70–77.

[6] See M. Gottfredson, T. Hirschi, The General Theory of Crime, Stanford University Press, Stanford, CA, 1990.

[7] N. James, How Crime in the United States Is Measured, Congressional Research Service (CRS), Washington, DC, 2008.

[8] Federal Bureau of Investigation, Crime in the United States, 2008, Table 8, Crime in the United States by State, by City, 2008. FBI, Washington, DC, 2008. Retrieved 9/12/2007 from www.fbi.gov/ucr/cius2008/data/table_8.html.

[9] J. Eterno, E. Silverman, The trouble with Compstat: pressure on NYPD commanders endangered the integrity of crime stats, New York Daily News, February 15, 2010. Retrieved 9/15/2010 from http://www.nydailynews.com/opinions/2010/02/15/2010-02-15_the_trouble_with_compstat.html.

[10] Federal Bureau of Investigation. Retrieved 8/1/2006 from http://www.fbi.gov/ucr/cius_04/offenses_cleared/index.html.

[11] Federal Bureau of Investigation. Retrieved 9/15/2010 from http://www.fbi.gov/ucr/cius2009/offenses/data/table_25.html.

[12] N. James, How Crime in the United States Is Measured, Congressional Research Service, Washington, DC, 2008.

[13] M. Wolfgang, R. Figlio, T. Sellin, Delinquency in a Birth Cohort, University of Chicago Press, Chicago, 1978.

[14] M. Tonry, L. Ohlin, D. Farrington, Human Development and Criminal Behavior: New Ways of Advancing Knowledge, Springer-Verlag, New York, 1991.

[15] D. Farrington, L. Ohlin, J. Wilson, Understanding and Controlling Crime: Toward a New Research Strategy, Springer-Verlag, New York, 1986.

[16] D. Farrington, L. Ohlin, J. Wilson, Understanding and Controlling Crime: Toward a New Research Strategy, Springer Verlag, New York, 1986, p. 2.

[17] Steven Levitt's economic analysis indicated that the rising use of abortion by poor women after abortion became legal led to a reduced number of unwanted children who were at the highest risk for becoming delinquents and criminals.

[18] See J. Pollock, Women, Prison and Society, Wadsworth/ITP, Belmont, CA, 2005.

[19] J. Lauritsen, K. Heimer, J. Lynch, Trends in the gender gap in violent offending: new evidence from the national crime victimization survey, Criminology 47(2) (2009) 361–401, 378. For a different view, see J. Schwartz, D. Steffensmeier, H. Zhong, J. Ackerman, Trends in the Gender Gap in Violence: Reevaluating NCVS and Other Evidence, Criminology 47(2) (2009) 401–427.

[20] From Crime in the United States, Table 43. Retrieved 9/15/2010 from http://www.fbi.gov/ucr/cius2009/data/table_43.html.

[21] Sourcebook of Criminal Justice Statistics. Retrieved 9/15/2010 from http://www.albany.edu/sourcebook/pdf/t2292009.pdf.

[22] Sourcebook of Criminal Justice Statistics. Retrieved 9/15/2010 from http://www.albany.edu/sourcebook/pdf/t2282006.pdf.

[23] Retrieved 6/2/2005 from http://www.gallup.com/poll/1603/crime.aspx.

[24] L. Bennett, The public wants accountability, Corrections Today 53 4(92) (1991) 94–95.

[25] The Sentencing Project, "Crime Punishment and Public Opinion: A Summary of Recent Studies and Their Implications for Sentencing Policy," [1999]. Available at http://www.sentencingproject.org.

CHAPTER 3

Why Do People Commit Crime?

WHAT YOU NEED TO KNOW

- Criminology is the study of crime and criminal motivation.
- Classical thinkers believed that humans were rational and chose crime because it was in their best interest to do so.
- Positivists look for the causes of crime and positivist theories fall into biological, psychological, or sociological categories.
- Biological theories identify certain genetic influences that may predispose some individuals to crime.
- Psychological theories can be subdivided into psychoanalytic, developmental, and learning theories.
- Sociological crime theories can be further divided into social structure theories and social process theories.
- Social structure theories identify societal elements as criminogenic and include subcultural theories, the strain/opportunity theory, radical/critical theories, social support, and social disorganization theories.
- Social process theories identify interactive processes between the individual and the environment as criminogenic and include differential association, labeling theory, control theory, the general theory of crime, and general strain theory.

CONTENTS

Almost everyone thinks they know why people commit crimes. Their answers may include family factors (bad parents), individual/personality factors (bad kids), peer factors (bad friends), and societal factors (bad economy/neighborhood). For hundreds of years, researchers have attempted to understand why some people choose to commit crimes. **Criminology** is the study of crime and

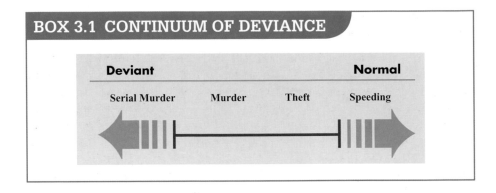

criminal motivation. It is usually a separate course in most college curriculums, and so, in this short chapter, we do not attempt to discuss all the various theories that have been proposed to answer this question. Instead, we will look at the types of theories that have been proposed and tested. Recall from the last chapter that the strongest predictors of crime are sex, age, and, to a lesser extent, race. Thus, any theory of crime should be able to explain why young men (and, for some crimes, young black men) are more likely than any other group to commit crimes (or perhaps only be arrested for them).

Another way to approach the study of criminology is to think of crime on a continuum of deviance, as displayed in Box 3.1. At one end are acts that are extremely rare. They are committed by very few people and happen infrequently, such as serial murder, sadistic killings, and serial rapes. At the other end of the continuum are acts that are committed by a large number of people quite frequently, such as speeding or perhaps minor income tax evasion (such as overstating the amount contributed to charity). All other crimes fall on the continuum in relation to how frequently they are committed and/or how many people commit the act. It seems reasonable that an explanation of why people commit crimes on the far left side of the continuum would more likely be individual theories; that is, explanations that are unique to the individual because they are so different from others. Therefore, psychoanalytic theories make more sense for these types of offenders. Crimes toward the right of the continuum may be explained by a wider range of criminological theories.

THE CLASSICAL SCHOOL VERSUS POSITIVISM

The Classical school is usually described by the contributions of Cesare Beccaria (1738-1794) and Jeremy Bentham (1748-1832) [1]. Both theorists, writing in the 1700s, operated under a fundamental assumption that men were rational and operated with free will. Therefore, the elimination of crime could be achieved by the threat of punishment for offenses, which would act as a deterrent to crime. Philosophers during this period did not view women in the same manner as men and viewed their mental abilities to be more akin to children; therefore, their discussions applied specifically to men.

Jeremy Bentham proposed that the justice system must administer punishment in such a way that it was slightly more punitive than the perceived profit of the crime contemplated (in order to deter individuals from attempting the crime). Bentham's "**hedonistic calculus**" called for punishment adjusted in this way for each offense. According to Bentham, punishment should be no more than necessary to deter. It should be adjusted upward in severity in relation to a decrease in certainty. Punishment that was swift, certain, and proportional to the potential profit or pleasure of the crime was most effective. The focus of these thinkers was on the legal system; the assumption was that everyone would respond to the legal system in a similar, rational manner. The Classical School is usually a historical preface to the theories of crime that developed after the rise of positivism.

Positivism

Positivism can be described simply as "scientific method" or the search for causes using scientific method. It is typically associated with Cesare Lombroso (1835-1909) [2], who is often referred to as the "grandfather of criminology." With Lombroso, the focus shifted from the legal system to the offender. The cause of crime, in fact, was assumed to lie in the individual. Lombroso believed that a few "born criminals" were born with genetic defects that made them commit criminal acts. It should also be noted that over the course of his career, he developed a more sophisticated typology of criminals. He recognized other types in addition to the purely biological criminal, and these types represented some of the same explanations we use today, such as opportunity, influence, and passion. Later positivists in the early 1900s also looked at individual causes, and both biological and psychological factors were examined. According to positivists, criminals were different from noncriminals and criminologists merely needed to understand those differences.

Cesare Lombroso (1836-1909)—Italian physician and psychiatrist—argued that there were "criminal types" distinguishable by physical characteristics. *Courtesy en.wikipedia.org*

Lombroso also wrote a book about criminal women [3]. Women were presumed to be biologically and psychologically different from men, which accounted for their lower crime rates. However, some women were evolutionary throwbacks, according to Lombroso, and these "primitive" women were criminal because, in his theory, all primitive women were more masculine and criminal than "modern" law-abiding women.

We can say that the field of criminology really began with the positivists because they initiated the search for differences between criminal men and women and law-abiding men and women. Their findings do not hold up over the passage of time and their scientific method was primitive, but their approach is still the basic approach of most criminologists today—that is, to seek out differences that motivate some people to choose crime.

BIOLOGICAL THEORIES OF CRIME

Recall that the three strongest predictors of crime—sex, age, and race—are biological constructs. Of the three, only race shows strongly different patterns crossculturally. Furthermore, race is mediated by inter-racial mixing so that most people do not represent pure racial phenotypes. Contrary to the complications race presents, the other two correlates are age and sex. Thus, it would seem that biology should be at least explored as a factor in crime causation. However, research on biological factors has been given little attention in most criminology textbooks. Part of the reason biological approaches in criminology have been so completely rejected is that there are serious policy implications for such theories. It is argued that such theories lead to **eugenics**, which is the idea of improving the human race through controlled procreation, and other forms of control repugnant to our democratic ideals.

Biological factors may be (a) inherited genetic traits, or (b) biological, but not genetic. For instance, a brain tumor that puts pressure on the violence center of the brain and results in irrational violence is obviously a biological cause of crime, but tumors are not thought to be inherited. Chemicals or other environmental toxins can also affect the brain and are non-genetic biological factors that may influence criminal choice. More controversial, however, is the idea that criminality is inherited.

A scientist examines a DNA model. *Blend Images via AP Images*

Is there a criminal gene? Of course not, but the argument of biological criminologists is that there are some inherited characteristics that predispose individuals to criminal choices [4]. The methodological problem has always been trying to isolate genetic influences from socialization influences. If you are like your mother or father, is it because you have inherited traits from them or because they raised you? Trying to separate these influences is very difficult.

Twin studies identify and track twins (both monozygotic twins who share a single egg and dizygotic who have separate eggs but a single sperm) and look to find concordance or discordance in such things as intelligence, delinquency, alcoholism, and other behavioral indices. **Concordance** occurs if both twins possess the affliction (e.g. alcoholism). Discordance means that the twins do not share the trait. Higher rates of concordance among monozygotic twins than dizygotic twins lend support to biological explanations because monozygotic twins share the exact same genetic makeup. Several studies have found higher concordance rates, but the problem remains that such similarity could be because monozygotic twins are treated more alike than dizygotic twin pairs [5]. Studies have also looked at the concordance between the criminality of children and their adoptive parents and biological parents. The best study would be of monozygotic twins separated from biological parents, and from each other, at birth, but obviously, such samples are extremely small.

We know that there are medical conditions that may be inherited. We also now know that certain forms of mental illness have a genetic component. It is also believed that a predisposition to alcoholism or addiction is inherited, and scientists believe they have discovered the "addiction gene" on the DNA strand. Further, it may be that certain personality traits, such as impulsivity and poor conditionability (or ability to learn), are also inherited. Personality traits, such as impulsiveness, aggressiveness, or and extroversion, have long been associated with delinquency/criminality. These traits do not inevitably lead to criminal choices, but they predispose the individual to such choices, especially when the individual grows up in criminogenic environmental conditions.

Hormones and brain chemistry

When a personality trait is believed to be inherited, scientists look for the actual physical components of the trait. These origins lie in the neural structures of the brain, brain chemistry, and hormones. For instance, if aggressive tendencies are inherited, it is possible that what is actually inherited is a higher-than-average level of testosterone, which has long been associated with aggression. A fairly impressive body of knowledge has developed on the correlation between testosterone and aggression, although such research has also been subject to heavy criticism. Although both men and women have testosterone in the body, men have about 10 to 15 times more testosterone than women. Therefore, many argue that when we observe male aggression, we are observing the effects of testosterone. Basic problems with such research include accurate measurements of testosterone, a valid definition and operationalization of the construct of aggression, and understanding the interactive effect of testosterone production, aggressive behavior, and environmental cues. Testosterone production seems to be moderated by environmental factors, and obviously the translation of aggressiveness to behavior is subject to social control, self-control, meanings ascribed to behavior, and learning, which may account for the ambiguous findings in this area [6].

Brain chemicals may also affect personality traits. A chemical found in the brain has intriguing qualities that may be linked to a predisposition to

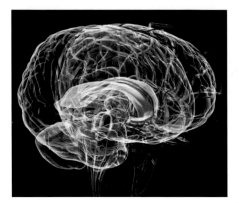

Brain anatomy. The cerebellum is purple, the corpus callosum is green.
© Roger Harris/Science Photo Library/Corbis

delinquency. Researchers have found that a low level of monoamine oxidase (MAO) is linked to psychopathy, alcoholism, sensation-seeking, impulsivity, extroversion, schizophrenia, and criminal behavior [7]. Men, on average, have about 20% less MAO than women, and this difference exists at all ages. Studies have reported findings that MAO levels are linked to delinquency. Boys with low MAO levels were found to be more impulsive and sensation-seeking than other boys and were more likely to have drug and alcohol problems [8]. Associations are consistently found between low MAO activity and various correlates of criminal behavior, such as impulsiveness, childhood hyperactivity, learning disabilities, sensation-seeking, substance abuse, and extroversion. MAO activity seems to be correlated with age, sex, and race. Testosterone evidently depresses MAO levels. In fact, testosterone levels are at their highest and MAO levels are at their lowest during the second decade of life (10 to 20, roughly corresponding to the crime-prone age years) [9].

Other research shows interesting connections between serotonin levels and negative emotionality and impulsivity [10]. Serotonin also seems to be linked with norepinephrine levels and, together, they may play a role in conditionability or the ability to learn [11]. There is evidence to indicate that individuals differ at a cellular level in their response to outside stimuli. Those with low levels of arousal tend toward behaviors that are risk-taking and sensation-seeking because these behaviors increase the cortical level of arousal. Risky behaviors are not necessarily antisocial. They could be sport-related activities or daredevil stunts. However, some individuals might be predisposed toward antisocial behaviors because these behaviors are exciting and produce the level of cortical arousal that extroverts seek. Thus, aggressive interactions, fast driving, shoplifting, robbery, and so on are risky and result in a thrilling rush of adrenalin that is much more pleasant for thrill seekers than thrill avoiders. Because thrill seekers need a greater level of stimuli to respond, they do not learn as well, and do not as readily absorb societal lessons that lead to law-abiding behavior [12].

One model that incorporated physiological processes and learning theory postulates that traits that have been linked to delinquency—specifically, impulsivity, hyperactivity, sensation-seeking, risk-taking, and low self-control—are linked to neurophysiological mechanisms. Risky activities may release more endorphins in certain individuals than others because of brain chemistry. The differential experience of endorphins means that such behaviors become more internally rewarded for some than others, with the corollary prediction that they will continue to engage in such behavior [13]. Sex differences exist in cortical arousal levels, and men, in general, are more likely to have low cortical arousal [14].

ADD, hyperactivity, and intelligence

There is consistent evidence that hyperactivity and attention deficit disorder (ADD) are correlated with delinquency. It has been reported that those diagnosed with hyperactivity as children were 25 times more likely to exhibit later delinquency [15]. Denno [16] also reports that delinquency is linked to overactivity, perceptual-motor impairments, impulsivity, emotional lability, attention deficits, minor disturbances of speech, intellectual defects (learning disabilities), clumsiness, neurodevelopmental lag, psychogenic factors, and minor physical anomalies. These features may be the result of genetic transmission, poor living environment, prenatal or birth trauma, or a combination of the above. It has been found that delinquents have significantly lower verbal skills, auditory verbal memory, interspatial analysis, and visual-motor integration in elementary school. Such early evidence of cognitive deficits indicates that it is not simply a delinquent "lifestyle" and/or drug use that causes subsequent lower cognitive abilities, but rather there may be problems at birth that affect the child's performance in school. Evidence indicates that many children outgrow predisposing factors, but those who do not are more likely to become delinquent.

It is interesting to note that ADD and hyperactivity tend to be more common for boys than girls. Boys and men experience a higher incidence of prenatal and perinatal mortality and complications, reading and learning disorders, and mental retardation, as well as left hemisphere deficits [17]. In general, male children are more prone to learning dysfunctions due to brain differences [18]. Is it possible that the greater tendency of young men to engage in risky and/or violent behavior is not only culturally induced, but also may have a biological component?

There are numerous, hotly debated issues involved in the research concerning intelligence. The first is whether intelligence can even be defined and/or measured. The next point of controversy, assuming that we can agree upon some definition of intelligence, is whether intelligence is inherited. Again, while some researchers maintain that the evidence is clear and convincing, others argue that the correlation in IQ scores between parents and children, between twins, or between siblings is simply the product of family environment or other social factors (such as poverty), rather than a product of inheritance. Finally, there is the issue of the relationship between intelligence and delinquency or criminality.

Most researchers accept that there is a correlation between intelligence scores and delinquency/criminality. Some researchers argue that the relationship is purely spurious, because both are affected by some other factors, that is, poverty, family dysfunction, or something else. Other researchers, however, believe that the relationship exists even after controlling for all other factors [19].

The relationship between intelligence and delinquency may be that intelligence affects school performance, which in turn affects delinquency because of opportunity (kids who drop out have more time to get into trouble). It could also be a direct relationship in that poor conditionability would lead to poor school performance, and poor conditionability would lead to poor socialization to law-abiding norms. Intelligence may be related to family and environmental variables as well as genetic inheritance. It could also be that the association we see is between intelligence and arrest, not delinquency. Recall that if we measure crime by official data, we are measuring not only the actions of the offender, but the actions of the system actor (to arrest or formally identify the offender as criminal). While some criminological studies use self-reports, many more use official data as their measure of criminality.

Summary

Theorists who support the idea of a biological predisposition to choose criminal behavior argue that personality differences do not inevitably lead to delinquency, no more than social factors inevitably lead to delinquency. The traits of impulsivity and thrill-seeking are due to biological differences, such as MAO and serotonin levels, as well as low cortical arousal. However, these biological differences merely predispose individuals to certain behavior patterns. The choice of crime versus other types of behaviors is influenced by social, familial, and environmental factors.

Biological theories can help explain the sex and age differential in criminality. There are sex differences in the relative levels of brain chemicals and hormones associated with delinquency. Furthermore, these chemicals and hormones fluctuate over the life course, therefore explaining why younger people are more impulsive and thrill-seeking than older individuals. These predispositions don't necessarily translate into delinquency, but there is a higher probability of such behavior when such biological predispositions exist.

PSYCHOLOGICAL THEORIES OF CRIME

Criminologists have largely ignored psychological theories of deviance and crime [20]. This is largely because criminology has emerged as a discipline from the field of sociology, not psychology. Psychological theories can be categorized into psychoanalytic theories, developmental theories, and learning theories. Of these, both developmental theories and learning theories have their correlates in sociological criminology, so to say that psychology is ignored in criminology textbooks is perhaps a misstatement of facts. Perhaps we could say that psychological theories are merely sociologized.

Psychoanalytic theories

Neither Sigmund Freud nor many of his followers had a great deal to say about crime. The psychoanalytic tradition would assume, however, that crime was the result of a weak superego or ego [21]. According to psychoanalytic theory, one does not develop in a normal manner when childhood trauma occurs or there is deficient parenting. Crime may occur because of unresolved feelings of guilt and a subconscious wish to be punished, or, more likely, because of weak superego controls over id impulses; that is, the individual cannot control impulses and pursues immediate gratification.

Generally, when a criminal commits very unusual or extreme acts, psychological explanations are utilized. The FBI has been instrumental in the growing use of "profilers" who construct psychological profiles of offenders based on the small sample of offenders who have been caught and interviewed. The book and movie *Silence of the Lambs* and many similar movies and television shows dramatize the work of psychological profilers. "Forensic psychologists" are used by many police departments for a variety of tasks, including offender profiling. As information is collected from these offenders, profiles are constructed and refined based on similarities and differences between them and how they commit their crimes. It should be noted, however, that the work of profilers is typically used for unusual criminals (such as serial or mass murderers, serial arsonists, or serial rapists). Furthermore, profiles are not infallible. Recall that the predicted profile in the Washington, D.C., sniper case was a white male 20 to 30 years of age, with a military background. John Malvo and John Mohammed did not fit the profile, but profiles are constructed from prior examples of such criminals, and the smaller the sample size, the greater the possibility of error [22].

The most obvious contribution of psychological theory to an understanding of criminality is the concept of **sociopathy** or **psychopathy**. The psychopath has been differentiated from the sociopath in the following way: "[the psychopath is] an individual in whom the normal processes of socialization have failed to produce the mechanisms of conscience and habits of law-abidingness that normally constrain antisocial impulses" and the sociopath as "a person whose unsocialized character is due primarily to parental failures rather than to inherent peculiarities of temperament" [23]. The *Diagnostic and Statistical Manual* (DSM-IV), a type of dictionary for mental health workers to diagnose and categorize all mental health problems, has replaced the terms "psychopathy" and "sociopathy" with the term "antisocial personality disorder." Regardless, these definitions describe an individual who is without a conscience and unable to form sincere, affectionate bonds with others. This describes many, but not all, of those who engage in criminal behavior.

Psychological explanations for behavior generally identify agreed-upon personality trait models (i.e., the big five: neutroticism, extroversion, openness to experience, agreeableness, conscientiousness), and then identify certain traits as associated with criminal propensity [24]. Interestingly, in the few applications of psychology to criminology, there is very little discussion of gender, other than to say that these personality dimensions occur in both genders [25]. Longitudinal studies note that the traits of sensation-seeking, overactivity, low self-control, emotionality, and callousness, as well as "negative emotionality," which include aggression, alienation, and anger/irritability as a stress reaction, are associated with persistent criminality [26]. While researchers note that the traits seem to equally predict male and female offending, it is also true that there are fewer female offenders; therefore, there are either fewer young women who possess the predisposing traits, at least to the degree that young men do, or alternatively, there are environmental mediators that operate differently between the sexes so that young men and women with similar personality traits experience life differently and, therefore, take different behavioral paths. In the Focus on Crime box, the crime of stalking is described. Does this crime lend itself to psychological or sociological explanations?

FOCUS ON CRIME: STALKING

About 14 in every 1,000 people were victimized by stalking in 2006. Stalking is behavior that is directed at a specific person that would cause a reasonable person to feel fear. Behaviors include making unwanted phone calls, sending unwanted letters or e-mails, following or spying on the victim, showing up where the victim is without a legitimate reason, waiting at locations where the victim is likely to go to, leaving unwanted items (flowers, presents), posting information or spreading rumors about the victim. None of these acts are criminal in themselves. There must be a pattern of behavior so that it can be assumed the perpetrator intends to cause fear in the victim. Some victims who experience a pattern of these behaviors do not express fear and they are considered by the National Crime Victimization Survey as victims of harassment rather than stalking.

Women were more likely to experience fear and, therefore, be victims of stalking, but both men and women were equally likely to be victims of harassment. Single or divorced individuals were the most likely targets. About a quarter of all victims reported cyberstalking. Three-quarters of the victims knew their stalker, and most were a former intimate. While most of the stalking victims reported being a victim of stalking for a year or less, 11% said they had been stalked for more than 5 years.

Almost half of all stalking victims experienced fear of what would happen next, and more than half of the stalking victims lost 5 or more days of work because of fear of the stalker. About one in five feared bodily harm to themselves or their relatives. About 40% of the stalkers threatened the victim or the victim's family, friends, or coworkers.

Stalking is primarily intra-racial and involves a lone offender. Perpetrators and victims are generally similar in age. Men were as likely to be stalked by a woman as a man, but female victims were significantly more likely to be stalked by a man (67%). About 10% of women and 16% of men were not able to identify the sex of their stalker. Thirty-six percent of the offenders had prior problems with law enforcement (according to the victims). Victims reported the offenders' motivations as anger, retaliation, spite, or a desire to control the victim.

Victims who reported that the stalking had stopped indicated that police had warned the stalker (15%) or they had talked to the stalker (13%) or someone else intervened (12%). About 10% had obtained a restraining order. Other crimes committed by the stalker against the victim included identity theft, property damage, breaking and entering, aggravated assault, simple assault, animal injury, and injury to a child.

Source: K. Baum, S. Catalano, M. Rand, *Stalking Victimization in the United States, Bureau of Justice Statistics, U.S. Department of Justice, Washington, DC, 2009.*

Developmental theories

Theories of development address both cognitive development and social development. The general hypothesis is that all individuals progress through similar stages of understanding and maturity regarding the world around them. Those who engage in criminal behavior have, for some reason, become "stuck" at lower stages of development. They are immature, either in their response to the world, their interactions with others around them, and/or in their putting self above others.

Piaget [27] and Kohlberg [28] are most commonly identified with the cognitive development field. Those who subscribe to the stage theory of cognitive development assume that the infant goes through qualitatively different stages of understanding. Only gradually does the child come to understand that others have needs and desires similar to him- or her-self. Higher levels of maturity are necessary to understand such abstract concepts as altruism and compassion. Kohlberg carried Piaget's work into moral development, arguing that cognitive development was necessary in order to develop a moral conscience, and understandings of right and wrong varied depending on what cognitive level one had reached. For instance, very young children understand that stealing is wrong only because parents have told them so. It is much later that they come to understand more abstract reasons for why stealing is wrong.

Later, Gilligan [29], a student of Kohlberg's, concluded that women tended to cluster at lower stages in Kohlberg's stage sequence than did men. Although controversial, her theory was that women followed a "different" morality and were more likely to continue to utilize themes of relationships and caring, while men moved on to principles and law-based models of morality. A similar approach to understanding male and female development can be seen in Stephanie Covington's model for female offender/addiction treatment programs, which is based on Karen Horney and Nancy Chodorow's earlier work. The thread that runs through this feminist psychology is the idea that women's psychological development occurs through relationships, while men's development normally involves separation. Thus, behavioral decisions for women (use of drugs/crime) are more influenced by relationships than the decisions made by men because psychological "normality" for men is separateness.

This work has seldom been applied directly in criminology to the question of why people choose criminality. One of the problems seems to be that one's ability to understand the moral implications of one's acts does not necessarily translate into behavior. That is, many people know something is wrong, but do it anyway. The research on moral stages, however, has been utilized in corrections, and it has been found that offenders can improve their moral reasoning given appropriate learning environments [30].

Learning theory and behaviorism

Basically, learning theory proposes that individuals act and believe the way they do because they have learned to do so. Learning takes place through modeling or reinforcement. **Modeling** stems from the desire to be like others, especially those whom one admires; therefore, children will act as they see their parents or peers act. The other form of learning is through **reinforcement.** That is, one will continue behaviors and beliefs for which one has been rewarded, and eliminate behaviors and beliefs that have been punished or not rewarded. Bandura [31], for instance, argues that individuals are not necessarily inherently aggressive, but rather learn aggression. He and others also point out that learning is mediated by intelligence and temperament. Personality traits such as impulsivity, aggressiveness, and emotionality affect one's ability to absorb learning.

One of the most enduring explanations of why women commit less crime, by both laypeople and criminologists, is the idea that they learn to be law-abiding and that the social sanctions against deviance for women and girls are much stronger than what boys or men would experience. If true, learning theory is perfectly consistent with the lower crime rates observed for women. Further, it also explains why women tend to cluster in consumer crimes, because women may be more likely to learn how to commit credit card fraud or check forgery than armed robbery. It might also explain why younger people commit more crime—we might suppose they haven't yet absorbed societal messages that condemn such behaviors.

Summary

Psychological theories concentrate on individual factors of criminal choice. More sophisticated theories also refer to environmental factors. So, for instance, Andrews and Bonta [32] developed a psychological theory of crime that includes the characteristics of the immediate environment and individual characteristics to explain crime choices. They point to the attitudes, values, beliefs, and rationalizations held by the person with regard to antisocial behavior, social support for antisocial behavior (perceived support from others), a history of having engaged in antisocial behavior, self-management and problem-solving skills, and other stable personality characteristics conducive to antisocial conduct. Then, they relate these to a behavioral explanation of criminality where rewards and costs of crime are mediated by these individual differences.

Such theories can only explain why women commit less crime if we presuppose that women learn different messages from society (learning theory) or develop different moral definitions (developmental theory). The theories are somewhat consistent with the age differential because it can be assumed that one continues to develop and learn through young adulthood and that maturity changes one's inclination to commit criminal acts. Also, it might be assumed that reward structures change during the life course and criminal choices may result in greater rewards for young people than for those with family and career responsibilities.

SOCIOLOGICAL THEORIES OF CRIME

If the focus of the classical school was the legal system, and the focus of the positivists was the individual, then the focus of early sociology was society itself. Societal factors were determined to be the causes of crime. However, while the classical school assumed all men would respond rationally to the deterrence of punishment, sociological theories offer more complicated assumptions.

Adolphe Quetelet (1796-1874) and Emile Durkheim (1858-1917) are credited as early sociologists who established the foundations of sociological criminology. Quetelet discovered that crime occurred in reasonably predictable patterns in society, thus supporting the notion that there was something about society that caused crime rather than crime occurring at random or because of individual causes. Emile Durkheim offered the principle that crime was normal and present in all societies. The absence of deviance or crime, in fact, was evidence of cultural stagnation.

Sociological theories can be further divided into social structure theories and social process theories. Societal factors that influence criminality may come from the social structure (i.e., elements of society that induce criminality), or the social process (i.e., the interactions between the individual and society that influence criminal choices). These are not very good distinctions because it is always the interaction between the individual and society that shapes behavior. Both approaches reject the idea of the "criminal as different." In these theories, it is assumed that anyone who happens to be exposed to these factors would become criminal; thus, the approach is similar to the classical school (which assumed sameness among individuals).

Social structure theories

Social structure theories identify some aspects of society as leading to criminal choices. The so-called Chicago school in the 1930s and 1940s truly began the study of societal influences on criminality when sociologists at the University of Chicago observed that crime occurred more often in **mixed zones** of the city. In these zones, residential, commercial, and industrial activity could be observed. The zones were also characterized by low home ownership, property damage, graffiti, and high rates of alcoholism, domestic violence, and mental health problems. Early sociologists discovered that these mixed zones always had higher crime rates, even though different demographic groups moved in and out of them over the decades. For instance, in the nineteenth century, Irish immigrants were the population living in the zones, but they eventually moved out, to be replaced by Eastern and Southern Europeans, and then blacks moving up from the South. Thus, it seemed that there was something about the zone, rather than the people who lived within it, that generated crime. Observers noted that subcultures existed in the mixed zone, and these subcultures promoted values and beliefs that were different from the dominant culture and encouraged criminal behavior (such as prostitution, gambling, and other forms of deviance).

Subculture theories and cultural deviance theories, first developed in the 1950s, observed that there are some groups in society who teach antisocial behaviors (instead of socializing its members to follow the norms of the dominant culture). If one lives in these areas of the city, then one will most likely become delinquent because the subculture defines such behavior as acceptable [33]. **Cultural deviance theory** identifies cultures that clash when individuals migrate to a new culture; that is, immigrants from India who sell their daughters into marriage in the United States are committing a crime, but in their culture, this behavior is not wrong. **Subcultural theories** look at subcultures that exist within the dominant culture but have different values and belief systems. Gangs are an example of a subculture, although this stretches the classic definition of a subculture, because members of any gang also participate and are socialized, to some extent, by the dominant culture as well. Women were largely ignored in early subcultural theories even though they obviously lived in the mixed zones alongside the boys and men who were being socialized to criminality. More recently, gang research has identified female gang members and female gangs, but there are mixed findings as to whether girls are increasing participation in gangs [34].

Another factor observed in the mixed zones was lack of opportunity. The individuals who lived in these neighborhoods had very little hope of economic success. **Strain or opportunity theory**, popularized in the 1960s, argued that lack of opportunity is the cause of crime. Individuals who are blocked from legitimate means of economic success, such as employment, family, or education, will choose crime [35]. A later application of the theory enlarged it to groups, so that those who were blocked from opportunities would form groups (gangs) distinct from those who had legitimate opportunities [36]. Because everyone is socialized to believe that they can and should achieve material success, those who do not have the means feel particular stress. In other cultures that are more static, that is, where the poor have no expectations or hope that they will achieve wealth, there is less pressure or inclination to use illegitimate means to get ahead.

If the strain/opportunity thesis was perfectly able to explain crime, then one would think that women should be more criminal than men because, arguably, they have had fewer opportunities to achieve financial success and, therefore, should experience more strain. On the other hand, if women's goals are different—for instance, to get married and to have children—rather than achieve economic success, then the theory would adequately explain the sex differential in crime. Whether this has ever been true, or whether it is true today, is a subject that many researchers have addressed. The results indicate that there are differences between men and women and strain may predict to some extent the criminal choices of both groups, but economic strain does not completely explain why some people commit crime, or why men are more likely to make criminal choices.

Radical, critical, or Marxist criminology was somewhat popular in the 1970s. This type of theory can also be considered a social structure theory because it identifies an element of society as criminogenic. Radical or critical criminology challenges the "science" of criminology and the nature of the exercise, concentrating as it does on the individual "deviant." Critical or radical criminology addressed the process of defining crimes and the nature of law as a method of social control by those in power. Under a Marxist theory of crime, crime exists in the capitalist society as "work." It is an essential element of capitalism. Typical criminal activity represents false consciousness; the "lumpen-proletariat" does not know who their true oppressors are; thus, they steal from and hurt each other. This approach would expand the definition of crime to activities engaged in by government and business; for instance, the death of workers because of unsafe working conditions should be defined as homicide.

Elements of **critical criminology** include an identification of class-based definitions of crime, a challenge to the ideology of equality, and the lack of objectivity in law [37]. Critics of these theories contend that their view of society is oversimplified and that power coalitions are more complicated and diverse than can be represented by such theories. Another criticism that can be made is that these types of theories are unable to explain the sex differential.

More recently, the ideas of the Chicago school have been revived with **social support theory** and **social disorganization theory**. Basically, both point to the community as a prime factor in crime causation. These theories tend to look solely at macrolevel factors that are correlated with crime causation. They are similar in that social support theory identifies elements of the society that provide emotional and practical support to the individual and proposes that the more support there is in a community, the less crime occurs [38]. Social disorganization theory states a similar assumption, arguing that communities that exhibit signs of disorganization and lack of cohesion are more likely to experience delinquency and criminality [39]. Thus, in both theories, crime is predicted in the neighborhoods and for the people who have few resources such as church, friendly neighbors, clubs, and other social organizations.

Social process theories

Social process theories focus on the individual's interaction with the world around him or her. Thus, relationships become a central feature of these theories. Social process theories have more in common in this respect with psychological theories and, in fact, many could be described as social psychological.

Differential association theory, introduced originally by Edwin Sutherland in 1939, is very similar to learning theory [40]. Differential association assumes that delinquency and criminality develop because of an excess of definitions favorable to crime offered by one's close associates. That is, if family and friends are criminal, profess criminal values, and teach criminal methods, one will become criminal. This theory assumes that learning takes place most importantly within intimate personal groups and that learning includes techniques of crime, as well as motives, drives, rationalizations, and attitudes. Later, others applied social learning principles to the theory to make it even more similar to learning theory [41].

In order for this theory to be consistent with the sex differential in crime, one must assume that girls and boys receive different societal messages, with girls less likely to be reinforced for delinquent behavior. Burgess and Akers argued that: "From infancy, girls are taught that they must be nice, while boys are taught that they must be rough and tough... Girls are schooled in 'anti-criminal behavior patterns'" [42]. Evidently all girls are taught from birth to conform to one model of female normality that is homogeneous across social, economic, and subcultural categories, while boys are exposed to a variety of different definitions of normality depending on class, race, and neighborhood. This broad assumption is a weakness of the theory. Further, the theory doesn't explain why crime is more common among young people and drops off after young adulthood because, if one learned criminal definitions, there is no reason to assume they would change after maturity.

Labeling theory relies on symbolic interactionism. The theory is unique from those discussed earlier in that, like radical criminology, it focuses attention on the official labeler as well as the deviant. This theory assumes that even though almost all of us have engaged in "primary deviance," only certain individuals are labeled as deviant. This results in their accepting and absorbing the deviant role and committing further delinquency because of the label [43]. Criticisms of labeling theory include the observation that no explanation for primary deviance is offered. Also, whether secondary deviance would not exist except for the labeling is probably untestable [44]. Labeling does not explain persistent criminality when offenders are not subject to labeling (such as undetected white-collar criminality) and ignores the fact that official intervention (such as prosecution and punishment) might deter individuals from future criminality.

Recall that the classical school assumptions disappeared with the rise of positivism in the 1800s. However, the premises of the classical school have been revived with **rational choice theory**. This modern-day theory presumes that criminals rationally choose criminal action because the immediate rewards outweigh uncertain punishments [45]. Burglars, for instance, are influenced by such facts as the affluence of the neighborhood, the presence of bushes, nosy neighbors, alarms, dogs, placement on the street, access to major traffic arteries, and other factors. They identify and target the houses where they have the best chance of success. Although the theory makes sense with burglars, and other purely economic crimes, it is more difficult to apply to other criminals.

Under the general heading of deterrence theory, a number of current criminologists continue to investigate the relative influence of deterrence; specifically, whether criminals choose to commit crime or remain law-abiding based on the threat of punishment. Modern deterrence theory is more complicated, however, than the simplistic approach of the classical school and recognizes the influence of individual factors that mediate how deterrent messages are received, such as low self-control or impulsivity, personal experience, belief systems, and perceptions of punishment. For instance, in order for a punishment to be a deterrent, there has to be an ability to control one's behavior and a perception that the threatened punishment is noxious. Because any type of punishment is experienced differently by different people, this makes predicting the effect of punishment much more difficult. These elements make the concept of deterrence more complicated than simply increasing the amount of punishment [46].

Routine activities theory is slightly different from rational choice, and might even be placed in the social structure category because it ignores criminal motivation, assuming that a motivated offender exists all the time [47]. According to these theorists, for a crime to happen, there must be a motivated offender, suitable targets of criminal victimization, and the absence of guardians of persons or property. Any changes in routine activities lead to changing opportunities for crime. For instance, the increase in the number of working women after WWII meant that more homes were left unattended during the day, and this created the opportunity for burglaries to occur. Most social process theories look at the motivation of the offender, but routine activity theorists argue that it is also fruitful to look at changes in opportunities or guardianship. Tests of this theory focus on demographic, macrolevel changes in society. However, it is difficult to identify any societal changes that occurred in the last decade that might have accounted for the dramatic drop in crime. Critics argue that, by not looking at the criminal motivations of the offender, this theory is incomplete.

Control theory, as presented by Travis Hirschi in 1969 [48], stated that the delinquent or criminal is one who is not controlled by bonds of society—specifically attachment, commitment, involvement, and belief. Attachment involves relationships; commitment involves the dedication to legitimate work and leisure activities; involvement measures actual time engaged in such activities; and belief refers to the agreement and acceptance of goals and rules of society. In the research that supported the development of control theory, Hirschi used self-report surveys of large numbers of young people and analyzed self-reported delinquency (validated by comparison to official records) and whether delinquency was correlated with the bonds to society described earlier. Control theory postulates that conformity occurs because of ties to society; deviance occurs when those ties are weak or nonexistent. Conformity is associated with good school performance, strong family ties, liking school, conventional aspirations, and respect for law.

Control theory provides a relatively adequate explanation for the sex differential in crime rates if we can assume that girls have more attachments and other bonds than boys. It is generally found that girls profess stronger ties to friends, family, and school, and they tend to possess more prosocial belief systems than boys. The theory is also consistent with the age correlate because one can assume that "bonds" to society increase as a young man matures and obtains a job, wife, and family.

In 1990, Hirschi and Gottfredson [49] presented a new theory: the **general theory of crime.** Actually, the two are not all that different. While control theory postulates that various bonds to society (attachment, commitment, belief, and involvement) control the individual and prevent delinquency, the general theory of crime proposes, simply, that individuals are born with and/or are raised to have different levels of self-control and those with low self-control are more likely to commit crime.

These authors propose that there are no real differences between serious and nonserious crimes, and disagree with the proposition that criminals are different from each other in their criminal orientation (i.e., career criminals versus occasional criminals). They propose that one variable explains all criminal offending and that variable is self-control. Gottfredson and Hirschi propose that people with low *self-control* commit criminal acts and a host of other dangerous and impulsive behaviors; people with more self-control do not. Low self-control types are also engaged in other activities indicative of low self-control, such as smoking, drinking, using drugs, gambling, having illegitimate children, and engaging in illicit sex [50].

White-collar criminality is a problem for this theory. The authors explained that white-collar criminals, like embezzlers, simply have less self-control than their professional colleagues who do not commit crimes. However, their argument that white-collar crime by professionals is relatively rare flies in the face of evidence that graft, fraud, and other forms of corporate criminality are widespread.

The major cause of a lack of self-control, according to these authors, is ineffective parenting. They argue that the conditions necessary to teach self-control include monitoring behavior, recognizing deviant behavior, and punishing such behavior [51]. Applications and tests of this theory of crime typically explore associations between other indications of low self-control and criminality. Not surprisingly, such associations exist, although some researchers argue that self-control adds nothing new to existing facts that have identified the association between crime and impulsivity and risk-seeking [52].

A major weakness of the theory is that it does not adequately explain the sex differential in crime unless one was to assume that women generally have more self-control than men [53]. It also is only consistent with the age-crime correlate if we assume that individuals increase their self-control as they age (but then it does not explain why some individuals do improve their self-control and why the persistent offenders do not). Another criticism of the theory is that it does not include any concept of the meaning of actions and how personal meaning interacts with and influences self-control. Values, motivations, and meanings interact with individual self-control, explaining why some people show a great deal of self-control in some areas and none in others. Further, there is a qualitative difference, it seems, in the acts labeled "criminal" and those merely injurious to one's health. Many people drink and smoke but relatively few commit victim-harming crimes. In other words, there are many more "weak" people than there are "harming" people; thus, even if we find that most criminals have low self-control, it does not follow that most people with low self-control are criminals.

Agnew [54] reformulated strain/opportunity theory (which was a social structure theory) into a social process theory by reinterpreting strain as an individual construct rather than an experience shared by the group or due to societal factors such as poverty. His **general strain theory** proposes that individuals who commit crime experience strain from not getting what they want, losing something that was important, or in other ways being in a situation that is experienced as noxious. In this theory, negative relationships that generate negative emotions, such as disappointment, fear, depression, and anger cause delinquency and individuals commit delinquent acts in order to relieve the strain of the negative emotions.

An entirely different direction to explaining crime is offered by Tom Tyler. Hirschi's earlier "bond theory" in the 1960s asked the question, "why do people obey the law?" and answered they do so because of their bonds to society like school and attachment to parents and a belief in their future. Tyler also asks the question, "why do people obey the law?" but his answer is that they do so when they believe in the legitimacy of the law and the legal institutions of society. It is a political theory as well as a criminological one because if there is widespread distrust and rejection of the legal institutions of society, then that bodes ill for the very security of a nation. Tyler also maintains that individuals are more likely to conform their behavior to the law when they believe in its legitimacy (i.e., people who disobey marijuana laws because they believe marijuana should be legal) or they distrust and reject the legal institutions of society (there is evidence to indicate that those who have more distrust of police are more likely to commit crime). Tyler also notes that legitimacy is tied to procedural justice; when people believe that the justice system is fair and just, there is more adherence to the law itself [55].

Summary

The beginning of criminology in this country occurred with the Chicago school of the 1930s. Sociological theories identify elements of society or the interaction of the individual with his or her environment as the reason that people commit crimes. These elements range from poverty and subcultures (in structural theories) to social bonds and negative emotions (in social process theories). While virtually none of these theories directly explains the sex or the age differential in crime rates, later researchers have attempted to apply them in such a way as to explain these crime patterns. Some seem better able to explain these crime correlates than others.

INTEGRATED THEORIES OF CRIMINOLOGY

Integrated theories combine elements of psychological theories and sociological theories, and even accept some elements of biological criminology in a more complicated and comprehensive approach to explaining criminal choices. The methodology typically associated with integrated theories is the cohort study, also called longitudinal research because it involves following a sample of individuals for a long period.

One finding of the longitudinal research studies is that there seem to be two separate groups of delinquents/criminals. The first group begins committing delinquent acts very early and these individuals are chronic and serious criminal offenders; however, the second "late onset" group drifts into delinquency during their teenage years and matures out fairly quickly. Their delinquency seems to be episodic and peer-influenced.

The following traits or characteristics seem to be correlated with the group who begin delinquency very early: low intelligence; high impulsiveness; child abuse victimization; harsh and erratic parental discipline; cold and rejecting parents; poor parental supervision; parental disharmony, separation, and divorce; one-parent female-headed households; convicted parents or siblings; alcoholic or drug-using parents or siblings; nonwhite race membership, low occupational prestige of parents; low educational level of parents; low family income; large family size; poor housing; low educational attainment of the child; attendance at a high delinquency school; delinquent friends; and high-crime area of residence [56].

Unfortunately, cohort samples for longitudinal studies often exclude women. This is especially unfortunate because the studies consistently identify correlates of delinquency such as attention deficit disorder (ADD) and hyperactivity, which are more prevalent among boys. Sex/gender differences may also be present in other factors related to criminal choices, such as sensation-seeking, low physiological arousal, intelligence, poor supervision and erratic discipline, and delinquent peers. By excluding women from the cohort sample, these studies are unable to determine the relative effects of these factors on male and female delinquency and criminality.

Denno [57] utilized biological and sociological factors in an integrated explanation of criminality and delinquency. She identified predisposing factors (that increase the likelihood of criminality), facilitating variables (that, in combination with predisposing, increase the likelihood of delinquency), and inhibiting variables (that counteract predisposing factors and decrease the probability of delinquency). At birth, individuals are already affected by such factors as culture, gender, prenatal maternal conditions, pregnancy and delivery complications, socioeconomic status, and family stability. By age seven, other factors, such as cerebral dominance, intelligence, and physical and health development, have influenced their predisposition to delinquency, and during the preteen and teen years, school behavior, achievement, and learning disabilities are affected by intelligence and influence, in turn, the likelihood of delinquency and, eventually, adult crime.

Robert Sampson and John Laub also present an integrated theory of delinquency, suggesting:

- A set of predisposing factors:
  - low family socioeconomic status, family size, family disruption, residential mobility, parent's deviance, household crowding, foreign-born, mother's employment;
- individual characteristics:
  - difficult temperament, persistent tantrums, early conduct disorder;
- and interactions with social control processes as the child develops:
  - family, lack of supervision, erratic/harsh discipline, parental rejection, school, weak attachment, poor academic performance, delinquent influences, sibling delinquent attachment, and peer attachment that leads to delinquency and incarceration.

These factors, in turn, lead to fewer social bonds, weak labor force attachment, and weak marital attachment that influences the continuation of crime and deviance [58].

Integrated studies are comprehensive in that they include precursors and facilitators of delinquency. In fact, most of the elements identified by all previous theories are incorporated into these integrated theories. While some may say that is the strength of these theories, others argue that it is a weakness because it makes the theory more complicated, and by using every explanation, in effect, there is no explanation that easily explains crime choice. On the other hand, it is probably unrealistic to assume that there is a simple answer to criminal behavior—or any human behavior, for that matter.

CONCLUSION

Courses in criminology cover a multitude of theories that have been created and tested to attempt to answer the question, "Why do people commit crime?" This chapter barely skims the surface of this material, but it provides some general descriptions of the types of theories that have been developed. Any good theory should be able to explain the sex and age differential, as well as why minorities are over-represented in street and violent crimes. In the Breaking News box, the "barefoot bandit" is an interesting case to try to apply the theories described in this chapter. Which theory best explains his conduct?

BREAKING NEWS: THE BAREFOOT BANDIT

Colton Harris-Moore was tagged by the media as the "barefoot bandit" because he was believed to be barefoot in some of the many burglaries he committed. The 19-year-old (in 2010) attained a somewhat iconic reputation by eluding authorities for 2 years while he burglarized homes in the state of Washington. At the height of his fame, his mother appeared on morning news shows and a Facebook page was created. He then expanded his travels by leaving the state, traveling through the Midwest to South Dakota, and furthered his exploits by stealing luxury cars, boats, and several airplanes (even though he had never taken flying lessons and crashed both planes). He is suspected of stealing an airplane in Indiana and flying it to the Bahamas where he crash-landed in a marsh. He then allegedly stole a yacht estimated to be worth about $650,000. In all, he is suspected of about 80 crimes. Harris-Moore was captured in July 2010 and almost killed in a hail of bullets as he tried to escape Bahamian authorities by stealing another boat and trying to outrun them. He gave up and was taken into custody, charged only with one count of illegal entry, and deported back to the United States in the fall of 2010. News reports indicate that federal prosecutors are trying to consolidate the charges that range across at least nine states and two countries to try him once for all of them. State prosecutors, however, reserve the right to try him on state charges after his federal prosecution. At least one prosecutor said he intends to.

Harris-Moore was first arrested at the age of 12 on Camano Island, a rural community north of Seattle. His mother raised him alone after the death of his stepfather when he was seven. His biological father evidently has never been in his life. She was quoted before he was captured as being "proud" of his exploits and said she wished he would get to a country that did not have an extradition treaty with the United States and send her a one-way ticket to join him. She also indicated that the authorities in Camano Island blamed him for crimes he did not commit and that she couldn't tell him what to do because he had a strong will, even when he was very young. Authorities who have been in contact with him say that he is very intelligent and not violent. Observers note that he may be facing 4 to 12 years for the federal crimes. His defense attorney thinks he should be recruited by the CIA. The Facebook page devoted to Harris-Moore now requests donations for his legal defense fund.

Sources: R. Owens, S. Netter, Barefoot Bandit' Colton Harris-Moore Back on U.S. Soil, Vows to Turn Life Around," ABCNews.com, July 14, 2010. Retrieved 9/15/2010 from http://abcnews.go.com/GMA/TheLaw/barefoot-bandit-colton-harris-moore-vowed-turn-life/story?id=11159980. J. Holtz, Judge Sets Nov. 15 Deadline to Indict Harris-Moore, HeraldNet.com, August 24, 2010. Retrieved 9/17/2010 from http://www.enterprisenewspapers.com/article/20100824/NEWS01/708249875/0/ETPZoneLT.

Generally, the field of criminology has de-emphasized biological and psychological factors of crime causation and focused solely on sociological causes of crime. More recent theories, such as the general theory of crime and general strain theory, bring the focus back to the individual and, thus, one can argue that the pendulum of scientific/criminological thought has swung from the legal system (classical) to the individual (positivist), to the society and neighborhood (Chicago school), and back to the individual (general theory). Integrated theories incorporate aspects of all three types of theories—biological, psychological, and sociological—and, arguably, provide the most complete answer to why people commit crimes. In Box 3.2, there are very brief descriptions of the theories discussed in this chapter.

The quest for reasons why people make criminal choices is ultimately for a practical purpose. We want them to stop. All criminology serves the practical purpose of developing policies and societal interventions that reduce crime. Thus, another way to discuss the theories presented in this chapter is to figure out the policy implications that follow from each theory. It seems clear that most theories support the idea of full employment and strengthening the family unit to ensure that all children grow up in stable homes where parents are able to discipline and monitor their behavior through strong, loving attachments. Whether this can ever be accomplished is a difficult question. The answer to why people commit crime and how we can reduce crime, in fact,

BOX 3.2 THEORIES OF CRIME

Biological

Nongenetic: idiopathic tumors, brain injuries, toxins
Genetic: testosterone, brain chemicals, neural conditionability, other inherited personality traits, such as impulsiveness

Psychological

Psychoanalytic: individual suffers trauma in childhood
Developmental: individual does not progress to mature social-interpersonal levels
Learning: individual is rewarded for criminal behavior

Sociological Theories

Social Structure Theories

Chicago School: individual lives in the mixed zone of a city where crime occurs
Cultural Deviance: individual is socialized to deviant norms
Strain: individual is blocked from achieving societal goals
Radical/Critical: individual is oppressed by capitalistic economic system
Social Support: individual lives in area with low social support

Social Disorganization: individual lives in area with indices of social disorganization

Social Process Theories

Differential Association: individual learns to be criminal
Labeling: individual is labeled a deviant and so lives up to the label
Rational Choice (Deterrence): individual weighs options and chooses crime
Routine Activities: crime occurs when there is motivated offender and opportunity
Control (Bonds): individual has few bonds to society
General Theory of Crime: individual has low self-control
General Strain Theory: individual suffers strain, which leads to crime
Trust in Procedural Justice: individual is more apt to obey the law when they believe in it
Integrated Theories: different aspects of the theories above explain crime at different periods in the life course

goes far beyond the criminal justice system. But then we knew that, because the criminal justice system is the social control institution that steps in when others (family, church, school) fail. If those institutions could be made stronger, there would be less need for the criminal justice system components, because there would be less crime.

Review Questions

1. What are the three strongest correlates of crime?
2. Differentiate between the classical school and the positivists.
3. What would be a way to study the relative effects of genetics and socialization?
4. What personality traits have been associated with criminality?
5. Distinguish between developmental theories and learning theories.
6. Distinguish social structure theories from social process theories.
7. Provide some examples of social structure theories and their policy implications.
8. What are the elements of critical or radical criminology?
9. Provide some examples of social process theories and their policy implications.
10. What are integrated theories? Describe.

VOCABULARY

classical school includes the contributions of Cesare Beccaria and Jeremy Bentham and the ideas that men were rational, operated with free will, and could be deterred from criminal acts

concordance measure of genetic influence; if one twin has an affliction (i.e., alcoholism), then so does the other twin. Discordance means that the twins are different

control theory Hirschi's theory that delinquents are not controlled by bonds to society, specifically attachment, commitment, involvement, and belief

criminology the study of crime and criminal motivation

critical criminology rejects definitions of crime and includes the idea that the legal system is a tool of the powerful

cultural deviance theory identifies crime as occurring when cultures clash, that is, when individuals migrate to a new culture

differential association theory Sutherland's theory that delinquency develops because of an excess of definitions favorable to crime

eugenics the idea of improving the human race through controlled procreation

general strain theory Agnew's theory that delinquency occurs because of strain from negative emotions that are caused by a number of "strains"

general theory of crime Gottfredson and Hirschi's theory that crime results from low self-control

"hedonistic calculus" Bentham's idea that punishment should be adjusted to slightly outweigh the perceived pleasure or profit from crime in order to deter people

integrated theories combine elements of psychological, biological, and sociological theories and explain crime over the life course

labeling theory focuses attention on the official labeler as well as the deviant and assumes that labeling creates secondary deviance

mixed zones zones where residential, commercial, and industrial activity are mixed and characterized by crime and other forms of disorder

modeling form of behavior change that occurs when one desires to be like others, especially those whom one admires

positivism "scientific method" or the search for causes using scientific method

psychopathy an individual without a conscience or habits of law-abidingness that normally constrain antisocial impulses

rational choice theory theory that criminals rationally choose criminal action because of immediate rewards

reinforcement form of learning in which behaviors and beliefs that are rewarded continue and behaviors and beliefs that are punished disappear

routine activities theory theory that for a crime to happen, there must be a motivated offender, suitable targets of criminal victimization, and the absence of guardians of persons or property

sociopathy persons whose unsocialized character is due primarily to parental failures rather than to inherent peculiarities of temperament

social process theories theories of crime that focus on the individual's interaction with the world around them

social disorganization theory theory that crime occurs in neighborhoods where there is no cohesion, transitory populations, and few indices of social support

social support theory theory that assumes crime occurs where social supports (both emotional and concrete) are absent

strain or opportunity theory theory that assumes that lack of economic opportunity causes crime

subcultural theories theory that deviant subcultures with different values and belief systems socialize individuals to crime

ENDNOTES

[1] J. Bentham, The rationale of punishment, in: R. Beck, J. Orr (Eds.), Ethical Choices: A Case Study Approach, Free Press, New York, 1843/1970, pp. 326–340.

[2] C. Lombroso, W. Ferrero, The Criminal Man, Patterson Smith, Montclair, NJ, 1895/1972.

[3] C. Lombroso, W. Ferrero, The Female Offender, Philosophical Library, New York, 1894/1958.

[4] O. Jones, Behavioral genetics and crime, in context, Law Contemp. Probl. 69(1) (2006) 81–100.

[5] D. Andrews, J. Bonta, The Psychology of Criminal Conduct, fourth ed. LexisNexis/Matthew Bender, Newark, NJ, 2006, pp. 128–129.

[6] E. Maccoby, C. Jacklin, The Psychology of Sex Differences, Stanford University Press, Stanford, University Press, Stanford, CA, 1994. See also J. Tedeschi, R. Felson, Violence, Aggression and Coercive Actions, American Psychological Association, Washington, DC, 1977; S. Mednick, K. Christiansen (Eds.), Biosocial Bases of Criminal Behavior, Gardner Press, New York, 1987; S. Mednick, T. Moffitt, S. Stack (Eds.), The Causes of Crime, Cambridge University Press, New York, 1991; A. Walsh, Intellectual Imbalance, Love Deprivation and Violent Delinquency: A Biosocial Perspective, Charles C. Thomas, Springfield, IL, 1974.

[7] H. Eysenck, G. Gudjonsson, The Causes and Cures of Criminality, Plenum, New York, 1991, p. 135. See also A. Walsh, Intellectual Imbalance, Love Deprivation and Violent Delinquency: A Biosocial Perspective, Charles C. Thomas, Springfield, IL, 1989, p. 140.

[8] A. Walsh, Intellectual Imbalance, Love Deprivation and Violent Delinquency: A Biosocial Perspective, Charles C. Thomas, Springfield, IL, 1991, p. 127.

[9] A. Walsh, Biosociology: An Emerging Paradigm, Praeger, Westport, CT, 1995, pp. 50–54. See also L. Ellis, Monoamine oxidase and criminality: identifying an apparent biological marker for antisocial behavior, J. Res. Crime Delinq. 28 (1991) 227–251.

[10] A. Caspi, T. Moffitt, P. Silva, M. Stouthamer-Loeber, R. Krueger, P. Schmutte, Are some people crime prone? Replications of the personality-crime relationship across countries, genders, races, and methods, Criminology 32 (1994) 163–195.

[11] A. Raine, The Psychopathology of Crime: Criminal Behavior as a Clinical Disorder, Academic Press, San Diego, CA, 1993, p. 93.

[12] H. Eysenck, G. Gudjonsson, The Causes and Cures of Criminality, Plenum, New York, 1989, p. 55.

[13] P. Wood, B. Pfefferbaum, B. Arneklev, Risk-taking and self-control: social psychological correlates of delinquency, J. Crime Justice 16 (1) (1993) 111–130.

[14] H. Eysenck, G. Gudjonsson, The Causes and Cures of Criminality, Plenum, New York, NY, 1989, p. 126.

[15] H. Sandhu, H. Satterfield, Childhood diagnostic and neurophysiological predictors of teen-age arrest rates, in: S. Mednick, T. Moffitt, S. Stack (Eds.), The Causes of Crime, Cambridge University Press, New York, 1987, pp. 146–168.

[16] D. Denno, Biology and Violence: From Birth to Adulthood., Cambridge University Press, New York, NY, 1990, p. 15.

[17] D. Denno, Biology and Violence: From Birth to Adulthood, Cambridge University Press, New York, NY, 1990, p. 17.

[18] T. Moffitt, The neuropsychology of juvenile delinquency: a critical review, in: M. Tonry, N. Morris (Eds.), Crime and Justice: A Review of Research, vol. 12, University of Chicago Press, Chicago, 1990, pp. 99–171.

[19] See T. Moffitt, The neuropsychology of juvenile delinquency: a critical review, in: M. Tonry, N. Morris (Eds.), Crime and Justice: A Review of Research, vol. 12, University of Chicago Press, Chicago, 2006, p. 112. See also D. Andrews, J. Bonta, The Psychology; of Criminal Conduct, fourth ed., LexisNexis/Matthew Bender, Newark, NJ, 1993, pp. 128–129; and A. Raine, The Psychopathology of Crime: Criminal Behavior as a Clinical Disorder, Academic Press, San Diego, CA, 1990.

[20] D. Andrews, J. Bonta, The Psychology of Criminal Conduct, fourth ed., LexisNexis/Matthew Bender, Newark, NJ, 2006.

[21] D. Andrews, J. Bonta, The Psychology of Criminal Conduct, fourth ed. LexisNexis/Matthew Bender, Newark, NJ, 2006.

[22] J. Holloway, The Perils of Profiling for the Media, American Psychological Association Online, 2003. Retrieved 5/24/2007 from http://www.apa.org/monitor/jan03/perils.html.

[23] D. Lykken, The Antisocial Personalities, Lawrence Erlbaum, Hillsdale, NJ, 1995, pp. 6–7.

[24] J. Miller, D. Lyman, Structural models of personality and their relation to antisocial behavior: a meta-analytic review, Criminology 39(4) (2001) 765–799.

[25] See J. Andrews, J. Bonta, The Psychology of Criminal Conduct, Anderson, New Providence, NJ, 2010, p. 195.

[26] T. Moffit, Males on the life-course-persistent and adolescent-limited antisocial pathways: follow-up at age 26 years, Dev. Psychopathol. 14 (2002) 179–207.

[27] J. Piaget, The Moral Judgment of a Child, Free Press, New York, 1965.

[28] L. Kohlberg, The Philosophy of Moral Judgment, Harper and Row, San Francisco, CA, 1981.

[29] C. Gilligan, In a Different Voice: Psychological Theory and Women's Development, Harvard University Press, Cambridge, MA, 1982.

[30] For a review of research, see J. Pollock, Ethics in Criminal Justice: Dilemmas and Decisions, fifth ed., Wadsworth, Belmont, CA, 2007.

[31] A. Bandura, Social Learning Theory, Prentice-Hall, Englewood Cliffs, NJ, 1977.

[32] D. Andrews, J. Bonta, The Psychology of Criminal Conduct, second ed., Anderson, New Providence, NJ, 2010.

[33] See, for instance, C. Shaw, H. McKay, Juvenile Delinquency and Urban Areas, University of Chicago Press, Chicago, 1934/1972.

[34] J. Pollock, Women, Prison, and Crime, Wadsworth, Belmont, CA, 2002.

[35] R. Merton, Social structure and anomie, Am. Sociol. Rev. 3(6) (1938) 672–682.

[36] A. Cohen, Delinquency in Boys: The Culture of the Gang, Free Press, New York, 1960. See also R. Cloward, L. Ohlin, Delinquency and Opportunity, Free Press, New York, 1955.

[37] See, for instance, I. Taylor, P. Walton, J. Young, The New Criminology, Harper and Row, New York, 1973; and R. Quinney, Critique of the Legal Order, Little, Brown, Boston, 1998.

[38] R. Bursik, H. Grasmick, Neighborhoods and Crime: The Dimensions of Effective Community Control, Lexington Books, New York, 1994. See also F. Cullen, Social support as an organizing concept for criminology, Justice Q. 11(4) (1993) 528–559.

[39] A. Reiss, M. Tonry, Communities and Crime, University of Chicago Press, Chicago, 1989. See also R. Sampson, W. Groves, Community structure and crime: testing social disorganization theory, Am. J. Sociol. 94 (1986) 774–802.

[40] E. Sutherland, D. Cressey, Principles of Criminology, Lippincott, Philadelphia, 1960/1966.

[41] R. Akers, Deviant Behavior: A Social Learning Approach, Wadsworth, Belmont, CA, 1966. R. Burgess, R. Akers, A differential association-reinforcement theory of criminal behavior, Soc. Probl. 14 (1973) 128–147.

[42] R. Burgess, R. Akers, A differential association-reinforcement theory of criminal behavior, Soc. Probl. 14 (1966) 142.

[43] See, for instance, E. Lemert, Social Pathology: A Systematic Approach to the Theory of Sociopathic Behavior, McGraw-Hill, New York, 1951.

[44] R. Akers, Deviant Behavior: A Social Learning Approach, Wadsworth, Belmont, CA, 1973.

[45] D. Cornish, R. Clarke, The Reasoning Criminal: Rational Choice Perspectives on Offending, Springer-Verlag, New York, 1986.

[46] See, for instance, M. Stafford, M. Warr, A Reconceptualization of general and specific deterrence, J. Res. Crime Delinq. 30 (1993) 123–135.

[47] L. Cohen, M. Felson, Social change and crime trends: a routine activities approach, Am. Sociol. Rev. 44 (1979) 588–608.

[48] T. Hirschi, Causes of Delinquency, University of California Press, Berkeley, 1969.

[49] M. Gottfredson, T. Hirschi, A General Theory of Crime, Stanford University Press, Stanford, CA, 1990.

[50] M. Gottfredson, T. Hirschi, A General Theory of Crime, Stanford University Press, Stanford, CA, 1990, p. 90.

[51] M. Gottfredson, T. Hirschi, A General Theory of Crime, Stanford University Press, Stanford, CA, 1990, p. 97.

[52] D. Longshore, S. Turner, J. Stein, Self-control in a criminal sample: an examination of construct validity, Criminology 34(2) (1996) 209–227.

[53] S. Miller, C. Burack, A critique of Gottfredson and Hirschi's general theory of crime: selective (in)attention to gender and power positions, Women Crim. Just. 4 (2)(1993) 115–134.

[54] R. Agnew, Pressured into Crime: An Overview of General Strain Theory, Oxford University Press, New York, 2007.

[55] T. Tyler, Why People Obey the Law, Princeton University Press, Princeton, NJ, 2006.

[56]   M. Tonry, L. Ohlin, D. Farrington, Human Development and Criminal Behavior: New Ways of Advancing Knowledge, Springer-Verlag, New York, 1991, p. 142.

[57]   D. Denno, Biology and Violence: From Birth to Adulthood, Cambridge University Press, New York, 1990.

[58]   R. Sampson, J. Laub, Crime in the Making: Pathways and Turning Points through Life, Harvard University Press, Cambridge, MA, 1993, p. 244.

Law Enforcement as Social Control

CHAPTER 4

Police in America

WHAT YOU NEED TO KNOW

- There are more than 20,000 state and local police agencies.
- There are about 1.5 officers for every 1000 citizens.
- Law enforcement includes many overlapping jurisdictional agencies.
- There are federal, state, county, and municipal law enforcement agencies.
- The first municipal police department was begun by Sir Robert Peel in London, England, in 1828.
- The first municipal police department in the United States was created in Boston in 1838.
- Two major functions of law enforcement are crime control and order maintenance.

Cops are our modern-day cowboys. Even though female officers have been integrated into patrolling for 30 years, the iconic police officer seems to share the traits of the "ideal man"—strong, courageous, and able to handle crises with calmness, authority, and integrity. It should also be noted that the image of the police officer is a mixed one. While the majority of the public's views are consistent with this description, there are neighborhoods and groups in this society where police have a negative image, the extreme of which would be a "jack-booted thug" who abuses his power against the poor and oppressed. Obviously, neither idealized image is accurate.

On television, the image of policing is largely drawn from characters who are detectives rather than patrol officers. This gives viewers the false impression that most of the investigative work—indeed, most of the "real" police work—is conducted by plainclothes detectives. This is not the case. The vast majority of police officers are patrol officers and, in reality, many crimes are solved by patrol officers, not detectives, either because the perpetrator is caught immediately or because the patrol officer acquires information that solves the crime.

Law enforcement in the United States is composed of a complex network of overlapping jurisdictions and agencies, all with the function of enforcing laws. There are federal, state, and local police agencies as well as special jurisdictional agencies. Increasingly, private police add to the numbers of individuals who enforce the law and protect the citizenry from crime and disorder.

Another major feature of policing is the existence of the dual goals of crime control and order maintenance. The image of policing emphasizes the crime-control function, while the reality is that most police work is in the nature of **order maintenance**, meaning tasks associated with keeping peace and order in society beyond crime control. We consider our police to be the 24-hour one-stop-shop for problem solving. Think about the types of calls police are called upon to attend:

- Traffic accidents
- Health emergencies
- Burglar alarms
- Crime reports
- Crimes in progress
- Domestic disputes
- Mentally disturbed citizens
- Noise violations
- Alcohol violations
- Abandoned vehicles
- Animal control issues
- Neighbor disputes
- Lost elderly citizens
- Lost and runaway children
- "Public welfare checks" (where police are asked to check on someone who isn't answering the phone)
- And cats in trees

Well, perhaps police dispatchers won't send officers out to the cat-in-a-tree call anymore, but that doesn't stop people from calling police for help in those situations. In fact, whenever we are in trouble, our first thought is probably to call 911. Police officers, then, have a day that may begin with a person suffering from Alzheimer's who has forgotten where they live or even what their name is, and ends with an alligator in someone's backyard pool that has just eaten the family's Chihuahua. Crime calls happen too, but car chases and catching burglars is not the day-to-day routine of most police officers. In fact, one might say that there is no such thing as a day-to-day routine.

POLICE: JUST THE FACTS

The Bureau of Justice Statistics reports that there are at least 17,876 state and federal police agencies in the United States with more than 1 million full-time state and local law enforcement personnel and 732,000 sworn personnel. This translates to about 249 officers for every 100,000 citizens. One survey of police agencies in 2004 identified 12,766 local police agencies, 3067 sheriff's agencies, 49 state law enforcement agencies, 1481 "special jurisdiction" agencies, and 513 other agencies (primarily constables unique to Texas). This figure does not include the numerous federal law enforcement agencies. Since 1992, state and local law enforcement personnel have increased by almost 30%. Most police officers work in municipal agencies (53%) [1].

> **INTERNET KEY**
>
> To find numerous reports on police and policing, go to the Bureau of Justice Statistics Web site, http://bjs.ojp.usdoj.gov and look at the section called Law Enforcement.

All police departments require officers to be citizens, and most have age restrictions—that is, applicants must be between 21 and under 35 to 40 to be hired. Some departments now require 60 or 90 college hours. There are written, physical, and psychological tests during the selection process. No one has ever gotten rich as a police officer—although cities vary widely; the average starting salary is about $31,700 [2]. Seniority and overtime can substantially increase the annual salary of an officer.

Increasing diversity in the ranks

The first black police officer was hired in 1861 [3]; however, the vast majority of officers from the late 1800s to mid-1900s were white. The recruitment and hiring of minority police officers increased in the 1960s and 1970s when there was a growing realization that departments needed to diversify their forces. During the 1960s, race riots gave the appearance of the police as "foreign" soldiers policing minority groups living in city ghettos. A concerted effort was made to make police departments more accurately represent the city and community that they policed, and this effort has resulted in some cities having a greater percentage of minority representation than others. Large cities have more minority representation than cities under 10,000.

The majority of police officers are still white (76.4%), but 11.7% are black (only somewhat smaller than their percentage of the total population). Another 9.1% of police officers are Hispanic, with the remaining 2.8% from other minority groups. The percentage of minority officers is substantially higher in large cities. While almost a quarter (24.4%) of officers in cities of 500,000 to a million were black, only 5.7% of officers serving towns of 2500 or less were black. Hispanic officers comprised a larger percentage in cities of a million or more (19.3%) and a much lower percentage in cities of 10,000 to 24,999 (3.0%) [4]. The first female police officer was hired in 1910, but her role was restricted to dealing with children and female prisoners. Early policewomen also performed clerical tasks. Policewomen were hired under a separate job category from male police officers, with separate hiring requirements. All that changed in the 1970s, when women were integrated into the patrol ranks. They joined women who, in increasing numbers, were entering other "nontraditional" professions, such as engineering, law, and construction [5].

By 1997, women represented 10.6% of all police officers [6]. Not a huge percentage, to be sure, but more than perhaps some ever thought there would be, given the early cold reception they received from their male colleagues. However, there has been very little increase in the percentage of women in law enforcement since the 1990s. In 2007, women still accounted for only about 13% of sworn officers. While 12% of local police departments' and 11% of sheriff offices' sworn personnel were women, only 6.5% of state agencies' sworn officers were women. As was the case with minority officers, the larger percentages of women are in large cities, not small towns. There are also large differences between cities, from Detroit with 27% women to Las Vegas with only 9%. About 15% of federal law enforcement personnel are women; for instance, 32% of the criminal investigators for the IRS and 19% of the FBI are women [7].

The first women hired in police departments have interesting stories of their early years when the public was skeptical of female officers, and some fellow officers were downright hostile to the idea of women joining their ranks. Some of the first female patrol officers experienced sexual harassment, some were the targets of hostile practical jokes, and some found that back-up was slow and/or that male partners tried to protect them rather than let them do their job.

There seems to be some residual doubt that women are as capable as men in meeting the requirements of the role. The IACP (International Association of Chiefs of Police) conducted a survey of its members, finding that 28% believed that women did not have the strength, capacity for confrontation, size, and ability to use force sufficient to be an effective police officer [8]. On the other hand, research studies indicate that in most measures, female officers are identical to their male counterparts. There are some interesting differences. For instance, women are less likely to use their firearms and they receive fewer citizen complaints [9].

HISTORY OF POLICING

It may surprise you to know that police agencies are a relatively recent phenomenon in the history of social order, beginning less than 200 years ago. Of course, there has always been a need to control crime and deviance, but that function was largely undertaken by the military, by private watchmen and guards, and by citizens themselves up until the 1800s.

We trace American policing back to the British "bobbie" and the "shire reeve" (sheriff). Early England was divided into shires and each shire had an authority figure called the **shire reeve**, or sheriff, who was responsible for tax collection and enforcing the king's peace. Another authority figure in early shires was the constable, who was responsible for the administration of shire courts and carrying out the orders of the magistrate. The constable was also responsible for keeping the **gaol** (jail) where prisoners were kept before being punished. There was no organized police force and citizens themselves participated in a watch system.

Bow Street Magistrate's Court, London. *Courtesy en.wikipedia.org*

By the 1800s, this informal system of crime control had become ineffective, especially in major cities like London. Henry Fielding, a magistrate in London, created the **Bow Street Runners** in 1748, which could be considered the first type of organized police force. Their first duties were to enforce warrants from the magistrate's court, but they eventually added crime

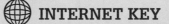 **INTERNET KEY**

For more information and historical pictures of the London Metropolitan Police Force, see http://www.met.police.uk/history/archives.htm.

detection and investigation. Eventually, their reach extended all over England when pursuing criminals. They also provided protection in the Bow Street area of London, especially after a mounted patrol was established by Fielding's successor.

In 1829, Robert Peel, the Home Secretary of England, convinced Parliament to pass the Metropolitan Police Act, creating the first police force as we know it today. They eventually became known as "**bobbies,**" referencing Peel's role in their creation. By 1839, the Metropolitan Force had absorbed the Bow Street Runners, the Bow Street mounted patrol, and the Wapping Marine Police. The Force was initially based in Scotland Yard with five more watch houses and 17 districts. In 1831, the Special Constables Act was passed, which added more officers to the force.

In the colonies, crime prevention was the responsibility of every citizen. Watch systems existed that were similar to those found in the early English shires. Boston holds the honor of having the first police department in this country, if one uses the date of origin of 1838 (when the first "day police" were hired), and not 1854 (when the police department was created as an agency separate from the constable's office). (See Box 4.1 for a timeline of the Boston Police Department's history.)

🌐 INTERNET KEY

For an interesting article that compares the *Gangs of New York* movie to the historians' descriptions of the "Five Points" area of New York City and the immigrant gangs of the period, go to http://news.nationalgeographic.com/news/2003/03/0320_030320_oscars_gangs.html.

New York City's police department was created in 1844. By the early 1800s, New York was overwhelmed with the dual problems of poverty and rising crime. The area of the Bowery, and especially the "Five Points" neighborhood, were the center of the problems that threatened to overrun the city. The power of the immigrant Irish gangs is fancifully portrayed in the hit 2002 movie *Gangs of New York*. Although there was growing support for an organized police force, citizens were suspicious of allowing such a centralized power. Still,

BOX 4.1 BOSTON POLICE DEPARTMENT: A BRIEF HISTORICAL CHRONOLOGY

1635: First night watch established.

1788: "Inspector of police" established.

1838: Both a day police and a night watch existed, completely independent of one another.

1852: Six-point star made of brass became the badge of the police.

1854: Boston Police Department established.

1858: Telegraph system linked the central office and police stations.

1861: "Full uniform" included the white gloves.

1872: The Great Boston Fire destroyed 776 buildings.

1873: First mounted patrol established.

1903: First use of an automobile for patrol. A Stanley Streamer touring car with a chauffeur and a higher back seat allowed the police officer to see over the area's back fences.

Source: *http://www.cityofboston.gov/police/about/history.asp.*

by 1845, the Mayor of New York had created a municipal police force with an initial staffing of 900 men.

New York's police force, like other city police departments, was very much influenced by politics. Police officers received appointments for several years, rather than being hired, and these appointments came through political patronage. Both the Democrats and the Whigs fought over the police department, and in 1857 the Whigs managed to get the state legislature to pass a bill creating the Metropolitan Police for the City of New York, Brooklyn, and Westchester County. The two police forces operated simultaneously and, at one point, even engaged in a large brawl in front of City Hall as the Metropolitan Force sought to arrest the mayor. The Metropolitan Force emerged as victor, but the police force was returned to municipal control in 1870 [10].

Theodore Roosevelt, later elected President of the United States, is pictured in 1895 while he was serving as New York City Police Commissioner. *Courtesy en.wikipedia.org*

One of the early police commissioners was Theodore Roosevelt. Starting in 1895, he began a series of reforms that included:

- Hiring based on skill and aptitude rather than political patronage
- The creation of disciplinary rules and enforcement
- Adopting an early form of fingerprinting
- Creating a bike squad
- Requiring officers to have pistol practice
- Instituting physical exams for officers
- Hiring the first female police matron to supervise female prisoners (Minnie Gertrude Kelly)
- Eliminating the practice of homeless people sleeping in the basements of the precinct offices in horribly unsanitary conditions [11]

> **🌐 INTERNET KEY**
>
> For an interesting web site that covers the history of the New York City Police Department, go to http://www.nycpolicemuseum.org/.

City police departments were slower to emerge in the West and the marshal was often the only law enforcement officer in early Western towns. For instance, a true city police department didn't emerge in Los Angeles until almost 1870. The precursor to the Los Angeles Police Department was the "Los Angeles Rangers," who were volunteers enlisted to help the county sheriff and marshal in the unruly times of the 1850s. Los Angeles was inundated with immigrants and others who were spurred by "gold fever" to come to the West Coast to make a fortune. The Rangers wore a white ribbon that indicated they served under the authority of the Council of Los Angeles. The "Los Angeles City Guards" succeeded the Rangers and wore the first official uniform. Vigilante justice was commonplace and early authorities were unable to keep order. Evidently, during the 1860s, a group of residents was successful in their request to the French government for protection.

This 1914 photograph depicts a uniformed policewoman of the era.
© CORBIS

For some period of time, French troops were deployed in the city to guard residents! [12]

In 1869, six officers were formally hired and paid out of city funds. Led by the city marshal, who also acted as dog catcher and tax collector, this early force was the beginning of the LAPD of today. The mounted patrol began in 1875 and existed until 1916. In 1876, the Board of Police Commissioners was formed and a police chief was hired after the marshal was killed by one of his own men. In 1885, the chief of police commanded 18 men and earned $150 a month. In 1886, two black officers were hired. In 1889, professional standards emerged with a new chief, John M. Glass, who instituted hiring standards and formalized training [13].

As the 1800s gave way to the 1900s, cities and towns grew, and most eventually created their own police departments. That process continues today and small towns sometimes make the decision to create a municipal police force, even if it is only a chief and one or two officers, rather than depend on the county sheriff's office for police protection. Sheriff's deputies provide patrol protection and crime investigation to unincorporated areas and small towns that do not have their own police department.

Policing in the twentieth century

Early police departments continued to be very influenced by politics through the 1930s. Positions were awarded through political patronage, and sometimes police campaigned in uniform for politicians running for re-election. Of course, if their candidate lost, they would have lost their jobs, and so there may have been, in some situations, more than a hint of coercion and corruption in their involvement with the political process. Police were implicated in coercing votes and stuffing ballot boxes [14].

Training was minimal, and police were paid very little. Some officers were corrupt and utilized their position for graft. While early police departments were involved in a range of community activities, such as running soup kitchens and pursuing moral reforms such as anti-alcohol campaigns, they were also involved in strike-busting and immigrant control, sometimes through extralegal and violent means [15]. In some cities with strong political machines, police might have been seen almost as a private security force serving only those in power. The control of the working and "immigrant classes" was not necessarily done with any degree of sensitivity or even legality [16].

🌐 **INTERNET KEY**

For an interesting description of the early days of the LAPD, go to the official Web site, http://www.lapdonline.org/history_of_the_lapd/content_basic_view/1107.

August Vollmer (1876-1955) is credited with beginning the process of professionalizing the police. He was elected marshal of Berkeley, California, in 1905 and later became its first police chief. During his long tenure with the Berkeley Police Department, he was instrumental in a large number of innovations in policing that spread across the country and led to police departments being considered more as professional crime fighters than "hired muscle" for political machines. Interestingly, he is also credited with beginning the first criminal justice department at the University of California at Berkeley, where he taught some of the emerging leaders in the field. (See Box 4.2 for a sample of his contributions to the fields of law enforcement and criminology.)

In effect, the "professionalization" of police resulted in a real, or at least perceived, shift of police loyalty from political bosses to the law itself [17]. Professionalization implied objectivity, professional expertise, and specialized training. The professionalization of police probably also led to the emphasis of the crime fighter role over order maintenance in following decades. Professionalization led to more training, hiring standards, and standard operating procedures.

By the 1960s, police were seen as professional crime fighters, but certain factors had combined to drastically change their relationship with the community. They were isolated in patrol cars instead of meeting and interacting with citizens while walking beats, and they had layers of bureaucracy that reduced their discretion when handling community problems. Professionalization may have led to police officers in some cities being seen as well-trained crime fighters, but it also made them seem more like soldiers than public servants.

Then in the 1960s, police departments around the country were faced with civil protests that challenged their ability to maintain public order. When civil rights protests began in the south, police were seen on television news shows using dogs and high-pressure water hoses on peaceful demonstrators. When race riots broke out in the cities of the north, police were seen by some as an

---

BOX 4.2 AUGUST VOLLMER AND THE BERKELEY POLICE DEPARTMENT

1906: Installed a basic records system
1906: Installed the first modus operandi (MO) system
1907: First use of scientific investigation (analysis of blood, fibers, and soil)
1907: First police academy was established
1911: First police motorcycle patrol
1913: Began to use automobiles for patrolling
1916: First school of criminology at University of California at Berkeley

1918: Began using intelligence tests in recruiting police officers
1920: First lie detector instrument developed and used
1921: Psychiatric screening used in recruitment
1924: One of the first single fingerprint systems
1925: Established crime prevention division and hired a policewoman

Source: *Berkeley Police Department Web site, http://www. ci.berkeley.ca.us/police/history/history.html.*

all-white force oppressing an all-black ghetto. The antipathy one finds between police departments and urban minority communities today has its roots as far back as the late 1800s when police were used to control the immigrant classes, but the more immediate origin is the 1960s race riots. In 1992, after the acquittal of police officers accused of beating Rodney King, Los Angeles erupted in a riot similar to those of the 1960s, making it apparent that race relations is a topic that continues to be problematic for police departments. Not all depart ments are successful at balancing community relations with crime-control strategies.

Because of the discord and conflict of the 1960s, police departments around the country sought to improve their relationships with minority communities through the recruitment and hiring of minority and female officers. They also created community relations and public information officers. Citizen advisory committees were started in some communities, and other attempts were made to make the relationship between the police department and the community it served more open and cooperative. These efforts continue today.

The Texas Rangers

In addition to municipal police departments, law enforcement agencies at the state level emerged in the early 1900s, but at least one police organization had a much earlier origin. While the Department of Public Safety in Texas was not created until 1935, the Texas Rangers, a unit of the state police, trace their origins back to 1823 when Stephen F. Austin hired 10 men to protect the frontier from Indians and bandits. In 1835, the provisional government of Texas created the first official Ranger force in preparation for the revolution against Mexico. By the 1880s, the Rangers had developed into a law enforcement agency rather than a paramilitary organization [18].

Although associated with some darker periods of Texas history, especially after the Civil War, the Rangers have attained an almost iconic image. Through the late 1880s and early 1900s, the Rangers were utilized as a statewide crime-fighting force. In 1935 when the Department of Public Safety was created, the Texas Rangers were absorbed into this larger agency. They are known as the oldest statewide law enforcement organization in the country.

 **INTERNET KEY**

For more information about the Texas Rangers, go to http://www.txdps.state.tx.us/TexasRangers/index.htm.

Of course, today, many television viewers associate the Texas Rangers with martial arts star Chuck Norris from the *Walker, Texas Ranger* television series, but some of the real Texas Rangers, from all accounts, may have been even more "larger-than-life" than the television character.

EXERCISE: IN THE STATE OF...

1. Choose a city in your state that has an official Web site for its police department, including the history of the department.
2. See when the department was created and review its early history.
3. Note hiring qualifications and starting salary if given.
4. Note the structure and organization of the department.
5. Repeat with the state police agency (state patrol or other name).

THE STRUCTURE AND ORGANIZATION OF POLICING

Local and state police agencies have adopted an organizational model based on the military, while federal agencies tend to have organizational structures more similar to other bureaucracies. The military command system found in state, county, and local law enforcement often uses the same ranks as one would find in the military (captain, lieutenant, sergeant). Information flows downward in a hierarchical pattern and the span of control principles are similar to the military, with each officer responding to his or her own chain of command. Some argue, however, that police organization is very different from the military, in that each officer has much more discretion and makes more decisions than the average soldier. This discussion of whether patrol officers are basically "foot soldiers" or whether they are autonomous decision makers is also present in the discussion of whether policing is a profession or an occupation. It seems clear that whatever one wants to call them, police officers on the street must be comfortable with a large degree of discretion and authority to handle a wide range of different situations.

Federal law enforcement

Unlike many other countries, the United States has no national police force. Part of the reason for this is the vast area encompassed within the borders of this country, but another reason is that, since the American Revolution, there has been a cultural hostility and suspicion of centralized power. This does not mean, however, that there are no federal law enforcement officers. In fact, there are more than 93,000 federal employees who have the authority to make arrests and are considered law enforcement officers. Prior to 2003, the Immigration and Naturalization Service (INS) employed the largest number of federal officers (19,101), followed by the Federal Bureau of Prisons (14,305), and then the U.S. Customs Service (11,634). The Department of Homeland Security (DHS) has absorbed both INS and the U.S. Customs Service, making the DHS the largest federal law enforcement agency today [19]. In 2004, U.S. Customs and

Border Protection employed 27,705; the Federal Bureau of Prisons 15,214; the FBI 12,242; and U.S. Immigration and Customs Enforcement 10,399 [20].

We are probably most familiar with the Federal Bureau of Investigation (FBI) and the Drug Enforcement Administration (DEA); however, there are numerous other federal agencies that employ law enforcement officers who have the power to make arrests and carry firearms. Box 4.3 shows some of these agencies.

As you might expect, these agencies have specific duties and missions. The U.S. Marshals Service, for instance, is responsible for seizing and maintaining property confiscated through civil and criminal forfeiture hearings, providing security for federal courtrooms and judicial officials, transporting federal prisoners, and protecting federal witnesses (some through the Federal Witness Protection Program).

The Department of Homeland Security (DHS), created in 2002, has absorbed a number of other agencies. As mentioned previously, the Immigration and Naturalization Service and the U.S. Customs Service are now under DHS. The functions of these two agencies have been reorganized, and now the agency primarily responsible for border protection is called U.S. Customs and Border Protection, and the other agency called U.S. Immigration and Customs Enforcement enforces immigration laws within the interior of the country. Other agencies absorbed by the Department of Homeland Security include the U.S. Coast Guard and the U.S. Secret Service. The Transportation Security

BOX 4.3 FEDERAL AGENCIES WITH LAW ENFORCEMENT OFFICERS

- U.S. Customs and Border Protection, 27,705
- Federal Bureau of Prisons, 15,214
- Federal Bureau of Investigation, 12,242
- U.S. Immigration and Customs Enforcement, 10,399
- U.S. Secret Service, 4,769
- Drug Enforcement Administration, 4,400
- Administrative Office of the U.S. Courts, 4,126
- U.S. Marshals Service, 3,233
- U.S. Postal Inspection Service, 2,976
- Internal Revenue Service, Criminal Investigation, 2,777
- Veterans Health Administration, 2423
- Bureau of ATF and Explosives, 2373
- National Park Service, 2148
- U.S. Capitol Police, 1535
- Bureau of Diplomatic Security, 825

- U.S. Fish and Wildlife Service, 708
- USDA Forest Service, 600

Also employing law enforcement personnel:

- Department of Agriculture
- Department of Commerce
- Department of Defense
- Department of Energy
- Department of Health and Human Services
- Department of the Interior
- Department of State
- Department of Transportation
- Department of the Treasury
- Department of Veterans Affairs

Source: *B. Reaves, Federal Law Enforcement Officers, 2004, Bureau of Justice Statistics, Washington, DC, 2006, p. 2.*

Administration (TSA) is a new agency charged with providing protection at airports. The same Act that created the DHS also changed the Bureau of Alcohol, Tobacco and Firearms (ATF), which is now the Bureau of Alcohol, Tobacco, Firearms and Explosives, and the law enforcement functions of the agency have been transferred to the Justice Department while the revenue functions remain with the Department of the Treasury [21].

Federal law enforcement agencies enforce federal laws. They share jurisdiction with state and local law enforcement agencies when an action is a violation of both federal and state law. The most common example of this is the sale of controlled substances. While smuggling drugs into the country is a federal crime, sales of controlled substances break both federal and state laws. That is the reason special task forces were created in the 1980s to investigate drug offenders. These task forces were staffed by federal and local officers so that their efforts would not be duplicated, or get in the way of each other's investigations.

> ### 🌐 INTERNET KEY
>
> For more information about federal law enforcement, see http://bjs.ojp.usdoj.gov/index.cfm?ty=pbdetail&iid=867

State law enforcement

State law enforcement agencies are typically called Highway Patrol, Department of Public Safety, or State Patrol, although their mission encompasses more than patrolling the state highways and issuing drivers' licenses. These statewide agencies usually have a state-of-the-art crime lab to assist smaller jurisdictions that have no analysis capabilities. They also provide assistance with investigation and detection to local agencies and carry out their own investigations when the criminal activity is statewide, especially if the criminal activity involves drugs or auto theft rings. The state agency may be the central repository for crime statistics, may have authority over gun registrations and investigations for licenses, and may have supervision over controlled substances registration. Box 4.4 contains Web sites for selected state law enforcement agencies. Generally their duties are similar, but there are some differences.

Many states also have limited jurisdiction law enforcement agencies. Examples include state agencies that enforce alcohol and tobacco laws, fish and game agencies that enforce hunting and other laws, and child support enforcement

BOX 4.4 SELECTED STATE LAW ENFORCEMENT AGENCIES

Alabama: http://www.dps.state.al.us/
New York: http://www.troopers.state.ny.us/
Oklahoma: http://www.dps.state.ok.us/

Washington: http://www.wsp.wa.gov/about/about.htm
Wisconsin: http://www.dot.wisconsin.gov/statepatrol/

agencies. State universities may have their own police departments (or they may use private security officers who are not police officers). Each state is slightly different in the type and the number of these agencies.

County law enforcement

Recall that one of the earliest law enforcement officials was the shire reeve, who was responsible for collecting taxes for the king, and keeping the king's peace in the shires (or counties) of England. The modern-day shire reeve is the county sheriff. Sheriffs are elected officials, but sheriff's deputies are hired through civil service selection procedures in a similar manner to municipal law enforcement officers. Usually, county sheriffs also have the responsibility of managing the county jail. In some jurisdictions, sheriff's deputies may be assigned either patrol duties or jail duties, but in other jurisdictions, the position of jailer is a different job from that of deputy. Sheriff's offices also serve warrants and civil documents, including eviction notices.

While sheriffs are elected, police chiefs are hired by the city manager and/or a city council and mayor. Both, however, have notoriously short average tenures, because both positions are lightning rods for public controversy. One of the most controversial sheriffs in the country is Sheriff Joe Arpaio in Arizona. The Breaking News box describes a recent controversy. A few counties also have county police agencies separate from the sheriff's office. These agencies are more like a municipal police agency and the police chief of this agency is not an elected official.

BREAKING NEWS: SHERIFF JOE MISUSED $80 MILLION?

Sheriff Joe Arpaio of Maricopa County, Arizona, is no stranger to media attention. His "get tough" style toward prisoners and his aggressive immigration round-ups have earned him admirers and critics. Some allege that he has used the power of his office to intimidate and harass political foes and critics. Liberal activists complain that his treatment of prisoners borders on unconstitutional. In September 2010, the county board of supervisors alleged that he had misused funds and instituted dramatic budget restrictions and oversight measures. They also fired the law firm that represented him in lawsuits against the board of supervisors and filed lawsuits against him. The board of supervisors' report indicates that trips to Puerto Rico and Belize were charged on county credit cards, there were upgrades to first-class airfares, and $2215 were spent at Disneyworld Yacht Club Resort. Other findings included training trips to Honduras costing $91,000 and the use of jail funds for non-jail-related sheriff's office expenditures that might be as much as $64 million. The sheriff's office may have also misused antiracketeering funds. New reports indicate that the board of supervisors has passed their findings onto the U.S. Attorney's Office.

Source: Y. Wingett, *Joe Arpaio's Office Misused Up to $80 Million, Maricopa County Says, The Arizona Republic, September 22, 2010. Retrieved 9/22/2010 from http://www.azcentral.com/news/articles/2010/09/22/20100922joe-arpaio-misused-funds-maricopa-county-says22-ON.html.*

Municipal law enforcement

When we think of the police, we typically think of the municipal police department. Most towns and cities of any size have their own police department. Small towns may have a police department of only three or four officers, while big-city police forces may number in the thousands, such as New York City at more than 38,000 officers. Most police *officers* work in the larger police departments, even though most police *departments* have fewer than 50 officers [22]. The majority of departments in the country are quite small; in fact, about 800 police departments have only one officer! [23]

Larger police departments are typically broken into divisions, such as patrol and investigation. Under the investigation division, there may be further subdivisions, such as homicide, juvenile, and vice. Other departments exist as well, including community relations, internal affairs, training, and research and planning. Some police departments have created special domestic violence teams, police squads specially trained to respond to the mentally ill, and other specialized teams. In smaller departments, of course, patrol officers are expected to be generalists and handle a large variety of calls.

Special jurisdiction law enforcement agencies

In your community, there may also be special or limited jurisdiction law enforcement agencies. Some cities have park police, airport police, housing police, or transit police. These agencies have the power to arrest, but their jurisdiction is limited to crimes that occur within or in relation to their specific jurisdiction.

Indian tribes may have their own tribal police forces that have exclusive jurisdiction on reservations. In fact, there is a completely separate justice system existing on some Indian reservations, complete with tribal police and a tribal court system. Even civil court matters are dealt with by tribal courts, and a state district court has no authority once a matter is deemed to be under the jurisdiction of these tribal courts.

> **⊕ INTERNET KEY**
>
> For information about the Oneida Indian Nation police department, go to http://oneida-nation.net/police.

Private law enforcement

Private security officers are not peace officers. They are paid with private funds rather than public dollars, and their primary duty is to provide protection and investigative services to the hiring entity, which might be a company, neighborhood, or private individual. We mention private security officers here only because many people misunderstand their power and assume that they have similar powers to those of public peace officers. The other reason that we must mention them is that there may be many more private security officers than police officers. There are probably more than 1.5 million individuals employed in private security, and private security expenditures are on track to be almost double that of public expenditures.

It should also be noted that there is overlap between private and public policing because public police officers are often hired as private employees of security companies. Because police are certified peace officers who can carry a weapon and use their arrest powers even when off-duty, they carry those powers with them into the private position. Otherwise, private security officers have no greater powers of arrest or use of force than an average citizen.

The American Society for Industrial Security (now ASIS International) is the largest professional organization for security professionals. Its Web site states that it was founded in 1955 and has more than 35,000 members worldwide. ASIS administers three certification programs. The Certified Protection Professional (CPP™) designation indicates board certification in security management. The Physical Security Professional (PSP™) and the Professional Certified Investigator (PCI™) are also offered [24].

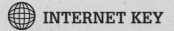 **INTERNET KEY**

For information about the American Society for Industrial Security, go to http://www.asisonline.org/about/history/index.xml.

THE FUNCTION OF POLICE IN SOCIETY

What is the function of police? You probably said crime control, but that is not a complete answer. Police officers are dispatched to many different types of calls and crime calls form only a portion of their workload. According to researchers, the majority of police work is divided among patrol, service calls, and paperwork. Further, only 13% of their time is taken up with potentially criminal matters, according to these authors [25].

It is common to identify crime control and order maintenance as the two major functions of law enforcement. Crime control includes all the tasks associated with preventing crime and enforcing the law. Patrol, responding to dispatched calls, investigating crimes, engaging in sting operations, arresting suspects, testifying in court, and all the other tasks associated with either preventing crime or catching criminals is included in the crime-control function.

Order-maintenance tasks include everything else police do. When police respond to a car accident and control traffic and see that the victims get medical treatment, this is order maintenance. When police are called by a worried mother to check on her college-age daughter because she hasn't answered her phone in three days, and they do so, this is order maintenance. When police drive slowly by a rowdy group of teenagers late at night, pull over, and watch until the teenagers disperse and go home, this is order maintenance. Police are present when there are medical emergencies, water rescues, traffic problems, public disturbances and organized protests, weather-related and other natural disasters, and civil defense. You will recall that after Hurricane Katrina, New Orleans police officers were expected to ignore the needs of their own families and stay on duty over the days and weeks following the flooding to provide victim rescue, crime control, and public order. The subsequent criticism of their performance should only serve to illustrate how much was expected of them [26]. This incident also shows how both law enforcement and order-maintenance functions are expected of the police. Police swung between being law enforcers (against looting) and service providers (when they broke into stores and distributed the goods to desperate citizens). Politicians ordered police to concentrate on lawbreaking, then they demanded that police emphasize saving lives even if it meant ignoring lawbreaking, and then, when the public attitudes toward looting became very negative, the politicians ordered the police (and the National Guard soldiers who had arrived) to emphasize law enforcement again. However, individual police officers in the flooded streets were the ones who had to choose between those sometimes conflicting role responsibilities in every situation, over the exhausting days that stretched into months.

A New Orleans resident reaches out to thank New Orleans Police Captain Marlon DeFillo, center, as Superintendent Eddie Compass, right, announces to the storm victims that food and water is on the way on September 2, 2005. *AP Photo/Dave Martin*

Order-maintenance and crime-control functions may overlap and even merge. When police are called to a neighbor dispute, this is order maintenance; but if they are unsuccessful in resolving the problem, it may turn into a crime when one neighbor decides to settle the argument with arson or a gun. A mentally ill person may complain to police that their brain is being scanned by an alien, which is obviously not a crime-control issue; however, if they do not respond in an effective manner to this complaint, the delusional person may decide that an innocent bystander is the alien and assault or even kill that bystander. When neighbors call police because there is a large group of "suspicious looking" people in a park late at night, not responding may result in nothing happening, or it may result in a series of vehicle burglaries or other crimes.

On the other hand, order-maintenance functions may be considered extralegal activities that exceed police authority. That group of people in the park late at night probably has every legal right to be there, at least until the official closing time. Do police use their coercive authority to "encourage" the people to disperse, satisfying the homeowners who are nervous, or do they allow the group to exercise their right to use a public park, satisfying the group members, but alienating the homeowners? These order-maintenance choices are sometimes difficult to make.

DISCRETION AND STYLES OF POLICING

Discretion can be defined as the power to make a decision among two or more choices. Patrol officers have a great deal of discretion in defining criminal behavior and deciding what to do about it. When police stop people for minor traffic violations, they can write tickets or give warnings. When they pick up teenagers for drinking or other delinquent acts, they can bring them in for formal processing or take them home. After stopping a fight on the street, they can arrest both parties or allow the combatants to work out their problems. One older study found that police do not make arrests in 43% of all felony cases and 52% of all misdemeanor cases [27]. More recently, researchers found that police officers make arrests in less than a third of all cases where they have the legal authority to do so [28]. The Focus on Crime box illustrates one crime that has seen major changes in the pattern of enforcement over the last 40 years. Historically, police have had a great deal of discretion in how to respond to drunk drivers, but today they face pressures from interest groups and the public so that there is much less discretion and many agencies employ a no-discretion policy when officers stop drivers who are suspected of being under the influence.

FOCUS ON CRIME: DWI

One of the most frequent crimes committed is driving under the influence or driving while intoxicated. This crime has seen major changes in perception and enforcement in the last 20 years. Through the efforts of Mothers Against Drunk Driving (MADD) and other interest groups, the penalties for drunk driving have been increased and enforcement is less discretionary than it used to be. Laws have also been changed to reduce the level at which one is considered legally intoxicated (from .10 to .08). Below is a table that illustrates the numbers of arrests for DUI, displayed as total arrests and then arrest percentage by sex.

While the table indicates there were about 80,000 more arrests for DUI in 2009 than in 1995, that does not mean that people are more likely to be arrested in recent years than in the past. The rate per 100,000 divides the arrests by the population and, so, in 2009 there were 463 arrests per 100,000 but in 1995 there were 526 arrests per 100,000. Thus, while DUI has not seen the dramatic decline in arrests that are recorded in other crime categories, there has been a decrease in this type of crime as well. From the table, we can see that women are more likely to be arrested today for DUI than in the past. Whether women's increasing percentage of total arrests is due to changes in behavior or changes in police officers' decisions to institute formal arrest is impossible to determine from any data source we have available, but it is probably a safe assumption that there has been a change in women's drinking and driving behavior.

	Total Arrests	% Male	% Female
2009	1,112,384	77	23
2008	1,110,083	79	21
2007	1,055,981	79	21
2002	1,020,377	83	17
2000	915,931	84	16
1995	1,033,280	85	15

Source: *FBI, Uniform Crime Reports, 1995-2009.*

Discretion allows different styles of policing to emerge. That is, departments may emphasize crime control or order maintenance, or they may emphasize other goals or objectives. Similarly, individual police officers seem to approach their job in different ways, emphasizing certain functions over others. These styles influence the decisions that are made in situations encountered on the street.

Wilson [29] developed a typology of policing behavior in regard to the frequency and type of interchange with the citizenry. He perceived these types as departmental types and they occurred, in part, because of the type of community the police department served.

1. The *legalistic model* describes a department with frequent, but formal, exchanges with the public. This is a "by-the-book" type of department that has a strong emphasis on rules and proper procedures. Police officers are not encouraged to use discretion in decision making. Relationships with the community are formal and legalistic. This type of model may be found in cities and larger towns.
2. The *service model* describes a department with frequent but informal exchanges with the public. Police officers are encouraged to use informal means of conflict resolution when appropriate and have stronger ties with the community. This model is common in small towns and suburban areas.
3. The *watchman model* is characterized by infrequent exchanges with the public. This department has less frequent interchanges with the public and makes distinctions between groups or types of individuals. Citizens who are deemed nonthreatening will be given a "pass" when caught doing something minor (like DUI or juvenile offenses), but for those who are outsiders or identified as troublemakers formal processing will be utilized.

Although Wilson's typology may appear to be dated today and may not describe police departments very accurately, there do seem to be differences between departments. Some police departments are known to be more or less likely to use force; some have better or worse relationships with minority communities; some are known to be progressive and some reactionary. Just as with all organizations, city police departments' reputations may lag behind reality and a department that encounters bad press, for instance, may suffer a negative reputation for years after the problems have been dealt with.

Other authors describe individual officers and their different performance styles. Muir [30] discussed four types of police officers and their willingness and acceptance of the use of force and coercion. According to Muir, the successful police officer is able to balance willingness to use coercion with an understanding of humankind, with empathy and sympathy toward the weaknesses of human nature. If officers overemphasize coercion, they become cynical and brutal; if they overemphasize understanding, they become ineffective. Sometimes, a young police officer's response creates internal conflict and eventually the officer will tend to avoid situations that create the need to make these choices; this kind of officer became either a *reciprocator* or an *avoider*. Finally, some young officers found ways to exercise coercion legitimately with care and competence; these officers became *professionals* [31]. Box 4.5 shows Muir's types.

Brown [32] also described four types of police officers. Instead of the use of force, this typology focused on how each officer uses the discretion that comes with the role.

1. *Old style crime fighters* are concerned only with action that might be considered crime control; therefore, they will ignore or slight calls that they do not consider "real" police work.
2. *Clean beat officers* seek to control all behavior in their jurisdiction and take ownership over everything that happens in the area. They may use extralegal or persuasive authority to get desired results.
3. *Service style officers* emphasize public order and peace officer tasks, perhaps over crime fighting. These individuals like the public service aspects of the job rather than the tasks that result in more antagonistic relationships with the public.
4. *Professional style officers* are the epitome of bureaucratic, by-the-book policing. They may enforce the law with little discretion and seldom give anyone "a break."

Of course, no police officer fits into these described types perfectly. These are descriptions of the different ways that people approach situations they encounter (or the way departments emphasize different goals). Research has explored

---

BOX 4.5 MUIR'S POLICE TYPOLOGY

1. *Enforcers* are willing to use force, but unable to empathize with citizens. They may use force too quickly and not understand when it is absolutely necessary and when it isn't.
2. *Professionals* are willing to use force, but able to empathize with citizens; therefore, they are able to use other means when appropriate. When force is necessary, they are effective but are always reluctant to use force except as a last resort.
3. *Reciprocators* are unwilling to use force because they empathize and identify with citizens. These officers attempt to get cooperation through negotiation,

bargaining, and persuasion, but, ultimately, are less effective when these methods do not work.

4. *Avoiders* are unwilling to use force, but not because they empathize with citizenry. Rather, they prefer to avoid situations that are dangerous or troublesome and do so by staying on simple calls longer than necessary, not responding to dispatches for all available officers and, in other ways, they avoid the potential for the use of force or coercion.

Source: W. Muir, *Police: Streetcorner Politicians*, University of Chicago Press, Chicago, 1977, p. 24.

interesting questions, such as whether race and gender affect one's style of policing, whether any of the styles are more associated with corruption, and many other issues related to performance issues. Most typologies incorporate the dual roles of crime control and order maintenance. A major change in policing that also addressed this issue occurred in the late 1980s and 1990s in the form of community policing.

COMMUNITY POLICING/PROBLEM-ORIENTED POLICING

Community policing is based on a belief that police should partner with communities to prevent and reduce crime. Around the early 1980s, James Wilson and George Kelling developed what came to be called the **"broken windows" theory** of crime. These researchers argued that signs of neighborhood disintegration and deterioration indicated to criminals that no one cared and no one would intervene in criminal acts; therefore, crime is higher in these types of neighborhoods. The more crime, the less community members invest in their neighborhoods, increasing the spiral of disorder, decay, and crime. Markers of such disintegration include abandoned homes, graffiti, loitering youth, drunks and homeless people on the street, and minor offenses like public urination. Herman Goldstein argued that the police had a role in strengthening the community, which would, in turn, increase the community's ability to prevent crime [33].

Eventually the theory that neighborhood disintegration would lead to crime led to community policing, order-maintenance policing, zero tolerance policing, and problem-oriented policing. Depending on the source, these various models of policing are described as the same, similar, or different. While zero tolerance policing has been heavily criticized and community policing has received negative press as ineffective, problem-oriented policing seems to remain a well-respected approach. We can offer some observations about possible differences between these types of policing. Community policing is a broader term that encompasses many different types of tactics and programs, all with the goal of officers and community members developing partnerships to solve some of the neighborhood's problems. Order-maintenance and zero tolerance policing are associated with William Bratton's campaign at the New York City Transit Police and then with the NYPD. This type of policing, based on "broken windows," deals with all public order crimes, such as graffiti, noise violations, public urination, and or aggressive panhandling, with full enforcement. The idea is that you arrest the "little" criminals and it prevents serious crime. There is no necessary partnership with the community to undertake this model of policing and, in fact, eventually the community rebels because police officers become perceived as too intrusive and oppressive as they enforce minor ordinances against everyone. Problem-oriented policing is a model that is consistent

---

BOX 4.6 COMMUNITY POLICING STRATEGIES

- Direct engagement with the community with greater information about neighborhood problems
- Freeing community police officers from responding to dispatched crime calls so they can engage in proactive crime prevention
- More visible police operations
- Decentralized operations that lead to greater familiarity with specific neighborhoods
- Encouraging officers to see citizens as partners

- Moving decision making and discretion downward to patrol officers
- Encouraging citizens to take more initiative in preventing and solving crimes

Source: *National Institute of Justice, Community Policing in the 1990s, NIJ Research Bulletin, U.S. Department of Justice, Washington, DC, 1992, p. 3.*

---

with community policing but not necessarily essential to it; problem-oriented policing can be used even by departments that don't buy into the community-police partnership that is the hallmark of community policing (See Box 4.6).

The purpose of all community policing efforts was to increase the partnership between the community and the police in crime prevention [34]. The programs loosely grouped under a community policing strategy attempted to get community members to assist in crime prevention efforts. These partnerships may have been as simple as "National Night Out," where neighborhood members were encouraged to go outside on a specified night and meet their neighbors, to more elaborate citizen-police partnerships that identified problems in the community and shared the responsibility to fix them. Community policing efforts have included the following:

- An increase in foot and bike patrols
- Storefront police stations
- Bilingual crime hotlines
- Prevention newsletters and watch programs
- Meetings with community members
- Citizen police academies
- D.A.R.E. and G.R.E.A.T. programs
- Officers with greater responsibility and autonomy dedicated to communities

Community policing efforts also emphasize the decentralization of policing. Neighborhood storefront police stations were given greater autonomy in prioritizing and solving the problems of that particular neighborhood. The police role expanded to include helping citizens get the city to respond to abandoned cars, broken streetlights, overgrown empty lots, and dilapidated houses. Permanent assignments rather than rotating shifts help police officers develop working relationships with citizens and encourage a feeling of responsibility for their assigned community.

Criticisms of community policing

Critics of community policing programs argued that they were ineffective in crime prevention for a variety of reasons. One reason was that they mistakenly assumed "community" could be defined purely geographically. That is, community policing programs might have targeted a particular neighborhood, drawing boundaries by crime rates, voting districts, or through some other means of establishing the border of the "community." However, people may be affiliated more through activity than "place." For instance, a family may not know its neighbors but be very active in a church that is three miles away [35]. More police presence in a particular geographic neighborhood may have deterred some crime, but it may not have been successful in strengthening the community sufficiently to prevent criminal decision making.

Community policing efforts may have failed because there was no "community" to join with, or because the partnership was nonexistent. Critics argued that some programs used the community as the "eyes and ears" of police, to gain political support, monetary assistance, and moral support; but they did not involve the community in power sharing or decision making [36]. Further, in some communities, police are seen as the enemy and the antipathy felt toward police overwhelmed any attempts to gain trust. Residents may not have liked criminals, but they liked police even less. In these neighborhoods, any partnerships needed to overcome the residual distrust and dislike before becoming workable.

Generally, evaluations of community policing efforts have been mixed. It seems that public satisfaction increased when a police department adopted community policing programs, but whether such approaches reduced crime is difficult to say. Some researchers argue that findings indicate the central organization and service delivery of policing never changed that much anyway [37]. Ironically, one of the major hurdles of community policing efforts was that the community police officer emphasized order-maintenance tasks rather than crime-control tasks. This may have been a less desirable role for many officers who preferred to see themselves as "crime fighters," regardless of the effectiveness of community policing efforts.

Zero tolerance policing has been mistakenly associated with community policing, but it is conceptually distinct. As mentioned earlier, this approach targets minor offenders. Critics contend that it is a policing approach that has the risk of biased enforcement against cultural groups that do not fit into the mainstream [38]. Street people, youth, and minorities are affected, but so, too, are "law-abiding" people who violate a city ordinance, such as parking or maintenance of property. In New York City, the zero tolerance approach taken by the police was touted as the reason crime in the city dropped substantially through the late 1990s and 2000s, but critics contend that the crime rate dropped in other places that did not implement zero tolerance. Further, the rate of citizen complaints during the same time period increased substantially, so there is a cost in citizen-police relations to zero tolerance that may not be justified by any proven link to reduced crime.

Problem-oriented policing

As mentioned above, problem-oriented policing has been associated with community policing and the approach is certainly consistent with community policing, but it can be removed from the community policing model and still have legitimacy. Generally, problem-oriented policing follows the so-called SARA model of problem solving. SARA stands for scanning, analysis, response, and assessment. It refers to how police should approach crime problems. Instead of simply patrolling and reacting to crime calls, police should be constantly scanning for problems by using crime reports and other sources of information to target a particular problem, for instance an increase in burglaries in a particular neighborhood. Then, the analysis phase identifies potential explanations for the crime problem and ways to address the situation to reduce crime. Response involves implementation, which might be increased patrol, targeted enforcement, or some other response. Finally, assessment measures whether the response was successful. Despite literally thousands of articles and news reports of various problem-oriented programs across the country, there are fairly few rigorous evaluations of its effectiveness, although those that have been done do indicate that problem-oriented policing is effective [39]. Interestingly, in at least one study that evaluated the methods used in responding to identified crime problems, it was found that situational prevention responses were more effective than simple arrest strategies, calling into question the effectiveness of the zero tolerance approach [40].

A new entry to the list of policing models is "intelligence-led policing." Once again, the phrase may mean different things to different people, but generally it is associated with policing efforts after 9/11 to increase their intelligence activities in order to proactively deal with the risk of terrorism. There has been federal money available for local and state police departments to hire intelligence analysts who utilize computers and a wide variety of information sources to identify and track potential threats. The main element to this model of policing is the proactive nature of the intelligence gathering and the blurring of lines between domestic crime prevention and terrorism.

CONCLUSION

Law enforcement in this country is a descendant of the London "bobbie" from the late 1800s. Most people think of municipal police officers when they think of police, but we should be aware that there are federal, state, and local law enforcement agencies. Police hold special powers in society and have a great deal of discretion in how they resolve the situations they deal with every day. We see a great deal of criticism of police, and we expect the men and women who hold these positions to conform to high standards of behavior, both on and off duty. We expect police to pursue both goals of crime control and order maintenance. In fact, we want police to be supermen (and women).

The surprising thing is that they do so well at this impossible task. According to the Gallup Poll, respondents placed police fourth highest in ranking professions on honesty and integrity (following only nurses, druggists, and medical doctors). About 60% of respondents had a "great deal of confidence" in the police (although there was quite a large difference between whites at 63% and blacks at 38%) [41]. The favorable ratings from the public are sometimes forgotten or overlooked when there are "front-page" conflicts between the police and the community, but it should be remembered that the vast number of police officers do their job competently and compassionately and the vast bulk of the public appreciate what they do.

Review Questions

1. Describe the two functions or goals of the police and provide some examples of each.
2. How many police agencies and police officers are there in the United States?
3. Describe early law enforcement in England.
4. Which cities began the first police departments in the United States? When?
5. Who is considered responsible for the "professionalization" of police and what does that term entail?
6. Describe the types of law enforcement agencies at the federal, state, county, and local levels. What are special jurisdiction agencies?
7. Describe Wilson's typology of police departments.
8. Describe Muir's and Brown's typologies of police officers.
9. What are the principles of community policing?
10. Distinguish between community policing and problem-oriented policing.

VOCABULARY

"bobbies" older term for London's police, which refers to Robert Peel's role in creating the force in 1829

Bow Street Runners begun in 1748 by Magistrate Henry Fielding in London and considered the first type of organized police force

"broken windows" theory (of crime) states that crime occurs when there are signs of neighborhood disintegration and deterioration indicating to criminals that no one cares and no one will intervene

community policing a model of policing based on a belief that police should join with communities to prevent and reduce crime; programs include community members assisting in crime prevention efforts

discretion the power to make a decision among two or more choices

gaol early English jail where prisoners were kept before being punished

order maintenance tasks associated with keeping order and peace in society beyond crime control

shire reeve or sheriff; was responsible for tax collection and enforcing the king's peace

ENDNOTES

[1] B. Reaves, Census of State and Local Law Enforcement Agencies, 2004, Bureau of Justice Statistics, U.S. Department of Justice, Washington, DC, 2007.

[2] M. Hickman, B. Reaves, Local Police Departments, 2003, Bureau of Justice Statistics, U.S. Department of Justice, Washington, DC, 2006.

[3] J. Kuykendall, P. Burns, The black police officer: a historical perspective, J. Contemp. Crim. Just. 1 (4) (1980) 103–113.

[4] M. Hickman, B. Reaves, Local Police Departments, 2003, Bureau of Justice Statistics, U.S. Department of Justice, Washington, DC, 2006, p. 13.

[5] S. Martin, Breaking and Entering: Policewomen on Patrol, University of California Press, Berkeley, CA, 1980.

[6] M. Hickman, B. Reaves, Local Police Departments, 2000, Bureau of Justice Statistics, Washington, DC, 2003, p. 4.

[7] L. Langton, Women in Law Enforcement, 1987-2008, Bureau of Justice Statistics, Washington, DC, 2010, p. 3.

[8] International Association of Chiefs of Police (IACP), The Future of Women in Policing: Mandates for Action, IACP, Fairfax, VA, 1998.

[9] L. Gaines, V. Kappeler, Policing in America, sixth ed., LexisNexis/Matthew Bender, New Providence, NJ, 2008.

[10] W. Andrews, The Early Years: The Challenge of Public Order, from 1845 to 1870, New York Police Department, 2007. Retrieved from http://www.ci.nyc.ny.us/html/nypd/html/3100/retro.html.

[11] W. Andrews, An Era of Corruption and Reform: 1870-1900, New York Police Department, 2007. Retrieved from http://www.ci.nyc.ny.us/html/nypd/html/3100/retro.html.

[12] Los Angeles Police Department. Retrieved 6/1/2007, from http://www.lapdonline.org/history_of_the_lapd/content_basic_view/1107.

[13] Los Angeles Police Department. Retrieved 6/1/2007, from http://www.lapdonline.org/history_of_the_lapd/content_basic_view/1107.

[14] J. Crank, Understanding Police Culture, Anderson Publishing, Cincinnati, OH, 2003.

[15] V. Kappeler, R. Sluder, G. Alpert, Forces of Deviance: Understanding the Dark Side of Policing, Waveland Press, Prospect Heights, IL, 1994, p. 41.

[16] S. Walker, A Critical History of Police Reform: The Emergence of Professionalism, Lexington Books, Lexington, MA, 1977.

[17] V. Kappeler, R. Sluder, G. Alpert, Forces of Deviance: Understanding the Dark Side of Policing, Waveland Press, Prospect Heights, IL, 1994, p. 49.

[18] Texas Department of Public Safety. Retrieved 6/1/2007 from http://www.txdps.state.tx.us/overview.

[19] B. Reaves, L. Bauer, Federal Law Enforcement Officers, 2002, Bureau of Justice Statistics, Washington, DC, 2003, p. 1.

[20] B. Reaves, Federal Law Enforcement Officers, 2004, Bureau of Justice Statistics, Washington, DC, 2006, p. 2.

[21] B. Reaves, L. Bauer, Federal Law Enforcement Officers, 2002, Bureau of Justice Statistics, Washington, DC, 2003, p. 5.

[22] M. Hickman, B. Reaves, Local Police Departments, 2000, Bureau of Justice Statistics, Washington, DC, 2003, p. 2.

[23] M. Hickman, B. Reaves, Local Police Departments, 2000, Bureau of Justice Statistics, Washington, DC, 2003, p. 4.

[24] ASIS International. Retrieved 6/8/2007 from http://www.asisonline.org/about/faqs.xml.

[25] S. Mastrofski, R. Parks, A. Reiss, R. Worden, Policing Neighborhoods: A Report from Indianapolis, National Institute of Justice, Washington, DC, 1999.

[26] C. Drew, Police Struggles in New Orleans Raise Old Fears, 2006, New York Times Online (6/13/2006). Retrieved 6/1/2007 from http://www.nytimes.com/2006/06/13/us/13orleans. html?ex=1307851200&en=b53088f98360e0d8&ei=5088&partner=rssnyt&emc=rss.

[27] G. Williams, The Law and Politics of Police Discretion, Greenwood Press, Westport, CT, 1984, p. 4.

[28] W. Terrill, E. Paoline, Non-Arrest Decision Making in Police-Citizen Encounters, Police Q. 10 (2007) 308–331.

[29] J.Q. Wilson, Varieties of Police Behavior, Harvard University Press, Cambridge, MA, 1968.

[30] W. Muir, Police: Streetcorner Politicians, University of Chicago Press, Chicago, 1977.

[31] W. Muir, Police: Streetcorner Politicians, University of Chicago Press, Chicago, 1977, p. 24.

[32] M. Brown, Working the Street, Russell Sage Foundation, New York, 1981, p. 224.

[33] H. Goldstein, Problem-Oriented Policing, McGraw-Hill, New York, 1990.

[34] P. McCold, B. Wachtel, Community is not a place: a new look at community justice initiatives, in: J. Perry (Ed.), Repairing Communities through Restorative Justice, American Correctional Association, Lanham, MD, 2002, p. 47.

[35] P. McCold, B. Wachtel, Community is not a place: a new look at community justice initiatives, in: J. Perry (Ed.), Repairing Communities through Restorative Justice, American Correctional Association, Lanham, MD, 2002, p. 40.

[36] P. McCold, B. Wachtel, Community is not a place: a new look at community justice initiatives, in: J. Perry (Ed.), Repairing Communities through Restorative Justice, American Correctional Association, Lanham, MD, 2002, p. 43.

[37] J. Zhao, N. He, N. Lovrich, Community policing: did it change the basic functions of policing in the 1990s? A national follow-up study, Justice Q. 20 (4) (2003) 697–724.

[38] C. Kubrin, Making order of disorder: a call for conceptual clarity, Criminol. Publ. Policy 7 (2) (2008) 203–214.

[39] D. Weisburd, C. Telep, J. Hinkle, J. Eck, Is problem-oriented policing effective in reducing crime and disorder? Criminol. Publ. Policy 9 (1) (2010) 139–172.

[40] A. Braga, Setting a higher standard for the evaluation of problem-oriented policing initiatives, Criminol. Publ. Policy 9 (1) (2010) 173–195.

[41] Sourcebook of Criminal Justice Statistics, Table 2.17.2009, Respondents' rating of the honesty and ethical standards of various occupations, and Table 2.12.2009, Reported confidence in the police. Retrieved 9/15/2010 from http://www.albany.edu/sourcebook/pdf/2172009.pdf, and http://www.albany.edu/sourcebook/pdf/2122009.pdf. 2009.

Police Operations

- Hiring qualifications for police departments typically include age restrictions, educational requirements, good credit history, no criminal history, physical fitness, and psychological stability.
- Although the police subculture is not as strong as it might once have been, the themes that run contrary to the formal mission of policing, including the "blue curtain of secrecy," are still present to some degree.
- Research shows that blacks are stopped more frequently than whites, but that they are not more likely to experience disrespectful behavior, at least initially, from the officers.
- Three areas of corruption include graft and gratuities, abuse of authority, and "noble cause" corruption.
- Three explanations of police deviance are individual explanations, organizational explanations, and societal explanations.
- Suggestions to reduce police corruption include better training, integrity testing, civilian review/complaint boards, and early warning or audit systems.

CONTENTS

What makes a good police officer? In this chapter, we will discuss how police departments select, train, and supervise their police officers. In a few cases, selection, training, and supervision fail, and police corruption occurs. It is important to realize, however, that the majority of the public have positive opinions regarding the police and the vast majority of police officers perform their role with integrity and competence. Most of the discussion in this and the following chapter emphasizes law enforcement at the local municipal level.

SELECTION

The qualifications for being hired by a police department typically include only a few absolute requirements. One major department, for instance, requires that applicants have the following qualifications:

- Be 21 to 44 years old
- Have put in 60 hours of college or possess an honorable discharge from the military
- Be a U.S. citizen
- Be height and weight proportionate
- Have a valid driver's license
- Have no more than two moving violations within the last 18 months
- Have no felony or class A misdemeanors
- Have no class B misdemeanors within the last 10 years
- Have a stable credit history

Applicants who meet these qualifications take a civil service test that they must pass with a score of 70 or higher. The next steps of the hiring process include a preliminary interview, physical agility test, polygraph test, criminal background check, interview, medical exam (including a drug test), and a psychological exam [1].

The hiring process is described as a "screening out" process rather than a selection process. In other words, all applicants are accepted and then screened out when factors indicate they would be inappropriate for policing. Factors that would screen out applicants include a lack of intellectual ability (failing the civil service exam), lack of responsibility (bad credit), lack of honesty (failing the polygraph test), lack of physical fitness (failing the physical test), or lack of mental stability (failing the psychological exam).

The psychological exam utilizes objective personality tests, such as the Minnesota Multiphasic Personality Inventory (MMPI), and a personal interview. The psychologist looks for personality characteristics such as aggressiveness, bias, or anxiety, which would indicate that the candidate is a poor fit for the job. On the other hand, there is no desired personality profile that all police departments use to look for candidates. Little research has been done to explore whether certain personality profiles are more or less successful in policing careers. The Inwald Personality Inventory (IPI) was developed to measure personality characteristics and behavioral patterns specific to fitness for law enforcement. The so-called Big Five personality traits (extroversion, neuroticism, agreeableness, conscientiousness, and openness) have been validated as reliable measures of personality and, of these, conscientiousness seems to predict good performance in other jobs and professions. Conscientiousness is related to the degree of organization, control, and motivation one has, and has been related to being organized, reliable, hard-working, self-governing, and persevering. There has been very little research, however, as to whether the trait accurately measures police performance success [2]. Generally, desirable traits and characteristics for officers include higher education, varied life experiences, cognitive problem-solving skills, communication skills, empathy, and respect for others [3].

In the past, height and weight requirements excluded women and some minorities from being hired by police departments. Stringent height and weight requirements have been struck down as discriminatory by the courts, so today you may see very short police officers. It is still acceptable to require that applicants be in good physical shape, however, and requirements that applicants be height and weight proportionate have generally been upheld. Applicants are also typically required to pass some form of physical fitness test. Although these vary from department to department, they usually involve some form of cardiovascular fitness (running), strength, and agility. There is some concern that physical ability tests unfairly exclude women or others who might otherwise make good police officers; however, studies have validated that such tests do measure bona fide occupational qualifications for police officers [4].

It is also ironic that although physical fitness tests screen out applicants at the hiring stage, many, if not most, police departments do not require officers to maintain physical standards once hired. It is difficult to make the argument that certain physical requirements are necessary to policing if employed officers are not required to maintain any level of fitness. Many advocate that physical standards be adopted by police departments, much as the military does, with gradations of fitness based on age. Arguably, departments could save money in insurance costs and lost time due to sickness and injury if officers were required to maintain height and weight ratios and cardiovascular fitness. These demands would reduce heart attacks or injuries when carrying out police duties.

A police personality?

One interesting topic that has been explored by researchers is whether there is such a thing as a "police personality." A related question is whether the career attracts people with certain personality characteristics, or whether the career changes people so that they develop such characteristics after working in the field. The so-called police personality has been described as having the traits of cynicism, authoritarianism, and suspiciousness. Some researchers have found police officers to be generally cynical, isolated, alienated, defensive, distrustful, dogmatic, and authoritarian [5]. There is conflicting research as to the prevalence of these traits. Another question is whether the traits exist before being hired or are acquired on the job [6]. Furthermore, it is not clear that any particular traits are associated with undesirable behaviors or less effective officers. These are important research questions and should be addressed.

TRAINING

Early officers had no training and were basically given a uniform and nightstick and told to go do their job. Training has expanded exponentially and today police departments require hundreds of hours of academy training. To be certified as a peace officer in most states, one must have graduated from a recognized academy and passed standardized tests that include academic subjects as well as skills training, such as firearms and driving.

Police officers receive training in departmental or regional academies. Smaller departments may prefer to hire individuals who have already received certification through attendance at a regional academy, but larger departments have their own academies and require all applicants to attend, even those who may already have certification. In-service training hours are required for all police officers to maintain their certification. This in-service training usually has content that is mandated by the state, and also optional training segments that can be selected by the department or individual officer. Departments train officers either by assigning them to required training at certain times during the year, or some departments allow the officer to choose training segments from a selection of course offerings, as long as they total the required number of hours.

Recruit training includes law, operations, mental health assessments, communication skills, domestic violence, firearms, physical combat, and driving skills, among other topics. In-service training may cover updates on laws related to policing, communication skills, forensic analysis topics, testifying, and many other topics.

Field training officer (FTO) programs started in 1972 [7]. This last portion of training pairs the new recruit with an FTO who supervises the trainee for a period that may range from weeks to months. **FTOs** are expected to help new academy graduates apply their academy training to real-life problems of the street. Some FTOs and others convey the idea that what one learns in the academy is irrelevant and now they will teach the recruit the way "it really is." Because most academy instructors are better versed in current law and departmental policies, it is usually a problem when this approach is taken. FTOs should be, and usually are, chosen for their ability to teach recruits good practices that will prevent citizen complaints and lawsuits against the department.

SUPERVISION

Most police officers start as patrol officers, although they may quickly transfer to "desk jobs," such as community relations. During the probationary period, officers may be fired at will; however, once the probationary period is over, civil service protections require that if an officer is to be fired, it must be for cause and there is a hearing and appeals process. Promotions typically take place through civil service tests and interview boards and, typically, if an officer is promoted to a higher rank, he or she must accept a transfer to whatever division has an empty position.

Sergeants are the front-line supervisors and are called whenever a police officer thinks it is necessary or is required to seek the advice or the authority of a supervisor. Sergeants are responsible for evaluating and contributing to performance reviews of officers. Sometimes, sergeants experience personal challenges in supervising and disciplining officers who they patrolled and/or partnered with before being promoted. It has been said that sergeants are the foundation of the department, and if sergeants do their job well, the department is usually in good shape. However, if sergeants do not supervise, if they allow patrol officers to ignore policies, or if they make decisions based on favoritism, then the department will be weaker because of it.

Police management training is often very advanced. Various organizations, such as the Police Executive Research Forum (PERF), provide research and training to improve administration and management. There is also training for police managers available through the Federal Law Enforcement Training Center (FLETC), which also conducts training internationally.

🌐 INTERNET KEY

To learn more about PERF, go to http://www.policeforum.org/, and for FLETC, to http://www.fletc.gov/.

Stress

Early research indicated that police officers experienced higher stress than most other occupations; however, this may not be the case. It is certainly true that policing has a few unique stressors not shared by most other occupations—that is, using or being a target of lethal force is not present in most occupations. On the other hand, other types of stress, such as dealing with bureaucracy, or unfair supervisors, are similar to other occupations and professions. Some researchers have concluded that police officers do not experience more stress than others [8]. Other research indicates that officers experience more stress from management over such things as being "second guessed," being punished for minor infractions, and not being rewarded than they do from the "operational" elements of policing (dealing with suspects and danger). In one study on police stress, it was found that officers experienced "organizational stress" (which included perceptions of supervisors being too rigid and oppressive with a corresponding lack of discretion) and that this stress reduced their performance [9].

Other researchers have found that individuals experience the stress of policing differently, and factors such as gender, age, and ethnicity seem to affect the ability to cope with the stressors [10]. Stress is an important issue because it may lead to **burnout**, which is when officers merely "go through the motions" of their job and may be susceptible to corruption. It can also lead to turnover when officers quit or retire early because of stress. This is unfortunate for the officer and also presents a high cost to the public, because training is expensive. Departments have responded to the reality of stress by offering psychological services and other departmental policies that encourage good coping skills.

Use of tasers

In 2008, 12,000 law enforcement agencies employed conducted energy devices (CEDs), commonly known as tasers. Using news stories as a source for measuring their use, researchers noted that reports of CEDs increased from 24 news stories in 2002 to 338 stories in 2006 [11]. Proponents of the devices argue that they have resulted in less injury to officers and suspects alike, and officers who use them avoid having to use lethal force. Opponents, such as Amnesty International, argue that they have been responsible for 300 deaths. Research indicates that the electricity that is conducted by the devices is not sufficient to seriously harm an individual, but there have been reports of serious injuries caused by falling and deaths occur because of pre-existing conditions. For instance, those who are under the influence of drugs may be more susceptible to injury. Also, if the taser is used multiple times on a person, there is a greater risk of injury [12].

The most troublesome news stories are those where the officer involved used the taser in a situation where it did not seem to be appropriate, as in stopping someone from being verbally disruptive rather than physically dangerous. Amnesty International reports that 36% of the use of CEDs were against verbally noncompliant individuals [13]. It also seems to be the case that officers do not receive as much training on the use of tasers as they undergo for firearms, and this may explain why some officers misuse the taser. Generally, the courts have determined that a reasonableness standard applies to the taser as with any use of force. The officer is not obligated to use the least serious level of force but he or she is obligated to use only that level of force (including the taser) that is reasonable given the nature of the threat. This means that the officer must feel threatened and the taser is not appropriate for gaining compliance.

Police use of lethal force and deaths of police

For close to 40 years, the number of police shootings has remained in the 300 to 450 per year range despite large increases in the national population and large increases in the number of police officers. The number of justifiable homicides by police was in the 400s in the 1970s, dropped to the 300s in the 1980s, and rose again to 450 in 1993. The total killed in 2009, 406, is higher than in any year from 2000 to 2008 (347 to 398), but was lower than in the mid-1990s [14]. It is interesting that police use of lethal force shows somewhat the same pattern as violent crime in that the highest number of individuals killed occurred just before the drop in violent crime in the latter half of the 1990s.

Police officers' responses to shootings have been the focus of research. Reactions vary depending on characteristics of the officer and the situational elements of the shooting, but many officers experience symptoms of stress. Police departments may require an officer to be evaluated by a mental health professional when he or she has been involved in a shooting incident because of well-established findings that shooting-related stress is likely [15].

When a police officer is killed, it is always a sobering reminder that the job is dangerous. In the fall of 2009, four Lakewood police officers,

Lakewood, Washington police officers (clockwise from top left) Greg Richards, Mark Renninger, Tina Griswold, and Ronald Owens are pictured in this handout released by the Pierce County Sheriff's Department on 11/29/2009. The four officers were shot and killed at a coffee shop in Tacoma, a Washington state suburb. **Source:** © HO/Reuters/ Corbis

a suburb in the Seattle-Tacoma area, were murdered as they sat doing paperwork in a coffee shop. There was no precipitating event to the shooting; a man simply walked in and shot all four officers and then escaped, although one officer managed to shoot the assailant before dying. He was killed two days later when a lone officer confronted him about a stolen car and he reached for his weapon. No motive for his deadly rampage was uncovered, other than he had been previously prosecuted and punished in the criminal justice system and had told family and friends that he was going to "kill some police" and to "watch the news." Six other people have been arrested for aiding and abetting his escape, including his ex-cellmate, who drove him away from the shooting, and his sister, who bandaged his gunshot wound. In 2000, Governor Mike Huckabee in Arkansas commuted his 108-year sentence for armed robbery and other violent crimes. He had been arrested for raping a child and had been released six days before the shooting.

The good news is that there were are fewer officer deaths today than in the 1970s. In 1975, with 600,000 officers, there were 156 deaths, but in 2009, with 900,000 officers, there were about 47 gunfire deaths. This translates

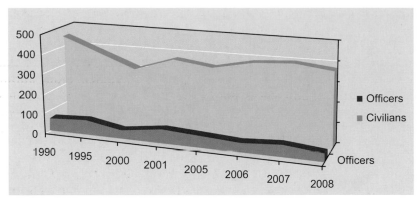

FIGURE 5.1
Justifiable homicides of civilians and deaths of police officers, 1990 to 2008.

to rates of 0.26 per 1000 in 1975, compared to 0.05 per 1000 in 2009; so officers are much less likely to be killed today than 30 years ago. Figure 5.1 does not display data from the 1970s, but one can see that the number of police killed has been as high as 75 in 1995 and as low as 41 in 2008, but the number killed seems to continue to be much lower than in past decades [16].

PATROL AND INVESTIGATION

In the last chapter we discussed the dual goals of crime control and order maintenance. **Reactive policing** describes activities that respond to crime when brought to the attention of the police through crime reports or complaints. **Proactive policing** is when police engage in active behavior to seek out crime, including undercover work, the use of informants, and sting operations.

Patrol

Patrol can be considered both reactive and proactive. Typically, patrol officers look for crime, but they also spend a great deal of time responding to dispatched calls for service. Responding to dispatched calls is obviously reactive crime control.

There has been interesting research that has focused on how effective patrolling really is. One of the most famous research projects in policing was the Kansas City Preventive Patrol Study. In this study, part of Kansas City, Missouri, was divided into three different areas. One area had no patrol at all—police only responded to dispatched calls. The second area had increased patrol, roughly five to six times the normal pattern. The third area was the control group, with normal patrols scheduled. Study authors found no significant differences among the three areas in level of crime or citizen satisfaction [17]. This does not mean, of course, that police have no effect on crime; but it does call into question the effectiveness of normal patrols.

Police departments may at times initiate **saturated patrols**, meaning that a certain neighborhood or area of town is targeted for frequent, perhaps even constant, patrol presence. The "hot spot" is identified through crime reports and the saturated patrol continues for a set period or until the crime reports are reduced to an acceptable level. Research has indicated that saturated patrols do work in reducing crime; there is a **residual effect**, meaning reduced crime continues after the saturated patrol ends; and there does not seem to be a **displacement effect**, meaning that crime merely moves to another area of the city [18].

Most police officers are engaged in general patrol and respond to dispatched calls. However, it would be a mistake to think of policing only in this light. Many departments are constantly trying innovative methods to more effectively serve the public. For instance, in the last chapter, we discussed problem-oriented policing, which has been implemented in many locales around the country. Departments also may have special units to deal with the mentally ill or domestic violence. One of the most difficult calls police respond to is when a mentally ill individual is threatening family members or other citizens. In some of these calls, police resort to using violent means to subdue the individual and then encounter criticism for doing so. Some police departments have responded to the challenge by training special officers to handle these calls. These officers are trained to identify the signs of mental illness. They also have received specific training in how to deal with the mentally ill, and what resources are available in the community to assist these individuals.

Some police departments also have special victim units, crisis teams, or domestic violence units that respond to calls that involve battered women, abused children, rape victims, and other specific types of calls. These specialized patrol units receive additional training and are sensitive to the needs of the targeted types of crime victims. As the Focus on Crime box indicates, domestic violence poses special problems for law enforcement and prosecution.

FOCUS ON CRIME: DOMESTIC VIOLENCE

Before the 1980s, domestic violence was rarely considered a crime. Law enforcement, generally, was described as treating domestic disputes as order maintenance calls, even when injuries were involved. If the injury was "severe," aggravated assault could be charged and the perpetrator could be arrested, but if the injury was not defined as severe, it was only misdemeanor assault and a police officer could not arrest unless the victim swore out a complaint. That changed in the 1980s when states passed "mandatory arrest" statutes that allowed officers to arrest without a complainant in cases of domestic violence even if the injury did not rise to aggravated assault.

The extent and nature of domestic violence is difficult to determine because the UCR does not identify this as a specific type of crime; therefore, domestic assaults are part of the general assault category. The NCS/NCVS does provide information on the victim-offender relationship, and the information cited in the rest of the box comes from these victim surveys.

Between 1993 and 1999, women accounted for 85% of victims of "intimate partner violence." The typical victim was young (16 to 24), although the typical victim of intimate partner murder was older (35 to 49). Victims were most likely to be separated from their partners at the time of the victimization (as opposed to divorced, widowed, or never married). In general, the lower the income bracket, the greater the likelihood of being a domestic violence victim. The most common type of violence was simple assault. Rates of intimate partner violence fell 41% from 10 per 1000 to 6 per 1000 between 1993 and 1999. In all age categories except 20 to 24, black and white women's rates of victimization were similar. While up to 38% of all female homicide victims in some age groups were killed by an intimate, at most, only 8% of male homicide victims were killed by an intimate partner. In this study of victims between 1993 and 1999, 53% of the assailants were current or former boyfriends or girlfriends, 30% were spouses, and about 14% were ex-spouses. In 81% of the cases, the assailant did not have a weapon. During these years, 5% of victims sustained serious injuries, 41% experienced minor injuries, and 4% were sexually assaulted. Only about half of these domestic violence incidents were reported to the police, with older victims less likely to report than younger victims.

The rate of intimate partner violence declined by more than 50% between 1993 and 2008. The rate of intimate partner violence against women was 4.3, against men it was 0.8, and the rate overall was 2.6 per 1000. Women continue to be victimized at a level much higher than men by intimate partners; the percentage of total incidents with women as victims remained at about 85%. About 83% of the intimate partner violence against men was committed by female offenders and about 99% of the violence committed against women was by male intimates. In 2007, intimate partners committed about 2340 homicides, which is about 14% of all homicides. About 70% of the victims were women. Women continue to be much more likely to be killed by an intimate than men. Of female homicide victims, 64% were killed by a family member or intimate (45% by an intimate partner), but only about 16% of male homicide victims were killed by a family member or intimate (5% by an intimate partner). Interestingly, while 72% of the intimate partner violence that involved male victims was reported to the police, only 49% of the intimate partner violence with female victims was reported to police.

Sources: *C. Rennison, Intimate Partner Violence and Age of Victim, 1993-1999, Bureau of Justice Statistics, U.S. Department of Justice, Washington, DC, 2001; S. Catalono, H. Snyder, M. Rand, Female Victims of Violence, U.S. Department of Justice, Washington, DC, 2009.*

One of the most publicized police management strategies has been the CompStat program. This approach was developed in New York City during the tenure of Chief William Bratton. Basically it uses computer-generated crime statistics and daily or weekly meetings of division heads to hold these managers responsible for the crime in their districts. Immediate feedback, in the form of crime reports, allows higher-level administrators to see who is and who is not successful in reducing crime. Critics argue that the program is nothing more than what has always occurred in good departments, and others suggest that the format may create pressure to "doctor" crime reports. However, advocates argue that it is an efficient, modern approach to policing that is based on management principles [19].

Undercover operations

Proactive policing is looking for crime before it happens, but without creating crime. There are a wide range of undercover activities engaged in by police. Some of these activities present opportunities for criminals to commit crimes so that they can be caught; other operations are designed to collect evidence once an investigation has centered on a particular suspect. Police officers may pretend to be drug dealers, prostitutes, "johns," crime bosses, friends, and perhaps even lovers, to catch criminals.

We can think of undercover operations as operating on a continuum of intimacy. The least personal relationships would be represented by a brief "buy-bust" incident in which the officer pretends to be a drug user and buys from a street dealer, and moments later an arrest is made. Similar set-ups are done to control street prostitution—policemen routinely pretend that they are "johns," and policewomen dress up as prostitutes. At the other extreme would be a situation in which an undercover officer develops a long-term relationship with the suspect.

Some argue that undercover operations that go on for a long time, and where others besides the suspect are misled, should not occur [20]. It is also true that these operations are difficult for the officer. Undercover officers have difficulty, at times, separating themselves from their cover and feel that they have deceived innocent people (if they become close to the family members of the suspects) [21]. Evidently, even other officers have difficulty seeing the undercover narcotics officer as an officer instead of drug dealer, and it has been reported that undercover officers have trouble integrating back into the department after a long operation [22].

In proactive investigations, the central question is: Who do police target and why? Police operations that provide opportunities for crime change the police role from discovering who has committed a crime to one of discovering who might commit a crime if given the chance. Some examples of "set-ups" include:

- A fake deer placed by the side of the road, used to entice overeager hunters, who are then arrested for violating hunting laws
- Police officer decoys dressed as drunks and "passed out" on sidewalks with money sticking out of their pocket to entice thieves

- Undercover officers, posing as criminals, entice doctors to prescribe unneeded medications that are controlled substances, such as Percocet and OxyContin
- Police set up fencing operations to buy stolen goods from unsuspecting thieves and burglars

Are only bad people tempted? If police cross a line in their undercover operations, it is called entrapment and we will discuss entrapment in the next chapter. Anything short of entrapment, however, is legally acceptable.

One type of sting operation is when police set up a fencing operation, receive stolen goods for a period of time, and then arrest all the burglars and thieves who brought the goods in to be sold. Some argue that this creates crime, but others counter by saying that the burglar would have taken their goods to another fence anyway. Another argument is that, despite the effectiveness of stings, government deception appears unseemly; the counterargument is that they are creative ways to catch criminals.

Informants are individuals who are not police officers, but who assist police by providing information about criminal activity, acting the part of a buyer in drug sales, or otherwise "setting up" a criminal act so that police may gather evidence against the target. Informants perform such services for some reward—money, to get charges dropped or reduced or, in some documented cases, for drugs supplied by an officer. They may do it to retaliate against the suspect for some wrong done to them. Informants typically are not middle-class, upstanding-citizen types [23]. They probably have engaged in criminal activities themselves, and they may even be currently committing crimes at the same time they are acting as informants. In some cases, the evidence they provide may be purely manufactured [24]. Some officers argue that they could not do their job without informants. There are other arguments, however, that the perceived value of informants is overstated [25]. The Commission on Accreditation for Law Enforcement Agencies (CALEA) has developed standards for working with informants.

THE SUBCULTURE OF POLICING

A **subculture** exists when a group has a different set of values, beliefs, and even language from the dominant culture. In the case of the police subculture, there is research that indicates that in some departments there is a "subculture" of policing that is different from, and in conflict with, formal departmental mission statements.

Researchers argue that the reason this subculture exists is the special nature of policing, including the following characteristics:

- Police typically form a homogeneous social group.

- They have a uniquely stressful work environment.
- They participate in a basically closed social system [26].

Police have tended to come from the same socioeconomic and ethnic groups, although diversity is more common today than in the past. Further, the work life of police officers is marked by shift work and special characteristics (such as dangerousness and stigma). Police officers' social lives tend to include other police officers. This can lead to closed viewpoints and **groupthink** (where no one feels free to offer competing viewpoints) [27].

The subculture of policing has been described by various researchers as including certain values or themes. This is a similar discussion to the one about a police personality, but instead of individuals with certain traits being attracted to policing or adopting traits afterward, the idea here is that the subculture is already established and individuals are socialized to the subculture.

Socialization is adopting the values and beliefs of one's culture (or subculture). The police subculture has been described as including the following traits:

- Stereotypical views of large numbers of citizens as troublemakers [28]
- Loyalty to colleagues over citizens or the department
- View that the use of force is acceptable even when not strictly legal
- View that police officer discretion should not be questioned
- View that the truth is relative and subject to protecting officers or crime control [29]

Another researcher identified the three dominant characteristics of the police culture as cynicism or suspicion (of everyone); the acceptance of the use of force when their authority is threatened; and the perception that they are victims of public misunderstanding and scorn, low wages, and unfair administrators [30].

Part of the police subculture involves the **"cop code,"** a set of informal rules for police officers that are not necessarily the same as those taught in the academy. The code has been described as including the principles found in Box 5.1.

Some argue that the police subculture is merely a mix of a conservative political viewpoint and a work culture that is not that much different from many other workplaces [31]. It also seems to be true that the subculture may not be as prevalent or extreme as it once might have been. Several factors contribute to the possible weakening of the subculture.

1. *Increasing diversity*: Many diverse groups are now represented in police departments, including blacks, Hispanics, women, and the college-educated. These different groups bring their own value systems into the police environment.

BOX 5.1 THE "COP CODE"

- "You cover your men: don't let any officer take a job alone"
- "Keep a cool head"
- "Don't backdoor it" (a prohibition against certain gratuities)
- Watch out for your partner first and then the rest of the guys working that shift
- Don't give up another cop
- Be aggressive when you have to, but don't be too eager
- Don't get involved in anything in another guy's sector
- Hold up your end of the work
- If you get caught off base, don't implicate anybody else
- Make sure the other guys know if another cop is dangerous or "crazy"

- Don't trust a new guy until you have checked him out
- Don't leave work for the next shift
- Protect your ass
- Don't give them too much activity
- Don't do the bosses' work for them
- Don't trust bosses to look out for your interest

Sources: W. Muir, Police: Streetcorner Politicians, University of Chicago Press, Chicago, 1977, p. 191; E. Reuss-Ianni, Two Cultures of Policing: Street Cops and Management Cops, Transaction, New Brunswick, NJ, 1983, p. 14.

2. *Police unions*: Unions formalize relationships between the line staff and the administration; thus, instead of subcultural (informal) methods for coping with perceived administrative unfairness, there are formal grievance procedures.

3. *Civil litigation*: Police officers face large monetary damages when gross negligence and perjury can be proven. They may be less likely to cover for a fellow police officer when faced with these possible sanctions.

More recently, researchers have found that there is substantial variation among officers and differences in their cultural views. Although there are some associations seen between certain values and gender and ethnicity, these associations are not strong. The researchers conclude that the police culture is less uniform and powerful today than it might have been in earlier decades [32].

Race relations and the police subculture

One of the most persistent criticisms of police is that they enforce the law in a discriminatory manner against minorities. This criticism persists despite the entry of minority officers in the ranks, and despite attempts by police departments to improve relations with minority communities. Some argue that police officers enforce the law differentially or that they withhold the protections and benefits of the law from certain groups [33]. The groups that believe they experience discrimination by police include the poor, gays, and minorities, especially blacks [34].

Some studies report that lower-class blacks have significantly more negative interactions with police. More than twice as many report disrespectful language or swearing by police officers in surveys [35]. Lower-class blacks have more negative opinions of police than do middle-class blacks [36]. Minorities that live in metropolitan areas, have less education, less income, are younger, and report more bad experiences with the police, not surprisingly, perceive more police misconduct and exhibit the highest endorsement of police reforms [37]. Areas of concentrated disadvantage showed the least satisfaction with police, but race was still a predictor, even when controlling for neighborhood characteristics [38].

The Project on Policing studies used 240 hours of observations of encounters with 3130 suspects in Indianapolis and St. Petersburg in 1996-1997. In this study, trained observers noted characteristics of these encounters, and the results were used to examine such things as police officers' use of force and disrespect. The authors provided a careful review of prior studies and noted that police disrespect had been linked in prior studies to those who were disrespectful or resistant, intoxicated, or mentally ill. In other words, the results tended to indicate that whether a police officer was disrespectful or not was associated with demeanor, rather than class or race [39].

Observers in the Project on Policing study noted that suspects were disrespectful toward police in 15% of encounters, while police were *initially* disrespectful toward suspects in only 5% of encounters (this percentage does not include police disrespect after a suspect-initiated disrespect). While only 5% of the citizens who did not initiate disrespect received it from the officers, 35% of those who initiated disrespect received it in turn. Contrary to other studies and popular opinion, these researchers found that minority suspects experienced less "disrespect" than white citizens [40].

The authors also reported that blacks in both cities appeared in the pool of encounters at roughly one and one-half times their percentage of the general population. In other words, even though blacks were no more likely to receive disrespect than whites when stopped, they were stopped one and one-half times as often as their population percentage would have predicted [41]. Racial profiling refers to the practice of stopping drivers based on a profile that is largely dependent on race. It has been condemned as discriminatory and will be discussed more fully in the next chapter.

The blue curtain of secrecy and the police subculture

The **blue curtain of secrecy** refers to the practice of police covering up the misdeeds of other officers and/or not testifying against them in administrative discipline hearings or legal proceedings. It should be noted that recent research indicates that this conspiracy of silence is breaking down [42]. There are interesting contradictions, however, because in a recent survey, while 80% of police officers did not think that the "code of silence" was essential for police trust and good policing, fully two-thirds reported that a "whistleblower" would suffer informal punishment from fellow officers. Further, more than half agreed that it was not unusual for police to ignore improper conduct on the part of other officers [43].

One of the greatest harms of police cover-ups is the damage that is inflicted on a police officer's credibility. Prosecutors can ordinarily rely on a jury to take police testimony as fact and believe police witnesses over nonpolice witnesses when there is contradictory testimony. When jury members believe that police officers lie, it is much more difficult for a prosecutor to obtain a conviction.

The "blue curtain of secrecy" may not exist in some departments or may exist at varying levels in different police departments. If it does exist, it occurs for various reasons. Officers feel loyalty toward each other. They also may believe that the officer's wrongdoing is not as serious as the discipline he would receive or equal the loss of an experienced officer to the department. There may be egoistic reasons as well, because the officer may believe that he or she has also committed acts that could be disciplined. Even good officers who have not engaged in misconduct may experience great anguish and self-doubt over turning in or testifying against friends and colleagues, and that is understandable. Loyalty is perhaps stronger in law enforcement than in other professions because police depend on one another, sometimes in life-or-death situations. Loyalty to one's fellows is part of the *esprit de corps* of policing and is an absolutely essential element of a healthy department, but it seems that it can also cause problems when some officers are protected from the consequences of their misconduct.

⊕ INTERNET KEY

For a Web site that provides more information on criminal justice ethics, go to the Institute for Criminal Justice Ethics at http://www.lib.jjay.cuny.edu/cje/html/institute.html.

FOCUS ON ETHICS

You are a young police officer and still patrolling with your FTO. One day you and your FTO are called to assist in an altercation at a fraternity house. When you arrive, there are about 30 people outside the house and two other patrol cars are there. It seems that most of the people are watching several young men who are physically struggling with the four officers who are already there. Your FTO jumps out of the car and immediately grabs one of two men who appear to be fighting with one of the officers. You also begin to wrestle with another man when he attempts to push you away from the others. After a short struggle, you manage to put handcuffs on him. Taking him to the car, you see that your FTO has a young man in the car and he is repeatedly hitting him in the face and head with his baton. The young man is trying to protect his face by squirming away and kicking at the officer, although he is handcuffed. Only when

FOCUS ON ETHICS—CONT'D

two other patrol cars arrive does your FTO stop hitting the man who, by that time, is bloody and almost unconscious. Later, there is an investigation into the incident spurred by reports that the police officers on the scene used excessive force. What, if anything, would you say to the investigating officers?

The informal practice of punishing individuals who come forward is an especially distressing aspect of loyalty. For the individual who tears the blue curtain of secrecy, subcultural sanctions can be extreme. This is not just true of law enforcement agencies, of course. In fact, sanctions against whistleblowers are so common that most states and the federal government now have laws designed to protect whistleblowers. In Box 5.2, two quotes show how the subcultural sanctions against whistleblowers remained virtually unchanged for more than 20 years in New York City.

POLICE CORRUPTION

The International Association of Chiefs of Police developed the Law Enforcement Code of Ethics and the Canons of Police Ethics, and many departments have used these or adapted them to their own situations. There are at least four major themes in the International Chiefs of Police Code. They are as follows:

1. The principle of justice or *fairness* is the single most dominant theme in the law enforcement code. Police officers must uphold the law regardless of the offender's identity. They must not single out special groups for different treatment.
2. A second theme is that of *service*. Police officers exist to serve the community and their role, appropriately and essentially, concerns this idea.

BOX 5.2 THE MORE THINGS CHANGE...

The problem is that the atmosphere does not yet exist in which honest police officers can act without fear of ridicule or reprisal from fellow officers...

—Frank Serpico, Knapp Commission, 1971

Source: *N. Hentoff, Serpico: nothing has changed, VillageVoice.com, 1999. Retrieved 11/4/1999 from http://www.villagevoice.com/issues/9944/hentoff.shtml.*

Cops don't tell on cops.... [I]f a cop decided to tell on me, his career's ruined... [H]e's going to be labeled as a rat.

—Police officer witness, Mollen Commission, 1994

Source: *S. Walker, Police Accountability: The Role of Citizen Oversight, Wadsworth, Belmont, CA, 2001, p. 32.*

3. The third theme is the *importance of the law*. Police are protectors of the Constitution and must not go beyond it or substitute rules of their own. Because the law is so important, police must not only be concerned with lawbreakers, but also their own behavior must be totally within the bounds set for them by the law.

4. The final theme is one of *personal conduct*. Police, at all times, must uphold a standard of behavior consistent with their public position. This involves a higher standard of behavior in their professional and personal lives than that expected from the general public. "Conduct unbecoming" is one of the most often cited discipline infractions and can include everything from committing a crime to having an affair or being drunk in public.

🌐 INTERNET KEY

To read the International Chiefs of Police Law Enforcement Code, go to http://www.lib.jjay.cuny.edu/cje/html/codes/codes-usa-organizational/lece-r.html.

Unfortunately, despite the code of ethics, and departmental efforts in selection, training, and supervision to minimize the occurrence of misdeeds on the part of officers, scandals do occur. Examples of widespread corruption have been uncovered by various committees and investigative bodies since the very beginnings of organized police departments.

EXERCISE: IN THE STATE OF...

Do a newspaper or Google search of your state to see if there have been any police corruption scandals. In what city did the scandal occur? What happened? What steps have been taken to respond to the problem?

New York City has experienced a series of police scandals that occurred in 1894, 1913, 1932 (the Wickersham Commission), 1949 (the Kefauver Commission), 1972 (the Knapp Commission), and 1993 (the Mollen Commission). NYPD has been in the news because of the Amadou Diallo case and the Abner Louima case in the past, and in 2010 the department was in the news again because of alleged harassment against Adrian Schoolcraft, a police officer who secretly taped supervisors ordering officers to meet quotas and make arrests even without probable cause [44]. The movie *Training Day* may be partially based on the Rampart scandal in Los Angeles. In this real-life incident, it was discovered that a group of officers belonging to a narcotics task force were shockingly similar to the crooks they were pursuing. They engaged in intimidation, planted evidence, and, in one instance, shot an unarmed suspect. They also vandalized houses they searched and once sprayed "L.A.P.D. Rules" on the wall of a house. The scandal came to light when one of the officers attempted to make a deal with prosecutors to get out of a drug prosecution and testified against the others, detailing all of their illegal activities.

Many other large cities have their own historical cycles of corruption and exposure. In the last several years, there have been police scandals in Chicago (as noted in the Breaking News box below), Baltimore, Indianapolis, New Orleans, Boston, Stoughton (Massachusetts), Minneapolis, Philadelphia, and Tulsa (Oklahoma). These scandals involve police officers taking money from drug dealers for protection, stealing from burglary sites, soliciting kickbacks, and planting evidence and perjury [45]. While the vast number of officers are honest and perform their job honorably, it is important to understand the structural elements that allow these instances of corruption to occur. It does seem to be the case that the most extreme cases of police corruption occur in large cities. Perhaps this is because there is more anonymity in large departments and it is more difficult to supervise all officers in all divisions and squads. Further, it is harder to develop a cohesive culture of integrity and service in larger departments with thousands of officers. We will discuss three areas of corruption: graft, abuse of authority, and "noble cause" corruption.

BREAKING NEWS: CHICAGO'S CRIMINAL COPS

In 2009, officers in a Chicago special operations unit were indicted for shaking down drug dealers for money. Seven officers pleaded guilty to felony theft or official misconduct, and most have received probation or only several months in prison for cooperating. The alleged ringleader, ex-cop Jerome Finnigan, has been charged in a murder-for-hire plot aimed at a fellow officer who was thought to be cooperating with investigators. Reports indicate that the federal investigation is continuing and may reach management, involving supervisors who either participated in the shakedowns or knew about them and did nothing.

Source: *P. Meincke, Cops plead guilty, sentenced in corruption cases, ABC.com, September 25, 2009. Retrieved 10/1/2009 from http://www.abclocal.go.com/wls/story?section=news/local&id=7033273&pt=print.*

Graft and gratuities

Graft refers to any exploitation of one's role, such as accepting bribes or protection money. Graft also occurs when officers receive kickbacks from tow truck drivers, defense attorneys, or bail bondsmen for recommending them. The Knapp Commission documented examples of a wide range of graft, including taking bribes for changing testimony or "forgetting," or phrasing answers in a way that would aid the defense [46]. Although there are some regional differences, bribery is considered one of the more serious forms of corruption by police officers. In one study, only theft from a crime scene was rated as more serious [47].

Gratuities are items of value received by an individual because of his or her role or position, rather than because of a personal relationship with the giver. The widespread practice of free coffee in convenience stores, half-price or free meals in restaurants, half-price dry cleaning, and so on, are all examples of gratuities. Although the formal code of ethics prohibits accepting gratuities, many officers believe there is nothing wrong with businesses giving "freebies" to a police officer.

The police obviously have discretionary authority and make judgments that affect store owners and other gift givers. This may explain why some think it is wrong for police to accept gifts or favors. It also explains why so many people do not see anything wrong with some types of gratuities, because police officers may not make decisions affecting the giver and, instead, are simply providing a service, such as responding to a burglary or disturbance call. There are extensive arguments relating to the ethics of taking gratuities [48]. What is not in dispute, however, is that the rules of most police departments expressly prohibit accepting them; therefore, officers who do accept them expose themselves to possible disciplinary sanctions.

Abuse of authority

Police abuse of authority comes in three different areas: physical abuse (excessive force, sexual assault), psychological abuse (disrespect, harassment, intimidation), and legal abuse (unlawful searches or seizures or manufacturing evidence) [49].

The most famous case of physical abuse is probably the use of force against Rodney King in Los Angeles, but the most shocking case was that of Abner Louima. Justin Volpe, an NYPD officer, sodomized Louima, who was handcuffed, with the handle of a bathroom plunger in a police precinct. The officer ended up in prison, but the larger question is how could the incident have happened in the first place? The fact is that despite departments' best efforts, some individuals who enter policing are predisposed to abuse their position or cannot handle the stress of policing and succumb to unlawful uses of force, often in retaliation for suspects' actions against them.

The use of force is usually perfectly legal—officers have the right to tackle a fleeing suspect, or hit back when they are defending themselves. Illegal or excessive force occurs when the officer goes beyond what is necessary to secure a lawful arrest, or has no lawful reason to use force at all. Excessive force appears to be more likely when victims challenge police authority—passing a patrol car, asking questions, challenging the stop, or intervening in the arrest of another [50].

After reviewing the research on the use of force and excessive force, a few generalizations can be made:

- Force is present in a small percentage of the total encounters between police and citizens (between 1.3% and 2.5% of all encounters, although rates vary widely between cities and between regions of the country) [51].
- A small percentage of officers seem to be responsible for a disproportionate percentage of the force incidents.
- Some studies do find an association between force and race or socioeconomic status, but other factors, such as demeanor, seem to be even more influential [52].

There is nothing more divisive in a minority community than a police shooting that appears to be unjustified. Cities are quite different in their shooting policies, and in their rates of civilian deaths. Earlier in this chapter, the number of justifiable homicides by police was displayed. It is important to note that all of these shootings were evaluated by police administrators, prosecutors and, in some cases, civilian review boards. In every shooting, the officer undergoes scrutiny from inside and outside the police department. In some cases, the ensuing strife between the police department and the community occurs because there are conflicting perceptions. If there is evidence that the officer's actions were unjustified, then he or she can be found guilty of a crime, that is, voluntary or involuntary manslaughter.

Another type of abuse of authority is when officers extort sex from female citizens. Egregious cases in the United States include rapes by officers on duty, and by jailers in police lock-ups. In a few instances, several officers have been involved in sexual misconduct and protected by departmental supervisors [53]. Peter Kraska and Victor Kappeler proposed a continuum of sexual invasion that ranges from some type of invasion of privacy to sexual assault. This range of behavior includes viewing victims' photos for prurient purposes to deception to gain sex, to sexual assault [54].

"Noble cause" corruption

In the "**Dirty Harry problem**," the question is whether it is acceptable for a police officer to inflict pain on a suspect in order to acquire information that would save an innocent victim (from the *Dirty Harry* movies of Clint Eastwood) [55]. This is a specific example of what is also called **noble cause corruption**, which occurs when officers employ unethical means to catch criminals because they believe it is right to do so. John Crank and Michael Caldero [56] argue that such practices as **"testilying"** (lying in affidavits or when giving testimony) and coercion occur because of **ends-oriented thinking**, which means that the person believes "the end justifies the means" regardless of how bad the means are.

Police officers behave this way when they place a high value on crime control, even over due process. The behaviors under the noble cause category are done by those who believe they are fulfilling their oath of protecting the public. Crime lab investigators and prosecutors may also engage in shortcuts and unethical acts in order to convict the perceived guilty. Prosecutors have been known to suppress evidence and allow perjured testimony, so it is not only police officers who feel compelled to break the law in order to further the noble cause of crime control [57].

"Testilying" is perjury and officers could get a prison sentence for committing this felony. Another effect of such actions is that officers who are caught lying jeopardize all the prior convictions based on their testimony. In many cases around the country, when it is proven that an officer has planted evidence or perjured himself, prosecutors must review all the cases in which that officer testified. In many cases, the suspect must be released and even convicted offenders may have their conviction overturned because of the taint of the officer's involvement. Even if these actions start out for noble reasons, eventually those involved end up lying to keep themselves out of trouble. Covering up personal misdeeds and protecting oneself by subverting the justice process is not noble.

Explanations for corruption

Explanations of corruption can be described as:

- Individual
- Institutional (or organizational)
- Systemic (or societal)

Individual explanations assume that the individual officer has deviant inclinations before he or she even enters the police department and merely exploits the position. The most common explanation of police officer corruption is the **rotten-apple argument**—that the officer alone was deviant and that it was simply a mistake to hire him or her. Such explanations support better selection procedures and better supervision for reducing the possibility of corruption.

Institutional (or organizational) explanations point to organizational problems. Some argue that police scandals are due to rapid hiring without proper background checks, a lack of supervision from front-line sergeants, and other issues [58]. Others argue that administrators can breed corruption by ignoring certain types of rule-breaking and incompetence [59].

The noble cause corruption discussed earlier is also a type of organizational explanation because officers lie or commit other unethical acts to catch criminals because of formal and/or subcultural support for such actions [60]. Organizational explanations are those that explain police corruption as being supported by the organizational culture, whether that be the "formal culture" or the "subculture."

A systemic (or societal) explanation of police deviance focuses on the relationship between the police and the public [61]. The public expects the police to enforce laws but sometimes believes that some people should be excused. When societal norms encourage differential application of the law, it supports police graft. Some police decide that a hypocritical public won't mind a few gambling operations, or a certain number of prostitutes, or even a few drug dealers, so they might as well accept protection money. As long as the general public engages in illegal activities (like gambling, prostitution, and drug use), it is no surprise that some police officers are able to rationalize not enforcing the law. In another vein, as long as the public relays a message that crime control is more important than individual liberties and rights, then we should not be surprised when some police act on that message and violate the law.

Reducing corruption

A wide range of suggestions has been offered that may reduce or minimize the chance of police corruption, including those found in Box 5.3.

Education has been offered as one suggestion to reduce police corruption, but education itself is certainly not a panacea. Ethics training in the academy, as well as part of in-service training, is common and recommended for all police departments today. There is also some doubt that these ethics training courses are successful. One author pointed out that after the Knapp Commission uncovered wide-ranging corruption in the NYPD, ethics awareness workshops

---

BOX 5.3   REDUCE POLICING CORRUPTION

- Increase the salary of police
- Eliminate unenforceable laws
- Establish civilian review boards
- Improve training
- Require more education
- Improve leadership
- Set realistic goals and objectives for the department
- Provide a written code of ethics
- Provide a whistle-blowing procedure that ensures fair treatment of all parties

- Create more oversight (i.e., civilian review boards)
- Integrity testing

Sources: E. Malloy, The Ethics of Law Enforcement and Criminal Punishment, University Press of America, Lanham, MD, 1982, pp. 37-40; J. Pollock, Ethical Dilemmas and Decisions in Criminal Justice, Wadsworth/ITP, Belmont, CA, 2007; H. Metz, an ethical model for law enforcement administrators, in: F. Schmalleger (Ed.), Ethics in Criminal Justice, Wyndam Hall, Bristol, IN, 1990, pp. 95-103.

were begun. Unfortunately, they have not stopped the periodic corruption scandals in the NYPD that have occurred since [62].

Some departments use **integrity testing**. Candidates are recruited straight from academies to investigate suspected officers [63]. This attempt to "police the police" involves setting up a situation in which the officer might commit a wrongful act. For instance, an officer responds to a report of an open door to an apartment, and when he checks it out, he sees money in plain sight. The scene is being monitored, however, to see if he takes the money. There are also tests whereby a wallet is turned in to see if officers would take money out of the wallet [64].

All departments have some form of internal affairs division. Some departments also have **civilian review/complaint boards**. Civilian review boards have been created in several cities to monitor and review the investigation and discipline of officers who have complaints filed against them. Citizens not connected to the police department sit on these committees, commissions, or boards to monitor how police investigate citizen complaints. There are many models for the idea of civilian review, and no one model has been reported to be more effective or better than any other [65].

Another idea is an **early warning or audit system**. Because research shows that a small number of officers are responsible for a disproportionate share of excessive force complaints and other types of citizen complaints, the idea is to identify these officers early. Early warning systems have been used by New Orleans, Portland, and Pittsburgh [66]. The early warning systems utilize number of complaints, use of force reports, use of weapon reports, reprimands, and other indicators to identify problem officers. Intervention may include greater supervision, additional training, and/or counseling.

Employee behavior is directly influenced by superiors. A supervisor cannot promote ethical ideals, and then act unethically and expect employees to act ethically. Thus, regardless of formal ethical codes, police are influenced by the standards of behavior they observe in their superiors. Police departments that have remained relatively free of corruption have administrators who practice ethical behavior on a day-to-day basis.

Even if leaders are not involved in corruption directly, encouraging or participating in the harassment and ostracism that is directed toward whistleblowers supports an organizational culture in which officers may be afraid to come forward when they know of wrongdoing. A different problem may be when certain people in the department do not receive punishment for behaviors that others would receive punishment for. This climate destroys the trust in police leadership that is essential to ensure good communication from the rank and file.

CONCLUSION

Police departments go to great lengths to hire individuals who do not have any obvious qualities that would prevent them from being good police officers. The screening tools include civil service tests, physical tests, and psychological tests. Then candidates are subjected to hundreds of hours of training in academies as well as annual in-service training. After selection and training, supervision is supposed to prevent officers from abusing their discretion and power. However, the discretion of policing creates opportunities and temptations to behave in unethical and even illegal ways.

The vast majority of police officers perform their job admirably, with a great deal of professionalism and integrity. Unfortunately, periodic scandals have occurred because of the actions of a few officers. There are types of corruption that are purely for self-interest, and then there is corruption that stems from the "noble cause" of crime control. Explanations for why some police officers engage in these practices can be categorized into individual explanations, organizational explanations, and societal explanations. Solutions to reduce or minimize corruption have included better training, and better supervision through such things as early warning systems. Perhaps the most important suggestion, however, is that police departments must strive to a make sure that police leadership promotes honesty and ethical behavior.

Review Questions

1. What are the typical hiring requirements for policing?
2. Describe the characteristics of the police personality.
3. Describe the training curriculum for police.
4. Describe research findings on police stress.
5. What were the findings of the Kansas City Preventive Patrol Study? Describe the research on saturated patrol efforts.
6. What are the arguments for and against undercover operations?
7. Describe the police subculture and cop code and why it may be breaking down today.
8. Describe the Project on Policing Study and its results.
9. What are the three areas of police corruption? Describe each.
10. Describe the three explanations for police deviance. Provide some suggestions for reducing or minimizing police corruption.

VOCABULARY

blue curtain of secrecy the practice of police covering up the misdeeds of other officers and/or not testifying against them

burnout when officers merely "go through the motions" of their job after experiencing prolonged stress

civilian review/complaint boards citizen groups that monitor and review the investigation and discipline of officers who have complaints filed against them

"cop code" a set of informal rules for police officers that are not necessarily the same as those taught in the academy

"Dirty Harry problem" the question of whether it is acceptable for a police officer to inflict pain on a suspect in order to acquire information that would save an innocent victim (from the *Dirty Harry* movies of Clint Eastwood)

displacement effect when crime merely moves from a heavily patrolled area to another area of the city

early warning or audit system identification system for finding problem officers early through tracking citizen complaints, use of force reports, and other markers

ends-oriented thinking the belief that "the end justifies the means"

FTOs field training officers

groupthink the situation in a group of decision makers where no one feels free to offer competing viewpoints

integrity testing setting up police officers with opportunities for lying or theft to see if they do so

noble cause corruption when officers employ unethical means to catch criminals because they believe it is right to do so

proactive policing active behavior to seek out crime

reactive policing activities that respond to crime when brought to the attention of the police through crime reports or complaints

residual effect the effect of saturated police patrols when crime continues to be at low levels even after saturated patrol programs have ended

rotten apple argument the explanation that it is only the individual officer who is deviant

saturated patrols when a certain neighborhood or area of town is targeted for frequent or constant patrol presence

socialization adopting the cultural values and beliefs of one's culture

subculture a different set of values, beliefs, and even language from the dominant culture

"testilying" lying in affidavits or when giving testimony to convict a criminal

ENDNOTES

[1] Houston Police Department. Retrieved 6/1/2007 from www.houstontx.gov/police/img/hr_chart.jpg.

[2] B. Sanders, Using personality traits to predict police officer performance, Policing: An International Journal of Police Strategies & Management 31(1) 2008 129–147; N. Claussen-Rogers, B. Arrigo, Police Corruption and Psychological Testing, Carolina Academic Press, Durham, NC, 2005.

[3] G. Cordner, K. Scarborough, Police Administration, seventh ed., Anderson, Burlington, MA, 2010, p. 159.

[4] G. Anderson, D. Plecas, T. Seeger, Police officer physical ability testing: re-validating a selection criterion, Policing 24(1) (2001) 8–32.

[5] C. Johnson, G. Copus, Law enforcement ethics: a theoretical analysis, in: F. Schmalleger, R. Gustafson (Eds.), The Social Basis of Criminal Justice: Ethical Issues for the 80's, University Press of America, Washington, DC, 1981, pp. 39–83.

[6] See the following section on police subculture.

[7] M. McCampbell, Field Training for Police: State of the Art, National Institute of Justice, Washington, DC, 1986.

[8] J. Storch, R. Panzarella, Police stress: state-trait anxiety in relation to occupational and personal stressors, J. Crim. Just. 24(2) (1996) 99–103.

[9] J. Shane, Organizational stressors and police performance, J. Crim. Just. 38(4) (2010) 807–818.

[10] R. Haar, M. Morash, Gender, race, and strategies of coping with occupational stress in policing, Just. Q. 16(2) (1999) 303–336.

[11] S. Chermak, Conducted energy devices and criminal justice policy, Criminol. Publ. Policy 8(4) (2009) 861–864; M. White, J. Ready, Examining fatal and nonfatal incidents involving the TASER, Criminol. Publ. Policy 8(4) (2009) 865–891.

[12] H. Williams, Are the Recommendations of the Braidwood Commission on Conducted Energy Weapons Use Sound Public Policy? Paper presented at the Academy of Criminal Justice Sciences Meeting, February 2010, San Diego, CA.

[13] Amnesty International, Amnesty International's Concerns about TASER Use: Statement to the U.S. Justice Department Inquiry into Deaths in Custody, Amnesty International, London, 2007.

[14] Federal Bureau of Investigation, Supplemental Homicide Reports, various years; C. Loftin, B. Wiersema, D. McDowall, and A. Dobrin, Underreporting of justifiable homicides committed by police officers in the United States, 1976-1998, Am. J. Public Health 93(7) (2003) 1117–1121.

[15] D. Klinger, Police Responses to Officer-Involved Shootings, U.S. Department of Justice, Washington, DC (grant #97-IJ-CX-0029), 2002.

[16] C. Long, Gun deaths tried to fray the thin blue line in '09, AP News Service, 2009. Retrieved 12/22/2009 from http://www.google.com/hostednews/ap/article/ALeqM5jq2tCn7DWNVZ. qLpr5ReGKkyc-C6gD9CHV3B80; Federal Bureau of Investigation, Law Enforcement Officers Killed and Assaulted, 1990-2009. Retrieved from http://www.fbi.gov/publications.htm.

[17] G. Kelling, T. Pate, D. Dieckman, C. Brown, The Kansas City Preventive Patrol Experiment: A Summary Report, Police Foundation, Washington, DC, 1974.

[18] L. Sherman, D. Weisburd, General deterrent effects of police patrol in crime 'hot spots': a randomized, controlled trial, Just. Q. 12(4) (1995) 625–648. See also D. Weisburd, L. Green, Policing drug hot spots: the Jersey City drug market analysis experiment, Just. Q 12(4) (1995) 711–735.

[19] M. White, Current Issues and Controversies in Policing, Allyn and Bacon, Boston, 2007.

[20] F. Schoeman, Privacy and police undercover work, in: W. Heffernan, T. Stroup (Eds.), Police Ethics: Hard Choices in Law Enforcement, John Jay Press, New York, 1985, pp. 133–153.

[21] G. Marx, Police undercover work: ethical deception or deceptive ethics? in: W. Heffernan, T. Stroup (Eds.), Police Ethics: Hard Choices in Law Enforcement, John Jay Press, New York, pp. 83–117; T. Mieczkowksi, "Drug abuse, corruption and officer drug testing, in: K. Lersch (Ed.), Policing and Misconduct, Prentice-Hall, Upper Saddle River, NJ, 1985, pp. 157–192; M. Baker, Cops, Pocket Books, New York, 1985, pp. 139–140.

[22] E. Conlon, Blue Blood, Riverhead, New York, 2004.

[23] N. South, Police, security and information: the use of informants and agents in a liberal democracy, in: S. Einstein, M. Amir (Eds.), Policing, Security and Democracy: Special Aspects of Democratic Policing, Office of International Criminal Justice (OICJ), Sam Houston State University Press Huntsville, TX, 2001, pp. 87–105.

[24] M. Curry, Faulty drug cases draw police inquiry, Dallas Morning News, February 21 (2002) 25A.

[25] C. Dunningham, C. Norris, The detective, the snout, and the audit commission: the real costs in using informants, Howard J. Crim. Just. 38(1) (1999) 6787.

[26] S. Scheingold, The Politics of Law and Order, Longman, New York, 1984.

[27] S. Scheingold, The Politics of Law and Order, Longman, New York, 1984, pp. 97–100.

[28] J. Van Maanen, The asshole, in: P. Manning, J. Van Maanen (Eds.), Policing: A View from the Street, Goodyear, Santa Monica, CA, 1978, pp. 221–240; S. Herbert, Morality in law enforcement: chasing 'bad guys' with the Los Angeles Police Department, Law Soc. Rev. 30(4) (1996) 799–818.

[29] L. Sherman, Learning police ethics, Crim. Just. Ethics 1(1) (1982) 10–19.

[30] S. Scheingold, The Politics of Law and Order, Longman, New York, 1984, pp. 100–104.

[31] S. Scheingold, The Politics of Law and Order, Longman, New York, 1984, p. 97.

[32] E. Paoline, S. Myers, R. Worden, Police culture, individualism, and community policing: evidence from two police departments, Just. Q. 17(3) (2000) 575–605.

[33] V. Kappeler, R. Sluder, G. Alpert, Forces of Deviance: Understanding the Dark Side of Policing, Waveland Press, Prospect Heights, IL, 1999, p. 175; D. Cole, No Equal Justice, Free Press, New York, 2000; S. Walker, C. Spohn, M. DeLone, The Color of Justice, Wadsworth, Belmont, CA, 1998; J. Crank, Understanding Police Culture, Anderson, Cincinnati, OH, 1994.

[34] V. Kappeler, R. Sluder, G. Alpert, Forces of Deviance: Understanding the Dark Side of Policing, Waveland Press, Prospect Heights, IL, 1994, pp. 176–184.

[35] R. Weitzer, Citizens' perceptions of police misconduct: race and neighborhood context, Just. Q. 16(4) (1999) 819–846.

[36] R. Weitzer, Racialized policing: residents' perceptions in three neighborhoods, Law Soc. Rev. 34(1) (2000) 129–157.

[37] R. Weitzer, S. Tuch, Reforming the police: racial differences in public support for change, Criminology 40(2) (2000) 435–456.

[38] M. Reisig, R. Parks, Experience, quality of life, and neighborhood context: a hierarchical analysis of satisfaction with police, Just. Q. 17(3) (2000) 607–630.

[39] S. Mastrofski, M. Reisig, D. McCluskey, Police disrespect toward the public: an encounter based analysis, Criminology 40(3) (2002) 519–551.

[40] S. Mastrofski, M. Reisig, D. McCluskey, Police disrespect toward the public: an encounter based analysis, Criminology 40(3) (2002) 534.

[41] S. Mastrofski, M. Reisig, D. McCluskey, Police disrespect toward the public: an encounter based analysis, Criminology 40(3) (2002) 543.

[42] T. Barker, Ethical police behavior, in: K. Lersch (Ed.), Policing and Misconduct, Prentice Hall, Upper Saddle River, NJ, 2002, pp. 1–25.

[43] D. Weiburd, R. Greenspan, Police Attitudes toward Abuse of Authority: Findings from a National Study, U.S. Department of Justice, Washington, DC, 2000.

[44] A. Baker, J. McGinty, NYPD Confidential, 2010, Nytimes.com, March 26, 2010. Retrieved 3/28/2010 from http://www.nytimes.com/2010/03/28/nyregion/28iab.html.

[45] J. Pollock, Ethics in Criminal Justice: Dilemmas and Decisions, Wadsworth/Cengage, Belmont, CA, 2011.

[46] P. Manning, L. Redlinger, Invitational edges, in: C. Klockars, S. Mastrofski (Eds.), Thinking about Police: Contemporary Readings, McGraw-Hill, New York, 1991, pp. 398–413.

[47] C. Klockars, S. Ivkovic, M. Haberfeld, The Contours of Police Integrity, Sage, Thousand Oaks, CA, 2004.

[48] J. Pollock, Ethical Dilemmas and Decisions in Criminal Justice, Wadsworth/ITP, Belmont, CA, 2007.

[49] T. Barker, D. Carter, Police Deviance, third ed., Anderson Publishing, Cincinnati, OH, 1994.

[50] V. Kappeler, R. Sluder, G. Alpert, Forces of Deviance: Understanding the Dark Side of Policing, Waveland Press, Prospect Heights, IL, 1994, p. 159.

[51] M. Ducrose, P. Langan, E. Smith, Contacts between Police and the Public, 2005, Bureau of Justice Statistics Report, April 29, 2007. Retrieved 5/15/2010 from http://bjs.ojp.usdoj.gov/index.cfm?ty=pbdetail&iid=653, 2002; J. Garner, C. Maxwell, C. Heraux, Characteristics associated with the prevalence and severity of force used by the police, Just. Q. 19(4) (2007) 705–745.

[52] J. Pollock, Ethical Dilemmas and Decisions in Criminal Justice, Wadsworth/ITP, Belmont, CA, 2007.

[53] D. McGurrin, V. Kappeler, Media accounts of police sexual violence, in: K. Lersch, Policing and Misconduct, Prentice-Hall, Upper Saddle River, NJ, 2002, pp. 121–142, 133.

[54] P. Kraska, V. Kappeler, To serve and pursue: exploring police sexual violence against women, Just. Q. 12 (1) (1995) 93.

[55] C. Klockars, The Dirty Harry problem, in: C. Klockars, S. Mastrofski (Eds.), Thinking about Police: Contemporary Readings, McGraw-Hill, New York, 1983, pp. 428–438.

[56] J. Crank, M. Caldero, Police Ethics: The Corruption of Noble Cause, Anderson Publishing, Cincinnati, OH, 2000/2005.

[57] J. Crank, M. Caldero, Police Ethics: The Corruption of Noble Cause, Anderson Publishing, Cincinnati, OH, 2000/2005.

[58] J. Dorschner, The dark side of the force, in: G. Alpert (Ed.), Critical Issues in Policing, second ed., Waveland, Prospect Heights, IL, 1989, pp. 254–274.

[59] P. Murphy, D. Caplan, Conditions that breed corruption, in: R. Dunham, G. Alpert (Eds.), Critical Issues in Policing, Waveland Press, Prospect Heights, IL, 1989, pp. 304–324.

[60] J. Crank, M. Caldero, Police Ethics: The Corruption of Noble Cause, Anderson Publishing, Cincinnati, 2000/2005.

[61] M. Johnston, Police corruption, in: D. Close, N. Meier (Eds.), Ethics in Criminal Justice, Wadsworth, Belmont, CA, 2007; J. Pollock, Ethical Dilemmas and Decisions in Criminal Justice, Wadsworth/ITP, Belmont, CA, 1995.

[62] E. Reuss-Ianni, Two Cultures of Policing: Street Cops and Management Cops, Transaction, New Brunswick, NJ, 1983.

[63] E. Reuss-Ianni, Two Cultures of Policing: Street Cops and Management Cops, Transaction, New Brunswick, NJ, 1983, p. 80.

[64] G. Marx, The new police undercover work, in: C. Klockars, S. Mastrofski (Eds.), Thinking about Police: Contemporary Readings, McGraw-Hill, New York, 1991, pp. 240–258.

[65] T. Prenzler, C. Ronken, Models of police oversight: a critique, Polic. Soc. 11 (2001) 151–180.

[66] T. Barker, Ethical police behavior, in: K. Lersch (Ed.), Policing and Misconduct, Prentice-Hall, Upper Saddle River, NJ, 2002, pp. 1–25; S. Walker, G. Alpert (2002). Early warning systems as risk management for police, in: K. Lersch (Ed.), Policing and Misconduct, Prentice Hall, Upper Saddle River, NJ, p. 224.

CHAPTER 6

Policing and the Legal Process

WHAT YOU NEED TO KNOW

- Four types of police-citizen interactions are consent stops, sobriety checkpoints, investigatory detentions, and arrest.
- Racial profiling occurs when police stop motorists or pedestrians based solely on their race. Studies show mixed findings as to whether minorities are stopped disproportionately.
- The Fourth Amendment protects us against unreasonable searches and seizures of our home, person, or papers by law enforcement officers.
- The types of searches include pat-downs, searches incident to arrest, exigent circumstance searches, auto searches, inventory searches, consent searches, and border searches. Plain-view seizures are not searches.
- The Fifth Amendment gives us the right to be silent when accused of a crime. The *Miranda* warnings are judicially created procedures to ensure that everyone knows of this and other rights.
- The three types of identifications are showups, photo arrays, and lineups.
- Entrapment occurs when someone who did not have a predisposition to commit a crime does so because of police actions.
- The exclusionary rule is the punishment imposed when police violate the rights of the accused; however, there are at least three exceptions: the good faith exception, the inevitable discovery exception, and the public safety exception.

Much of the training that police officers receive in recruit training as well as in-service classes relates to the law. The authority of the police officer derives from the law, but the law also sets limits on the powers of the police. Most of the case holdings that will be discussed in this chapter have set restraints on the power of the police to stop, detain, search, or question. Some argue

Crime and Justice in America, Second Edition

that these court decisions have "handcuffed" the police from doing their job. Actually, there is no research to indicate that many cases have been lost or arrests have not been made because of the due process protections recognized and/or created by the Supreme Court.

STOPS AND ARRESTS (SEIZURES)

When can police stop and question someone? One answer is any time that the person consents to stop and answer their questions. However, the more important question is when can they stop and question someone who doesn't want to be stopped? The answer to that question is when they have reasonable suspicion that a crime has been or is about to be committed. We can distinguish four types of situations in which police have the legal authority to "seize" individuals:

1. ■ **Consent stops**: individual consents to stay and talk to police officers but could leave at any time
2. ■ **Sobriety checkpoints**: everyone, or some random selection of individuals, is stopped for a very brief check of driver's license and registration to evaluate driver for intoxication or other impairment
3. ■ **Investigatory detentions**: the police have *reasonable suspicion* that a person is engaged in or about to commit a crime; they can stop that person, ask for identification, and conduct a superficial search for weapons
4. ■ **Arrest**: the police have *probable cause* that the person committed a crime or traffic violation; search may be conducted for weapons and evidence of crime if an arrest occurs

Consent stops

A large number of police-citizen interactions occur because the citizen agrees to stop and talk to police officers. When police stop someone on the street and ask what they are doing, it is a consent stop unless the individual is not free to leave. Similarly, if a police officer asks someone if they can look into their bag, it is a consent search unless the person says "no" and the officer does it anyway. When the police ask someone to accompany them to the station for questioning, it is a consent visit unless they make it clear that the person will be arrested if they don't come. The police do not need any level of suspicion or probable cause to ask people to talk to them or ask to search, but the person can also refuse to comply with such requests.

On the other hand, some courts have held that police can't stop automobile drivers and say that it is a consent stop. The situation of stopping a moving car is different because it affects a person's movement more completely than a pedestrian stop. Therefore, police need at least a reasonable suspicion before they stop a moving automobile (unless it is at a fixed checkpoint). In most cases, they stop a car only after they have seen a traffic violation, however minor. Once the driver has committed a traffic violation, police have probable cause to arrest (even if only a traffic offense) and can stop the car.

Sobriety checkpoints

The Supreme Court has allowed police departments to engage in "fixed checkpoints" or "sobriety checkpoints" to protect us from drunk drivers. The rationale for allowing such stops is that the inconvenience to the public is minor, the governmental interest in stopping drunk drivers is high, and the stops are not conducted in a way that could be arbitrary and capricious. Every driver must be stopped or police must use some random system for stopping some drivers, if not all drivers. Further, the checkpoints can only occur with supervisory approval.

So far, fixed checkpoints have been acceptable only when the goal is to stop drunk drivers. Courts have not allowed such checkpoints to be used to identify drug offenders (away from border areas) or other criminal suspects [1].

Investigatory detentions

One of the earliest cases that set the boundaries of the police power to stop was *Terry v. Ohio* [2] in 1968. In this case, a police officer observed Mr. Terry walking around a bank several times and peering in the window. While the officer did not have probable cause to arrest, he did have a reasonable suspicion that Terry was "casing" the building for a robbery or burglary. The officer stopped and searched Terry, and found a gun. He was convicted of an unlawful weapons charge. He appealed the conviction, arguing that the gun should have been excluded because the stop and search were unlawful in that there was no probable cause that he had committed a crime. The Supreme Court held that the search was lawful because the stop was lawful. According to the Court, police officers can stop and detain someone briefly to investigate a potential crime if they have reasonable suspicion that a crime had been, or was going to be, committed. Furthermore, police officers had a right to search for weapons to protect themselves while they were conducting a brief investigation.

The case clearly supported the right of police officers to detain individuals for short periods of time, and to question and even search them for weapons, if there were enough facts to support reasonable suspicion. The stop must be brief and not inconvenience the citizen unreasonably. The courts have never created a bright-line test for what a reasonable length of time might be as it depends on the circumstances of the stop and other factors. Generally, for instance, when an officer has reasonable suspicion that there are drugs in a car and the driver does not consent to a search, the officer may be able to detain the driver for the period of time it takes to bring out drug dogs unless it would take several hours for them to arrive. Furthermore, a police officer's "hunch," without any factual basis, that an individual was going to commit a crime would not be sufficient to justify such a stop. Interestingly, however, the Supreme Court stopped short in this case of requiring the individual to answer the officer's questions. Justice White said, in his concurring opinion, that the person stopped is not obliged to answer questions and his refusal cannot be used to justify an arrest.

However, 36 years later, in *Hiibel v. Sixth Judicial District Court of Nevada* [3], the Supreme Court upheld a Nevada statute that made it illegal to refuse to give police officers one's name, when they had reasonable suspicion that the detainee was involved in a crime. The Court held that this law did not violate the Fourth or Fifth Amendments to the federal Constitution. In the *Hiibel* case, the detainee was stopped by police responding to a report that a woman had been assaulted. It turned out that Mr. Hiibel had been in an argument with his daughter, who had gotten out of his car and walked home. When police arrived, he refused to give his name even after they threatened him with arrest. He was subsequently arrested, fined $250, and appealed the conviction all the way to the Supreme Court, arguing that citizens shouldn't have to give their name to police when they have not been arrested. The Supreme Court did not agree. The Court held that as long as police have a reasonable suspicion to stop someone, a state statute that requires an individual to simply give their name does not violate the Fourth or the Fifth Amendments to the Constitution. You should understand, though, that some state statutes only require an individual to give identification when there is *probable* cause that a crime has been committed—in other words, when police have enough evidence to arrest the suspect.

EXERCISE: IN THE STATE OF...

Look in the penal code for your state and find out if there is a statute that requires a person to give their name to police officers when asked. Do police need *reasonable suspicion* or *probable cause* if there is such a statute?

Racial profiling

Racial profiling occurs when the decision to stop a driver (or pedestrian) is based on a "profile," and the major element of this profile is race. Profiling began when federal agents developed a profile of drug smugglers to assist border patrol and customs agents in airports. The list of indicators included behavior as well as demographic indices, including race. Behaviors such as nervousness, traveling with a one-way ticket, traveling without baggage, and so on, were combined with race to create the "drug smuggler profile." The profile was adapted to highway drivers by state patrol officers who were attempting to stem the flow of drugs up through the interstates in Florida, Georgia, Texas, and other Southern states [4]. Eventually, the term "racial profile" was coined because, at least for some officers and some departments, race became the predominant element in deciding which drivers to stop.

Eventually, the practice of police officers stopping, detaining, and searching minority motorists disproportionately to their population was believed to be so prevalent that advocates argued that a new "crime" had been created called DWB (driving while black). There was a strong enough public backlash that in 1999 President Clinton condemned the practice, and congressional hearings were held to investigate how widespread the practice was. The result of federal attention was that many states passed legislation that required police departments to collect demographic information on police stops in order to determine whether they were done in a discriminatory manner that violated state and federal constitutional rights.

It cannot be ignored that there is a widespread perception that police stop minorities more often than whites. In one study authors found that race and personal experience with racial profiling were the strongest predictors of attitudes toward the police [5]. There are difficult methodological problems involved in analyzing the extent of racial profiling. Just because certain groups may be stopped more often does not necessarily mean they are being targeted: there may be more individuals in that group, they may drive more, they may commit more traffic offenses, they may be more likely to drive in high-crime areas, and so on. If one is comparing the rate of stops with population figures, it is important to know how many stops were of residents, as opposed to non-residents passing through the area. Alternatively, if one is using agency information on stops, the information may not be complete because it may count only stops that resulted in tickets or searches. The Supreme Court has upheld the right of police officers to stop individuals when they use profiles that utilize race as *one factor* of several that, together, may establish reasonable suspicion for a brief investigatory detention [6]. It is also important to note that most traffic stops occur after a traffic violation has been observed, so police have a legal right to stop the driver. Opponents argued, however, that police engage in **pretextual stops**, which refers to the practice of using a minor traffic violation to stop the individual and, in the course of the traffic stop, look for other evidence of wrongdoing, specifically by a search—usually a consent search. According to some research, minorities are more likely to be stopped with "pretextual stops." When this practice was the basis of a court challenge, however, the Supreme Court upheld the right of officers to stop for minor traffic violations, even if the main reason for the stop was the officer's desire to search based on a racial profile [7].

By 2000, public opinion had solidified against the practice and police were heavily criticized for racial profiling. Some researchers argued that it was an inefficient use of police resources anyway because the "hit rate" for finding drugs was lower for blacks than for other groups [8]. Despite several decades of research, researchers still can't seem to agree as to whether racial profiling even exists, much less its prevalence. There do seem to be replicated findings that even if black drivers are not stopped more often than their proportion of the driving public would indicate, the percentage of stops that result in searches is higher for blacks, as is the number of times an arrest occurs after a stop. It also is probably true that the public scrutiny that focused attention on the practice resulted in true changes in patterns of stops with fewer blacks being stopped without reasonable suspicion [9]. Ironically, about the time that law enforcement began developing formal policies against racial profiling and public opinion had shifted against it, the tragedy of September 11, 2001, occurred. After the terrorist attacks, those who looked like they were Middle Eastern were subject to increased scrutiny before they boarded airplanes. In some cases, individuals were denied entry when other passengers complained that they would not fly with men who looked like they might be suicide bombers. Many people who objected to racial profiling when the targets were blacks suspected of drug smuggling, believe that it is acceptable toward those of Middle Eastern extraction, especially when they are flying on commercial airliners. We will discuss the challenges of policing in the age of terrorism in Chapter 15.

Arrest

Police officers have the legal authority to arrest individuals when they have probable cause to believe that the person has committed a crime. In some states, misdemeanor arrests must be based on an arrest warrant supported by a criminal complaint filed by a victim or a police officer. However, usually if the misdemeanor is committed in the presence of an officer, the police officer can arrest the suspect without a criminal complaint having been filed. Except for a "hot pursuit" exception, if officers need to enter a private dwelling to arrest the suspect, they must first obtain an arrest warrant.

Arrest is the power to hold someone against their will. Police officers may be guilty of unlawful arrest only when there is evidence of maliciousness. Otherwise, if the arrest turns out to be invalid or in error, the officer can use a "good faith" defense.

An interesting fact is that police officers don't necessarily have a legal obligation to arrest. In fact, the decision to arrest is one of the least studied areas of criminal justice. Generally, police officers use their discretion, and in many cases where there is legal authority to arrest, officers choose not to. Most of us have not received a traffic ticket when we deserved one; this is an example of police discretion. Even when more serious offenses occur, police may choose not to arrest, unless there is a specific law that compels arrest. For instance, some states have passed "mandatory arrest" laws in domestic violence cases that require police officers to arrest when there is probable cause that future violence will occur.

When has an arrest occurred? If a reasonable person would not feel free to leave, then an arrest has occurred. There are no "magic words" that are required to create the arrest. If a police officer puts handcuffs on an individual and places him or her in a patrol car, that person has been arrested without having to hear the words "you are under arrest." On the other hand, if someone is asked to come in to the police station to talk about a crime, they are not under arrest unless a reasonable person would not feel free to leave. In fact, that is the so-called *Mendenhall* test: an arrest has occurred when a reasonable person does not feel free to leave.

You may not realize that a traffic ticket is an alternative to a custodial arrest. You have committed a crime and the officer may arrest you and take you into custody; however, in all states, there is enabling legislation that allows the officer, instead, to give you a citation or "ticket to appear," which operates in lieu of a custodial arrest. You still have to appear in court (or admit guilt by paying the fine). The Supreme Court has upheld the right of police officers to utilize full custodial arrests in minor traffic violations, even when the maximum penalty involved is only a fine [10]. The Supreme Court has also held that evidence obtained from a search incident to arrest may still be admitted into evidence even if the arrest itself is invalid because state law does not allow arrests in those particular offenses [11].

Police are authorized to use force to accomplish an arrest and it is unlawful to resist an arrest (which would be a crime in addition to the original crime). Police cannot, however, use lethal force to subdue a suspect if there is no reason to believe the suspect poses a danger to the officer or others. The case of *Tennessee v. Garner* [12] involved the police shooting of an unarmed teenager who was running away from them after being caught burglarizing a home. The Court held that it was a violation of the Fourth and Fourteenth Amendments to shoot at a fleeing suspect if the only reason for the shooting was to stop him or her from escaping and there was no evidence that the suspect would be dangerous to others.

SEARCHES

The **Fourth Amendment** protects citizens against the unreasonable intrusion by government agents into one's private home or papers. The Fourth Amendment states:

> The right of the people to be secure in their persons, houses, papers, and effects, against unreasonable searches and seizures, shall not be violated, and no Warrants shall issue, but upon probable cause, supported by Oath or affirmation, and particularly describing the place to be searched, and the persons or things to be seized

INTERNET KEY

For an interesting Web site about the Bill of Rights, go to http://www.archives. gov/exhibits/charter/bill_of_rights.html.

In all Fourth Amendment cases, the guideline for the Court's reasoning is whether there is a reasonable expectation of privacy on the part of the individual. Additionally, the court balances the individual's right to privacy against the state's right to investigate and prevent crimes (or for other substantial governmental interests).

When it was written, the Fourth Amendment protected us as citizens from unlawful searches by federal agents. Indeed, the Bill of Rights (the first 10 Amendments to the Constitution) only protects us against violations by federal actors, not from the actions of state or local agents. The Fourteenth Amendment was ratified in 1868 after the Civil War. It states:

> … all persons are citizens of the United States and of the state wherein they reside. No state shall make or enforce any law which shall abridge the privileges or immunities of citizens of the United States; nor shall any state deprive any person of life, liberty, or property, without due process of law…

The **due process clause** tells states they cannot "deprive any person of life, liberty or property without due process of law." What constitutes due process of law depends on what is at stake, but it basically means that whenever the government seeks to deprive an individual of life, liberty, or property, there must be procedural protections.

The Fourteenth Amendment was the basis for the **incorporation** of some of the protections from the First, Fourth, Fifth, Sixth, and Eighth Amendments to citizens who may be faced with actions by state or local government agents. In other words, through a sequence of court cases, the Supreme Court held that, although when written, the protections only applied to actions by the federal government, the Fourteenth Amendment created due process rights that created fundamental protections against local police actions as well. For instance, because of *Mapp v. Ohio* [13], Fourth Amendment protections now apply when a search is being conducted by city police officers (not just federal law enforcement agents), and, because of *Gideon v. Wainwright* [14], the Sixth Amendment right to counsel now applies when the prosecution is by a state rather than the federal government. These rights have been "incorporated" as have most of the other rights detailed in the Bill of Rights. It is important to remember, however, that not all rights in the Bill of Rights apply to us as state citizens; the rights that do apply to us as state citizens are those that have been judicially recognized under a test as to whether they are essential as fundamental liberties.

Law enforcement agencies cannot search your house or papers without probable cause, and in many cases probable cause is ensured through the issuance of a warrant. A **magistrate** (any judicial figure authorized to issue a warrant) must evaluate the evidence brought to him or her by police officers and conclude that there is probable cause to search. The search warrant comprises the legal authority to do so. On the other hand, there are many exceptions to the warrant requirement, which will be discussed later. The standard is always probable cause, however, and even if police officers do not need a warrant to search for evidence, they always need to show probable cause that evidence or instrumentalities of the crime will be at the location they want to search (Box 6.1).

Surveillance, Wiretaps, and Other Electronics

One typically thinks of only physical searches as being protected by the Fourth Amendment, but wiretaps and some forms of electronic surveillance are also treated as searches because they also intrude upon the privacy of citizens. Arguably, before police "bug" your house, tap your phone, or record your actions, they should have some justification for doing so. Crimes against wiretapping by private citizens go back as far as the telegraph in the late 1800s, and restrictions on police using such devices have been in place for decades [15].

Although there are some exceptions, states generally follow federal law in allowing some wiretapping and eavesdropping; specifically, when there is consent by at least one party, and when law enforcement has the proper authorization from the court. Cases involving wiretapping, as in all Fourth Amendment cases, involve one's reasonable expectation of privacy. One of the earliest cases was *Katz v. United States* [16]. In this case, the Supreme Court held that police officers must have a warrant before placing a wiretap on a public telephone because people using public phone booths had a reasonable expectation of privacy. On the other hand, individuals talking in a public park do not have a reasonable expectation of privacy if police officers sitting close by can hear

---

BOX 6.1 SAMPLE SEARCH WARRANT

State of Ohio, _____ County, ss:

To the sheriff (or other officer) of said County, greetings:

Whereas there has been filed with me an affidavit, of which the following is a copy (here copy the affidavit).

These are, therefore, to command you in the name of the State of Ohio, with the necessary and proper assistance, to enter, in the daytime (or in the nighttime) into (here describe the house or place as in the affidavit) of the said _____ of the township of _____ in the County aforesaid, and there diligently search for the said goods and chattels, or articles, to wit:

(here describe the articles as in the affidavit) and that you bring the same or any part thereof, found on such search, and also the body of ____, forthwith before me, or some other judge or magistrate of the county having cognizance thereof to be disposed of and dealt with according to law.

Given under my hand this _____ day of _____, 2008

_____, Judge, County Court

Source: *Ohio Revised Code Annotated § 2933.25. Form of search warrant. Copyright © 2007 by Matthew Bender & Company, Inc., a member of the LexisNexis Group.*

without the aid of any electronic listening devices, but officers must obtain a warrant before using any electronic equipment that amplifies sound from distances [17]. Individuals in jails have no reasonable expectation of privacy when they use jail phones, especially when there are signs stating that calls may be monitored and recorded [18]. The USA PATRIOT Act and federal laws governing law enforcement investigations of terrorists expand regular law enforcement guidelines and will be covered in Chapter 15. While state agents must comply with both the federal minimum standards and any additional restrictions imposed by their state, federal investigators are governed by federal regulations and laws [19].

Police, like criminals, have embraced technology. In all cases where police use increasingly sophisticated devices for listening, recording, and surveilling citizens, courts use the basic guidelines of "expectation of privacy" and "reasonableness." In *Kyllo v. United States* [20], for instance, the Supreme Court held that a thermal-imaging device that was able to measure the amount of heat coming from a house was a "search" and required a warrant. The Court held that individuals had a reasonable expectation of privacy in their own home and a right to expect that police are not using electronics not available to the general public to measure sound, heat, or anything else coming out of their private home. Note that police can use such equipment, but they must develop probable cause first and seek a warrant from a magistrate before "searching" using the equipment.

Another issue that has emerged is whether police can use GPS-tracking devices and/or obtain information from telecommunications companies that track locations from personal cell phones. There are two ways cell phones can be used to track locations: the first is to triangulate data from cell phone towers used, and the second is when the cell phone is equipped with GPS, which then can provide the cell phone's exact location. Police have used cell phone location information in murder cases to impeach suspects' alibis and to place a suspect near the location of the body or place of kidnapping. Police may obtain a warrant for such information, but the legal question is whether they should be able to obtain the information from your cell phone company without a warrant. On the one hand, there is an argument that individuals agree to disclose their location to their cell phone provider and, because it is provided to this third party, there is no privacy right to such information at all. On the other hand, most would probably agree that cell phone users would not agree that their location has no privacy protections at all. The position taken by law enforcement is that the Patriot Act authorized the use of pen registers with less than probable cause, which allow law enforcement to collect "dialing, routing, addressing, or signaling information" from telephones/cell phones, and location information falls under signaling information. If courts accept this argument, then law enforcement need only show that such information is "relevant" to an ongoing investigation [21].

As for GPS-tracking devices, one argument is that the GPS device merely assists law enforcement who could also follow the suspect; therefore, it is similar to binoculars or telescopes, which have been ruled acceptable tools to aid human senses. The other argument is that they are a "search" and, as such, require a magistrate's approval in the form of a warrant. There is no Supreme Court opinion in these areas and there are conflicting lower court opinions, so it is an interesting and unsettled area of law [22]. What is clear, however, is that law enforcement will continue to utilize the latest technology available to accomplish the goals of public safety, as the Breaking the News box indicates.

BREAKING NEWS: UTILIZING TECHNOLOGY TO CATCH CRIMINALS

Police in Los Angeles County are partnering with UCLA researchers to practice what some have called "predictive policing." Analysts use extremely sophisticated algorithms based on past criminal incidents to predict where and when crime will occur. Another application is to conduct computer analysis of criminals themselves to predict their movements and behaviors based on past patterns. It is a twenty-first-century version of the pin maps of crime that some departments might have used 50 years ago. In the ideal scenario, computers would provide continuous data to officers about likely criminal events, including locations and types of crime. Police promise that the science merely gives them probabilities that crime will occur and that they must prove probable cause that an individual has committed a crime or is about to commit a crime before an arrest can be made.

Source: J. Rubin, Can Crime Be Stopped Before It Even Starts? *Los Angeles Times*, September 26, 2010, reprinted in *Austin American-Statesman*, September 26, 2010, B1, B4.

Physical searches

The law on searches and when warrants are required is somewhat complicated, but the first thing to understand is the type of searches that exist. In Box 6.2, there are descriptions of some types of searches and the legal justification for each type of search. Searches that do not require warrants are pat-downs during a *Terry* stop, searches incident to arrests, and "exigent circumstances" searches.

BOX 6.2 SEARCHES

1. *Search for weapons to protect officers during investigative stops—"pat-downs"*

When an officer stops an individual who is acting suspiciously, the officer must have a reasonable suspicion that criminal activity has or is about to take place. If the stop is justified and the officer has a reasonable suspicion that the suspect may have a weapon, then the officer has a right to "pat down" the subject for his or her own protection. The search is limited to a tactile search for weapons. If something feels like a weapon, the officer can remove it from a pocket and if other contraband is found during the search, that evidence can be used against the suspect (*Terry v. Ohio* [23]).

2. *Search for weapons and evidence upon lawful arrest*

When a suspect has been placed under a lawful arrest, officers have the right to search the person and immediate vicinity of the person for weapons and contraband and evidence

Continued

BOX 6.2 SEARCHES—CONT'D

of the crime. This is to ensure that evidence is not destroyed by the suspect or others. This search is more intrusive than the pat-down search, but is justified by the arrest (*Chimel v. California* [24]).

3. *Exigent circumstances*

All exigent circumstance exceptions are based on logic and reasonableness. Basically, the exception recognizes that there are some circumstances where getting a warrant is impossible because the suspect will flee, the evidence will be destroyed, or there is some other good reason to allow the officer to search without a warrant. Note that it is *not* an exception to probable cause. The officer must still have probable cause that the suspect has engaged in a crime, but it provides an exception to the requirement to obtain a warrant before undertaking a search.

The **hot pursuit exception** is a type of exigent circumstances search. It refers to situations where police officers are following a fleeing suspect who has just committed a crime or they have probable cause to believe he has just committed a crime. If waiting for a warrant will result in the escape of the suspect or the destruction of evidence, they may pursue the suspect into a dwelling and search for him or her. If they see contraband or the fruits of the crime during the course of the search for the suspect, they may seize that evidence as well (*Warden v. Hayden* [25]).

Another exigent circumstance is when police have cause to believe someone is in danger. If police officers hear screaming from inside the home, they can enter the home without permission and without a warrant to protect the suspected victim. Even if they turn out to be wrong (e.g., the screaming was coming from the television), the entry is legal; therefore, any contraband seen by the police is subject to seizure and use as evidence against the homeowner. As soon as they are aware that there is no danger to anyone, however, they must stop the search. Only evidence that is seen during the course of the legitimate entry can be used in any subsequent prosecution.

4. *Automobile Searches*

Automobile searches are a type of exigent circumstance search, but the line of court cases became so complicated that they require a separate discussion. Recall that exigent circumstances exist when there is a real danger that the suspect will flee or the evidence will be destroyed. Both of these circumstances exist when an automobile driver is stopped and there is probable cause to believe that there is evidence of a crime or contraband inside the car. Earlier cases distinguished between a car and the trunk, and a car and any containers in the car, but, finally, the Supreme Court held that when a police officer had probable cause to believe a crime had been committed using or within the automobile, then that auto could be searched, along with any containers found inside, including containers (such as purses) owned by passengers. Later, another case expanded that provision to when the probable cause applied only to a container that happened to be in a car [26]. Therefore, when a police officer stops a car because of a minor traffic violation and smells marijuana, or observes any other evidence of a crime that rises to probable cause, he or she may search the car and any bags, purses, or backpacks found in the car (*United States v. Ross* [27]). Another type of automobile search occurs when the driver and/or passengers are arrested. Then, officers may conduct a search of the automobile under a search incident to arrest because the court has held that anywhere in the automobile may be within reach of the suspect (*New York v. Belton* [28]). Police officers possibly have made arrests on extremely minor traffic offenses and violations simply in order to obtain the power to search the automobile as a search incident to arrest. In *Arizona v. Gant* [29], the Supreme Court held that officers must show either that there was a danger to the officer and the search was for weapons, or there was evidence related to the arrest that might be destroyed before they could search an automobile. Thus, if someone was arrested for a traffic violation and there was nothing to indicate the officer might be in danger, then a search of the car would be unwarranted. Note, however, that this does not change the holding of the earlier cases and if officers have probable cause that there has been a crime or is going to be a crime committed and there is evidence of such in the car, they can still search it under exigent circumstances.

5. *Inventory Searches*

An inventory search is not a search for evidence—it is simply a search to identify and record any possessions, especially valuables, found inside a car or other vehicle that is impounded by a law enforcement agency. If contraband or

BOX 6.2 SEARCHES—CONT'D

evidence is found during a routine inventory search, it can be used against the suspect. On the other hand, an inventory search does not include taking the panels off the inside of the car or deconstructing it in any way. If police choose to do this type of search, they should obtain a warrant.

6. *Consent Searches*

Probably most searches are conducted because the individual has given the law officer consent to search. Even without probable cause, if a police officer asks to look into a driver's trunk, and the driver opens it, then the search is legal because the driver has given consent. Similarly, if a police officer asks someone to empty their pockets and they agree to do so, the officer doesn't need probable cause for this type of consent search. Only if the consent is clearly coerced would any contraband or evidence be excluded in this type of situation (*Schneckloth v. Bustamonte*) [30].

7. *Plain View Seizures (These are not searches!)*

When an officer has legal authority to be in a particular place, then anything that can be seen with the aided or unaided eye is subject to seizure. This is not considered a search and, therefore, requires no legal justification other than the legal right to be there. For instance, when an officer responds to a domestic disturbance call and is allowed into a home, then anything he or she sees in the home, such as drugs on the table, is subject to seizure and used for prosecution. When an officer is in a public hallway in an apartment building and peers through an uncurtained front window and sees narcotics, this is a plain view situation and he may use this information to get a search warrant. However, if a police officer comes into a yard with "no trespassing" signs posted and comes onto the porch and stands on a box to peer into a window, that is considered a search and any evidence or "fruits" of the evidence obtained from such a "search" will be excluded. The "open fields" doctrine, however, states that even when homeowners put up "no trespassing" signs and enclose fields by fences, if the field can be seen from the air, it falls under plain view and officers would not need a warrant to search.

8. *Border Searches*

There are greater police powers to search at the borders of this country. The argument, of course, is that there is a great need to protect the country's borders and if people choose to go across a border, they therefore choose to be subject to the greater powers of search by border agents. We are all familiar today with the metal detectors and even pat-downs by TSA officers when traveling through airports. These pat-downs are done without probable cause or even reasonable suspicion because flying isn't a right and one implicitly consents to such searches by choosing to fly. Our bags are sniffed by drug dogs and we may be asked to open our luggage to be searched by customs or border agents.

In cases where officers have reasonable suspicion, they may detain an individual in an airport or a border for a reasonable period to determine if a crime is being committed. When individuals are suspected of smuggling drugs, they may be detained and searched. They may be asked for consent to an ultrasound of their stomach and, if they refuse, be monitored when they go to the bathroom to see if drugs are being carried in their body. These invasions of privacy are done without warrants only because airports are considered similar to borders and we all have a reduced expectation of privacy when crossing the border. Highway border stops may even be 100 miles inside the border, yet the same justification applies (*United States v. Martinez Fuerte* [31]).

Requirements for a warrant and informants

When police officers need a warrant to search a house, person, or business, they must prove probable cause that they will find contraband or evidence of a crime. They must state what they expect to find and where they expect to find it with specificity. In other words, they cannot make application to a magistrate for a search warrant based on a hunch, a suspicion, or state that they need

U.S. Forest Service public information officer Alan Barbian points to trees marijuana farmers cut down in the Chequamegon-Nicolet National Forest to grow pot, August 20, 2010, near Marinette, Wisconsin. The Marinette County Sheriff's Department said that deputies found the growth in the central section of the county during a ground search. *AP Photo/Todd Richmond*

to look but don't know exactly what might connect the individual to a crime. If they are looking for drugs, they must say so; if they are looking for particular papers, they must say so, and so on. They must prove to the magistrate that they have credible evidence that rises to probable cause to believe that they will find the target of the warrant where they say it will be.

In *Illinois v. Gates* [32] the Supreme Court addressed the question of whether the police could use the information provided by an anonymous informant in order to secure a search warrant. In this case, the officers learned from an anonymous informant that a couple would be driving back from Florida. The information provided the travel dates, the description of the car, and the fact that they would be carrying a large amount of drugs. All turned out to be true. Before this case, police were required to show the credibility of the informant through either the content of the information (i.e., how detailed it was) or the credibility of the informant (i.e., how many times he or she had told the truth in the past). In the *Illinois v. Gates* case, the court created a "totality of circumstance" test, which basically means that if the totality of the informant's tip, even an anonymous tip, indicates that the information is likely to be true, then police will be able to obtain a search warrant.

INTERROGATION

The Fifth Amendment to the United States Constitution states, in part:

> No person … shall be compelled in any criminal case to be a witness against himself…

The Fifth Amendment was written by our founding fathers to prevent courts from using evidence obtained by force, coercion, and torture. Before the twentieth century, the Fifth Amendment was interpreted to mean the right not to be forced to speak. Then, in the twentieth century, the Supreme Court developed a broader interpretation of the Fifth Amendment that included the right of the individual to remain silent. Furthermore, the choice to remain silent cannot be used against an individual by a prosecutor who might use it to infer guilt. As with the Fourth Amendment, the Fifth Amendment protects citizens (from being compelled to give testimony against themselves) in *federal* prosecutions, and the right had to be "incorporated" to us as state citizens in state prosecutions.

The Supreme Court in *Miranda v. Arizona* [33] implemented a requirement that procedural safeguards should exist that ensured that all suspects knew their privilege against self-incrimination. The procedural safeguards developed in *Miranda* meant that an individual subject to custodial interrogation must first be warned of his rights, including his right to remain silent, before the commencement of any type of questioning; thus, the famous *Miranda* warning, as set out in Box 6.3.

What this means for police is that the Miranda warning must be given before they can conduct an interrogation of a suspect held in custody. The requirement of police to give *Miranda* warnings is widely misunderstood, however, and in many situations where police are interacting with the public, there is no requirement for the warnings to be given. For instance:

- When police arrive after receiving a crime report, they will question a number of people to get information about the alleged crime. No warnings are required because no one is a suspect and no one is in custody.
- When police ask someone to come into the station house to talk to them about a crime, but the person is not officially in custody (is free to leave), warnings are not required.
- When a suspect is arrested but the police do not question him or her, and the suspect volunteers information about the crime, no warnings are required (but are recommended).

Interrogations occur when the investigation has narrowed to one or a few suspects and the questioning is directed specifically at uncovering evidence or obtaining a confession. Interrogations can occur even if the officer is not asking the suspect specific questions but engages in words or actions designed to elicit a confession [34]. In more recent cases, the Supreme Court has considered the use of deception and other mental tricks used by police on suspects in order to get them to confess or provide evidence. The use of the "father confessor" approach (a sympathetic paternal figure for the defendant to confide in) or "Mutt and Jeff" partners (a "nice guy" and a seemingly brutal, threatening officer) are other ways to induce confessions or obtain information [35]. Officers may not threaten a suspect with physical harm, but they can threaten harsher charges or a recommendation for the death penalty if the suspect does not cooperate.

BOX 6.3 MIRANDA WARNING

You have the right to remain silent. If you give up this right, anything you say can and will be used against you in a court of law. You have the right to an attorney during questioning. If you cannot afford an attorney, one will be appointed for you by the court. Do you understand these rights?

These methods do not violate the suspect's rights; however, once the right to an attorney is invoked, the interrogation should cease until an attorney is present. It should be noted that, after indictment, the right to an attorney comes from the Sixth Amendment and is part of the defendant's "trial rights," but the right to an attorney during a preindictment interrogation stems from the Fifth Amendment. The right to an attorney during interrogation is largely to protect the defendant from coercive methods that overcome his or her Fifth Amendment right to remain silent. It is called a "prophylactic" right, meaning that it is largely to prevent the violation of another right—in this case, the right not to be forced to incriminate oneself. Generally, questioning must cease when the suspect requests a lawyer, but, recently, the Supreme Court has held that the suspect must be explicit in his request. In another case, the Court held that questioning can resume after a time even if the suspect has not seen an attorney. The Court has also held that the strict wording of the *Miranda* warning is not necessary. Observers note that the current Supreme Court seems to be moving in a direction that will dilute the power and practice of the original *Miranda* decision; however, *Miranda* warnings are now so entrenched in our national culture and police practice that court decisions probably will not change standard police practices at this point [36]. In an interesting example of the pervasiveness of American television and movie crime dramas, foreign law enforcement officials describe suspects who demand their rights to an attorney and to remain silent, even when no such rights exist in that country.

🌐 INTERNET KEY

For a very useful and interesting Web site devoted to the Supreme Court, where you can even hear recordings of Supreme Court cases and research case holdings, go to http://www.oyez.org/.

LINEUPS

A lineup is when the suspect is placed with other individuals in order for the victim to identify him or her. In *United States v. Wade* [37], the Supreme Court held that the defendant's attorney must be present at a lineup in order to make sure that it was not biased against the defendant. On the other hand, if the lineup occurs at an earlier phase of the investigation and the suspect has not been indicted, then there is no requirement for an attorney to be present [38].

Other forms of identification procedures include **showups** and **photo arrays**. Showups are frowned upon and should only occur when circumstances are such that it is unlikely that the victim-witness would make a mistake in identifying the suspect. In the most common example, a victim calls the police and provides a description, the suspect is found nearby and is immediately brought to the victim for identification, that is, "Did this guy take your purse?" Showups have the potential for biasing the witness and, therefore, are not used except in circumstances similar to the example given above. In the photo array, a suspect's picture is placed on a page with other pictures of similar-looking men or women. The photo array is, perhaps, the best method of identification to ensure admission of the identification because the array can be admitted into trial as evidence and jury members can see for themselves that the array was not biased and did not unfairly target the suspect as the potential offender.

SEIZURES OF BLOOD, TISSUE, HAIR, SALIVA, AND HANDWRITING SAMPLES

The popular *CSI* television series indicates that police agencies use sophisticated scientific analysis of physical evidence to prosecute criminals. This may or may not be true, but it does raise interesting new questions regarding seizures. Can police obtain one's blood, hair, saliva, or handwriting for forensic examination? These are searches and seizures of a sort; therefore, the Fourth Amendment applies. It has also been argued that this is a Fifth Amendment issue because giving one's blood, for instance, may be akin to giving testimony against oneself. The courts have disagreed with the latter presumption, however, distinguishing physical evidence (such as blood or DNA) from testimonial evidence (confession). One cannot be compelled to confess, but one can be compelled to give a DNA sample.

If the collection of body evidence is not intrusive (i.e., picture, handwriting or voice exemplar, fingerprint), then police merely need the legal justification to hold the person (it can be reasonable suspicion if the collection can be done without taking the individual to the police station). Even blood samples may be taken in DWI cases without consent and without a warrant when there is no time to obtain one and the blood is taken following standard medical procedures. However, generally police must obtain a court order to collect body fluids. Courts give approval for these seizures when the government successfully argues that their need for the evidence outweighs the individual's right to privacy over their own body [39]. This argument is easy to make when it is for a swab for DNA or a blood sample, but it is much harder to argue that the government's interest outweighs the individual's when the request is for surgery to recover a bullet.

In the television shows, the actors frequently obtain DNA from discarded soda cans or coffee cups. Although it is questionable that such tricks always will result in usable DNA, the practice does not violate any rights. The analogy would be when someone discards garbage and then police pick up the garbage and

Actress Lindsay Lohan arrives at the Beverly Hills Courthouse to attend a probation status hearing on May 24, 2010, in Beverly Hills, CA. She pleaded no contest in August 2007 to two counts each of DUI and being under the influence of cocaine, along with a reckless driving charge. *AP Photo/Damian Dovarganes*

find evidence. The Supreme Court has held that there is no reasonable expectation of privacy over one's discarded garbage and, by analogy, none over a discarded soda can [40].

Crime labs have recently been the targets of investigations because of alleged shoddy laboratory procedures and possible bias in testimony [41]. Other labs across the country have also been the subject of news reports. While sometimes the criticism has been simple incompetence and shoddy work practices, in other allegations, it appears that the lab examiners, who are sometimes employees of the police or sheriff's departments, and sometimes employees of independent labs, are engaged in "noble cause" corruption by working with police departments to arrive at desired results.

In 2009, the National Academy of Sciences issued a 225-page report on forensics and crime labs across the country. It was a highly critical report, incorporating the descriptions of many cases of innocent people convicted because of faulty scientific evidence. The authors concluded that crime labs lacked certification and standards, and that many forensic disciplines, including most of those described earlier, were not grounded in classic scientific methods; DNA analysis was the exception. Much of the problem is in pattern recognition (of fingerprints, bite marks, tool marks, etc.). There is no agreed-upon scientific standard for when to conclude a match, and human errors are introduced when the examiner knows the evidence is obtained from a suspect. The report calls on Congress to establish a national institute of forensic science to accredit crime labs and require that analysts be certified.

🌐 INTERNET KEY

To read about the report by the National Academy of Sciences on forensic labs, go to http://www.nap.edu/catalog.php?record_id=12589.

Because juries place a great deal of faith in laboratory findings, it is imperative that the highest standards of competence and ethics be applied to crime laboratories that test forensic evidence.

ENTRAPMENT

As discussed in Chapter 4, some police work involves proactively searching out crime before it happens. In one type of undercover operation, police offer opportunities for individuals to commit crimes rather than wait for them to do so. Bribery, drug sales, prostitution, and obscenity laws are areas that are particularly prone to the use of undercover officers offering the opportunity to commit the crime to unsuspecting individuals.

In legal terms, **entrapment** occurs when an otherwise innocent person commits an illegal act *because of* police encouragement or enticement. The entrapment defense argues that even if the defendant *committed* the crime, he or she should not be punished because government agents *created* the crime. Two approaches have been used to determine whether entrapment has occurred.

The **objective approach** examines the government's participation and whether it has exceeded accepted legal standards. For instance, if the state provided an "essential element" that made the crime possible, or if there was extensive and coercive pressure on the defendant to engage in the actions, then a court might rule that entrapment had occurred. The **subjective approach** looks at the defendant's background, character, and predisposition toward crime. If the offender is believed to have a predisposition to commit crime, then the police actions cannot be said to have entrapped the individual.

The defense of entrapment was first recognized by the U.S. Supreme Court in *Sorrells v. United States* in 1932 [42]. The Court held that when the "criminal design originates with the officials of the government" and they give the idea of the crime to the defendant, then the defendant has a legitimate defense. In early cases, if police played too large a role in the crime, for instance, by providing essential ingredients or creating the idea of the crime and providing all the materials for it, then it was held that they "entrapped" the defendant. This was the so-called objective test of entrapment.

This objective test was replaced by the subjective test in *United States v. Russell* [43]. In *Russell*, the Supreme Court changed the focus of the test from government actions to the "predisposition" of the offender. If the offender was predisposed to commit the crime, then it did not matter what the government did. Only when the offender was a true innocent who had no predisposition to commit the crime, could entrapment serve as a defense under this new test of entrapment.

Entrapment is an affirmative defense, which means that the defendant must raise the defense and offer some level of proof before the state is required to argue and offer evidence that the police actions did not constitute entrapment [44]. Some states have codified the defense in their penal codes, such as Colorado's Criminal Code [45], as shown in Box 6.4.

The federal government and most states follow some version of the subjective predisposition test. However, a minority of states continue to apply the objective test and a few combine the tests and require that the defendant prove

---

BOX 6.4 COLO. REV. STAT. § 18-1-709

The commission of acts, which would otherwise constitute an offense, is not criminal if the defendant engaged in the proscribed conduct because he was induced to do so by a law enforcement official or other person acting under his direction, seeking to obtain that evidence for the purpose of prosecution, and the methods used to obtain that evidence were such as to create a substantial risk that the acts would be committed by a person who, but for such inducement, would not have conceived or engaged in conduct of the sort induced. Merely affording a person an opportunity to commit an offense is not entrapment even though representations or inducements calculated to overcome the offender's fear of detection are used.

both elements (government activity and lack of predisposition) and at least one state (New Mexico) requires the defendant to prove either one or the other [46].

The line between police conduct that amounts to entrapment and merely affording an opportunity for the defendant to commit the offense is often a fine one. In drug cases, the general rule is that if the defendant has been involved in drug crimes in the past, then he or she is predisposed to such crimes and is not entrapped when he or she buys or sells to an undercover officer or informant.

Of course, providing the standard does not necessarily make the determination easy. Sometimes, there is legitimate disagreement about whether the actions of law enforcement officers constituted entrapment. In one case, the Supreme Court held that a man who had ordered two magazines (*Bare Boys I* and *Bare Boys II*) was not predisposed to purchase child pornography and was entrapped by federal agents because they had been sending mailings to him for *three years* under several fictitious company names [47]. The dissent argued that his magazine orders indicated a predisposition, but the majority of the court held that the fact that it took three years to finally get him to order something was evidence that he did not have a predisposition to unlawfully obscene materials.

Police engage in a wide variety of situations where they provide the opportunity to commit a crime. They may pretend to be:

- Individuals offering public officials a bribe in return for special treatment
- Drug sellers (or buyers)
- Prostitutes (or "johns")
- Children in Internet chat rooms offering to meet a predator for sex
- Fences encouraging the theft of certain types of automobiles
- Hit men who are willing to kill for money (or an individual wanting to hire someone to kill)
- Someone who can provide cable service for free
- A drunk on the street with money sticking out of his pocket

Generally, the guideline for which of these situations constitutes entrapment is whether the person who succumbs to the temptation had a "predisposition" to commit the crime. It may be the case that some crimes are particularly difficult to investigate and prevent without some level of undercover work on the part of federal or state officers.

EXCLUSIONARY RULE

What happens when an officer violates the rights of a citizen by ignoring a warrant requirement, putting the individual in a biased lineup, or using physically coercive or other illegal interrogation tactics? The Supreme Court has held that the court's response to such violations will be to exclude the evidence obtained from the illegal action.

In the 1914 case of *Weeks v. United States* [48], the Supreme Court excluded evidence obtained in violation of the Fourth Amendment by federal officers, but the ruling did not bar state or local police from using illegal evidence. Then in 1961, in *Mapp v. Ohio* [49], the Court extended the ruling to state and local police as well. In the *Mapp* case, Dolree Mapp's home was searched by officers looking for explosives or other evidence of revolutionary activity. They said they had a warrant, but they didn't. The officers found no explosives but did find some pornography in her basement and they arrested her for that. In the subsequent court trial and appeal, she argued that the evidence should have been excluded because it was obtained through an illegal search. The Supreme Court agreed, and eliminated the **silver platter doctrine**, whereby state and local officers, who were not bound by the *Weeks* decision, obtained evidence illegally and handed it to federal officers "on a silver platter." The *Mapp* decision extended the exclusionary rule to all law enforcement officers, whether they are federal, state, or local.

This decision, along with the *Miranda* decision, has been heavily criticized by those who argue that the rulings "handcuff" the police from doing their job and that criminals should not go free because of police mistakes or errors in judgment. On the other hand, there is no credible evidence that these decisions have affected criminal investigations and court processing to any great degree. Furthermore, the Supreme Court has recognized several exceptions to the exclusionary rule that allow evidence to be admitted when police actions are reasonable.

Exceptions to the exclusionary rule

There are times when evidence is obtained unlawfully but admitted anyway. In several cases, the Supreme Court held that there was either minimal harm in the violation or the exclusion would generate more harm than letting in the evidence. In all of these cases, the evidence was admitted despite a constitutional violation.

1. *The "Good Faith" Exception*

In 1984, the Supreme Court decided in *United States v. Leon* [50] that if the officer relied in good faith on a warrant, and that warrant turned out to be faulty, then evidence obtained under the warrant would still be admitted. In this case, the warrant was faulty because it was granted without meeting the probable cause standard. Therefore, the warrant issued by the magistrate was without legal authority. On the other hand, the court stated that the police officer should not be punished because the magistrate erred, and, therefore, the evidence would be admitted under this "good faith" exception.

2. The "Inevitable Discovery" Exception

Under this exception, if the state can show that the evidence would have been found anyway without using the illegally obtained evidence, then the information may be admitted as evidence. Basically, the argument here is that the evidence shouldn't be excluded because it would have been discovered inevitably anyway [51].

3. "Public Safety" Exception

Even though interrogations are supposed to be prefaced by a *Miranda* warning, in some situations when police officers do not give the warning, the information obtained from questioning can be used as evidence anyway. In *New York v. Quarles* [52], police officers had cornered a suspect in a grocery store. They demanded to know where he had hidden a gun he had been seen carrying, and they argued that they did so because they were afraid that citizens in the store might find the weapon and be hurt. He pointed out where he had hidden the gun and it was used as evidence against him. When he appealed, arguing that the question was an interrogation for evidence and therefore the gun should be excluded, the Supreme Court held that the officers' question was for public safety reasons, not for evidence collection, and the evidence could be admitted.

Arguably, these cases and others show that police and the courts don't have to be adversaries. Law enforcement is ultimately all about law. Generally, case decisions are made by balancing the needs of crime control against individual due process protections. If police officers don't believe in the law or only think it should apply to some and not others, then it is difficult to see how this approach cannot but hurt the process of justice.

CONCLUSION

In this chapter, we have examined a number of different legal principles as applied to police practices. In general, the government's intrusion into one's personal privacy is restricted. The Fourth Amendment requires police officers to have probable cause before they search a person's private papers or home. This protection has been held to include searches made by technology. Police do not necessarily need a warrant, but they do need probable cause if the activity is defined as a search. There are times when no warrant is needed, such as when evidence is in plain view or when there are exigent circumstances. The Fifth Amendment gives individuals the right not to incriminate themselves during the court process and also during the police investigation, but it does not protect against being compelled to provide physical evidence, such as blood or DNA.

Courts have also held that individuals should not be enticed to commit a crime and then be arrested for it. If it is shown that the suspect had no predisposition to commit the crime and it was only the police action that caused him or her to violate the law, then the defense of entrapment can be used.

If police overstep their authority and ignore the rights recognized by the courts, then evidence obtained can be excluded from any court proceeding against the defendant. However, courts have recognized several exceptions to the rule, including the good faith exception, the inevitable discovery exception, and the public safety exception.

Review Questions

1. Describe the four types of stops or seizures and the legal justifications required for each type.
2. What are the methodological problems in studying racial profiling?
3. What is the Bill of Rights? What does the Fourth Amendment say?
4. Do police need search warrants to wiretap? Can they use thermal-imaging equipment against a homeowner without a warrant? Can they do the following without a warrant: Obtain blood samples from a suspect? Get a picture of a suspect? Require handwriting samples? Hair samples? Fingernail scrapings?
5. What are the types of searches and what legal justification is necessary for each?
6. When can police use anonymous informants to support an affidavit for a search warrant?
7. When must the *Miranda* warning be given and when is it not needed?
8. What are the three procedures used for victims to identify suspects?
9. What two tests are used to determine if entrapment has occurred?
10. What is the exclusionary rule? Describe the three exceptions recognized by the Supreme Court.

VOCABULARY

arrest custodial seizure when police have *probable cause* that a person committed a crime

Bill of Rights the first 10 amendments to the Constitution; as written, they only protected citizens against violations by federal officers, but not by state or local agents of the law

consent stops interactions when the individual doesn't have to, but consents to stay and talk to police officers

due process clause appears in the Fifth and the Fourteenth Amendments to the Constitution; states that no person shall be deprived of life, liberty, or property without due process of law

entrapment when a person, who is not predisposed to commit crime, commits an illegal act because of police encouragement or enticement

fixed checkpoints police stop everyone or employ random stops of individuals for a very brief license and registration check (usually for deterring DWI)

Fourth Amendment protects citizens against intrusion by government agents into one's private home or papers

hot pursuit exception exception to the warrant requirement when police chase a suspect into a home

incorporation approach of the Supreme Court to apply Bill of Rights protections from the First, Fourth, Fifth, Sixth, and Eighth Amendments to citizens who may be faced with actions by state or local government agents

investigatory detentions when police officers have a *reasonable suspicion* that an individual has or is about to commit a crime, they can stop the person, ask for identification, and conduct a pat-down search for weapons

magistrate any judicial figure authorized to issue a warrant

objective approach defines entrapment by examining the government's participation in the crime and whether it has exceeded accepted legal standards

photo arrays suspect's picture is placed with others for victim identification

pretextual stops the practice of using a minor traffic violation to stop the individual and, in the course of the traffic stop, look for other evidence of wrongdoing

racial profiling occurs when reasonable suspicion to stop a driver (or pedestrian) is based on a "profile" with the major element of this profile being race

showups type of identification where officers bring suspect to the victim and ask the victim to identify the offender

silver platter doctrine referred to situation when state and local officers, who were not bound by the Fourth Amendment, would hand evidence to federal officers "on a silver platter"

subjective approach definition of entrapment that looks at the defendant's background, character, and predisposition toward crime; those with a predisposition cannot be entrapped

ENDNOTES

[1] J. Kanovitz, M. Kanovitz, Constitutional Law, twelfth ed., LexisNexis/Matthew Bender, New Providence, NJ, 2010.

[2] 392 U.S. 1, 1968.

[3] 124 S. Ct. 2451, 2004.

[4] D. Harris, Review essay/profiling: theory and practice, Crim. Just. Ethics 23 (2) (2004) 51–57.

[5] R. Weitzer, S. Tuch, Perceptions of racial profiling: race, class, and personal experience, Criminology 40 (2) (2002) 436, 443.

[6] *United States v. Martinez-Fuerte*, 425 U.S. 931, 1976.

[7] *Wren v. United States*, 517 U.S. 806, 1996.

[8] D. Cole, J. Lamberth, The fallacy of racial profiling, New York Times, May 13, 2001, A19.

[9] G. Alpert, R. Dunham, M. Smith, Investigating racial profiling by the Miami-Dade police department: a multimethod approach, Criminol. Publ. Policy, 6 (1) (2007) 25–47; P. Warren, D. Tomaskovic-Devey, Racial Profiling and Searches: Did the politics of Racial Profiling Change Police Behavior, Criminol. Publ. Policy 8 (2) (2009) 343–370.

[10] Atwater v. City of Lago Vista, 532 U.S. 318, 2001.

[11] Virginia v. Moore, 553 U.S. 164, 2008.

[12] 471 U.S. 1, 1985.

[13] Mapp v. Ohio, 367 U.S. 643, 1961.

[14] Gideon v. Wainwright, 372 U.S. 335, 1963.

[15] Berger v. New York, 388 U.S. 41, 87 S. Ct. 1873, 18 L. Ed. 2d 1040, 1967.

[16] 389 U.S. 347, 1967.

[17] Malpas v. State, 16 Md. App. 69, 695 A.2d 588, 1997.

[18] United States v. Friedman, 300 F.3d 111 2d Cir., 2002.

[19] United States v. Pratt, 913 F.2d 983 (1st Cir. 1990), *cert. denied*, 408 U.S. 1028, 111 S. Ct. 681, 112 L. Ed. 2d 673, 1990.

[20] 533 U.S. 27, 2001.

[21] T. Stapleton, The electronic communication privacy act and cell location data: is the whole more than the sum of its parts? Brook. Law Rev. 73 (2007) 383–400.

[22] M. Dolan, N. Lennon, K. Munoz, Use of cell phone records and GPS tracking, Chicago Bar Assoc. Rev. 24 (2010) 38–50.

[23] 392 U.S. 1, 1968.

[24] 395 U.S. 752, 1969.

[25] 387 U.S. 294, 1967.

[26] Acevedo v. California, 500 U.S. 565, 1991.

[27] 456 U.S. 798, 1982.

[28] 453 U.S. 454, 1981.

[29] 556 U.S. __, 2009.

[30] 412 U.S. 218, 1973.

[31] 428 U.S. 543, 1976.

[32] 462 U.S. 213, 1983.

[33] Miranda v. Arizona, 384 U.S. 436, 1966.

[34] Rhode Island v. Innis, 446 U.S. 291, 1980.

[35] J. Pollock, Ethical Dilemmas and Decisions in Criminal Justice, Wadsworth/ITP, Belmont, CA, 2007.

[36] Florida v. Powell, __ U.S. __ (Decided Feb. 23, 2010); Maryland v. Shatzer, __ U.S. __ (Decided Feb. 24, 2010); Berghuis v. Thompkins, 130 S.Ct. 2250 (2010).

[37] 388 U.S. 218 1967.

[38] Kirby v. Illinois, 406 U.S. 682, 1972.

[39] Schmerber v. California, 384 U.S. 757, 1966.

[40] Greenwood v. California, 486 U.S. 35, 1988.

[41] K. Axtman, Bungles in Texas crime lab stir doubt over DNA, Christian Science Monitor, April 18, 2003. Retrieved April 21, 2003 from http://www.csmonitor.com/2003/0418/p03s01-usgn.html.

[42] 287 U.S. 435, 1932.

[43] 411 U.S. 423, 1973.

[44] McGowan v. State, 671 N.E.2d 872 (Ind. 1996).

[45] Colo. Rev. Stat. § 18-1-709 (2002). See also § 18-1-710, which provides that entrapment is an affirmative defense.

[46] See State v. Little, 435 A.2d 517 (N.H. 1981); England v. State, 887 S.W.2d 902 (Tex. Crim. App. 1994); State v. Vallegos, 945 P.2d 957 (N.M. 1997).

[47] Jacobsen v. United States, 503 U.S. 540, 1992.

[48] 232 U.S. 383, 1914.

[49] 367 U.S. 643, 1961.

[50] 484 U.S. 897, 1984.

[51] Nix v. Williams, 467 U.S. 431, 1984.

[52] 467 U.S. 649, 1984.

[53] Miranda v. Arizona, 384 U.S. 436, 1966.

3

The Law as Social Control

CHAPTER 7

Law and Society

WHAT YOU NEED TO KNOW

- The purpose of law is to define and enforce the norms of society. It is declarative as well as purposive.
- Criminal law and civil law used to be combined, but today they have separate purposes and objectives.
- The three types of harm that law protects us from are harm to self, harm to others, and harm to society's morals.
- The three paradigms of law are the *consensus*, the *conflict*, and the *pluralist* paradigms.
- Common law has been largely supplanted by statutory law.
- Laws must not violate constitutional rights, specifically those rights specified in the Bill of Rights.
- Crimes can be classified as felonies, misdemeanors, and treason.
- Crimes must include an *actus reus* and a *mens rea*.

We take the law for granted, but it is important to take a moment to think about the purpose and origins of law. Why are certain behaviors defined as crimes? In this chapter, we will answer these questions and others before moving on to describe in more detail the American court system.

THE DEFINITION AND PURPOSE OF LAW

The law serves as a written embodiment of society's norms and morals. It is said to be declarative as well as purposive. That is, it declares the correct behavior in a society, but it also serves as a tool for enforcement. It cautions against certain types of behavior and warns of the consequences of ignoring the warning.

Natural law refers to the belief that some laws exist in the natural world and can be discovered by reason. For instance, some behavior is believed to be intrinsically wrong (*mala in se*), such as murdering an innocent. Other behaviors are prohibited in certain societies, but are not inherently wrong. They are called *mala prohibita* [1].

We can trace the history of law back to very early codes, such as the Code of Hammurabi (ca. 2000 BCE), which mixed secular and religious rules of behavior. These codes also standardized punishments. Early codes of law did not differentiate between what we might call public wrongs and private wrongs. Today, we have separated criminal law (public wrongs) and civil law (private wrongs).

Criminal law is the branch or division of law that defines crimes and provides for their punishment. In a criminal case, the state pursues justice to preserve the public peace. On the other hand, in civil law a person seeks a remedy against their perceived wrongdoer by bringing a civil, or *tort*, action. Torts are personal wrongs. Some examples of torts are assault, defamation, intentional infliction of emotional distress, and arson. *Torts* and *crimes* are not synonyms. While there is a great deal of overlap between crimes and torts, some crimes are not torts, and some torts are not crimes.

With torts, the emphasis is on adjusting the conflicting interests of individuals to achieve a desirable social result. The aggrieved party is the plaintiff and he or she must pay for the cost of the trial, although if he or she wins, the court may order the defendant to reimburse the plaintiff for costs incurred. There may also be punitive damages assessed in addition to compensatory damages. For example, if Ann hits Bob, causing him bodily injury, Bob may bring an action in court for recovery of expenses and for compensation for losses incurred. The state may also initiate an action against Ann for assault and battery and prosecute the case in criminal court. You may remember that there was a successful civil suit against O.J. Simpson for wrongful death *after* his acquittal in criminal court. It is entirely possible for a defendant to "win" in one court and "lose" in the other, partially because of the different burdens of proof in civil versus criminal court. In earlier times, however, these two different legal systems were combined. The remainder of our discussion in this chapter refers to criminal law, not civil law.

The purpose of criminal law

Why are some acts defined as crimes and punished? Blackstone, a famous English jurist, defined crime as "an act committed or omitted in violation of public law, either forbidding or commanding it" [2]. Specifically, the objectives of criminal law in a free society are to:

- Make it possible for individuals to coexist in society
- Define the wrongs that are considered necessary to protect the individuals

(3) ■ Define the method of determining guilt or innocence
(4) ■ Designate the type of punishment or treatment following conviction for violating the laws of society [3]

The purpose of criminal law is to protect society so that members of that society can be reasonably secure. There is always a balance to be achieved between the rights of the individual and the protection of society. The **social contract**, a concept originating with Thomas Hobbes and John Locke in the Age of Enlightenment, describes how individuals give up certain liberties in return for being protected by society. We give up the "right" to steal what we want in return for society's protection against our being victimized by others. We agree to follow the law but, in return, society should impose laws that are minimally intrusive upon our individual liberties.

There are three forms of harm that criminal law protects against:

(1) ■ Protection from the harm caused by others
(2) ■ Protection from the harm caused by ourselves
(3) ■ Protection of societal morals

The most obvious protection that the criminal law provides is protection against harm caused by others. Laws against homicide, rape, theft, and arson offer obvious protections. If we are harmed, these laws ensure that the offender will be punished if caught. Some legal writers identify a second set of wrongs that are not harmful but are offensive. Laws against public indecency or public disturbance are not directed to necessarily harmful behaviors but, rather, behaviors that are offensive to the majority of the population. One might say, then, that these "harm" our sense of order rather than threaten our physical security. The second form of protection that the law provides is protection against harm caused by ourselves. So-called **paternalistic laws** protect us against our own foolish behavior. Seat belt laws are one example of a paternalistic law. Although you may prefer to drive your car without such a restraint, you will be punished with a fine if you do so.

The third form of protection the law provides is protection of societal morals. We used to have many more laws that protected societal morals. Laws against businesses operating on Sunday, blasphemy, and adultery may all be relics of the past, but some of our current laws (gambling, pornography, prostitution) still have the major purpose of enforcing society's morals.

When a Georgia state law prohibiting sodomy (homosexual intercourse) was upheld by the Supreme Court in 1986 in *Bowers v. Hardwick* [4], the rationale was protection of society's morals. The Supreme Court upheld the right of the state to criminalize such behavior because they found that general societal morals condemned such behavior. However, in *Lawrence v. Texas* [5] in 2003, the Supreme Court overturned the earlier case. The majority held that the Texas law that criminalized homosexuality was unconstitutional. Evidently, just 17 years later, society's morals had changed to the extent that the law did not reflect societal morals. More recently, there has been a great debate about whether the law ought to recognize and legitimize same-sex marriages. The underlying justification that both sides employ is the protection of society's morals, or legal moralism. Laws related to obscenity, pornography, gambling, prostitution, and even drugs may be justified under legal moralism. Even though legal moralism may be a legitimate justification for laws, privacy rights may conflict with the government's right to enforce morality. It should also be noted that whether an action is moral or immoral is a different question from whether there should be laws and governmental sanctions regarding the behavior. In some cases, individuals may agree that a particular action is immoral but at the same time believe that the government should not have the power to restrict an individual's choice. For instance, some who advocate decriminalization of drugs do so because of cost effectiveness or libertarian reasons, not necessarily because they approve of drug use. Also, it seems fairly obvious that the state loses its moral authority to condemn gambling, for instance, when there is a state lottery. Laws that are based on the rationale of moral harm are usually the most controversial of all laws, and they have been, and continue to be, subject to shifts in public opinion and concern.

🌐 **INTERNET KEY**

For a Web site that approaches drug abuse as a medical problem rather than a criminal problem, go to http://drugabuse.gov/nidahome.html.

PARADIGMS OF LAW

A **paradigm** is a "fundamental image of the subject matter within a science.... It subsumes, defines, and interrelates the exemplars, theories, and methods/ tools that exist within it" [6]. In other words, a paradigm is a way of organizing knowledge. It is a broad perspective that shapes the way we process information. There are at least three paradigms (or perspectives) of law that can be identified: the consensus paradigm, the conflict paradigm, and the pluralist paradigm.

The **consensus paradigm** views society as a community consisting of like-minded individuals who agree on goals that are important for ultimate survival. This view sees the law as an aid to the growth and survival of society. Emile Durkheim (1858-1917), one of the first sociologists, wrote that criminal law represents the consensus of citizens [7]. We define an action as criminal because the majority of the populace holds the opinion that the behavior is wrong. An alternative view would be that the law is educational and teaches us what is wrong. In either case, the function of criminal law is the maintenance of social cohesion. Law defines who is "normal" and who is deviant.

The consensus view would point to evidence that we all agree, for the most part, on what behaviors are wrong and the relative seriousness of different types of wrongful behavior. In criminology, the consensus view is represented by classical thinkers such as Bentham and Beccaria, who relied on the accepted definitions of crime in their day. In fact, most criminologists (except radical or conflict criminologists) accept the legal definitions of crime, without questioning why some behaviors are defined as criminal.

In the consensus paradigm, we all pretty much agree with what is defined as wrong. Law reinforces social cohesion. It is also seen as value-neutral and objective; in other words, it is not used against any particular group for the benefit of another.

The **conflict paradigm** views society as being made up of those who have power and those who don't. Rather than perceiving law as representative, this perspective sees law as a tool of power holders that they use for their own purposes, which are to maintain and control the status quo. The law is seen as an instrument of special interests.

In this paradigm, it is believed that laws are written by power holders and tend to be against the interests of those who have no power [8]. Advocates of the conflict paradigm would point to laws against only certain types of gambling, or against the use of only certain types of drugs, as evidence that the ruling class punishes only the activities of other classes.

One example of differential definitions and enforcement that would support the conflict view is that federal drug laws passed in 1986 imposed more severe sanctions on crack cocaine than on powder cocaine. Many believed it was not merely a coincidence that crack cocaine, which is more likely to be the drug of choice for minorities (being cheaper), was punished at a rate 100 times more than powder cocaine, which is typically associated with Caucasians and social elites. In 2009, Congress rescinded that sentencing law and replaced it with one that reduced the disparity between the types of cocaine to 18:1. While the conflict view may explain the original dramatic disparity, it does not easily explain why Congress responded to those who objected to the sentencing structure that treated crack users so much more harshly. The pluralist paradigm, however, may better explain the response.

The **pluralist paradigm** shares the perception that society is made up of competing interests; however, pluralism describes more than two basic interest groups. Power may also shift when interest groups form or coalitions emerge. These power shifts occur as part of the dynamics of societal change. Thus, Mothers Against Drunk Driving, for instance, was a grassroots group that amassed enough political power to change DWI laws. In the ever-changing political landscape, small groups may create power by forming coalitions or aligning themselves with more powerful groups. In this view, determining who has the power to create law is much more complicated than the simple "powerful versus powerless" scenario described by the conflict view. Using the drug-sentencing disparity example, when enough interest groups combined together to put pressure on Congress, the law was changed.

Paradigms are subtly powerful in that they influence and shape the way we process information. If we hold a consensus perspective, we accept laws as they are passed and handed down to us from our representatives, with the assumption that they must be fair if they were the result of the legislative process. Conflict theorists are more critical of existing legislation and are able to see that some laws are passed because of hidden agendas, but their perspective that all law is the product of the powerful "pulling the strings" of government is probably not as realistic as the pluralist paradigm.

THE CREATION OF LAW

Recall that our system of laws in the United States is especially complex, because the criminal law is derived from English common law, statutory law, and our own case law tradition, split into 50 different state jurisdictions, the federal system, and thousands of counties and municipalities.

Most of the present-day crimes in the various states have their origins in the so-called **common law** of England. This was the law that developed in the early English case decisions. William the Conqueror (1066) and his son, Henry I (1100-1135), are generally credited with the development of a national court system that involved judges who traveled across England and provided guidance to local magistrates. The effect was a gradual consistency in court decisions that led to the establishment of similar decisions in similar cases, which became known as the "common law." Eventually, judges decided the cases that came before them according to established principles from prior cases. In 1765, William Blackstone published *Commentaries on the Laws of England*. This work was the most comprehensive written source of the common law at the time, and is still cited as a legal source.

Common law became the starting point for American criminal law. Gradually, states passed their own criminal codes that supplanted the common law, but if a particular code was silent on an issue, many courts would fall back to common law principles. For instance, in the 1970 case of *Keeler v. Superior Court*, the defendant was prosecuted for intentionally killing his wife's unborn child by kicking her in the stomach. However, because the California statute in question defined homicide as the killing of a "person," and the common law definition of person did not include the unborn, Keeler could not be prosecuted for the death of the fetus [9]. This led to California and other states changing their criminal code by redefining "person" to include a fetus, or creating the new crime of feticide. However, the decision in the *Keeler* case had to be made based on common law definitions because the California Penal Code was silent on the issue.

Today, <u>almost all crimes in all states are "statutory crimes," meaning that the state criminal code defines it as a crime.</u> When a legislative body (federal or state) determines that certain conduct is undesirable and should be forbidden, a bill is prepared describing what conduct should be prohibited. This is introduced in the House of Representatives or the Senate, and is voted upon by the elected members of the legislative body. If both houses of the legislature approve the bill, it then goes to the governor or the president for consideration and approval. If the chief executive officer signs the legislation, it then becomes a law to be enforced by those involved in the justice process. Even if the chief executive officer refuses to sign (in other words, vetoes the bill), the bill may become law if enough members of the legislative body approve it, overriding the veto. <u>The legislature is permitted to define criminal offenses in any way it chooses, as long as the law is not arbitrary and does not violate the state or federal Constitution.</u>

> ### 🌐 INTERNET KEY
>
> To view a few selected state penal codes, go to http://www.statutes.legis.state.tx.us/Index.aspx (Texas); *http://www.legis.state.wv.us/WVCODE/Code.cfm?chap* = 61&art = 1 (West Virginia); *http://www.leginfo.ca.gov/cgi-bin/calawquery?codesection* = pen&codebody = &hits = 20 (California).

As discussed in the first chapter, states have primary **police power**, which is <u>the authority to enact and enforce legislation to protect the health, welfare, morals, and safety of the people of the state.</u> Recall that the Tenth Amendment to the Constitution was added to make clear that the powers not delegated to the United States by the Constitution would remain in the states, respectively, and the people. The Tenth Amendment states:

> The powers not delegated to the United States by the Constitution, nor prohibited by it to the States, are reserved to the States respectively, or to the people.

The <u>federal government, supposedly, has no inherent police power.</u> In the federal system, there have also never been common law crimes, because the federal government only has the power that is delegated to it by the Constitution. However, Congress may pass laws that are related to one of the express powers granted to the federal government by the Constitution. The enumerated powers granted to the federal government are found primarily in Article I, Section 8 of the Constitution. Certain crimes, such as <u>treason,</u> are <u>federal crimes</u> because the Constitution grants to the federal government the specific right to define and prosecute treason. Other crimes are consistent with other enumerated powers. For example, under the power to regulate interstate and foreign commerce, Congress has created federal crimes such as transporting stolen vehicles (interstate), kidnapping (with the element of interstate transport), and counterfeiting because they are said to affect interstate commerce. Drug smuggling comes from the federal power to protect our borders, but other drug laws are justified under the power to regulate interstate commerce. In the last 30 years, the number of new federal laws has increased dramatically with attendant increases in the federal law enforcement, judicial, and correctional systems.

🌐 INTERNET KEY

To look at the United States Criminal Code, go to http://www.law.cornell.edu/uscode/18/usc_sup_01_18.html.

Cities, counties, townships, and municipal corporations also have limited authority to make and enforce rules and regulations. State legislatures have given these units of government the power to create laws as long as the regulations and ordinances do not conflict with the U.S. Constitution, the state constitution, or the laws of the state. The state may withhold, grant, or withdraw powers and privileges as it sees fit. City ordinances may vary quite a bit and are constantly being updated and revised in response to citizens' concerns, as the breaking news story shows.

BREAKING NEWS: BIKINI-CLAD BARISTAS AND CITY ORDINANCES

The state of Washington deserves its reputation as coffee central, not only for being the home to Starbucks, but also for leading the nation in consumption of coffee and pioneering the drive-through coffee stop. Another trend, started in Washington in the early 2000s, has spurred imitators around the country. In the last several years, the issue has gained more attention as residents in several towns in Washington may be surprised to find that the barista serving their morning coffee might be wearing a bikini, black lace lingerie, or, in a few places, even less. Business owners came up with the idea to increase revenue. And, evidently, it has with some employees making as much as $300 a day in tips. Some residents, however, have been less than supportive of the new business model. The issue was that the coffee places did not fit under "sexually oriented business" ordinances and, therefore, could not be regulated by rules that, for instance, barred the business from certain distances away from schools and residences. Some towns have found that their existing indecency or lewdness ordinances do not prohibit baristas from dressing in a manner some would say is barely appropriate for a beach. Snohomish County, including the city of Everett, was home to several of the new coffee drive-throughs. In 2010, five baristas were arrested under prostitution charges for letting customers touch them for money. Other towns are scrambling to pass new lewdness ordinances that would prohibit the businesses or specify exactly what can be shown and what must be covered. Some citizens welcome the ordinances; others argue that town leaders should be addressing "real problems," and if people don't like the idea of breasts with their brew, to simply stay away.

Source: O. Lei, *Bikini Baristas Under Scrutiny as Federal Way Discusses Lewd Conduct Law, NWCN.com, September 17, 2010. Retrieved 9/28/2010 from http://www.nwcn.com/news/washington/Bikini-Baristas-Under-Scrutiny-as-Federal-Way-Discusses-Law-103190609.htm.*

It should become clear by now that "law" in this country is a complex system of overlapping jurisdictions. There is the United States Criminal Code, which describes all federal criminal laws; the criminal codes of the 50 states; and thousands of city and county codes. Another code of law is the Model Penal Code, which was created by the American Law Institute. It is not the law in any state, but rather serves as a guide to state lawmakers. The American Law Institute is an association of judges, lawyers, and law professors and they created the **Model Penal Code** in 1962 with revisions and commentary being added through 1985. The MPC is helpful as a general outline of criminal law because it is difficult to compare the different laws of the 50 states and the federal government.

> ⊕ **INTERNET KEY**
>
> For an introduction to the Model Penal Code, go to http://www.law.upenn.edu/fac/phrobins/intromodpencode.pdf.

CONSTITUTIONAL CHALLENGES TO THE CREATION OF LAWS

The federal government, states, and municipalities do not have the power to pass a law that violates one of the rights granted by the United States Constitution. Specifically, protections are found in the first 10 amendments, which make up the **Bill of Rights**. We are protected against laws that are vague, punish behavior after the fact (**ex post facto laws**), or infringe upon our freedom of expression, association, or religion. Furthermore, laws that treat people in a discriminatory manner or that unreasonably infringe upon individual privacy rights are prohibited. A summary of the rights granted in the Bill of Rights appears in Box 7.1.

BOX 7.1 BILL OF RIGHTS

First Amendment: freedom of religion, expression, association

Second Amendment: right to bear arms

Third Amendment: right not to have soldiers quartered in people's homes

Fourth Amendment: right to be free from unreasonable governmental search and seizure

Fifth Amendment: right to be free from compulsory self-incrimination, federal right to grand jury, protection against double jeopardy, due process

Sixth Amendment: right to an impartial jury trial that is speedy and public, with specified due process elements

Seventh Amendment: right to trial in suit at common law, jury to be trier of fact

Eighth Amendment: right against excessive bail, right to be free from cruel and unusual punishment

Ninth Amendment: states "The enumeration in the Constitution, of certain rights, shall not be construed to deny or disparage others retained by the people."

Tenth Amendment: reserves all other powers not specifically delegated in the Constitution to the states

Vagueness challenges

It is a fundamental principle of criminal law that the legislation must not be vague, meaning that there is some reasonable doubt as to the meaning of the law. In vagueness challenges, the law is criticized as being so unclear as to what is prohibited that reasonable people would not have proper notification that some act was wrong.

In *City of Chicago v. Morales*, the Supreme Court struck down an antigang law passed by the Chicago City Council in order to control gang activity. The law/ordinance prohibited those "believed to be criminal street gang members" from "loitering in any public place." Criticisms of this law centered on the vague nature of identifying who were street gang members, and the vagueness of the terms "loitering" and "public place" [10]. The majority of the Court, however, objected to the fact that it was solely within the police officer's discretion to define when loitering was occurring. The Supreme Court, in this case, indicated that there may be antigang laws that could pass the vagueness test, but they needed to be written in a way that definitely stated what actions would be defined as criminal.

Basically, the right to be free from vague and overbroad laws comes from the Fifth and Fourteenth Amendments. Both amendments provide that an individual should receive "due process of law" before being deprived of life, liberty, or property. The Fifth Amendment provision has been interpreted to provide protection against due process violations by federal actors (such as the FBI), and the Fourteenth Amendment provision protects us from due process violations by state governmental actors (such as your municipal police). **Due process** has been defined as the procedures designed to protect against error in the governmental deprivation of life, liberty, and property. Due process includes the right to notice (to know what we are being accused of). Obviously, in order to have notice, a law must be clear and not subject to arbitrary definitions.

A very recent successful vagueness challenge was in *Skilling v. United States* [11]. Jeffrey Skilling, one of the executives of Enron who ended up in prison after the collapse of the huge energy company, challenged his federal prosecution under the so-called honest services law. The federal law makes it a crime to "deprive" your employer of the right to your honest services. The federal law was used successfully in many corruption cases and was especially useful to prosecutors when they could not prove specific bribes

Snohomish County Sheriff's deputy Bud McCurry, right, talks with a man wearing a sweatshirt with a "13" on it, February 18, 2010, in Everett, WA while on patrol as a member of his department's gang unit. The number 13 is often associated with the Sureno group of street gangs. Even as worries about gangs in smaller communities continue to grow, state legislators have had difficulty enacting new laws and rules to combat gangs. *AP Photo/Ted S. Warren*

or kickbacks were received or offered in return for specific acts, although they could prove a pattern of behavior that rose to a level that deprived employers, shareholders, or voters of the honest services of the accused. The Supreme Court in June 2010 held that the law was void for vagueness, arguing that a reasonable person would not know when they violated the law. The holding spurred many public corruption defendants to file challenges to their convictions.

Equal protection challenges

The Fourteenth Amendment to the Constitution prohibits the government from treating "similarly situated" people differently.

In this October 23, 2006, file photo, former Enron CEO Jeff Skilling, left, leaves the federal courthouse with his attorney Daniel Petrocelli, right, after being sentenced to 292 months in federal prison. A federal appeals court is considering whether Skilling will receive a new trial. *AP Photo/David J. Phillip*

> No State shall make or enforce any law which shall abridge the privileges or immunities of citizens of the United States, nor shall any State deprive any person of life, liberty, or property, without due process of law, nor deny to any person within its jurisdiction the equal protection of the laws.

The government must have a very good reason for treating different racial, ethnic, or religious groups differently under the law. If a law that is neutral on its face differentially affects only one group of people, it would also be scrutinized.

In 1967, the Supreme Court struck down Virginia's **miscegenation laws**, which made it a crime to marry someone of a different race [12]. The groups at issue were those who wished to marry a person from the same race compared to those who wished to marry someone of a different race. The Court held that the state did not have a reason that was sufficiently important to justify treating these groups differently and the holding invalidated all miscegenation laws in not only Virginia, but also the other states that had them. This case is used as a precedent case for those who argue that laws prohibiting same-sex marriages are unconstitutional in that they treat same-sex couples differently from heterosexual couples.

In the case *In re Michael M.*, a California statutory rape law was challenged. The argument was that the law violated equal protection because it treated male and female actions differently by defining the crime in such a way that only men could be perpetrators and only girls could be victims [13]. In this case, the Supreme Court upheld the law because the parties were *not* considered similarly situated, in that only female victims could become pregnant, and the law's imputed purpose was to prevent teenage pregnancy. Generally, laws that treat men and women differently have been struck down, such as laws that had different drinking ages (*Craig v. Boren*) [14]. However, in

Rostker v. Goldberg [15], the Supreme Court upheld the law that only required young men, not young women, to register for the draft. In equal protection cases, a law that treats groups differently can be upheld if (a) the groups are not "similarly situated," or (b) if the reason for the difference passes the so-called "strict scrutiny" standard, which requires that the government have a substantial and important government purpose and the difference is narrowly tailored to meet that purpose.

Ex post facto challenges

The U.S. Constitution and state constitutions specifically prohibit ex post facto laws. The two sections of the federal Constitution that relate to ex post facto laws are Article I, Section 9, which provides that "no bill of attainder or ex post facto law shall be passed," and Section 10, which provides that "[n]o state shall ... pass any ex post facto law" [16].

These provisions were added to the Constitution of the United States and similar provisions have been added to the constitutions of the respective states to prohibit legislative bodies from punishing a person for an act that was neither a crime nor punishable when the act was committed, or from increasing the punishment after the fact. Two critical elements are necessary to establish an ex post facto claim:

- The law must be retrospective—that is, it must apply to events occurring before its enactment.
- It must disadvantage the offender affected by it [17].

A mere procedural change in the law, not increasing punishment, or not changing the elements of the offense, does not result in an ex post facto violation. A law may be invalid as ex post facto toward a particular person who committed an act before its enactment, but that does not affect its validity generally. Such legislation would be ex post facto in relation to persons who committed the act prior to the enactment of the legislation, but would be upheld when applied to persons who commit the same act after the legislation.

First Amendment challenges

Neither the states nor the federal government can pass a law that limits First Amendment rights. As you know, the First Amendment protects our freedoms of speech, association, and religion.

> Congress shall make no law respecting an establishment of religion, or prohibiting the free exercise thereof; or abridging the freedom of speech, or of the press; or the right of the people peaceably to assemble, and to petition the government for a redress of grievances.

The government has a right to pass laws that do not unduly interfere with these rights. Thus, for instance, if our speech creates an imminent danger to others, it can be prohibited and even punished. One does not have the right to incite a riot. On the other hand, an ordinance that makes it criminal to simply *verbally* (not physically) object to the arrest of another has been ruled as unconstitutional in that it infringes upon free speech [18].

In *Texas v. Johnson*, an individual was arrested and punished under a Texas statute that made flag burning illegal. The Supreme Court ruled that the law violated First Amendment rights because flag burning was defined as symbolic speech [19]. This case decision is still controversial and a large number of people believe that burning the American flag, even if done as a protest, should be criminalized. In response, Congress has considered a proposal for a constitutional amendment that would criminalize flag burning. Other constitutional challenges may involve the First Amendment protections of religion, speech, or association. Generally, one has the right to speak, associate freely, and practice one's religion without state interference. However, laws can be passed if the behavior in question harms others or intrudes unduly on governmental interests in safety and order. These areas can raise interesting questions in how to balance individual freedoms and societal interests. Should worshipers, for instance, be allowed to sacrifice goats as part of their religion, or should they be bound by animal cruelty laws? Should followers of certain religions be allowed to have multiple wives, or be subject, as everyone else, to bigamy laws? If your religion uses peyote, as do some Native American groups, are you exempt from state and federal drug laws that criminalize the use and possession of this controlled substance? These challenges to created laws are always difficult and are resolved by balancing individual interests against government interests.

Privacy challenges

The right to privacy is not identified specifically in the Constitution, but has been recognized by the Supreme Court in various case decisions. Basically, the Justices' position in these decisions has been that the framers of the Constitution meant that privacy rights should exist, based on their language in certain amendments, such as the Fourth Amendment. One of the most important cases that established the protected right of privacy against governmental interference was *Griswold v. Connecticut* [20]. In that case, the Supreme Court struck down Connecticut's criminal law that punished the distribution of information regarding birth control and contraceptives to married couples. According to Justice Douglas, the First, Third, Fourth, Fifth, Ninth, and Fourteenth Amendments can be read to construe a privacy right that restricts the government from interfering with private decisions of procreation by a married couple.

The balance between individual liberty and governmental interest in these cases is typically the right to privacy versus protection of society's morals. Laws against drugs, pornography, gambling, and prostitution have been challenged under the privacy rationale, but generally have lost to the argument that the government's interest in societal safety justifies such laws. Laws against sodomy (same-sex sexual intercourse) have been abolished as a violation of privacy rights. As discussed earlier, in *Lawrence v. Texas*, the Supreme Court struck down the sodomy law of Texas as unconstitutionally infringing on the individual's right to privacy. Many commentators believed that the decision in *Lawrence* signaled that other privacy challenges would be successful as well, but differences exist between lower federal courts as to how the holding should apply to other privacy issues. For instance, a law in Alabama prohibits the sale of "any device designed or marketed as useful primarily for the stimulation of human genital organs …" and it was similar to a law in Texas that prohibited the sale of "obscene devices," defining "with intent to sell" as having more than six devices. In challenges to these laws using *Lawrence* as precedent, the Fifth Circuit struck down the Texas law as infringing on privacy, while the Eleventh Circuit upheld Alabama's law [21]. The Supreme Court refused to hear an appeal from the Eleventh Circuit case.

THE ELEMENTS OF A CRIME

If a law is not struck down because it violates one or more constitutional rights, it is enforceable as a crime. All crimes are classified as felonies, misdemeanors, or treason. These classifications are important not only in determining the degree of punishment, but also when determining the authority of justice personnel to take action. For example, in some states, law enforcement officers may not make misdemeanor arrests unless the offense was committed in their presence (or they had an arrest warrant).

According to most authorities, crimes punishable by death or by imprisonment in a state prison or penitentiary are **felonies**. A crime may be made a felony by reference to the punishment attached, or it may be made a felony by a statute that specifically says that it is a felony. When an offense is not designated by statute as either a felony or a misdemeanor, but a specific punishment is prescribed, then the grade, or class, of the offense is determined by the punishment. Generally, felonies are punishable by at least 1 year in prison.

Misdemeanors are offenses for which the punishment is other than death or imprisonment in a state prison or that have not been designated felonies by statute. A person convicted of a misdemeanor will ordinarily be incarcerated in a local jail or be required to pay a fine, but will not be sent to a state penitentiary. What is defined as a felony in one state may be a misdemeanor in another, except for the most serious crimes, such as murder, robbery, and rape, which are always felonies.

Treason is the only crime that is described in the Constitution. Because those who commit treason threaten the very existence of the nation, it is given a higher classification than a felony. According to the Constitution:

> Treason against the United States shall consist only in levying war against them, or in adhering to their enemies, giving them aid and comfort.

Also, the Constitution provides that no person shall be convicted of treason unless on the testimony of two witnesses to the same overt act, or on confession in open court.

Each crime, as defined in a criminal code, must include a specific prohibited act (or omission). This principle is referred to as the *actus reus*. The law does not punish mere criminal thoughts, nor does it punish a person for who he or she is. Each crime's definition includes a physical act or, in some instances, a failure to act. The physical act must be voluntary, such as pulling the trigger of a gun or breaking into a house to commit theft. There have been a few cases in criminal law in which the act was deemed to be not "volitional" or voluntary on the part of the perpetrator. Examples of acts that are not considered voluntary include actions taken during epileptic seizures or spasms, reflexive actions, or actions taken while sleepwalking or in some other form of "unconscious" state.

In some cases, the crime consists of a failure to act, such as a failure to register for the draft or failure to prepare income tax returns. An omission to act can only constitute a crime when there is also a legal duty. Legal duties are created by:

- Statute
- Relationship
- Contract
- Voluntary assumption of care

Examples of statutory duties are, for instance, the duty to file tax returns and the duty (of convicted sex offenders) to register in sex-offender registries. Failure to perform these duties is a crime in itself. Other statutory duties include:

- Stop and render assistance if involved in a traffic accident
- That of "mandated reporters" to report child abuse
- The duty of peace officers to enforce laws

Certain relationships also carry duties. The most obvious and common is the duty of a parent to care for a minor child. Care includes not only feeding and housing your child, but also providing medical care and ensuring that school-age children receive an education. In about 28 states, "filial responsibility" laws exist. These statutes create a duty for adult children to financially provide for one's aged and infirm parents if one is able to do so. In some states, a defense can be offered that the parent abandoned the child before the age of majority. Despite the fact that these state statutes exist, they are rarely enforced; in 11 of these states, *no one* has ever been prosecuted for failing to care for their elderly and infirm parents [22].

Contractual duties arise when one person receives something of value in exchange for a duty to care for others. If they are negligent in that duty, criminal culpability may be created. Examples of contractual duties exist between the following actors:

- Lifeguards to swimmers
- Child care provider to those in their care
- Doctor to patient

If a person who has no statutory, relationship, or contractual obligation to render aid but chooses to begin administering assistance, then they may create a duty for themselves. For instance, unless a state has a Good Samaritan law, there is no statutory duty to stop and render assistance if one sees a traffic accident (unless one is involved in the accident). However, if a driver does stop and begins to help, then they must not abandon their effort if it would leave the victim in a worse condition than before. If one sees a person in distress on the street, there is no duty to render aid; however, if the passerby helps the person in distress to a park bench or helps them to a doorway, or in any other way moves them away from where they might have received assistance from others, then the duty to continue care has been created. The rationale is that abandoning one's effort would leave the victim in a worse condition than before.

Another element of every crime, in addition to the *actus reus*, is a criminal state of mind, or **mens rea**. Under common law, each crime possessed a *mens rea*, but the language used in old English cases and early state statutes and cases in this country was not uniform; thus, for instance, the necessary intent for homicide was defined as malicious, premeditated, depraved indifference, depraved heart, or wanton disregard. The Model Penal Code condensed all the myriad definitions of *mens rea* into only four enumerated mental states. In all states that have adopted the Model Penal Code, statutes clearly specify that the actor must have acted *purposely, knowingly, recklessly,* or *negligently*. Further, the definitions of these terms do not vary state by state; they always mean the same thing. The definitions of these terms are as follows:

- *Purposely:* when the actor intends the act and intends to cause the result
- *Knowingly:* when the actor is aware of the nature of his conduct and is aware of the practical certainty of the result of his conduct
- *Recklessly:* when the actor knows of, but consciously disregards, an unjustifiable risk (and the action involves a gross deviation from a reasonable standard of conduct)

- *Negligently:* when the actor is unaware of, but *should have been* aware of, an unjustifiable risk (and the action involves a gross deviation from a reasonable standard of conduct)

One other concept important to criminal *mens rea* is the principle of **transferred intent**. This can be remembered as "bad aim" intent because the classic example is that if the defendant intends to kill victim A, but misses and kills victim B instead, he will be guilty of first-degree murder (for B's death) and attempted murder (for trying to kill A). The intent to kill was transferred to the actual victim.

If you examine any crime in your state's criminal code, you should be able to identify the specific *actus reus* and the *mens rea* required for criminal culpability. In Table 7.1, several serious crimes are given with the mens rea and actus reus attached. Obviously, these represent only a small portion of the crimes in any jurisdiction. It is important to remember that these definitions may not match exactly your state's definition. Each state's penal code may define the crimes in slightly different ways. If the *mens rea* is not specifically stated, case law usually assumes the legislators meant "knowingly." The state exercise allows you to compare the definitions provided against your own state's definitions of the crimes.

Table 7.1 Crimes and Mental States

Crimes	Mens Rea	Actus Reus
Homicide, first degree	Purposely	Did an act that resulted in the death of another (and intended the result)
Homicide, second degree	Knowingly	Did an act that resulted in the death of another either intentionally or with knowing it was an almost inevitable outcome
Voluntary manslaughter	Knowingly	Did an act that resulted in the death of another (and intended the result but with provocation)
Involuntary manslaughter	Recklessly	Did an act that resulted in the death of another by engaging in behavior where the risk was known to the defendant
Rape/sexual assault	Knowingly	Penetrated the sexual organ of another with the use or threat of force, against the consent of the victim
Robbery	Knowingly	Took something of value from another in their presence with the use or threat of force
Burglary	Purposely/with intent	Breaking and entering with the intent to commit a felony inside
Theft	Purposely/with intent	Taking something from another, without consent, with the intent to permanently deprive

---

EXERCISE: IN THE STATE OF...

Find the criminal code for your state and determine the following:

1. Has the code completely replaced common law, or does it "supplement" common law (meaning that common law would be applied if any particular issue was not contained in the code)?
2. Is there a law prohibiting sodomy? As it is written, does it conflict with the Supreme Court's holding in *Lawrence v. Texas?*
3. When is theft/larceny a misdemeanor and when is it a felony?
4. What are the *actus reus* and *mens rea* of the crime of burglary, according to your criminal code?

RECENT ISSUES IN CRIMINAL LAW

Controversies concerning the law and its implementation occur all the time. Abortion has continued to be a divisive issue for the country and for the Supreme Court. Although *Roe v. Wade* [23] ruled that the Texas law against abortion unconstitutionally infringed upon a woman's right to choose, subsequent cases refined and restricted the "right" to abortion. Today's Supreme Court may very well overturn the *Roe* decision completely. In *Gonzales v. Carhart* [24], decided in April 2007, the Supreme Court upheld the Partial Birth Abortion Ban Act of 2003. In this decision, the justices held that prohibiting this type of abortion did not unduly interfere with a woman's right to privacy. In the coming years, the Supreme Court will hear challenges to new state laws that further limit abortions, which is why the selection of new Supreme Court justices is such a hotly debated issue. The recent additions of Sonia Sotomayor and Elena Kagan are groundbreaking in that there are, for the first time, three women on the Court, and Sotomayor is the first Latina.

The issue of whether abortion should be a crime is a *substantive* legal issue, meaning that the substance of the law is the issue, that is, *should* abortion be considered a crime? There are also *procedural* legal issues, typically concerning the nature and extent of due process. For instance, in *Boumediene v. Bush* [25], the Supreme Court decided whether the United States' prisoners in Guantánamo Bay should be subject to military commissions instead of federal courts. They decided that the detainees could not be held without the right of habeas corpus and that the military commissions did not provide sufficient due process. The decision had nothing to do with their guilt or the particular crime they might be determined to be guilty of, but, rather, determined that the procedure involved violated rights recognized by American law. One need only look in the newspaper to see current legal controversies. Should hate crimes be extended to gender? Should same-sex marriages be legal? Should Congress pass laws that make it a federal crime to give aid to foreign organizations defined as terrorist (even if some other activities are philanthropic)? Should concealed firearms be allowed on college campuses? Should there be a crime that holds owners of dogs that maul victims criminally culpable? Should medical marijuana laws override federal drug laws? The point is that the law affects you every day and it is a dynamic entity. It constantly changes in response to current events and political and social influences.

FOCUS ON CRIME: MEDICAL MARIJUANA USE—CRIME OR CURE?

Is buying and selling marijuana prescribed by a doctor and to use as a medical treatment illegal? Yes and no. Yes in some states, no in other states, and yes in all states as far as federal law is concerned. The Federal Bureau of Investigation reports that there were an estimated 1,663,582 arrests for drug abuse violations in 2009. Of these arrests, only 18% are for sales or distribution and the majority (82%) are for possession. Of the possession arrests, almost half (45%) were for marijuana; thus, the vast number of drug arrests in this country are for possessing marijuana. About 15 states, including California, Oregon, Vermont, Rhode Island, and New Mexico now have laws that legalize the use of marijuana when it is medically prescribed, and about that number have decriminalized it to some degree. The Gallup Poll shows that in 2005, 78% of Americans were in favor of medical marijuana laws and, in 2009, 44% were in favor of completely legalizing the drug. The federal drug laws have not been changed, but under the Obama administration, the Department of Justice has shifted its enforcement to deemphasize marijuana prosecutions in the states that have passed these laws. Proponents argue the time has come to recognize that marijuana presents some health benefits for individuals who cannot ingest other forms of pain medicine. Opponents to such laws argue that there are other safer methods, and that medical marijuana dispensaries are nothing more than legalized drug shops, and they bring an undesirable element to the community and serve as a gateway to other drugs. While the controversy continues, more than 600,000 people are arrested every year for marijuana possession.

Sources: *UCR, 2009, retrieved 9/29/2010 from http://www.fbi. gov/ucr/cius2009/data/table_29.html and Arrests for Drug Abuse Violations from http://www.fbi.gov/ucr/cius2009/arrests/index. html; Gallup Poll Sourcebook of Criminal Justice Statistics, 2005, Table 2.69.2005, Respondents' attitudes toward making marijuana legally available for doctors to prescribe, http://www.albany.edu/ sourcebook/pdf/t2692005.pdf, and Table 2.67.2009, Attitudes toward legalization of the use of marijuana, http://www.albany.edu/ sourcebook/pdf/t2672009.pdf.*

CONCLUSION

Society has law in order to protect the citizenry from harm. Criminal law is the branch or the division of law that defines crimes, their elements, and provides for their punishment. In a criminal case, the state (or federal government) is the plaintiff, and the purpose of the prosecution is to preserve the public peace or address an injury to the public at large. It can be distinguished from civil law.

The protections of law fall into the three areas: protection from harm from others, protection from harm from oneself, and protection of society's morals. Paradigms of law are descriptions of perspectives concerning the basic function in society, and include the consensus, conflict, and pluralist paradigms.

Most present-day crimes in the various states had their origins in the common law of England. This was the law developed in the early English court decisions and modified by English legislative bodies. Common law became the starting point for our criminal law, but has now largely been supplanted by statutory law as found in state and federal criminal codes.

Once the legislative or judicial branch of government decides that certain conduct is prohibited or required, criminal justice personnel are charged with enforcing those laws, and have the responsibility to do so until the laws are repealed or declared unconstitutional. Constitutional challenges fall into the areas of vagueness, equal protection, ex post facto, First Amendment, and privacy challenges.

Crimes are also classified as felonies, misdemeanors, and treason. According to most authorities, crimes punishable by death or imprisonment in a state prison are felonies, while crimes not amounting to felonies are classified as misdemeanors. Each crime's definition includes a prohibited action (the *actus reus*) and the requisite state of mind (*mens rea*).

Law is dynamic and it changes depending on public opinion and shifting public morals. On any given day, one could identify numerous legal issues in the daily newspaper or from an analysis of current events. Without law, there could be no crime.

Review Questions

1. What is the purpose of law? What three types of harms does law protect us from?
2. Distinguish between criminal and civil law.
3. What is a paradigm? Describe the three paradigms of law.
4. Distinguish between common law and statutory law.
5. What are the most common constitutional challenges? Describe them.
6. When can government define private behavior as criminal without violating freedom of speech, association, or religion?
7. Distinguish felonies, misdemeanors, and treason.
8. What are the two elements of a crime? When does a failure to act constitute the *actus reus* of a crime?
9. What are the four different criminal states of mind?
10. Describe some current legal issues in your state.

VOCABULARY

actus reus the specific prohibited act (or omission) that constitutes a crime

Bill of Rights the first 10 amendments to the Constitution

civil law the branch of law that seeks to resolve differences between individuals and repair damages or compensate victims

common law early case law of England

conflict paradigm views society as being made up of competing and conflicting interests

consensus paradigm views society as a community consisting of like-minded individuals who agree on what is a crime

crime an act committed or omitted in violation of public law, either forbidding or commanding it

criminal law the branch or division of law that defines crimes and provides for their punishment

due process the procedures designed to protect against error in the governmental deprivation of life, liberty, and property

ex post facto laws laws that punish behavior after the fact

felonies crimes punishable by death or by imprisonment in a state prison or penitentiary

mala in se behavior that is intrinsically wrong

mala prohibita behavior that is prohibited in certain societies but not inherently wrong

mens rea criminal state of mind (purposive, knowing, reckless, negligent)

miscegenation laws laws that made it a crime to marry someone of a different race

misdemeanors offenses for which the punishment is other than death or imprisonment in a state prison

Model Penal Code created by the American Law Institute, it is a guide or model code but has no legal authority

natural law refers to the belief that some law is inherent in the natural world and can be discovered by reason

paradigm a fundamental perspective of a subject matter

paternalistic laws laws that protect us against our own behavior, such as seat belt laws

pluralist paradigm view that society is made up of many competing interests that ultimately control the definition of laws

police power the authority to enact and enforce legislation to protect the health, welfare, morals, and safety of the people of the state

social contract a concept originating with Thomas Hobbes and John Locke in the Age of Enlightenment that describes how individuals give up certain liberties in return for being protected by society

torts personal wrongs

transferred intent "bad aim" intent; the intent is transferred from what the perpetrator meant to do to what he actually did do

ENDNOTES

[1] J. Mackie, Ethics: Inventing Right and Wrong, New York, Penguin, 1977, p. 232.

[2] W. Blackstone, Commentaries, vol. 4, 1769, p.15, as cited in J. Klotter, J. Pollock (Eds.), Criminal Law, Newark, NJ, LexisNexis/Matthew Bender, 2007.

[3] J. Klotter, J. Pollock, Criminal Law, Newark, NJ, LexisNexis/Matthew Bender, 2007, p. 3.

[4] 106 S. Ct. 2841, 1986.

[5] 539 U.S. 558, 2003.

[6] R. Rich, Essays on the Theory and Practice of Criminal Justice, Washington, DC, University Press of America, 1978, p. 1.

[7] E. Durkheim, Types of law in relation to types of social solidarity, in: V. Aubert (Ed.), Sociology of Law, London, Penguin Press, 1969, p. 21.

[8] J. Sheley (Ed.), Exploring Crime, Belmont, CA, Wadsworth, 1985, p. 1; R. Quinney (Ed.), Critique of the Legal Order, New York, Little Brown, 1974, pp. 15–16.

 [9] Keeler v. Superior Court, 470 P.2d 617 (Cal. 1970).

[10] 119 S. Ct. 1849 1999.

[11] Skilling v. United States, 561 U.S. __ (08-1394), 2010.

[12] Loving v. Virginia, 388 U.S. 1, 1967.

[13] 450 U.S. 464, 1981.

[14] 429 U.S. 190, 1976.

[15] 453 U.S. 57, 1981.

[16] U.S. Const. Art. I, §§ 9 and 10, Cl. 1.

[17] United States v. Abbington, 144 F.3d 1003 (6th Cir. 1998); Myers v. Ridge, 712 A.2d 791 (Pa. 1998).

[18] City of Houston v. Hill, 482 U.S. 451, 1987.

[19] 491 U.S. 397, 1989.

[20] 381 U.S. 479, 1965.

[21] Williams v. Morgan, 478 F.3d 1316 (11th Cir. 2007); Reliable Consultants v. Earle, 517 F.3d 738 (2008).

[22] See Caring for our parents in an aging world: sharing public and private responsibility for the elderly, N.Y.U. J. Legisl. Publ. Policy 5 2001 563–595.

[23] 410 U.S. 113, 93 S. Ct. 705, 35 L. Ed. 2d 147, 1973.

[24] 550 U.S. 124, 2007.

[25] 553 U.S. 723, 2008.

CHAPTER 8

Courts in America

WHAT YOU NEED TO KNOW

1   Each state generally has trial courts, intermediate appellate courts, and a supreme or highest court.
2   Trial courts are separated into courts of general jurisdiction and courts of limited jurisdiction. Courts of general jurisdiction may include special courts such as community courts, domestic violence courts, or drug courts.
3   Appeals allege legal errors in the proceedings leading to conviction. They may end up in the federal court system when there is a federal constitutional issue at stake.
4   Defense attorneys for indigents are provided through a public defender system, an appointment system, or by contract attorneys.
5. Judges may be elected officials or appointed. The Missouri Plan, or some version of it, is the most common method of appointment.
6. The federal system also has trial courts (federal district courts), appellate courts (circuit courts or courts of appeals), and a court of last resort (Supreme Court).
7. The Supreme Court hears only a small fraction of the cases that are appealed to it. When the Court chooses to hear a case, a writ of certiorari is issued.

CONTENTS

COURT SYSTEMS

There are 50 states and 50 different court systems in this country (not to mention Puerto Rico and the federal court system). Generally, each state has trial courts, intermediate appellate courts, and a supreme court or court of last

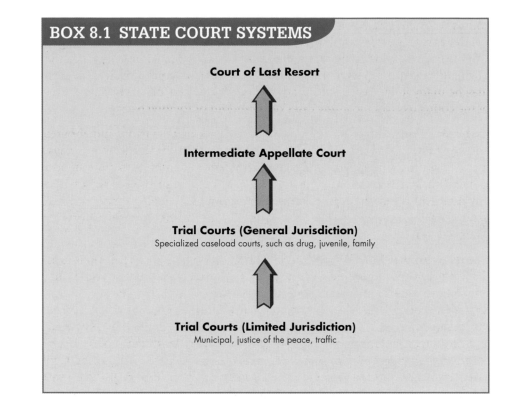

BOX 8.1 STATE COURT SYSTEMS

Court of Last Resort

Intermediate Appellate Court

Trial Courts (General Jurisdiction)
Specialized caseload courts, such as drug, juvenile, family

Trial Courts (Limited Jurisdiction)
Municipal, justice of the peace, traffic

resort that hears final appeals. Trial courts can be further separated into courts of general jurisdiction and courts of limited jurisdiction. Box 8.1 shows the basic outline of the court systems in most states.

The names of each level of the court system can vary considerably from state to state. "Supreme" may refer to the court of last resort, or, in some states, this term refers to trial courts. "Circuits" may refer to the intermediate appellate courts or the trial courts. That is why it is best to become familiar simply with the general categories of:

- Trial courts (limited jurisdiction and general jurisdiction)
- Intermediate appellate courts
- Courts of last resort

Jurisdiction

Courts have subject matter jurisdiction and geographic jurisdiction. **Subject matter jurisdiction** refers to the type of case that can be heard in each type of court; this is defined by legislation. Courts must also have **geographic jurisdiction** over the case. In criminal cases, this means that the crime must have taken place in the court's geographic jurisdiction. If the prosecutor does not prove this essential fact, the defendant must be acquitted. In California and many other states, the geographic boundary for each court is the county; however, in some states, a district or circuit may encompass more than one county [1]. In larger jurisdictions, there may be many judges, each with their own courtroom, for that jurisdiction. Each of the courts receives incoming cases on a random or rotating basis.

General jurisdiction courts are the courtrooms of television and movies, and they are what most people think of when they think of courts. These courts typically try felonies and have the power to sentence to state prison. General jurisdiction courts also try civil cases, although the courts are usually divided, so that there are Civil trial courts and criminal trial courts. These general jurisdiction courts may be called district courts, superior courts, or some other name.

Courts of limited jurisdiction can be found in all but six states [2]. Their jurisdiction is limited to specific types of cases. For instance, municipal courts may only adjudicate city ordinances and misdemeanors. There may be special traffic courts that only hear traffic violations up to a certain level of seriousness. Justices of the peace exist in some states and may hear minor misdemeanors and ordinance violations as well as civil cases. The judges/magistrates in such courts may also hold first appearances and arraignments for felony cases. Civil cases are usually limited to low-dollar claims (small claims courts). The powers of such courts are set by legislation, and their jurisdiction may be limited to a county, part of a county, city, or municipality.

Specialized courts

Juvenile and/or family courts may exist in your state and are typically courts of general jurisdiction, only with a specialized caseload. Probate courts (handling matters of estates and wills) may also exist in your state. In states without such specialized courts, such cases are heard in regular trial courts (courts of general jurisdiction). There are also a growing number of **community courts**, which may be courts of limited jurisdiction, but more often are courts of general jurisdiction, meaning that they may handle up to and including felony criminal matters. The focus of such courts tends to be on juvenile and minor criminal cases. These courts are part of the **restorative justice** movement and the defining feature of this type of court is a focus on "problem solving." The goal of the restorative justice approach is to resolve each situation by meeting the needs of victims and offenders alike [3]. Restorative justice models are not interested simply in assessing guilt or innocence and determining punishment—the goal is to address underlying issues that might have led to the offense and also to make sure the victim is "made whole" again and fully recovered from the offense. Community courts fit well with community policing because both are interested in strengthening the community's ability to respond to such problems as delinquency and crime. Typically, community courts use alternative sentencing models to achieve the restorative justice goals.

Noelle Bush, center, daughter of Florida Governor Jeb Bush, leaves the courtroom of Judge Reginald Whitehead following her completion of a court-ordered drug program, Friday, August 8, 2003, in Orlando, Florida)
AP Photo/Scott Audette

Relatively new to the scene are **drug courts**, which are typically courts of general jurisdiction, but with a specialized caseload of drug cases. Drug offenses form a huge portion of the workload of criminal courts. What is also true, it seems, is that drug offenders are repeat customers of the justice system, returning again and again on probation revocations. By 2000, more than 400 drug courts were established in most of the 50 states. The judges in these alternative courts identify first-time drug offenders, sentence them to drug testing and treatment programs, and then monitor the offender's progress through the program. If the offender successfully completes the program, he or she may be diverted from incarceration and their conviction may also be erased [4]. In other jurisdictions, offenders may be sentenced to regular probation, but they receive specialized prosecution and monitoring.

Drug courts have undergone dramatic growth since the first one was developed in Dade County, Florida, in 1989. They are described as an outgrowth of community-based justice programs and the system's response to the criticism that our nation's prisons and jails are filled with nonviolent drug users who need treatment, not punishment [5]. One of the distinguishing characteristics of drug courts is that the judge stays involved with the offender through the period of supervision, which usually includes drug treatment. The major goal of drug courts is to break the cycle of drug use rather than simply administer punishment.

Some studies have shown that offenders who go through drug courts are more likely to complete drug treatment programs and have lower recidivism rates than offenders who are sentenced through regular court processes [6]. However, at this point, the research is mixed, with just as many evaluations showing no difference as those that find that drug courts reduce recidivism, as compared to regular court processing. In a study of a Cincinnati drug court, researchers found that drug court participants were more likely to get probation than a comparison group, and the comparison group was more likely to receive intensive supervision probation [7]. While there was no difference in drug arrests between the drug court participants and the control group (30.8% vs. 37.4% were rearrested), there was a significant difference in theft/property arrests (18.4% vs. 31.7%) [8].

Another study looked at whether biweekly review sessions with the judge had an effect on recidivism. In some drug courts, there is minimal interaction between the offender and the judge, but this study looked at a program where the judge met much more frequently with the offenders. The findings indicated that biweekly hearings reduced recidivism among high-risk offenders, but not low-risk offenders [9].

In a cost-effectiveness study, researchers concluded that cost savings in a drug court in Multnomah County, Oregon, saved taxpayers close to $500,000 for every 100 participants [10]. In one review of several drug court evaluations, the authors concluded that effectiveness would be increased if the courts:

- Used objective risk and need instruments
- Used behavioral and cognitive treatment strategies
- Made sure the level of treatment was matched to the offender
- Provided aftercare
- Maintained quality control over treatment options [11]

In the same way that drug courts siphon away drug offenders for specialized prosecution and seek to break the cycle of drug addiction, domestic violence courts have been created to do the same thing with domestic violence offenders. Domestic violence refers to assaults that occur between intimates, either in a spousal (husband-wife), familial (parent/caregiver-child/dependent), or intimate (boyfriend-girlfriend or same-sex partners) relationship.

These courts have developed because of the growing awareness of the problem of domestic violence and the system's reaction to it. Mandatory arrest policies, for instance, have led to an increase in prosecutions for domestic assaulters, taxing the courts and filling jails and prisons with offenders. The impetus for domestic violence courts came from the Violence Against Women Act, which created federal funding for the implementation of the courts. Domestic violence courts increase coordination among the courts, police, and social service agencies, and adopt a "therapeutic approach" to justice [12]. In 1998, there were more than 300 domestic violence courts or specialized processes for handling domestic violence cases across the country [13]. The concept of a specialized court recognizes the unique interpersonal issues involved in domestic violence and emphasizes treatment for the batterer and services for the victim. These courts employ both sanctions (punishment) and services for greater effect. Recognizing the unique nature of domestic violence, these courts may also handle restraining or protective orders and even child custody and visitation issues to provide a comprehensive judicial response to the problem of violence in the home.

In the few studies that have been undertaken, domestic violence courts were found to reduce recidivism over traditional court processing. In one study, recidivism in the domestic violence court sample was 6% compared to a control sample of 14% [14]. On the other hand, another study showed that the creation of a domestic violence court increased the number of arrests for domestic violence. This was explained as the result of law enforcement becoming sensitized to the issue, as well as being more likely to arrest, knowing that the domestic violence court was available as a resource. The study also found that participants in the domestic violence court were significantly less likely to recidivate than those who went through traditional court processing. The conclusion of the study described earlier was that a "coordinated community response" to domestic violence, involving the police, courts, and social services, reduces recidivism [15]. In a more recent study, a court program for offenders in Albuquerque, New Mexico, was found to reduce recidivism as compared to a matched sample who did not go through the court program [16].

State trial courts

If one were to enter a trial court in most states, it would be easy to identify the judge, the prosecutor(s), and perhaps the defense attorney(s). One could also identify the bailiff, who may be either a sheriff's deputy or a court employee. Typically, there is also a court administrator who handles the nonjudicial aspects of the court, including scheduling and caseload processing. The court clerk handles legal filing of court orders, may collect court fees, and schedules the trial docket. In larger jurisdictions where there are many judges, one of the trial judges also serves as a presiding or administrative judge and handles the managerial and the budgetary aspects of the court system in that jurisdiction.

What may surprise a person who visits one of these courtrooms is the amount of time when "nothing is happening." Of course, something may be happening, but it is not recognizable as a trial. The judge may be meeting in chambers with attorneys, or conducting a pretrial motion hearing to determine if certain evidence should be allowed. Other activities that take place in trial courts are first appearances, preliminary hearings, and arraignments. You might, for instance, see a large number of individuals marched in, wearing jail uniforms, for the judge to arraign. Judges may also "take pleas," meaning that the defendant, his or her attorney, and prosecutor stand before the judge and submit the documentation of a plea bargain. This affidavit includes a confession and the prosecutor's recommendation for sentencing and serves as the sole evidence supporting the conviction. In busy courtrooms, defense attorneys may be conducting business in the back of the courtroom, or going inside "the bar" (the area in front of the defense and prosecutor's tables) to talk to the court clerk about court orders or other business. This may be happening even while the judge is on the bench and involved in a proceeding. Some judges run a very formal courtroom, but others have more relaxed rules.

The combined state and federal trial courts convict well over a million offenders each year. In 2006, 1,132,290 defendants were convicted of a felony in state trial courts, and 69% were sentenced to jail or prison [17]. Of these, 18% were convictions for a violent crime, 28% were convictions for a property crime, and 33% were convictions for a drug offense [18].

There is tremendous variation among judges in how many trials are conducted each year, even within the same jurisdiction. While some judges may clear up to a dozen cases off their **docket** (cases assigned to their court) each month, others take a more leisurely pace. Many states now allow cameras and audio equipment in the courtroom, but jury deliberations continue to be held in private. Despite the presence of cameras and news footage, most people's perception of what happens in a courtroom is shaped by the countless television shows and movies that find courtroom drama so compelling.

> **🌐 INTERNET KEY**
>
> For an interesting Web site that provides information about state courts, go to the National Center for State Courts' Web site at www.ncsc.org/.

Appellate courts

As you know, defendants who are convicted may appeal only if there has been some error in the proceedings. In some states, there are several intermediate courts of appeal, distributed geographically across the state. While the court of last resort in any state is usually a very old institution, probably dating back to the beginning of statehood and the state constitution, intermediate appellate courts are more recent additions and serve to reduce the highest court's caseload. About 40 states have these intermediate courts [19]. California has the largest number of intermediate courts, divided into nine divisions with more than 100 judges. Most of the time cases are heard by a panel of three judges, rather than the total number of judges in each division.

The highest court in the state, or court of last resort, is often called the state supreme court. Texas and Oklahoma are the only two states that split their court of last resort into two courts, including one that hears criminal appeals (court of criminal appeals), and one that hears civil appeals (supreme court) [20]. In most states, there are seven justices that sit on the court of last resort (28 states), although some states have nine (five states), and others only five (16 states) [20].

EXERCISE: IN THE STATE OF...

1. Go to http://www.ojp.usdoj.gov/bjs/pub/pdf/sco04.pdf.
   This is a report titled *State Court Organization 2004* by the Bureau of Justice Statistics. (There is no more recent report available at this time.)
2. Find your state's page in the state-by-state section. Describe your state's court structure.
3. What is the trial court called? How many trial courts are there? How many appellate judges are there in your state? What is the court of last resort called?
4. Another source that provides similar information is http://www.ncsconline.org/D_Research/Ct_Struct/.

A good rule of thumb is that trial courts decide upon facts, and appellate courts rule on points of law. However, this is not completely accurate because trial courts also make rulings on interpretations of law. The most important thing to remember is that an appeal can only be filed because of an error of law. Appellate courts never retry facts. Thus, the guilt or innocence of a defendant is never the issue, only whether there was some legal procedural error, or violation of a state or federal constitutional right, during the proceedings. Further, even when an error exists, an appellate court may rule that it is "harmless" and did not affect the outcome of the case.

In most states, the intermediate appellate court must review all appeals filed from trial courts (at least in criminal cases). That does not necessarily mean that there is any type of hearing. The court may review the appellate brief and find it is without merit and deny a full hearing. If an intermediate appellate court denies review or an appellant loses their appeal at this level, they can appeal to the court of last resort. In many states, the court of last resort has discretion to review or not review the many appeals filed. In these situations, appeals are reviewed by panels of the full court, and there must be a certain number of justices who vote to hear the case before it receives attention from the full court. Capital cases, however, carry a mandatory appeal and review process.

When an intermediate appellate or court of last resort hears an appeal, oral arguments will be scheduled. In these proceedings, the petitioner's attorney (the one who filed the appeal) and the respondent's attorney (typically the state is the respondent) will present their arguments to the appellate judges and answer questions from them. There are no witnesses or evidence presented because the only issues are points of law.

When a petitioner loses in a court of last resort, there is a possibility that he or she may file a further appeal in the federal court system. This is the case if there is a federal constitutional issue that the state's ruling has not addressed or ruled against. Petitioners must exhaust all state remedies before turning to federal courts. After exhausting state appeals, the appellate attorney may begin again by filing the appeal in federal court. The ultimate court of last resort, of course, is the Supreme Court. There are also tribal courts in many states that are independent of the state in which they reside. These courts adjudicate offenses that take place on Indian reservations and/or that involve members of the tribe. The following is a list of the states that do not have formally recognized tribes and tribal courts: Arkansas, Delaware, Georgia, Hawaii, Illinois, Indiana, Kentucky, Maryland, Missouri, New Hampshire, New Jersey, Ohio, Pennsylvania, Tennessee, Vermont, Virginia, and West Virginia.

PROSECUTORS

A district attorney (prosecutor) is usually an elected official (except in Alaska, Connecticut, the District of Columbia, and New Jersey) [21]. In all but the smallest jurisdictions, there are also assistant prosecutors who also try cases, but are hired and not elected. In larger jurisdictions, they may number in the hundreds, and the elected district attorney never actually prosecutes a case, but rather acts as the policy director and CEO of the office.

There are about 2344 state court prosecutors' offices, employing 78,000 attorneys, investigators, and support staff. This does not include county or city prosecutors who prosecute in courts of limited jurisdiction. Our conception of prosecutors' offices is probably shaped by television and movies, which tend to portray large jurisdictions such as New York City and Los Angeles. In reality, most offices are quite small. In 2005, most prosecutors' offices nationwide employed 10 or fewer people. In some offices, prosecutors served on a part-time basis, maintaining their own private law practice as well. Most prosecutors' offices receive both state and county funding [22]. Table 8.1 provides some information on prosecutors' offices from the most recent report available through the Bureau of Justice Statistics.

In very rare cases, special prosecutors are appointed by the governor or attorney general when it is believed that a local prosecutor has a conflict of interest or the prosecution involves a case that crosses jurisdictional lines. Such special prosecutors can also be found at the federal level. (You may recall that at

Attorney General Eric Holder speaks at a forum on intellectual property theft, December 14, 2010, at the Eisenhower Executive Office Building across from the White House in Washington. *AP Photo*

Table 8.1 State Court Prosecutors' Offices, 2005

Full-Time Offices (Population Served)					
	All offices	**1,000,000 or more**	**250,000-999,999**	**Under 250,000**	**Part-time offices**
Number of offices	2344	42	213	1515	574
Median 2004 population served	36,515	1,475,488	449,685	42,263	12,764
Total staff size	9	419	105	10	3
Salary of chief prosecutor	$85,000	$149,000	$125,000	$95,000	$42,000
Budget for prosecution	$354,755	$33,231,705	$6,034,575	$388,544	$132,586

Source: *D. Rottman, S. Strickland, State Court Organization, Washington, DC, Bureau of Justice Statistics, 2006.*

the federal level Kenneth Starr was a prosecutor investigating charges against President Clinton, and U.S. Attorney Patrick Fitzgerald was appointed to investigate and prosecute the exposure of Valerie Plame as a CIA agent. He eventually obtained a conviction against I. Lewis "Scooter" Libby for lying in the congressional investigation.) In some larger jurisdictions, the prosecutor's office is divided into divisions. The most common divisions are the misdemeanor division and the felony division. There may also be specialized caseloads, such as sexual assault or domestic violence caseloads. Prosecutors may be attached to a specific court and always appear before the same judge in the same courtroom, following a case from first appearance through sentencing. Alternatively, prosecutors may be assigned different stages of the process, so that they may deal with only preliminary hearings or only first appearances and pass the case on to those who specialize in litigation for the trial portion.

Although about 75% of chief prosecutors are full time, in the smallest towns, they may be part-time prosecutors and have a part-time private law practice as well. There may be conflicts of interest when the duty to prosecute an alleged offender conflicts with the prosecutor's duty to clients or social and business contacts. The role of a part-time prosecutor in a small town is very different from the district attorneys in large cities like New York, Chicago, or Houston, which have hundreds of assistant prosecutors.

The role of any prosecutor is quite different from that of the defense attorney. While the defense attorney's role is to protect the rights of the accused, the prosecutor has the ethical duty to "seek justice"—and this does not necessarily translate into "get a conviction." Prosecutors must balance office resources, the relative seriousness of the crime, and the desires/needs of the victim and community when making decisions about whether and how to prosecute. Not all cases that begin with arrest are prosecuted. In fact, prosecutors drop many cases without prosecution, and this decision-making ability is one of the least studied areas of the criminal justice system.

> 🌐 **INTERNET KEY**
>
> For more information about prosecutors, go to a report by the Bureau of Justice Statistics at http://bjs.ojp.usdoj.gov/content/pub/pdf/psc05.pdf.

Why would a prosecutor choose not to pursue prosecution? In most cases, it is because he or she believes there is not enough evidence to obtain a conviction. In other cases, evidence may be present, but the offense is considered not very serious and there is no public pressure for prosecution. The prosecutor has legal discretion to prosecute or not. It is important to remember that not all crimes are always prosecuted "to the fullest extent of the law."

Prosecutors typically do not make as much money as attorneys in private civil practice; their salaries are closer to those of criminal defense attorneys. The largest prosecutors' offices often have graduates of the finest law schools willing to be hired for much less than they might earn in private practice because of the opportunity to practice their litigation skills. An assistant prosecutor in a city such as Houston, New York, or Chicago may try more cases in a year than an average civil attorney tries in a lifetime. The career path of prosecutors is often to spend several years in the prosecutor's office, and then use the skills developed there in a lucrative private litigation practice. In fact, in the most recent survey of prosecutors, 72% reported problems in retaining experienced assistant prosecutors [23].

Each state also has an attorney general who is the state's chief legal officer. Attorneys general may have personnel who enforce child support enforcement; they may have lawyers that represent the state's citizens in consumer protection, antitrust, and utility litigation; they enforce federal and state environmental laws and represent the state and state agencies in criminal appeals and statewide criminal prosecutions. Finally, counties and cities also each have either appointed or elected attorneys who handle criminal cases under these jurisdictions.

> **🌐 INTERNET KEY**
>
> For a Web site that further describes attorneys general, go to www.naag.org/.

DEFENSE ATTORNEYS

Defense attorneys are favorite characters for television and movie script writers. They are portrayed as tireless crusaders for the downtrodden or sleazy "hacks" willing to do anything to help their clients avoid their just punishment. The reality, of course, resembles neither of these two extremes. Defense attorneys, for the most part, help the system work by helping individual defendants navigate the complex and confusing world of the justice system. Clients are more likely to receive due process because of defense attorneys.

Most defense attorneys are not superstars who appear in the newspaper frequently, although there are a few of these celebrities, such as Alan Dershowitz, who is also a professor at Harvard Law School. Defense attorneys tend to be on the lower rungs of earning ladders for graduates of law schools. Criminal law is not a favored specialty of lawyers; less than 10% of all lawyers have a full-time criminal practice. Most attorneys who do take criminal cases also carry a general law practice.

The Supreme Court holding in *Gideon v. Wainwright* (1963) [24] recognized a Sixth Amendment right to an attorney when a defendant was facing a felony conviction, and later, in *Argersinger v. Hamlin* (1972) [25], the Court held that all indigent offenders facing incarceration had a Sixth Amendment right to counsel (an attorney). This requirement meant that states needed to develop ways of providing defense counsel to all defendants facing jail or prison. The two most common ways are appointed counsel systems and

> **🌐 INTERNET KEY**
>
> To find information about your own state's method for delivering indigent defense services, go to http://public.findlaw.com/library/state-public-defenders.html.

public defender offices. All states except Maine have either a state or county public defender system (although most states also have appointed attorneys to supplement the public defenders) [26].

Appointed counsel systems occur when each trial court judge (or the jurisdiction as a whole) holds a list of attorneys approved to be appointed to indigent defendants. Assignments are given on a rotating or other basis. Attorneys get on this list by volunteering or, in a few cases, all attorneys in the jurisdiction are on the list. These attorneys are in private practice and have private clients as well as court appointments.

In public defender systems, the defense attorneys are full-time employees of a public defender office. They may be either county or state employees, or employees of a private nonprofit agency that holds a contract from the state for indigent defense. In 2007, 22 states had state-based public defender offices. Public defender systems are more common in urban areas, while appointed counsel systems are more common in suburban and rural areas. In 2007, there were 957 public defender offices in 49 states and the District of Columbia.

🌐 INTERNET KEY

For more information about public defenders, go to a Bureau of Justice report at http://bjs.ojp.usdoj.gov/content/pub/pdf/spdp07.pdf.

A third form of indigent defense is the contract attorney model. This is similar to the appointed counsel model, except that, instead of distributing cases to all the attorneys on a list, one or two attorneys take all of the indigent cases for a set contract amount. These attorneys may or may not also have a separate private practice, depending on how many cases are part of the indigent caseload. This model has proven to be attractive to some jurisdictions because it may be less expensive than the appointed counsel model and is useful in jurisdictions that do not have enough indigent cases to justify a public defender office.

The general thought is that individuals who are defended by a public defender or appointed counsel do not receive the same quality of legal assistance as those who are able to hire their own private attorneys. While the findings of researchers are mixed, it seems to be the case that indigents are more likely to receive a sentence to jail or prison and are more likely to plead guilty when they have counsel provided to them, but they receive shorter terms than those with privately retained attorneys [27].

Other research indicates that, at least in the federal system, appointed attorneys perform considerably worse than public defenders. They evidently bill for more hours per case, are less qualified, and achieve worse results for their clients. They cost the public, in the aggregate, about $61 million more than if public defenders had taken the cases. Suggested reasons for the difference between appointed attorneys and public defenders are that public defenders have more experience in criminal law and have a better relationship with prosecutors [28]. In another study, it was found that individuals in Harris County

(Houston), Texas, who hired their own attorney never received the death penalty, unlike those with appointed counsel. Further, those who hired attorneys for at least some portion of their defense were significantly less likely to receive the death penalty than those who had no private attorney for any portion of their defense. The authors concluded that the appointment system should be reformed and substituted with a public defender system [29].

In a 2008 report concerning public defense sponsored by the Department of Justice, the Bureau of Justice Assistance, and the National Legal Aid & Defender Association, it was noted that in the last 30 years there had been substantial improvement in the coverage of public defender programs; however, there were still problems. The conclusions included the following:

- There are still large numbers of defendants who never speak to an attorney.
- There are many individuals who receive ineffective counsel.
- There are resource deficits in many states.
- There is intense pressure on defendants and their lawyers to plead guilty.
- There has been an elevation or criminalization of minor infractions that has increased workloads.
- There is little respect for the public defense function in the system [30].

Defendants also have the right to defend themselves. A **pro se defense** is when the defendant chooses to defend himself (or herself). This is very rare, and often the judge will insist that an attorney sit with the defendant to provide legal advice anyway. Judges must balance the right of the individual to use a pro se defense and the need for competent counsel, if for no other reason than to forestall an appeal based on incompetent counsel.

FOCUS ON ETHICS

You are a recently graduated attorney and feel very lucky to have been hired as one of three contract attorneys for the district court in your hometown. While you didn't necessarily think you would ever work as a criminal defense attorney, you know that the experience in the courtroom will be very valuable when you move on and start a practice of your own. One of the indigent defendants assigned to your caseload is a guy who already has two prison terms. He is being prosecuted for "indecency with a child." After interviewing him and reading the police reports, you believe that there are some problems with the prosecution's case. For one thing, the child belonged to the defendant's ex-girlfriend and witnesses are available that will testify that she said she was going to "get even" with him for their break-up. Furthermore, it appears that he was held and questioned by the police without being informed of his *Miranda* warnings. Obviously, as a two-time convict, he knew his rights, but it was possible that this fact alone might be enough to exclude his comments made to police about when he was alone with the child. On the other hand, you don't necessarily believe that he didn't do it, especially because of his history. Also, the judge has indicated that he wants the guy to go away for a long time. In effect, the judge let you know that he doesn't want you to put up a strong defense that might stand in the way of a conviction. What should you do?

JUDGES

As described earlier, judges may be either trial judges in courts of general jurisdiction or courts of limited jurisdiction, or they may be appellate judges in intermediate courts or the court of last resort in the state (the state supreme court).

Judges may be either elected or appointed. About one-third of all state trial judges receive their position through a general nonpartisan election (33.3%). Roughly another third (31.4%) are chosen through some form of merit selection process. Another 17.6% are elected through partisan elections. The rest obtain their judgeships through legislative appointments, gubernatorial selection, or other means [31].

They typically serve fixed terms, although in a few states their terms are for life or at least until retirement age. The **Missouri Plan** is a merit selection process of appointing judges that involves a nominating process by statewide (for appellate) and local (for trial judges) committees. These committees send the nominees' names to the governor, who makes the appointment. The appointee then faces an election after one year, running against his or her own record. While 37 states use some form of nomination process, the remaining states still use general elections. In some of those states, the elections are partisan (with judges running as Democratic, Republican, or Independent), and in others the elections are nonpartisan. The Breaking News box describes observations that even in states that have merit selection processes, judges are feeling the pressure of interest blocks today.

BREAKING NEWS: POLITICAL PRESSURE AND JUDGES

News reports have indicated that judges are feeling the pressure as interest groups target them for unpopular legal decisions. States in which judges are elected have seen judicial elections become as heated as other contests with ever-increasing amounts of money spent to win elections. Even judges in states that have merit selection processes feel the pressure as groups have organized to contest their appointments. It is reported that in the 16 states that have retention elections, the amount of money that will be spent in the 2010 race will equal all the money spent in the last decade. In these states, judges are appointed and then have an election after a year so voters can vote either "yes" or "no" to the judge's continued service. In Iowa, a merit selection state, the decision to uphold same-sex marriages has placed three of the judges as targets of a well-funded right-wing conservative group who seeks to remove them. In Iowa, there have only been four judges removed in nearly 50 years. Whether it is abortion, consumer protection legislation, or same-sex marriage, judges are finding that their decisions have spurred opposition, such as a group in Colorado called "Clear the Bench." In these judicial contests, it appears that competence is less relevant than their past judicial decisions.

Source: A. Sulzberger, *Voters moving to oust judges over decisions, New York Times Online, September 25, 2010. Retrieved 9/25/2010 from http://www.nytimes.com/2010/09/25/us/politics/25judges.html.*

Typically, the constitution and statutes of a state specify residency, age, and legal credentials as requirements to serve as a judge. Many states require judges to receive continuing legal education beyond that necessary for all lawyers in the state. Nineteen states have formal procedures for evaluating the performance of judges.

Trial judges

Trial judges may preside over courts of general jurisdiction or limited jurisdiction. They may be family court judges, juvenile judges, criminal judges, or civil judges; or, in other jurisdictions, they may try all these kinds of cases in the same courtroom. Judges of limited jurisdiction (county courts, municipal courts, justices of the peace) may sit only part-time. Some of these magistrates may not even need to be lawyers to hold the judicial position (although this is rare). Some jurisdictions may occasionally hire retired judges to help with overloaded dockets.

Trial judges are basically like umpires in the justice process. They make decisions on rules of evidence and procedure. If a defendant decides to plead guilty (as the vast majority of defendants do), the judge must ensure that the confession is voluntary and that there is other evidence, in addition to the confession, upon which to convict the defendant. The judge, in these cases, must decide whether to agree with the prosecutor's recommendation for sentencing. Most pleas come after a **plea bargain**, in which the defendant agrees to plead guilty in return for a favorable sentencing recommendation.

In cases that go to trial, the defendant may choose to have a **bench trial**, which means that there is no jury and the case is tried solely to the judge. The judge not only ensures that rules are followed, but also determines guilt or innocence in these trials. Most felony trials, however, include a jury. Judges carry great weight with the jury and jurors may be influenced by any obvious bias the judge displays toward either the defense or the prosecution. The ideal judge is someone who is neutral and objective and makes decisions based on law rather than favoritism.

The judge may be called upon to rule on any pretrial motions, which will be described in the next chapter. It may be the case that one of the attorneys files a motion for **recusal**, asking the judge to step out of the case and assign it to another judge because he or she has a conflict of interest or cannot make an objective decision about the case. Interestingly, it is the judge who gets to rule on his or her own bias in this hearing, although if the attorney loses the motion, and the defendant is convicted, the decision may be appealed.

During the trial, judges rule on objections, based on rules of procedure in that jurisdiction. Some of the more common objections made during a trial are that the evidence does not have a proper foundation (meaning that the attorney has not obtained, through questioning witnesses, the proper level of proof that the item is what it is purported to be), the question asks something that is irrelevant or prejudicial, or the attorney was "leading" the witness (meaning that they were answering the question or suggesting the answer to the witness).

Although the jury determines guilt or innocence, the judge does have the power to throw out a guilty verdict if he or she finds that there is not sufficient evidence to support a judgment of guilt, as a matter of law. If a guilty verdict occurs, the judge may also be obliged to sentence the offender, although in some states juries have this function. Judges (or juries) must sentence within the statutory guidelines for sentencing.

If an offender is sentenced to probation, the judge maintains control over the defendant. Probation officers periodically submit progress reports to the court. The sentencing judge will ultimately be the one to close the case, either by revoking probation and sending the person to prison, by agreeing to an early release, or by recognizing that the offender has served the full term of probation.

Appellate judges

There are about 1335 appellate judges in the country. Their terms range from 4 to 16 years, but Rhode Island judges have a term for life, and judges in Massachusetts and Puerto Rico have terms that last until age 70 (the mandatory retirement age) [32].

Appellate judges may not be as newsworthy as their brethren in trial courts, but their decisions are, in some ways, much more powerful. Appellate courts overturn trial verdicts when they recognize errors of law and/or constitutional violations. Much of their caseload consists of civil appeals, but they also hear criminal appeals. One of the issues, in fact, when appointing or electing a judge, is whether they have any experience in civil and/or criminal law. While civil procedure and criminal procedure rules have many similarities, there are differences and, thus, a civil judge who aspires to become an appellate judge may have had no experience trying or judging criminal law cases, or vice versa.

Typically, appeals are heard by three-judge panels, and, if the three-judge panel denies relief, the petitioner may appeal to have the case heard **en banc**, meaning with the full number of appellate judges, or, in a state with more than one appellate jurisdiction, with all of the justices in that jurisdiction. It is typically from the ranks of state appellate judges that federal justices are selected.

THE FEDERAL SYSTEM

The discussion up to this point has been a description of state court systems, but there is also a parallel federal court system. Recall that federal crimes are listed in the United States Criminal Code. There are federal law enforcement agencies, such as the DEA and FBI, assigned to enforce these laws. When someone is arrested for a federal crime, they will be prosecuted in a federal court. The federal court system is similar to the state court system in that there are trial courts (magistrate courts and U.S. district courts), intermediate appellate courts (courts of appeals), and, finally, the court of last resort, the Supreme Court.

The United States military has its own judicial system. Each of the branches of the military has its own court of military review. Military law is set out in the Uniform Code of Military Justice. Decisions may be appealed to the United States Court of Military Appeals and, ultimately, to the Supreme Court. Procedures, rules of evidence, and even crimes are different in the military justice system. One of the interesting differences is that the defense and the prosecutor for a case are assigned out of the same office (the adjutant general's office).

The United States attorney is the federal equivalent of a district attorney or state prosecutor. There are about 94 U.S. attorneys [33], attached to the 94 U.S. federal district courts, which are the federal trial courts. There are also specialized courts that have limited jurisdiction over matters such as tax and patent law.

In 2007, U.S. attorneys supervised 88,742 cases, down from the 141,212 cases in 2004. Most cases are drug offenses (37%), followed by immigration offenses (20%). Other types of cases prosecuted in federal courts include property offenses (15%) and weapons offenses (10%). About 96% of federal defendants submitted guilty or no-contest pleas [34]. Box 8.2 describes the federal court system.

A federal case can be appealed to the court of appeals. The country is divided into 12 circuits, each with its own court of appeals. Table 8.2 shows the circuit courts of the United States. These justices hear appeals from the federal district courts, as well as state cases that allege a violation of constitutional rights.

All federal judges are nominated by the president after receiving recommendations from the U.S. senators in that jurisdiction. The nominees must go through a confirmation process by the United States Senate. Once confirmed, they may hold their position for life, unless they are impeached by Congress.

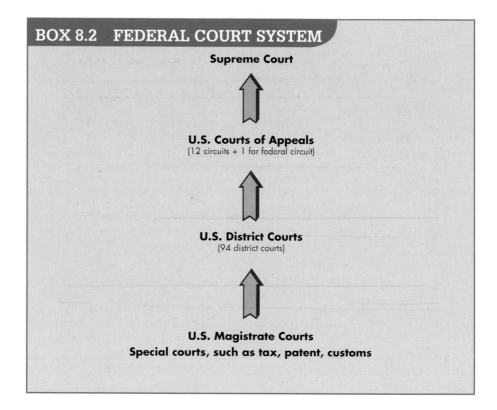

BOX 8.2   FEDERAL COURT SYSTEM

Supreme Court

U.S. Courts of Appeals
(12 circuits + 1 for federal circuit)

U.S. District Courts
(94 district courts)

U.S. Magistrate Courts
Special courts, such as tax, patent, customs

The United States Supreme Court is the highest court in the land. The nine Justices on the Supreme Court hold their position for life. The current members of the court are:

- Chief Justice John Roberts
- Samuel Alito
- Ruth Bader Ginsburg
- Stephen Breyer
- Clarence Thomas
- Anthony Kennedy
- Antonin Scalia
- Sonia Sotomayor
- Elena Kagan

INTERNET KEY

For an interesting Web site on the Supreme Court, go to http://www. supremecourt.gov/.

President Barack Obama appointed Justices Sotomayor and Kagan. President George W. Bush appointed Roberts and Alito. President Bill Clinton appointed Ginsburg and Breyer. President George H.W. Bush appointed Thomas. President Ronald Reagan appointed

Seated left to right: Justice Clarence Thomas, Justice Antonin Scalia, Chief Justice John G. Roberts, Justice Anthony M. Kennedy, Justice Ruth Bader Ginsburg. Standing left to right: Justice Sonia Sotomayor, Justice Stephen G. Breyer, Justice Samuel Anthony Alito, Jr., Justice Elena Kagan. *Collection of the Supreme Court of the United States, Photographer: Steve Petteway*

Kennedy and Scalia. Cases are often decided on a 5-4 vote indicating a strong ideological split on the court with "conservative" justices (Thomas, Scalia, Thomas, and Alito) often voting together and "liberal" justices (Ginsburg, Breyer, Sotomayor, and Kagan) voting together, with Justice Kennedy often the swing vote. Although this is a simplistic description of the Court and sometimes these voting patterns do not predict holdings, it is true that the confirmation of Supreme Court Justices is an extremely partisan affair. Despite the ideal that judges make decisions solely by legal precedent or legal analysis, most people agree that judges' decisions are influenced by their own ideas and belief systems.

The Supreme Court is the only court that was established by the United States Constitution. Article II states:

> The judicial Power of the United States, shall be vested in one supreme Court, and in such inferior Courts as the Congress may from time to time ordain and establish. The Judges, both of the supreme and inferior Courts, shall hold their Offices during good Behavior, and shall, at stated Times, receive for their Services a Compensation which shall not be diminished during their Continuance in Office.

Table 8.2 Federal Judicial Circuits

Circuits	Territory
District of Columbia	District of Columbia
First	Maine, Massachusetts, New Hampshire, Rhode Island, Puerto Rico
Second	Connecticut, New York, Vermont
Third	Delaware, New Jersey, Pennsylvania, Virgin Islands
Fourth	Maryland, North Carolina, South Carolina, Virginia, West Virginia
Fifth	Louisiana, Mississippi, Texas, District of the Canal Zone
Sixth	Kentucky, Michigan, Ohio, Tennessee
Seventh	Illinois, Indiana, Wisconsin
Eighth	Arkansas, Iowa, Minnesota, Missouri, Nebraska, North Dakota, South Dakota
Ninth	Alaska, Arizona, California, Hawaii, Idaho, Montana, Nevada, Oregon, Washington, Guam
Tenth	Colorado, Kansas, New Mexico, Oklahoma, Utah, Wyoming
Eleventh	Alabama, Florida, Georgia

Article III specifies the jurisdiction of the court.

> The judicial Power shall extend to all Cases, in Law and Equity, arising
> under this Constitution, the Laws of the United States, and Treaties
> made, or which shall be made, under their Authority; — to all Cases
> affecting Ambassadors, other public Ministers and Consuls; — to all
> Cases of admiralty and maritime Jurisdiction; — to Controversies to
> which the United States shall be a Party; — to Controversies between
> two or more States; — between a State and Citizens of another State;—
> between Citizens of different States; — between Citizens of the same
> State claiming Lands under Grants of different States, and between a
> State, or the Citizens thereof, and foreign States, Citizens or Subjects.

Article III goes on to specify that, in some cases, the jurisdiction of the Supreme
Court shall be original (meaning that the case can be brought directly), but in
other cases, the jurisdiction is appellate (meaning that the Court can only hear
appeals after the case has been litigated in a lower court).

> In all Cases affecting Ambassadors, other public ministers and Consuls,
> and those in which a State shall be Party, the supreme Court shall
> have original Jurisdiction. In all the other Cases before mentioned,
> the supreme Court shall have appellate jurisdiction, both as to Law
> and Fact, with such Exceptions, and under such Regulations as the
> Congress shall make.

The Court rarely exercises original jurisdiction and almost all case decisions
are those that occur when the Court issues a **writ of certiorari**, which means
to bring the case forward. Because most of the cases appealed to the Supreme
Court fall into the area of discretionary review, the Court does not have to hear
them. When four or more justices agree to hear a case, the Court issues the writ
of certiorari. Typically, the Court will only hear cases when there is a split in
Federal Circuit Courts over a particular legal issue.

The term of the Court begins on the first Monday in October and lasts until
October of the next year. Approximately 8000 petitions are filed with the Court
in the course of a term. In addition, some 1200 applications of various kinds
are filed each year that can be acted upon by a single justice [35]. Of all these
cases, the Court issues written opinions in only about a hundred or so cases.

It is important to note that only decisions of the Supreme Court are clearly
and absolutely "the law of the land." In all other legal questions or issues, you
cannot assume that you know the law in your state and jurisdiction unless you
research case decisions in your particular jurisdiction. In textbooks, for instance,
you may read cases from a court opinion from a federal circuit that does not
encompass your state, or the supreme court of another state, or from a state
intermediate court of appeals from a jurisdiction in your state, but one that

does not include your city or town. In these cases, the holding or the principle of law that is set by the court may or may not be the law in your jurisdiction. The holdings in other jurisdictions are only "persuasive," not "authoritative" when the same legal issue comes up. The Supreme Court's opinions, however, apply instantly and absolutely to all jurisdictions in the country. For this reason, these nine individuals on the Court are sometimes called the most powerful people in the country.

CONCLUSION

In this chapter, we have described the state and federal court systems. State systems typically involve state trial courts of general and limited jurisdiction, intermediate appellate courts, and state courts of last resort. These last courts are the state equivalent of the U.S. Supreme Court. Specialized courts exist, such as family or juvenile court, community courts, drug courts, and domestic violence courts. District attorneys (prosecutors) are usually elected, but their assistant prosecutors are not. Most prosecutors' offices employ less than 10 people, but some large cities have hundreds of prosecutors. Judges may be elected or appointed. If appointed, typically a form of the Missouri Plan is utilized.

The federal court system operates in parallel to state systems, and federal crimes (and civil matters relevant to federal laws or that cross state lines in jurisdiction) are prosecuted in these courts. There are 94 federal districts, each with their own trial court and a U.S. attorney (and assistants) to prosecute federal crimes. Federal cases (and some state cases that allege constitutional issues) can be appealed to federal courts of appeals and, ultimately, to the Supreme Court.

Review Questions

1. Describe the three layers of courts in each state. Describe the two types of trial courts and give examples.
2. Describe three specialized courts.
3. Describe subject matter and geographic jurisdiction.
4. How does the restorative justice approach change the traditional mission of the court system?
5. What are the findings regarding the effectiveness of drug courts?
6. When can you appeal a case? Give examples.
7. What are the three methods for providing defense counsel to indigents? What are the two cases that established the right to counsel for indigents?
8. About how many states still elect their judges? What is the Missouri Plan?
9. Describe the federal court system.
10. Explain the origin and powers of the Supreme Court.

VOCABULARY

bench trial a trial in which there is no jury and the case is tried solely before the judge

community courts may be a court of limited or general jurisdiction and address juvenile and minor criminal cases in a more "restorative" way by trying to solve problems rather than assess guilt and punishment

courts of limited jurisdiction handle specific and limited types of cases, such as municipal ordinances and traffic violations

docket the cases assigned to a particular court

drug courts are typically courts of general jurisdiction, but with a specialized caseload of drug cases

en banc the full number of appellate judges in the jurisdiction

general jurisdiction courts have broad subject matter jurisdiction and typically try felonies and have the power to sentence to state prison

geographic jurisdiction the civil case or crime must have taken place within the geographic boundaries of the court's power

Missouri Plan a method of appointing judges that substitutes a nominating process by nominating committees and appointment by the governor

plea bargain when the defendant agrees to plead guilty in return for a favorable sentencing recommendation

pro se defense when the defendant chooses to defend himself or herself

recusal when a judge steps out of a case and assigns it to another judge because he or she may be biased

restorative justice focus is "problem solving" and involves a range of innovations in the justice system, including alternative sentencing such as restitution and the like

subject matter jurisdiction refers to the type of case that can be heard in each type of court; this is defined by legislation

writ of certiorari "to bring the case forward," is an order to provide the U.S. Supreme Court with the case in order for it to be heard

ENDNOTES

[1] D. Rottman, S. Strickland, State Court Organization, Bureau of Justice Statistics, Washington, DC, 2006, p. 4.

[2] D. Rottman, S. Strickland, State Court Organization, Bureau of Justice Statistics, Washington, DC, 2006, p. 4.

[3] P. Casey, D. Rottman, Problem Solving Courts: Models and Trends, National Center for State Courts, Washington, DC, 2003.

[4] J. Petersilia, Reforming Probation and Parole, American Correctional Association, Lanham, MD, 2002, p. 4.

[5] S. Listwan, J. Sundt, A. Holsinger, E. Latessa, The effect of drug court programming on recidivism: the Cincinnati experience, Crime Delinq. 49(3) (2003) 389–411.

[6] J. Petersilia, Reforming Probation and Parole, American Correctional Association, Lanham, MD, 2002, p. 5.

[7] S. Listwan, J. Sundt, A. Holsinger, E. Latessa, The effect of drug court programming on recidivism: the Cincinnati experience, Crime Delinq. 49(3) (2003) 389–411.

[8] S. Listwan, J. Sundt, A. Holsinger, E. Latessa, The effect of drug court programming on recidivism: the Cincinnati experience, Crime Delinq. 49(3) (2003) 400.

[9] D. Marlow, D. Festinger, P. Lee, K. Dugosh, K. Benasutti, Matching judicial supervision to clients' risk status in drug court, Crime Delinq. 52(1) (2006) 52–76.

[10] M. Carey, W. Finigan, A detailed cost analysis in a mature drug court setting, J. Contemp. Crim. Just. 20(3) (2004) 315–338.

[11] S. Johnson, D. Hubbard, E. Latessa, Drug courts and treatment: lessons to be learned from the 'what works' literature, Correct. Q. Manag. 4(4) (2000) 70–77.

[12] A. Gover, J. MacDonald, G. Alpert, Combating domestic violence: findings from an evaluation of a local domestic violence court, Criminol. Publ. Policy 3(1) (2003) 109–132.

[13] L. Levy, M. Steketee, S. Keilitz, Lessons Learned in Implementing an Integrated Domestic Violence Court, National Center for State Courts, Williamsburg, VA, 2001.

[14] A. Gover, J. MacDonald, G. Alpert, Combating domestic violence: findings from an evaluation of a local domestic violence court, Criminol. Publ. Policy 3(1) (2003) 111.

[15] A. Gover, J. MacDonald, G. Alpert, Combating domestic violence: findings from an evaluation of a local domestic violence court, Criminol. Publ. Policy 3 (1)(2003) 119.

[16] W. Pitts, E. Givens, S. McNeeley, The need for a holistic approach to specialized domestic violence court programming: evaluating offender rehabilitation needs and recidivism, Juv. Fam. Court. J. 60(3) (2009) 1–22.

[17] Bureau of Justice Statistics. Retrieved 6/1/2007 from http://www.ojp.usdoj.gov/bjs/.

[18] S. Rosenmerkel, M. Durose, D. Farole, Felony Sentences in State Courts, 2006, Statistical Tables, Bureau of Justice Statistics, Washington DC, 2009.

[19] Bureau of Justice Statistics. Retrieved 6/1/2007 from http://www.ojp.usdoj.gov/bjs/.

[20] D. Rottman, S. Strickland, State Court Organization, Bureau of Justice Statistics, Washington, DC, 2006.

[21] C. DeFrances, Prosecutors in State Courts, Bureau of Justice Statistics, Washington, DC, 2001.

[22] D. Rottman, S. Strickland, State Court Organization, Bureau of Justice Statistics, Washington, DC, 2006.

[23] S. Perry, Prosecutors in State Courts, Bureau of Justice Statistics, Washington, DC, 2006.

[24] 373 U.S. 335, 1963.

[25] 407 U.S. 321, 1972.

[26] L. Langton, D. Farole, State Public Defender Programs, Bureau of Justice Statistics, Washington, DC, 2010.

[27] C. Harlow, Defense Counsel in Criminal Cases, Bureau of Justice Statistics, Washington, DC, 2000.

[28] A. Liptak, Study reveals gap in performance of public defenders, Austin American-Statesman, July 14, 2007, A9.

[29] S. Philips, Legal disparities in the capital of capital punishment, J. Crim. Law Criminol. 99(3) (2009) 717–756.

[30] Bureau of Justice Assistance, Public Defense Reform since Gideon: Improving the Administration of Justice by Building on Our Successes and Learning from Our Failures, Bureau of Justice Assistance, Washington, DC, 2008.

[31] American Judicature Society, Judicial Selection in the States, American Judicature Society, Des Moines, IA, 2004.

[32] Bureau of Justice Statistics. Retrieved 6/1/2007 from http://www.ojp.usdoj.gov/bjs/.

[33] U.S. Department of Justice, United States Attorneys. Retrieved 6/1/2007 from http://www.usdoj.gov/usao/offices/usa_listings2.html#n.

[34] Bureau of Justice Statistics. Retrieved 6/1/2007 and 10/1/2010 from http://www.ojp.usdoj.gov/bjs/.

[35] Supreme Court of the United States. Retrieved 6/1/2007 from http://www.supremecourtus.gov/about/briefoverview.pdf.

CHAPTER 9

Due Process: Arrest through Sentencing

- Due process refers to the protections designed to minimize governmental error in the deprivation of life, liberty, or property.
- Due process rights are created by the Fifth and Fourteenth Amendments to the Constitution.
- The steps of the criminal justice system include arrest, booking, first appearance, preliminary hearing, arraignment, trial, and sentencing.
- An indictment is the charging document used by grand juries, while the information is the charging document of prosecutors.
- Plea bargaining occurs in more than 90% of all cases.
- A trial includes pretrial motions, jury voir dire, opening statements, direct examinations, cross-examinations, rebuttal witnesses, and closing statements.
- The sentencing hearing has been determined to be a "critical stage" of the proceeding; therefore, a Sixth Amendment right to an attorney exists.
- The goals of sentencing include punishment, incapacitation, rehabilitation, and deterrence.

CONTENTS

DUE PROCESS

What is the purpose of the court process? Obviously, we expect the courts to determine guilt or innocence and assess punishment, but the most important function of the court is to minimize or avoid errors in identifying and punishing offenders. Many people are impatient with the "slow wheels" of justice and the many rules and appeals that must be adhered to before punishment can commence. There is a very good reason for such procedures, however, and the reason is to prevent error. Recall that the concept of **due process** refers to procedural protections that guard against errors when the government seeks to deprive anyone of life, liberty, or property.

Due process is perhaps the most important civil right guaranteed to us by our Constitution. We have certain protections when governmental actors want to take something from us, whether it is life, liberty, or property. These protections don't stop the deprivation, but they do make it more likely that government actors make these decisions in a fair, unbiased, and non-arbitrary manner. Before being punished, for instance, criminal defendants deserve a fair trial that is designed to minimize any chance that the defendant is innocent. Even after conviction, offenders have some due process rights that remain before further deprivations during the correctional process.

The Fifth Amendment guarantees due process rights to us, as citizens of the United States, against any deprivations that occur through the actions of the federal government. Similar due process rights are incorporated through the Fourteenth Amendment to us as state citizens, guarding against actions by state actors (which includes local municipal police).

> Fifth Amendment. No person shall be held to answer for a capital, or otherwise infamous crime, unless on a presentment or indictment of a Grand Jury, except in cases arising in the land or naval forces, or in the Militia, when in actual service in time of War or public danger; nor shall any person be subject for the same offence to be twice put in jeopardy of life or limb; nor shall be compelled in any criminal case to be a witness against himself, nor be deprived of life, liberty, or property, without due process of law; nor shall private property be taken for public use, without just compensation.

> Fourteenth Amendment. All persons born or naturalized in the United States and subject to the jurisdiction thereof, are citizens of the United States and of the State wherein they reside. No State shall make or enforce any law which shall abridge the privileges or immunities of citizens of the United States; nor shall any State deprive any person of life, liberty, or property, without due process of law; nor deny to any person within its jurisdiction the equal protection of the laws…

Due process is not a static concept. What is considered appropriate due process depends on the nature of the deprivation. First, something must be identified as a "protected liberty interest." This means that whatever the state or federal government wants to take away or do to a person must affect a protected interest. One's life is always a protected liberty interest, as is one's liberty. Any deprivation of these will always deserve some due process. However, some things are not protected. If it is not a protected liberty interest, then no due process is necessary. For example, prisoners have no right to be in any particular prison, so they have no procedural protections when prison authorities decide to transfer them, even if it is to a harsher prison [1]. On the other hand, if officials want to quarantine a citizen because of an infectious disease, the law allowing such confinement also specifies the process due before such a deprivation of liberty can occur. In general, due process is designed to minimize governmental errors in any decision to deprive anyone of life, liberty, or property.

Once it is decided that the object of the deprivation is a protected liberty interest, the question becomes: "What process is due?" Due process is a continuum and the greater the deprivation, the more process is due, while the less serious the deprivation, the less due process is required. So, for instance, when the government attempts to take away your property, as in an IRS action, or when you are denied Social Security benefits, then some due process applies, but it is much less than that required before the government can take away your life with a death sentence. The reason is obvious—the more serious the deprivation, the more important it is to make sure that no errors are made. Therefore, more steps exist to make sure the decision is accurate. Due process never protects you against governmental deprivations. The purpose is to protect *against errors* in the decision to deprive. Thus, the steps before a long prison sentence or an execution are taken to ensure that the guilty verdict is accurate and the punishment just. Due process is not limited to criminal justice applications. Eminent domain, for instance, is a procedure whereby the government has the power to take away one's land; however, there are due process requirements, including a public hearing and finding that the public benefit outweighs the loss to the individual. Also, the landowner must receive a fair market value before his land is taken.

Obviously, when a person is punished by the criminal justice system, the government must meet the demands of due process. In Box 9.1, showing the continuum of due process, we see that punishments range from the most serious (execution) to the least serious (fines). Criminal defendants have certain rights to a fair trial guaranteed by the Sixth Amendment. The Sixth Amendment states that the accused deserves a speedy and public trial, by an impartial jury. Further, each defendant has a right to be informed of the nature of the charges, to have the opportunity to confront and cross-examine the accusers and witnesses, and to have the assistance of counsel. Sentencing has been determined to be part of the trial process; therefore, the right to counsel continues through the sentencing hearing.

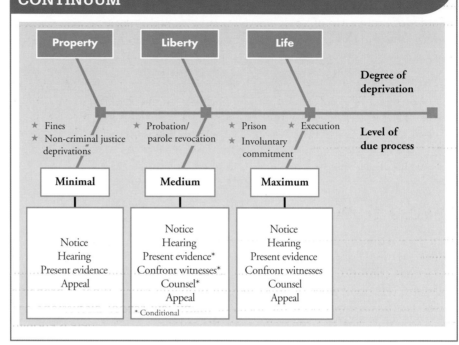

BOX 9.1 FOURTEENTH AMENDMENT DUE PROCESS CONTINUUM

It should be understood, however, that the Sixth Amendment "trial rights" are only an example of due process. The framers of the Constitution evidently thought it necessary to specifically identify the rights of the individual when facing the awesome power of the government.

> Sixth Amendment. In all criminal prosecutions, the accused shall enjoy the right to a speedy and public trial, by an impartial jury of the State and district wherein the crime shall have been committed, which district shall have been previously ascertained by law, and to be informed of the nature and cause of the accusation; to be confronted with the witnesses against him; to have compulsory process for obtaining witnesses in his favor, and to have the Assistance of Counsel for his defence.

Indeed, the criminal justice system is only one example of due process. Any time the government interferes with the life, liberty, or property of an individual, due process applies. The rights provided by the Sixth Amendment end at the point of sentencing; however, due process protections (from the Fourteenth and Fifth Amendments) apply even after sentencing. The rights of probationers, parolees, and others are determined by the nature of the deprivation. In a series of court cases, the Supreme Court has dealt with a variety of issues regarding how much process is due when the government seeks to deprive a criminal offender of some form of liberty interest *after* sentencing, such as being moved to punitive segregation, having probation or parole revoked, or losing "good time."

Due process also applies before the trial. Pretrial diversion, being held before booking, and being arrested implicate due process rights because they involve various types of deprivations. In this chapter, we will examine the steps of the criminal justice process from arrest through sentencing, but with an eye to these steps as they represent deprivations, and the due process rights attached to each step to protect us from governmental error.

ARREST TO TRIAL

An arrest is a deprivation of liberty; therefore, due process applies. What process is due? Before an arrest can be made, there must be **probable cause** that the suspect has committed a specific crime. Arrests can be made with or without a warrant, but both types of arrest require probable cause. What is probable cause? The answer has been the focus of many law school discussions and courtroom speeches, but, generally, probable cause means that there is enough evidence to indicate that the offender is "probably" guilty.

Recall that police officers can also temporarily detain individuals in **investigative detentions**. These brief deprivations of liberty only require reasonable suspicion. The reason the level of proof is less is because the level of deprivation is lower. The Supreme Court has not established a bright-line test of what is a reasonable period of detention [2]; however, lower court case decisions have drawn the parameters of what is considered reasonable. For instance, is being held for 2 hours on the side of the road while the police officer waits for a drug dog to inspect the car for drugs a reasonably short period or an unreasonable deprivation of liberty? To know the answer to that question, you would have to do legal research in your jurisdiction. If the length of the detention becomes unreasonable, and the person is not free to leave, then the deprivation becomes a de facto arrest. If the police officer does not meet the probable cause standard, then the arrest is an illegal deprivation of liberty.

The legal remedy for an improper arrest is that any evidence obtained directly from that arrest can be excluded under the exclusionary rule. If maliciousness can be proven, an individual subject to a false arrest may also pursue a civil judgment against the individual officer, and even the department, if there was complicity on the part of superiors.

Booking

Booking typically involves transporting the suspect to the lockup or county jail and filling out appropriate paperwork before the individual enters the facility. Booking is a due process step only in the sense that some errors of identity may be discovered at this point when fingerprints are taken. In rare cases, individuals are arrested because of outstanding warrants for others with the same name and birth date. If fingerprints are on file for the true offender, the booking process may be instrumental in discovering this mistake. Generally, however, booking is an administrative procedure to accommodate the needs of the jail or confinement facility. Individuals may also be kept in **lockups** for a short period. These temporary holding cells are in police stations.

Initial appearance

As mentioned earlier, every person taken into custody must see a magistrate within a reasonable period, usually within 48 hours. In *Riverside v. McLaughlin* [3], the Supreme Court ruled that, unless there were special circumstances, the initial hearing must take place within 48 hours of arrest. This is in order to ensure that the detention of the individual is legal, that is, that the charging documents are in order, there is probable cause for the arrest, and there is no clear abuse of power. Generally, this hearing is a fairly *pro forma* experience.

One of the major functions of the initial appearance is to notify the accused of the charges against him or her. One of the first elements of due process is notice. It is impossible to defend yourself unless you know what it is you are being accused of. The accused is usually provided with a copy of the complaint or charging document at this point. The magistrate also recites the *Miranda* warnings again to make sure that the defendant understands them.

The hearing magistrate, who may be a judge of any level from municipal court to state district court, will begin to assess whether the accused is indigent and will need an attorney provided by the state. Jurisdictions typically use some form of a questionnaire that asks the defendant to show assets and debts in order to determine **indigency**, which simply means without appreciable assets. The other major function of the hearing is to assess bail or offer some other form of pretrial release.

Bail or release on recognizance

The adjudicatory process sometimes takes months or even years to complete. Until it is over, it is obviously important that the suspect/defendant remain in the jurisdiction. For this reason, many are kept in jail until a conviction, dismissal, or acquittal occurs. However, if other means are sufficient to ensure that the individual does not disappear, then pretrial detention is unnecessary. The bail hearing is the due process designed to minimize error in the decision regarding this deprivation of liberty. The judge determines how likely it is that the defendant will **abscond** (escape the jurisdiction), and then determines whether to offer a pretrial release option, and/or what level of bail is the lowest necessary to ensure presence at trial.

It must be understood that bail is merely a way to ensure presence at trial. There is no constitutional right to bail, although the Eighth Amendment prohibits excessive bail.

> Eighth Amendment. Excessive bail shall not be required, nor excessive fines imposed, nor cruel and unusual punishments inflicted.

The individual pledges money and/or property that is forfeited if they do not appear. Bail is supposed to be set based on the threat of escape. More serious crimes carry with them more serious punishments; therefore, bail is set higher because it is assumed that defendants have more reason to run when facing more serious punishments.

The amount of bail for each suspect is determined not only by the seriousness of the crime, but also by the characteristics of the defendant. Homeownership, employment, and residential stability indicate that the suspect is a low risk for flight (unless the crime is very serious); however, if the offender is unemployed, has no family in the area, and has no place to stay prior to trial, there is a high probability that he or she will flee. Of course, there is also the high probability that they cannot afford bail either, and so these individuals would probably remain in jail.

There are a variety of bail/surety alternatives involving the courts and/or private bail bonds providers:

1. Direct/full bail
2. Private bail bonds—secured (requiring collateral) or unsecured
3. Court surety programs—secured (requiring collateral) or unsecured
4. Release on recognizance

Some defendants may be able to post the full amount of bail; however, most do not have the ability to offer that amount of cash. Most often, defendants or their families contract with bail bonds agents who often demand collateral from the defendant (i.e., house, car, money) in return for the bond agent signing a promissory note to the court. If the defendant does not appear, the bond agent must pay the full amount of the bail. Bond agents receive a fee even if the defendant appears; thus, even if the defendant is acquitted of all charges or the charges are dropped, they still have to pay the bond agent for the right to be released prior to court proceedings. In other instances, bond agents do not require collateral; they take on the risk of having to pay the court the full amount if the defendant absconds. In return for their assumption of this risk, the bond fee may be higher.

In some jurisdictions, the court cuts out the private bond agents and allows the defendant to offer the collateral directly to the court, along with a percentage (typically 10%), of the full amount of bail. If the defendant does not appear, then the deposit and the property are forfeited. In a very few jurisdictions, courts offer an unsecured bond option where the defendant promises to pay the full amount but it is unsecured by collateral. In both types of these court surety programs, if the defendant does appear, he or she pays only a small administrative fee. These programs, where they exist, save defendants quite a bit of money. Even in the areas where there are court surety programs, private bail bonds agents still have a role because defendants typically must meet fairly stringent background characteristics in order to be eligible for the **court surety program**, and all others who have bail granted must resort to the private vendor if they want to be released prior to trial.

The problem is that many defendants do not have any collateral. They do not have financial resources to equal the bail amount and, therefore, are not eligible for programs that require collateral. Thus, it is argued that the poor spend pretrial time in jail while those who have money do not, regardless of their risk of flight. That does not seem fair; thus, back in the 1960s, the Vera Institute of Justice funded the Manhattan Bail Project. This was the first formal **release on recognizance (ROR) program**. Defendants who could not afford bail but who seemed to be good risks were identified. In the course of one study period (1961-1964), the project evaluated 10,000 defendants for release; 4000 were recommended for release; 2195 were released; and only 15 did not show up for a court appearance. In general, ROR programs find that the failure-to-appear rates for those in the program are similar to those on bail [4].

In a study of pretrial release in 75 of the largest counties between 1990 and 2004, it was found that 62% of felony defendants were released prior to their case disposition. Beginning in the late 1990s, financial forms of prerelease became more common than nonfinancial (bail was more common than ROR). Most of those who were not released (five out of six) had bail set, but could not meet the financial conditions. The study also found that about a third of all pretrial releases were charged with misconduct, about a quarter for failure to appear, and about a sixth for a new offense. Characteristics associated with the likelihood of committing a new crime included being under age 21, having a prior arrest record, having a prior felony conviction, being released on an unsecured bond, or being part of an emergency release to relieve jail crowding. About 50% of those who were released on some form of emergency release had some form of misconduct, followed by 30% of those who were released on an unsecured bond. About a quarter of those who failed to appear were still fugitives after 1 year [5].

In 1984, Congress passed the Federal Bail Reform Act [6]. This bill allowed for the preventive detention of federal defendants. **Preventive detention is when the individual is incarcerated before trial, not because of a fear that they will abscond, but because of a perceived risk to the public if they are in the community.** With the federal preventive detention measure, judges can consider the offense, the weight of the evidence, the history and character of the defendant, ties to the community, drug history, and the nature and seriousness of danger to the community. They may determine that the risk to the public is too great to allow the offender to remain in the community prior to trial, and the offender will be held without bail. This seems to be contrary to the due process concept of "innocent until proven guilty," but there is at least some due process in that there is a separate preventive detention hearing where the magistrate weighs the risk and makes the determination.

The power to deny bail and hold under the preventive detention bill was challenged in *United States v. Salerno* [7]. The Supreme Court upheld the right of the federal government to hold individuals without bail, finding that, although the Eighth Amendment prohibited excessive bail, it did not prohibit a determination that no bail would be offered. The federal preventive detention power is held by federal judges and used for federal defendants. Your state probably has similar legislation allowing for the preventive detention of suspects in state prosecutions.

Preliminary hearing

The preliminary hearing may also be called the preliminary examination, probable cause hearing, bindover hearing, or some other term. This type of hearing is sometimes combined with the initial hearing, but more often it takes place several days later. While defendants would not necessarily have an attorney at the initial appearance, they must have one at the preliminary hearing.

As stated before, the initial appearance is a due process step to identify whether any clear abuse of power has occurred and to establish bail so that the accused might have the opportunity to remain free during the adjudication process. In the preliminary hearing, a judge or a magistrate rules on the strength of evidence by determining whether the prosecutor has shown that there is probable cause the defendant committed the crimes charged. The defense is not obligated to do anything at a preliminary hearing. If they choose, they can present evidence or witnesses, and they may cross-examine prosecution witnesses, but it is solely the prosecutor's burden to prove that there is enough evidence to go forward with the prosecution.

Defense attorneys utilize the preliminary hearing as a tool of discovery. Discovery involves finding out about the evidence the prosecutor plans to use at trial. The preliminary hearing gives the defense a brief introduction to the evidence the prosecutor has, whether that be forensic evidence, witness testimony, or expert reports. On the other hand, prosecutors tend to provide only enough of their evidence in order to convince the judge that there is probable cause.

If the charges are dismissed at this point, the prosecutor is free to continue to try to make a case. **Double jeopardy**—the right not to be tried for the same offense—does not "attach" or become an issue until a jury is empaneled. About half of cases are dismissed before trial, although some are refiled when there is more evidence [8].

Information or grand jury indictment (methods of charging)

Many people are confused about the difference between a grand jury and a petit jury. A petit jury is the type of jury you see in the courtroom determining guilt or innocence. You will not usually ever see a grand jury. These individuals are selected by the presiding or administrative judge and tend to be "good citizens known to the court." They sit for a month, 6 months, or even a year, for one day or an afternoon a week. The grand jury listens to cases brought before them by the prosecutor. The prosecutor may bring in witnesses to question, or just describe the evidence in the case, and then they determine whether there is probable cause to go forward.

If a grand jury decides that there is probable cause, they return an **indictment**. It is the charging instrument of the grand jury. If they do not believe that the prosecutor has proven probable cause, they will **no bill** the case, meaning that there is no indictment. Not all states have grand juries. The Fifth Amendment guarantees the right of grand jury review to federal defendants, but the right has not been "incorporated" to state citizens (those facing prosecution by states). Only about half of the states use grand juries. In some of these states, the right, at least for felony defendants, is guaranteed by the state constitution (New York, Ohio, and Texas). In other states, there is an option to go to the grand jury for indictment; otherwise, the prosecutor will issue the charging instrument.

The other method of charging is an **information**. An information is the charging instrument issued by the prosecutor when a grand jury indictment is not used. There is still due process because the prosecutor has had to show probable cause to a magistrate or a judge in the preliminary hearing. If the prosecutor is successful in proving probable cause at the preliminary hearing, he or she will issue an information charging the defendant and setting the stage for trial.

Arraignment and plea bargaining

The next step in the proceedings is the arraignment. Here, the defendant is formally notified of the charges against him or her and asked for a plea. If the defendant accepts a plea bargain, the arraignment may become the end of the process with the judge accepting the plea and setting punishment. As you probably know, about 90% of criminal defendants plead guilty. Most do so in return for a recommendation for a reduced sentence. Judges are not bound to accept the prosecutor's recommendation for sentencing, but they do so in the vast majority of cases. If a judge takes a plea, typically, the only evidence is an affidavit of the defendant admitting guilt. Attached to this legal document is the prosecutor's recommendation for sentencing. If the judge does not agree to the recommendation, the defendant has a right to withdraw the confession. The prosecutor is also barred from agreeing to a sentence and then retracting the agreement once he or she has obtained a confession. On the other hand, the Supreme Court has generally upheld cases where the defendant was forced to choose between a plea bargain and the possibility of the death penalty.

Although plea bargaining has been widely criticized, the interesting thing is that it is criticized by both sides of the political spectrum. Conservatives criticize plea bargaining as resulting in lenient sentences, while liberals criticize it as violating the presumption of "innocent until proven guilty," and creating pressure for innocent suspects to plead guilty. Plea bargaining allows the system to dispose of a tremendous number of cases without the expense of further adjudication.

In this July 26, 2007, file photo, Atlanta Falcons quarterback Michael Vick leaves the federal courthouse in Richmond, Virginia following his arraignment. *AP Photo/ Haraz N. Ghanbari*

Pretrial motions

Typically, after the arraignment, but before the beginning of the trial, if the case isn't plea bargained, there may be a number of pretrial motions. A **motion** is simply a request that the judge order something to be done or not done. For instance, the defense may file a motion to exclude evidence. The defense attorney would have to show either that the evidence was obtained illegally and should be excluded, or that the evidence is more prejudicial than probative (meaning helpful to prove). Generally, prior prison sentences or prior accusations are excluded because they are highly prejudicial and don't prove that the defendant did this particular crime, although, in some cases such evidence might come in as evidence of a pattern of criminal behavior. The motion is a **motion in limine**, which is a motion to bar the mention of something that might be prejudicial during the trial, but has no bearing on guilt or innocence in the case, such as a prior prison term.

Another pretrial motion is a **change of venue**, which is a request for the trial to be moved to another jurisdiction because of a belief that any jurors from the locale where the crime took place would be too biased to render a fair verdict. This is also a motion typically filed by the defense.

Either side might, but rarely does, file a motion for the judge to **recuse** him- or herself. This motion basically argues that the judge is not able to conduct the trial in a fair and unbiased manner because of some conflict of interest. The attorney who files a recusal motion hopes that the judge will grant it and remove him- or her-self from the case and give it to another judge.

Other pretrial motions judges may be called upon to decide are motions for severance of defendants when two or more defendants are being charged and tried together, but a defense attorney wants to separate out his or her defendant to be tried separately. Another motion is to force discovery, when the defense believes the prosecution has something that they are not sharing and the defense has a legal right to have access to it. Finally, perhaps the most common motion is a motion for continuance when one side or the other requests that the trial date be delayed for some reason.

TRIAL

If there is no plea agreement, a criminal case will end up in trial. Actual trials usually don't have the same drama as television trials, but there is a reason why they are used so frequently by scriptwriters. Most cases that go to trial are when the defendant has been accused of murder, rape, or another serious crime, and is facing a long prison sentence or perhaps even a death sentence. In a way, defense attorneys and prosecutors are like dramatists themselves in the way they put witnesses on the stand to tell the story that they want the jury to believe.

INTERNET KEY

For an interesting Web site about famous trials throughout history, go to http://www.law.umkc.edu/faculty/projects/ftrials/ftrials.htm.

In a criminal case, the state has the burden of proving the guilt of the accused beyond a reasonable doubt. That means that the prosecution has the responsibility to prove each of the elements of the crime with which the accused is charged. For example, the crime of burglary generally has these elements: breaking and entering, the dwelling, of another, with intent to commit a felony therein.

If the prosecution fails to prove any element of the crime beyond a reasonable doubt, but proves the other elements, the accused may sometimes be found guilty of a lesser crime. But ordinarily, if the prosecutor is unable to prove all elements beyond a reasonable doubt, the person charged cannot be convicted of the crime. Also, recall that the prosecutor must also prove that the offense took place within the geographic jurisdiction of the court.

In a civil case the degree of proof is a "preponderance of the evidence"; but in a criminal case, the degree of proof is "beyond a reasonable doubt." In some states, the exact wording of the charge to the jury dealing with the standard of proof is stated by statute. In other states, there is no such requirement, and in fact, the judge does not have to explain the term at all.

The "beyond a reasonable doubt" standard is a constitutional requirement. In 1970, the Supreme Court left no doubt about the requirement in the holding of *In re Winship*:

> Lest there remain any doubt about the constitutional stature of the reasonable-doubt standard, we explicitly hold that the Due Process Clause protects the accused against conviction except on proof beyond a reasonable doubt of every fact necessary to constitute the crime with which he is charged [9].

In most cases, the defense has no burden of proof at all, and can merely remain silent and argue that the prosecutor has not proven beyond a reasonable doubt that the defendant committed the crime. In certain cases, however, the defense may argue an **affirmative defense**, such as coercion, self-defense, entrapment, mistake, alibi, or insanity. In these cases, the defendant's attorney must offer proof (usually by a preponderance) before the jury can consider the defense [10]. For instance, in many states, once a defendant proves his or her insanity by a preponderance of evidence, the prosecution has the ultimate burden of disproving insanity (by the beyond a reasonable doubt standard). The jury instructions will indicate that the jury must consider whether the defendant is insane and whether the prosecutor proved beyond a reasonable doubt that the defendant was not. In 1984, as part of the Comprehensive Crime Control Act, Congress enacted legislation titled the Insanity Defense Reform Act of 1984. This section of the Code shifts the burden of proof to the defendant in federal prosecutions and sets the level at *clear and convincing*, a level of proof higher than preponderance, but lower than beyond a reasonable doubt [11].

In other situations in which the defendant claims an affirmative defense, the state may require that the defense be proven by either a preponderance or clear and convincing evidence. The Supreme Court in 1987 upheld an Ohio law that required the defendant to prove self-defense by a preponderance of evidence [12]. Although the defendant may be required to meet the preponderance or clear and convincing burden to submit the defense to the jury, it is still up to the prosecutor to prove beyond a reasonable doubt that the defendant is guilty of each element. In our Focus on Crime, we will examine homicide, a crime that usually results in a trial because of the seriousness of the offense and resulting punishment.

FOCUS ON CRIME: HOMICIDE

Homicide, as it is represented by national statistics, includes murder and non-negligent manslaughter and is defined as the willful killing of another. The homicide rate has been decreasing since the mid-1990s except for a few years of spikes (e.g., the chart shows those killed in the 9/11 attacks). One source of information about homicide is the Bureau of Justice Statistics (the source of the chart). However, the National Crime Victim Survey does not provide any information about homicide. Another source is the Uniform Crime Reports, published by the Federal Bureau of Investigation. Homicide is one of the nine "index crimes" of the UCR and trend and rate information is available. In addition, the FBI also publishes "Supplementary Homicide Reports," which provide more information about the crime.

In the 2009 report of crimes, the FBI reports that 77% of homicide victims were men. About half (48.7%) of victims were white, with about the same percentage black (48.6%), and the remainder of other races. About half (48.6%) of homicides were single offender/single victim incidents. As for offenders, most were men (89.7%), and 51.7% were black (a substantial percentage of homicide offenders were unknown; therefore, race and gender could not be established). About 71% involved firearms. About a quarter of homicides involved family members and about half of victims were killed by someone they knew of the homicides where relationships between victim and offender were known. In about 43% of the cases, there was no information on the victim–offender relationship. The most common motive for homicides (of the cases where this information was recorded) was arguments (41%). Only 22% of homicides occurred during other felonies (rape, robbery, burglary, etc.).

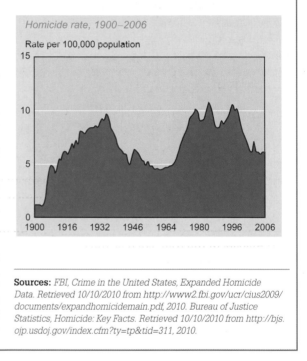

Homicide rate, 1900–2006

Rate per 100,000 population

Sources: *FBI, Crime in the United States, Expanded Homicide Data. Retrieved 10/10/2010 from http://www2.fbi.gov/ucr/cius2009/documents/expandhomicidemain.pdf, 2010. Bureau of Justice Statistics, Homicide: Key Facts. Retrieved 10/10/2010 from http://bjs.ojp.usdoj.gov/index.cfm?ty=tp&tid=311, 2010.*

Jury panels and voir dire

As you know, the Sixth Amendment gives criminal defendants the right to a trial by a jury of their peers. This has been interpreted by a line of court cases to mean that the jury pool must be pulled in such a way as to not clearly exclude any particular group, not necessarily that the jury panel represent the demographic characteristics of the defendant.

You may have been called to jury duty. Typically, jurisdictions use voter registration, driver's licenses, or motor vehicle registration lists to pull jury panels. Once called to perform jury duty, you may or may not actually serve on a jury. Depending on the jurisdiction, you may be on call for a day or a week (perhaps having the option to call in each morning to check to see if you are needed). If a judge in that jurisdiction is starting a trial, he or she will call for a jury panel of up to 50 people (depending on the case, the number of peremptory challenges, and the size of the jury in that jurisdiction).

Most jurisdictions allow for certain exemptions from jury duty. If one has minor children at home, is a full-time student, or is past a certain age, they are generally exempt. Some states have automatic occupation exemptions; others do not. Typically, jury members must be citizens, not have a criminal record, and be of "sound mind."

We tend to think that juries must be 12 individuals who vote unanimously to convict the defendant, but there is no constitutional right to a 12-person jury [13]. States may require only eight people to be on a jury (Arizona and Utah), or six (Connecticut and Florida), at least in noncapital cases. There is also no constitutional right to have a unanimous verdict. Some states do not require unanimous jury verdicts (Louisiana and Oregon) [14].

After the jury panel has been seated, the defense and prosecuting attorneys have a chance to examine the jury cards that jury panel members have filled out. These provide quite a bit of information about each panel member, including marital status, age, occupation, income, number of children, and so on. A translation of **voir dire** is something like "to see to say," but it basically means to speak the truth and it is the process by which attorneys quiz prospective jurors to find out if their biases prevent them from judging the evidence fairly. The first question that is asked is whether jury members know any of the principal players in the trial, such as the victim, the offender, either attorney, or the judge. Then attorneys ask questions relevant to the particular case. For instance, if the defendant was charged with negligent manslaughter because he killed someone in an accident after a night of drinking, the defense attorney is going to want to know the drinking habits of the prospective jurors and whether any of them had a relative who had been killed by a drunk driver. Attorneys may ask any questions that may uncover any biases that prospective jurors may have either for or against the defendant.

State statutes set the number of **peremptory challenges** for the prosecutor and the defense attorney. Peremptory challenges allow the attorney to reject the juror without having to show a particular reason. However, the attorney cannot use race as a reason to reject someone. The Supreme Court said in *Batson v. Kentucky* [15] that attorneys who used race as a reason to reject prospective jurors violated the equal protection clause of the Fourteenth Amendment. In subsequent cases, the Court also rejected the use of race by the defendant (as opposed to the prosecutor as in *Batson*) and gender. **Challenges for cause** are unlimited, but there must be a reason why the juror would be biased in the trial. The attorney has to state what the objection is, and the judge will consider the challenge and agree and dismiss the juror, or disagree and allow the juror to remain.

After each attorney has identified the jurors he or she has rejected under the peremptory challenges, and the judge has dealt with any requests to strike jurors for cause, the remaining jurors are called up one at a time to the jury box until it is filled with the appropriate number and, in some instances, alternates. Once the jury is seated, the trial can begin.

EXERCISE: IN THE STATE OF...

Find out how many jurors are required for your state. Also, check to see if your state requires a unanimous jury verdict. Finally, find out how many peremptory challenges are allowed for both the defense and the prosecution. You can obtain this information in your state's rules of criminal procedure, which may be online. If not, see if there is a copy in your library. You can also use a Bureau of Justice Statistics publication titled *State Court Organization—2004*, available at http://bjs.ojp.usdoj.gov/index.cfm?ty=pbdetail&iid=1204.

Opening statements

The opening statements are the attorneys' opportunity to address the jury as to what they should be looking for in the presentation of evidence. Each attorney seeks to educate the jury as to his or her version of the events. They need to convince the jury of their version through evidence that consists either of witnesses who testify to what they have seen, heard, or experienced, and/or expert witnesses who can offer opinions and judgments, at least within the confines of their expertise. The opening statement gives the attorney a chance to talk directly to the jury and tell them what they are going to hear. The defense often asks that their opening be deferred to the beginning of the defense's case.

Presentation of evidence

You have probably seen innumerable trials on television shows and movies. Some are fairly accurate and some are not. Generally, you know that the prosecution presents the state's case first. Witnesses are put on the stand, and the prosecutor goes through a **direct examination**, which is the questioning of his or her own witness. The questions cannot be leading (telling the witness the answer or making a statement); they cannot ask for an opinion, they cannot ask for **hearsay** (something that the witness did not hear, see, or experience directly), although there are many exceptions to this rule. They also cannot ask for something that would be unduly prejudicial or otherwise not be allowed into evidence.

After the prosecutor has finished questioning the witness, the defense may **cross-examine** the witness. These questions have pretty much the same rules, but there is the opportunity to ask leading questions, such as, "Isn't it true that on the night of July 15, you had so much to drink that you were not able to see the defendant clearly across the parking lot of the bar?"

After the defense has finished the cross-examination, the prosecutor has the opportunity to question again over any material that was brought up in the cross-examination. This process continues until all witnesses have been examined. Then, the prosecutor has the chance to present any rebuttal witnesses that might be appropriate. This might occur if the defense has elicited some information from one of the witnesses that the prosecutor can show is irrelevant or untrue or just to shed additional light on the information. Rebuttal witnesses respond directly to the facts already in evidence.

The presentation of the defense's case comes next, beginning with the opening statement if the attorney reserved the right to give one. The direct examination, cross-examination, and rebuttal witnesses occur in the same order. After all witnesses are finished testifying, there are closing arguments.

An instance where the prosecutor has an advantage over the defense is that they are allowed to have the first closing statement and then are able to speak to the jury again after the defense's closing statement. This is because prosecutors have the burden of proof in a trial. In the closing, each side summarizes the evidence in a way that supports their version of the case. They emphasize certain portions of the evidence, and they comment on the weight of the evidence. Attorneys cannot mention any facts not in evidence.

After the closing, the judge reads to the jury an instruction. The instruction to the jury is written by the judge with both attorneys suggesting text. It may include definitions of legal terms. It may ask them to choose between two or more different levels of culpability. For instance, in a homicide case, the instructions may give the jury the choice between finding the defendant guilty of murder in the first degree, second degree, or even manslaughter. If the judge decides that there is evidence that indicates the lower levels of guilt, then the jury will be able to make the decision. The rules for instructions are different among the states, but it is basically the guidelines, rules, or verdict available for the jury to follow in their deliberation.

If the jury cannot reach a verdict, it is called a "hung jury" and the prosecutor may decide to try the case again. This would not be double jeopardy because the trial is not officially over yet. If the jury comes back with an acquittal, it does not mean the jury members necessarily believe the defendant is innocent, it means that they did not believe the prosecutor proved the case beyond a reasonable doubt. If the jury comes back with a guilty verdict, the next step is sentencing.

BREAKING NEWS: BLAGOJEVICH TRIAL ENDS IN HUNG JURY

In 2010, the federal case against Illinois Governor Rod Blagojevich ended in a hung jury on 22 of 23 counts and a mistrial was declared. Because there was no verdict of acquittal, the prosecutors may retry the remaining charges. The governor's attempt to get something in return for his appointment to fill President Obama's U.S. Senate seat led to a wide-ranging prosecution including charges under RICO (Racketeer Influenced and Corrupt Organizations Act). The jury convicted Blagojevich on one count of lying to federal investigators. The U.S. Attorney's office indicates that it will retry Blagojevich on some of the counts that resulted in a hung decision based on information that the jury had only one holdout and had voted to convict 11-1.

Source: M. Davey, Blagojevich Trial Ends Fitzgerald's Successes, New York Times Online. Retrieved 8/21/2010 from http://www.nytimes.com/2010/08/20/us/20fitzgerald.html.

Appeals

The most important thing to remember about appeals is that the defendant can appeal only if legal errors occurred during the trial or the process leading up to the trial. If, for instance, police officers interrogated the defendant and obtained a confession without giving him the *Miranda* warnings, that would be grounds for an appeal. Or, if, during trial, the judge made incorrect legal rulings, or if there was some attempt to improperly influence the jury, that would be grounds for appeal. The defense attorney must "preserve" the error by objecting to it during the trial. If he or she does not object, then in most cases the error will not be able to be used as grounds for an appeal. All defendants have a right to an attorney for the first "direct" appeal. If there are subsequent appeals, then the defendant must pay for the attorney. If there is an alleged violation of the Constitution then, after state appeals are exhausted, there can be an appeal in the federal courts. Generally, this is done through the writ of habeas corpus, which basically alleges unlawful imprisonment. In some cases, the writ is used when a prisoner believes the prison or the holding facility is operated in a way that is violative of the Constitution, but in other cases, it is used when the allegation is that the person ought not to be held at all because of an error at trial.

The appellate courts evaluate the alleged error and determine whether to take the case and, if they do, both parties will file a written brief and engage in oral argument before the court. If the appellate court does not find for the appellant (defendant), then that decision can be appealed to a higher court up to the state's highest court. If the appellate court does find for the appellant (defendant), then the state can appeal the decision. Sometimes, the appellate court agrees with the appellant but determines that the error was "harmless" and did not affect the outcome of the trial.

SENTENCING HEARING

Depending on the state, judges or juries may sentence convicted felons and misdemeanants. In both cases, statutory guidelines limit the discretion of the judge or jury in what type of sentence can be imposed, and how long the sentence may last. A sentencing hearing is a "critical stage" of the trial process, meaning that the courts have held that a defendant must have an attorney present if they are facing the possibility of a jail or prison sentence. There are, however, relaxed rules of evidence. Hearsay may be admitted, as when people testify about the character of the offender. Victim statements may be read, which allow the victim or the victim's family to state how the crime has affected them.

In most states, presentence reports are also used in order to give the judge or the jury more information about the offender before a sentence decision is made. A presentence division in a probation agency conducts presentence investigations, and they provide information on the offender's criminal, educational, family, and work history. In Figure 9.1, a presentence report is described.

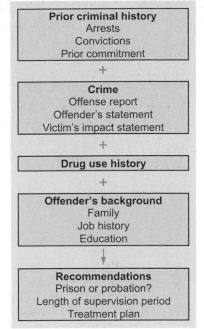

FIGURE 9.1
Presentence report.

We have a system in which there are several concurrent goals of sentencing. They include:

- *Punishment*: we believe that criminals must be punished because they deserve it.
- *Deterrence*: we believe that what we do to offenders will make others decide not to commit crime and will also encourage the offender not to commit additional crime.
- *Rehabilitation*: we believe that programs and what is done to the offender in the system may create some internal change that will make him or her become more law-abiding.
- *Incapacitation*: if nothing else, we believe that we should hold the offender in a manner that will prevent him or her from committing any crimes, at least for that period of time.

Theoretically any sentence, or every sentence, should achieve one or more of these goals. An offender who is sent to prison is certainly incapacitated and each of the other goals is possible—especially, of course, punishment.

Types of sentences

The most important sentencing decision is whether the offender is sent to prison or receives probation. This "in or out" decision is governed by state statute. The decision may come about through a plea agreement or it can be

BOX 9.2 SENTENCE ALTERNATIVES

1. *Split sentence*—a short period in jail followed by probation supervision (also called "shock probation")
2. *Halfway house placement*—either as a condition of probation or as a stand-alone sentence
3. *Boot camps*—military-style camps utilizing physical fitness and discipline
4. *House arrest with electronic monitoring*—usually as a condition of probation but sometimes may be a stand-alone sentence
5. *Fines*—either a stand-alone sentence or as a condition of probation

the decision of a judge or, in a few states, a jury. Besides the "in or out" (of prison) decision, sentencing decisions can include other forms of confinement or supervision. Box 9.2 illustrates some types of sentences.

It should also be remembered that a community corrections placement might result in additional or different sanctions during the course of the supervision period. For instance, if an offender is sentenced to probation, and one of the conditions is to submit to drug tests, a failed test may result in a judge adding a residential treatment center stay to the conditions of probation. Weekend jail may be added to a probationer's sentence if he or she has violated the terms of the probation, but the judge doesn't think it is serious enough to warrant revocation and a prison sentence. At any time during the probation sentence, a court proceeding to change the conditions may be initiated. Although the probation officer does not have the power to change the conditions or revoke probation, he or she can file a violation report and ask the prosecutor for a motion to revoke probation hearing. The judge is the only person who can revoke or change the conditions.

Indeterminate, determinate, and "structured sentencing"

An *indeterminate sentence* is one where the release date is unknown. The judge sets a period as provided for by statute, such as 5 to 15 years. How much of that is served depends on another agency, typically a paroling authority. This group of decision makers looks at the offender's behavior in prison. An offender may serve a small portion or the majority of the range of years, depending on the parole board (or paroling authority) decision.

A *determinate sentence* is when the release date is fixed. Determinate sentencing systems typically also set the amount of punishment for each crime by statute. The judge has little flexibility and, once there is a conviction and decision to send to prison, the judge must use the sentence specified by the statute. There is often a very small range for the judge to adjust the sentence by making it shorter or longer.

Indeterminate sentences have been around since the early reformatories in the late 1800s and early 1900s. They were the most prevalent sentencing structure in the 1960s and 1970s. However, critics argued that indeterminate sentences were unfair; conservatives claimed offenders were getting out of prison too early, and liberals complained that there was no accountability or predictability in who was getting out in what amount of time. Beginning in the late 1970s and 1980s, various forms of determinate or structured sentencing have taken the place of indeterminate sentencing in many states. The goals of structured sentencing have been listed as:

- Increase fairness in sentencing
- Reduce unwarranted disparity in decision to imprison or sentence length
- Establish truth in sentencing
- Balance sentencing policy with limited correctional resources [16]

In Box 9.3, there is a map of the United States showing which states have eliminated parole and instituted determinate sentencing.

Mandatory sentences are often embedded in a state's indeterminate sentencing structure. They are passed to control the sentencing discretion for certain specific crimes, usually because the crimes are heinous or have captured public attention. For instance, in a state that has an otherwise indeterminate sentencing system, there may be a mandatory jail sentence for third-conviction DUIs, or there may be a mandatory prison term for violent felonies that involve the use of a weapon. All 50 states have at least one type of mandatory sentence. Along with these types of sentences, some states have three-strikes legislation that allows a prosecutor to prosecute repeat offenders as three-strike (or second-strike) offenders with much longer prison terms attached. About half of all states have some form of three-strikes (habitual felon) sentencing statutes [17].

Sentencing guidelines

Sentencing guidelines were introduced in the early 1980s as a measure to reduce sentence disparity. Guidelines may be mandatory or discretionary. They present the presumed amount of time an offender should serve in prison given the nature of the crime and a risk factor score. Federal sentencing guidelines include a number in the first column that corresponds to the seriousness of the offense and the number of prior convictions across the top row. Judges must look up the seriousness of the current offense and the number of priors to find the number of months to sentence an individual.

If sentencing guidelines are discretionary, the guidelines are only advisory, and the judge or sentencing body may ignore them. If they are mandatory, then typically, there is a provision for the sentencing authority to enter into

BOX 9.3 UNITED STATES—TYPES OF SENTENCE STRUCTURES

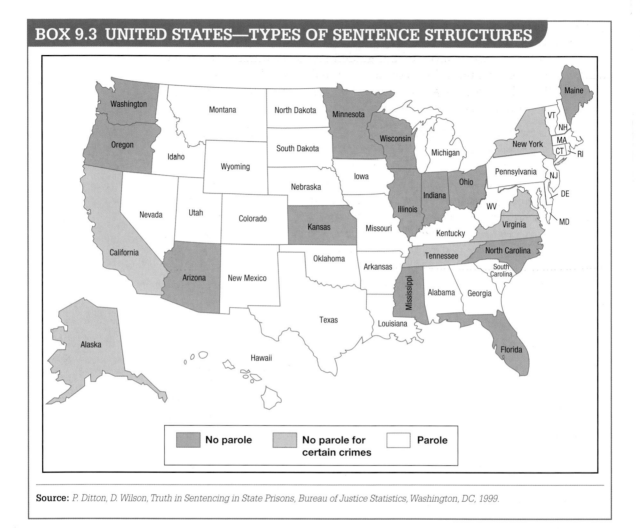

Legend: No parole | No parole for certain crimes | Parole

Source: P. Ditton, D. Wilson, *Truth in Sentencing in State Prisons*, Bureau of Justice Statistics, Washington, DC, 1999.

INTERNET KEY

For more information about state sentencing guidelines, go to http://www.ncsconline.org/csi/PEW-Profiles-v12-online.pdf.

the record the reason why they depart from the guidelines. As of 2008, 21 states had some form of sentencing guidelines [18].

In 2005, the Supreme Court called into question the legality of mandatory guidelines. The first case dealt with the state of Washington's mandatory guidelines. In 2004, in *Blakely v. Washington* [19], the Court invalidated the use of the guidelines to determine sentence length when elements not introduced and proven in court were used, such as number of priors or use of a weapon. This decision created doubt that the U.S. Sentencing Commission Guidelines, used with federal offenders, would be upheld in a challenge. The Federal Sentencing Reform Act of 1984 (effective 1987) had created a federal sentencing guideline structure. By 1992, federal parole was phased out in favor of the guidelines' determinate sentencing structure, although the federal system still included time off for good behavior, and allowed for downward or upward movement in sentence length depending on mitigating or aggravating factors.

The federal guidelines were challenged in an appeal similar to the Washington case, and, in *United States v. Booker* [20], the Supreme Court ruled that federal sentencing guidelines could only be advisory, and not consider facts "not in evidence" to determine sentence length. The reason for this is that due process rights require the government to prove the elements it uses to determine a sentence. Many of the elements in a sentencing guidelines structure are not entered into the record, the defendant does not get a chance to refute them, and they do not have to meet any burden of proof. Consequently, the Supreme Court decided that the due process rights of an offender were violated when the sentences in the guidelines were considered to be mandatory rather than advisory.

Split sentencing

In the 1980s, a new type of sentencing came onto the scene that allowed judges to use imprisonment and also keep control of the offender. Variously called split sentencing, shock probation, shock incarceration, or other terms, the idea was to be able to sentence the offender to a short period in jail or prison, and then put them on probation, thereby allowing the judge to keep control over the offender through the entire period of supervision. Petersilia [21] reports that probation is combined with jail or a prison sentence in 27% of felony cases. In this type of sentence, the average jail sentence length is 6 months and the probation supervision length is 40 months.

Probation versus prison

There is a widespread belief that most criminal offenders get a slap on the wrist in the sentencing process. However, according to national statistics, 69% of those convicted in 2006 were sentenced to incarceration, either to jail or prison. About 27% received probation, and about 4% received a fine or something other than probation or incarceration as the sole method of punishment. Of those sentenced to some form of incarceration, the average sentence was 4 years, 11 months. Drug offenders received a prison sentence of, on average, 7 years, 3 months if they were federal defendants, and 2 years, 7 months if they were state defendants [22]. In the last several decades, probation has been surpassed by prison or jail as the most frequent sentence handed down in felony courts.

Sentence disparity

There seems to be good evidence that young, black males are not only more likely to engage in some types of crime (street crime such as robbery and homicide), but that they are also more likely to be sentenced harshly because of a perception that they are more dangerous, whether they are or not.

Studies that examine the interaction among race, age, and gender find that the combination of these variables affects sentencing patterns more than any one individually. For instance, older black men are less likely to receive disproportionately severe sentences than young black men. Women, on the other hand, are sentenced fairly uniformly regardless of age. Race is less important as a factor in sentencing older rather than younger offenders, and for men rather than women. Steffensmeier and his colleagues [23] have examined the interplay of these variables in several studies and find that race does seem to affect sentencing, but it influences sentencing mostly for young men.

There has also been a lot of research on whether women receive leniency in sentencing. The so-called chivalry effect refers to the perceived practice of giving women lighter sentences than men who commit similar crimes. The research that has been directed to this question has had mixed findings, but generally it seems that for some women, and for some crimes, there might be a tendency to assess shorter sentences, but the practice is not uniform. For some women, especially young women, minority women, and those who commit violent crimes, sentencing may actually be harsher than for men [24].

Too much due process?

There have been many complaints over the years that the Supreme Court and criminal justice system have swung too far toward protecting defendant rights against the rights of victims for swift and certain justice. Ultimately, this is a question of opinion. It is also important to note that "too much" due process has evidently not resulted in a complete absence of errors in the deprivation of life or liberty. Some estimates indicate that between 1% and 3% of those in prison are actually innocent or innocent of the specific charges they were convicted of. The Innocence Project refers to groups of attorneys and other volunteers in many states who take cases of inmates claiming innocence. To date, they have been instrumental in exonerating 250 inmates, usually through

Cornelius Dupree, Jr., center, raises his hands in celebration with his lawyer Nina Morrison, left, and attorney Barry Scheck in Dallas on Tuesday, January 4, 2011. Dupree served 30 years for rape and robbery before being exonerated by DNA evidence. *AP Photo/ Mike Fuentes*

the use of DNA testing. Some of these individuals had been incarcerated for decades, and some were days away from being executed before found to be innocent. The reasons for their false convictions and imprisonment are usually a combination of eyewitness error, prosecutorial misconduct, defense attorney ineffectiveness, and false confessions (usually because of coercion). After reading the stories of some of these individuals (available through the Innocent Project Web site), it is difficult to argue that we have too much due process in the system.

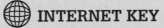 **INTERNET KEY**

To read more about the Innocence Projects, go to http://www.innocenceproject.org/?gclid=CK_-vdyKy6QCFQ5O2godgy9KEg.

CONCLUSION

In this chapter, we more fully described how the criminal justice system is a series of steps designed to protect against error in the court process. Due process protections come to us through the Fifth and Fourteenth Amendments. The Sixth Amendment gives us specific due process rights when faced with criminal prosecution, including a right to a jury of peers, and counsel. It is important to remember, however, that our due process rights go far beyond the Sixth Amendment, and are implicated any time the government attempts to deprive us of life, liberty, or property.

The steps of the criminal process begin with arrest and booking, continue through initial appearance, preliminary hearing, indictment or information, arraignment, and trial and sentencing. At each step, the process is designed to minimize or eliminate any errors that the government may make.

Review Questions

1. What is due process and what is the source of due process protections?
2. What are the steps from arrest to trial? (Describe each step.)
3. What are the four kinds of bail or surety programs?
4. What is the difference between an information and an indictment?
5. What are some examples of pretrial motions?
6. What are the steps of a trial?
7. What is an affirmative defense? Give some examples.
8. What is included in the PSR?
9. What are at least six different types of sentences? Describe sentencing guidelines and split sentencing.
10. What are indeterminate and determinate sentencing structures? Give examples of states that have indeterminate systems and states that have determinate systems.

VOCABULARY

abscond escape the jurisdiction, leave without permission

affirmative defense defenses where the defense must provide evidence to reach a certain level of proof (typically preponderance) before a jury can consider it; examples include self-defense, entrapment, and insanity

challenges for cause unlimited number of challenges either by defense or prosecution if they can prove that a prospective juror is not able to assess the evidence fairly at trial

change of venue a request for the trial to be moved to another jurisdiction because of a belief that any jurors from the locale where the crime took place would be too biased to render a fair verdict

court surety programs alternative to bail where the court administers a secured or unsecured bond in lieu of private bail

cross-examination the questioning of the other side's witness

determinate sentence a sentence where the release date is fixed by statute; judges have little flexibility and must use the sentence specified by the statute

direct examination the questioning of your own side's witness

double jeopardy the right not to be tried or punished twice for the same offense

due process procedural protections that guard against errors when the government seeks to deprive anyone of life, liberty, or property

hearsay something that you did not hear, see, or experience directly

indeterminate sentence a sentence where the release date is unknown; the judge sets a period as provided for by statute, such as 5 to 15 years, and another agency, typically a paroling authority, makes the release decision

indictment the charging instrument of the grand jury

indigency without appreciable assets

information the charging instrument issued by the prosecutor

investigative detentions brief deprivations of liberty when police officers have a reasonable suspicion that a crime has occurred, or is about to occur

lockups temporary holding cells, usually in a police station

mandatory sentences sentences specified by statute but only for certain specific crimes, usually because the crimes are heinous or have captured public attention; examples include mandatory jail sentence for third DWI, and mandatory 10 years added to sentence when gun is used

motion a request that the judge order something to be done or not done

motion in limine motion asking that something not be mentioned during the trial because it would prejudice the jury

no bill the finding of the grand jury when the prosecutor has not proven probable cause

peremptory challenges statutory number of challenges to prospective jurors without having to identify any specific bias

preventive detention pretrial detention because of a perceived risk to the public

probable cause when there is enough evidence to indicate that guilt is more probable than not

recuse(al) when the judge is not able to conduct the trial in a fair and unbiased manner because of some conflict of interest

release on recognizance (ROR) program prerelease without bond for good-risk defendants in lieu of bail

voir dire to say the truth; the process by which attorneys question prospective jurors to determine their ability to be fair and unbiased during trial

ENDNOTES

[1] Meachum v. Fano, 427 U.S. 215 (1976).

[2] United States v. Sharpe, 470 U.S. 675 (1985).

[3] 500 U.S. 44 (1991).

[4] S. Maxwell, Examining the congruence between predictors of ROR and failures to appear, J. Crim. Just. 27 (2) (1999) 127–141.

[5] T. Cohen, B. Reaves, Pretrial Release of Felony Defendants in State Courts, Bureau of Justice Statistics, National Institute of Justice, Washington, DC, 2007.

[6] 18 U.S.C.A. § 3141 et seq. 1996.

[7] 481 U.S. 739 (1987).

[8] B. Boland, P. Mahanna, R. Sones, The Prosecution of Felony Arrests, 1988, Bureau of Justice Statistics, Washington, DC, 1992.

[9] In re Winship, 397 U.S. 358, 90 S. Ct. 1068, 25 L. Ed. 2d. 368 (1970).

[10] State v. Babers, 514 N.W. 2d 79 (Iowa,1994).

[11] Title 18 U.S.C. § 17.

[12] Martin v. Ohio, 480 U.S. 228, 107 S. Ct. 1098, 94 L. Ed. 2d 267(1987).

[13] Williams v. Florida, 399 U.S. 78 (1970).

[14] Apodaca v. Oregon, 406 U.S. 404 (1972).

[15] Batson v. Kentucky, 476 U.S. 79 (1986).

[16] National Center for State Courts, State Sentencing Guidelines: Profiles and Continuum. Retrieved 10/10/2010 from http://www.ncsconline.org/csi/PEW-Profiles-v12-online.pdf, 2008.

[17] J. Travis, J. Petersilia, Reentry reconsidered: a new look at an old question, Crime Delinq. 47(3) (2001) 294.

[18] J. Travis, J. Petersilia, Reentry reconsidered: a new look at an old question, Crime Delinq. 47(3) (2001) 294.

[19] 542 U.S. 296 (2004).

[20] 543 U.S. 220 (2005).

[21] J. Petersilia, Reforming Probation and Parole, American Correctional Association, Lanham, MD, 2002, p. 29.

[22] S. Rosenmerkel, M. Durose, D. Farole, Felony Sentences in State Courts, 2006—Statistical Tables, Bureau of Justice Statistics, U.S. Department of Justice, Washington, DC, 2009.

[23] D. Steffensmeier, J. Ulmer, J. Kramer, The interaction of race, gender, and age in criminal sentencing: the punishment cost of being young, black and male, Criminology 36(4) (1998) 763–797.

[24] For a review of this literature, see J. Pollock, Women, Prison and Crime, Wadsworth, Belmont, CA, 2002.

Juvenile Justice and Corrections

CONTENTS

Nathaniel Brazill brought a gun to school and shot a well-liked teacher in the face, killing him. He was 13. The jury was asked to decide if he committed premeditated murder. Is a 13-year-old capable of "cold-blooded murder?" Throughout a good portion of this country's history, we have excused juveniles from their crimes because of a belief that their immaturity prevented them from engaging in the calm, rational deliberation that is required for criminal (and moral) culpability. It is the same reasoning that supports laws which prevent juveniles from drinking alcohol or buying cigarettes, voting, or serving in the military. Others argue that 13-year-old know right from wrong and should be held accountable for their actions. Brazill's jury found him guilty of second-degree murder, and he was sentenced to serve 28 years in prison. The juvenile justice system is a separate and parallel justice system to the adult criminal system. Many police departments have specialized juvenile divisions; states have specialized juvenile courts; and the juvenile corrections system is separate from the adult corrections system. The terminology in the juvenile justice system is different, as is its origin, history, and mission. A fundamental difference between the two systems is the emphasis placed on the culpability of the offender and the system's role in changing behavior. Children are believed to be less responsible for their actions than adults. In this chapter, we will review the juvenile justice system with special attention to how it differs from the adult system.

THE HISTORY OF THE JUVENILE JUSTICE SYSTEM

As most people know, juveniles are dealt with in a separate judicial and correctional system from adults, operating under the legal concept of *parens patriae* (literally "parent of the country"), which refers to the state's power to take the place of the parent in situations of abuse or neglect. While there are many parallels between the systems, most characterize the juvenile system as more lenient, forgiving, and more oriented toward rehabilitation than the adult justice system. The spirit of the juvenile justice system is based on the notion that young people are more malleable than adults and can be reformed; further, that the culpability of very young offenders is less than that of adults.

The juvenile system handles both **delinquents** (those who commit an act that is defined as a crime by the penal code) and **status offenders** (whose behavior is prohibited only because they are juveniles, such as running away, truancy, breaking curfew, or being "incorrigible"). In some cases, juveniles who are taken into state custody have done nothing wrong. They have been declared either neglected or abused and the state takes the child away from the parent for their own protection. There is an idea that youth who lack supervision and/or who are difficult to control will graduate to more serious forms of delinquency; thus, most states have created the authority to intervene upon a finding that the juvenile fits the description of CHINS, PINS, or MINS (children in need of supervision, persons in need of supervision, minors in need of supervision). However, this special attention to young people did not always exist.

Before the 1800s, children received very little protection or special treatment from society or the legal system. Only children under the age of seven were presumed to be incapable of criminal culpability; all others were punished similar to adults. In the early jails of this country, children and adults were housed together.

Gradually, there came recognition that children should receive greater protections and that the state should step in when parents either could not or would not provide a safe and nurturing environment. The **child saver movement**, as described by Platt [1], involved upper-middle-class women who took on, as a reform project, the terrible living conditions of immigrant children in Northeastern cities. These orphaned and/or poverty-stricken children roamed the streets as beggars and engaged in petty crimes to survive. In the late 1800s and early 1900s, the child saver movement resulted in states creating solutions such as foster care, orphanages, houses of refuge, and, eventually, the juvenile justice system.

The first juvenile court was established in Chicago in 1899, and, by 1919, almost all states had created a separate judicial system for youth [2]. Very soon afterward, juvenile probation was established. The concept of a separate system for juveniles was based on the idea that children were different from adults—in their culpability and in their vulnerability. Originally, the differences between children who committed crimes and children who were neglected or abused by their parents were de-emphasized because of the idea that all were in need of care.

Status offenders, who might not have done anything other than run away from an intolerable home life, were housed with juvenile delinquents, who could have been serious offenders. In the 1970s, many recognized the injustice of this situation. The 1974 Juvenile Justice and Delinquency Prevention Act mandated, among other things, that neglected/abused children and status offenders needed to be removed from secure detention facilities. Further, if there was a determination that a status offender be sent to a residential placement, then there had to be a sight-and-sound separation between status offenders and juvenile delinquents if housed in the same facility. This led to a substantial decrease in the number of status offenders housed in secure detention, and the incentive to find community placements for those who posed no threat to the community.

The other major development was a shift in perception that, even though the mission of the juvenile system was to help the young offenders, they still deserved due process. The Supreme Court decided a sequence of cases in the late 1960s and 1970s that established due process rights for juveniles and led to a greater formalization of the court process. These cases are described in Box 10.1. Other due process rights have not been accorded to juveniles, however, including the right to a trial by jury.

BOX 10.1 SUPREME COURT CASES ON JUVENILE RIGHTS

Kent v. United States 383 U.S. 541 (1966)
   Required a hearing before waiver to adult court
In re Gault 387 U.S. 1 (1967)
   Required some due process in juvenile proceedings
In re Winship 397 U.S. 358 (1970)
   Required juvenile courts be held to the "beyond a reasonable doubt" standard in finding of guilt, instead of the preponderance standard
McKeiver v. Pennsylvania 403 U.S. 528 (1971)
   Decision that juveniles did not require a jury trial under the Sixth or Fourteenth Amendments

An increase in juvenile crime in the 1980s and early 1990s led to a "toughening" of the system, with more institutional placements and more judicial waivers to adult court (sending youth to adult criminal courts to be tried and punished). Depending on the state, the juvenile who is adjudicated in adult court may serve their sentence in an adult facility; thus, we have come almost full circle back to where we were before the child saver movement more than a century ago.

ZERO TOLERANCE AND JUVENILES

Lionel Tate was 12 years old when he killed a 6-year-old by breaking her neck, imitating what he saw while watching pro wrestlers. His attorneys argued that he had not meant to hurt her and was just playing. It seems very possible that he did not mean to hurt the girl, and prosecutors must have thought so too, because they offered him a sentence of 3 years in a juvenile facility, 1 year of house arrest, and 10 years of probation. However, because he was a juvenile, his mother made the decision for him to refuse the plea bargain and go to trial, evidently assuming the jury would acquit him or find him guilty of a lesser crime. Instead, the jury found him guilty of first-degree murder, and he was sentenced to a mandatory term of life without parole [3].

On January 29, 2004, after an appeal seeking a retrial, the prosecutor and the defense reached a plea agreement whereby Tate pleaded guilty to second-degree murder, with a sentence of three years in juvenile custody and one year of house arrest. Because he had already served that amount of time, he was released. In 2006, Tate was convicted of committing armed robbery and is now back in prison for a probation violation.

The Tate case illustrates a number of issues in the juvenile justice system today. First, the practice of waiving very young offenders to adult courts with concomitant adult punishments has been a matter of some controversy. Second, there is the sad reality that such offenders are very likely to recidivate with some research indicating that those who are sent to adult correctional facilities are more likely to recidivate than those who remain in the juvenile system. Finally, the extreme sentence given to Tate, despite evidence indicating a lack of deliberate intent indicates the zero tolerance that has swept the nation when considering crimes by juveniles.

In the 1980s and 1990s, there was a real and perceived increase in juvenile crime. While youth may not have been the "super predators" that some pundits claimed, there was a spike in violent crime fueled by easy access to handguns and the crack markets in urban areas. Minority youth were especially affected by the increased crime—both as victims and offenders. Even though such violence was largely confined to inner cities, the perception that youth were out of control spurred many states to enact new laws or change existing laws to increase the controls and sanctions over juveniles. These laws included the following:

Lionel Tate, front right, is escorted from court after his sentencing hearing, Friday, March 9, 2001, in Fort Lauderdale, Florida. The boy who was 12 when he killed a little girl while imitating professional wrestlers, was sentenced to life in prison without parole; however, the sentence was later reduced and Tate was released. He has since been returned to prison for armed robbery.
AP Photo/Lou Toman

- Curfew laws
- Parental responsibility laws
- Antigang laws
- Juvenile boot camps
- Gun laws
- Removing laws that seal juvenile records
- Waiver laws (allowing waiver to adult courts)
- Concurrent jurisdiction laws (extending criminal court jurisdiction to more crimes)

Even though the violent crime spike in the mid-1990s had already started to decline, the 1999 Columbine High School shooting and others (Springfield, Oregon, 1998; Santee, California, 2001) solidified the pervasive view that juvenile crime was growing and the juvenile justice system was too lenient. At about the same time (late 1990s), the zero-tolerance approach was being touted as a way to reduce crime. This policing strategy (described in earlier chapters) found its way into the schools as well, so that full prosecution of minor crimes on the street became translated to full prosecution and suspension for minor misconduct in the school, in the hope that this would prevent more serious violent crimes on school grounds.

In some cases the zero-tolerance approach toward expressions of violence has reached extreme levels that many believe are counterproductive. A 10-year-old girl who whispered "I could kill her" after she wet her pants because her teacher refused to let her go to the bathroom, a 10-year-old who said "I oughtta murder his face" when a classmate messed up his desk, a classmate who uttered a threat after he was pushed, a 9-year-old boy who shot a wad of toilet paper, and a kid in the school cafeteria line who warned his classmates if they ate all the potatoes he would "get them" were all suspended for these "threats of violence." Many of these children now have criminal records for such acts. In all, 50 suspensions in six weeks occurred in one school district after the county prosecutor met with school officials and told them they had no discretion in reporting threats to authorities. Some parents and other observers believe that this response is unwarranted. The American Bar Association has passed a resolution condemning zero-tolerance policies that allow no discretion in defining children's acts as criminal [4].

Ironically, the zero-tolerance approach gained momentum during a period when juvenile crime was actually declining. Violent crime arrests of juveniles decreased by 8% and property crime arrests decreased by 11% between 1994 and 1998 [5]. In 2001, the murder rate was at a 15-year low, and the burglary and robbery rates were at 20-year lows [6]. The Bureau of Justice Statistics indicates that between 1993 and 2005, the number of serious violent offenses committed by persons aged 12 to 17 declined 61%, while those committed by persons older than 17 fell 58% [7]. Thus, the decade of 1995-2005 was a time when the majority of the public believed that juvenile crime was increasing and becoming more violent, and legislation and public responses to juvenile crime were becoming increasingly harsher, while in reality the rate of juvenile crime was declining at dramatic levels.

Zero-tolerance policies in schools have resulted in many more suspensions than before the implementation of such policies. According to one source, the percentage of students suspended at least once in grades K through 12 has nearly doubled over the last four decades (from 3.7% to 6.7%). The percentage of black children suspended is 15%. In 2006, almost a third of black boys (28%) were suspended, compared to 10% of white boys. Study authors caution that the numbers probably under-represent what is happening because school districts do not report all suspensions [8]. In many cases, a suspension leads to the student dropping out of school, forever handicapping his or her future. Some have argued that the increased suspension rates have occurred partially in response to national pressure to increase scores on standardized tests. If the lower-performing students are suspended, they do not have to be counted in the school's averages [9]. Another major change that has taken place on school grounds is the presence of "school safety officers" who may be assigned by the local police department or be peace officers employed by the district. What has occurred is a "formalization" of discipline so that a fistfight between two boys in junior high that might have been dealt with by the school principal is now handled by the school safety officer, with citations for public disturbance-fighting, and the involvement of the municipal court. This formal court intervention may occur with or without a school suspension. Recently, the North Carolina Supreme Court held that a school district could not suspend students and deny them alternative school placement or home tutoring without substantial reasons [10]. Up to this point, school districts did not have to give any reason for denying alternative schooling options. Advocates for youth herald this as a breakthrough and persuasive authority in other states that have similar cases. It may be a harbinger that the tides may be shifting once again to treat youth differently from adults with a more reformative rather than punitive mission.

Interestingly, the public has never supported purely punitive approaches toward juveniles despite the rhetoric of politicians. In studies of public opinion, there has continued to be a great deal of support for rehabilitative responses to juvenile crime. One study found, for instance, that respondents were as likely to be willing to pay for rehabilitative programs as incarceration for youthful offenders. In this study, 72% of respondents were willing to pay for rehabilitation for serious juvenile offenders, 65% supported early childhood prevention efforts, and 59% were willing to pay for longer sentences for youthful offenders [11].

> **⊕ INTERNET KEY**
>
> For information about the juvenile justice system and juvenile crime, go to the web site for the Office of Juvenile Justice and Delinquency Prevention at http://www.ojjdp.gov.

JUVENILE CRIME

Consistent with the dramatic decline of crime discussed in an earlier chapter, juveniles' crimes have also decreased, quite dramatically for some groups and in some crime categories. Table 10.1 shows juvenile arrests as a percentage of total arrests for certain selected crimes. One can see that in most crime categories, their share of total arrests has gone down. In motor vehicle theft, for example, their percentage of the total number of arrests

Table 10.1 Juvenile Arrests (Selected) as a Percentage of Total Arrests

Crime	1996 (%)	2005 (%)	2009 (%)
Total	19	15	14
Murder/manslaughter	14.5	9	9
Forcible rape	17	15.8	14
Robbery	31	24.7	25
Aggravated assault	14.6	13	11
Burglary	38.6	26	25
Larceny-theft	35	26	24
Motor vehicle theft	42.8	24	24
Violent crime	17.9	15.2	14
Property crime	36	26.4	25

Source: *Uniform Crime Reports, adapted from Table 32: Ten-Year Arrest Trends, 2005 and 2009. Retrieved 3/1/07 from http://www.fbi.gov/ucr/05cius/data/table_32.html and 10/10/2010 from http://www.fbi.gov/ucr/09cius/data/table_32.html.*

is almost half what it was 10 years ago. Thus, not only have the number of juvenile arrests declined, their *share* of arrests has also declined in most crime categories as shown in Table 10.1.

Juvenile arrest rates reached their peak in the early 1990s and have decreased since then. In 2008, there were 2.11 million arrests of juveniles (under 18). The overall juvenile arrest rate (per 100,000) was lower in 2008 than in 1980 [12]. For instance, arrests of juveniles declined for the following crimes between 1999 and 2008:

- Murder (declined by 9%)
- Forcible rape (declined by 27%)
- Robbery (declined by 25%)
- Aggravated assault (declined by 21%)
- Burglary (declined by 14%)
- Larceny-theft (declined by 17%)
- Motor vehicle theft (declined by 50%) [13]

The peak in violent crime came about 1995 and the decline occurred very rapidly. Figure 10.1 shows the violent crime arrest pattern for juveniles. There was a slight increase in the violent crime index rates for 2005 and 2006, but since 2006, the rates have been declining again (except for robbery). For property crime, the peak of arrests for juveniles occurred earlier and there has been greater stability in the arrest rates through the 1980s and first half of the 1990s, at which time the rates began to decline. Figure 10.2 shows that the juvenile arrest rate for Property Crime Index offenses declined more than 50% between 1980 and 2008. Between 1999

FIGURE 10.1

Juvenile arrest rates for violent crime index offenses, 1980-2005.
Source: *Office of Juvenile Justice and Delinquency Prevention, March 19, 2007, OJJDP Statistical Briefing Book. Available at http://ojjdp.ncjrs.org/ ojstatbb/crime/JAR_Display. asp?ID=qa05200.*

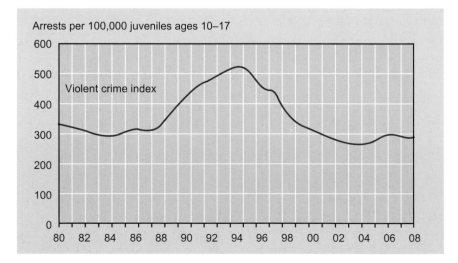

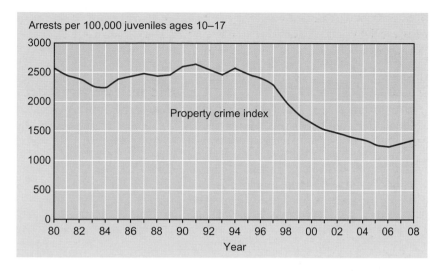

Arrests per 100,000 juveniles ages 10–17

FIGURE 10.2
Juvenile arrest rates for property crime index offenses, 1980-2008.
Source: *Office of Juvenile Justice and Delinquency Prevention, March 19, 2007, OJJDP Statistical Briefing Book. Available at http://ojjdp.ncjrs.org/ojstatbb/crime/JAR_Display. asp?ID=qa05200.*

and 2008, the number of arrests for larceny-theft declined by about 17% [14]. However, in the last several years, arrest of juveniles for property crimes has increased slightly.

A very important component of juvenile delinquency is membership in juvenile gangs. Our Focus on Crime box discusses gang involvement and gang delinquency.

Female juvenile offenders

Girls comprise about 30% of all juvenile arrests. This is a higher proportion than in many past decades. Programming has been aimed primarily at male juvenile offenders because they are the majority of the offender population. Theoretical research indicates that girls and boys may come to delinquency from different paths. Girls involved in the juvenile justice system are very likely to have experienced physical abuse (about 61%) and sexual abuse (about 54%). More than half have attempted suicide. A substantial number have been diagnosed with one or more psychiatric disorders [15]. Even more so than boys, delinquent girls come from dysfunctional backgrounds. In one study, it was found that girls involved as wards of the state in the child protective services system were four times more likely to be subsequently delinquent, while boys who had been in care were only twice as likely to be adjudicated as delinquent [16].

Girls' arrest rates followed generally the same pattern of increase and decline over the last 20 years as boys' rates, but at a substantially lower level. Girls' arrests did not decline as dramatically as did boys' arrests and, in some crime categories, they are higher than they were 20 years ago. In Figure 10.3, the trend of juvenile arrests for girls and boys is presented, but note that the

FOCUS ON CRIME: JUVENILE GANGS

It is important to remember that membership in a juvenile gang does not automatically mean the juvenile is also committing delinquent or criminal acts. A good portion of gang activity is noncriminal, especially for female gang members. However, juvenile gangs have been associated with a range of criminal activity, up to and including murder. Gangs are identified as the primary distributor of drugs in the United States, although this statement includes adult gangs as well as delinquent gangs.

There are two ways to estimate the impact of juvenile gang membership on crime. The first is to identify which crimes (or what percent of crimes) are committed by gang members. This is not possible through the Uniform Crime Reports because law enforcement agencies do not record that information. The Bureau of Justice Statistics reports on the National Crime Victim Survey, which does ask victims about the gang affiliation of the perpetrator. This source tells us that about 6% of all violent crimes were perpetrated by a gang-related offender (according to the victim). This is down from 9% in 1993. The second method would be through self-reports. Researchers ask youth if they are members of gangs, and they also ask what crimes they have committed and then evaluate the association. Estimates indicate that gang members commit three times as much crime as non-gang members. Girl gang members commit more crime than non-gang-related boys, but much less crime than male gang members.

Gangs are primarily found in inner-city urban areas, but suburban and rural areas also report the presence of gangs. Findings from longitudinal studies support the "affiliation" theory over the "selection" or "birds of a feather" theory of the association between gang membership and delinquency. This means that they have found that juveniles would be less likely to commit delinquent acts if they did not belong to a gang, not that juveniles predisposed to delinquency seek out gang membership. This study also found that the typical factors associated with gang membership, like poverty, family structure, low self-esteem, and high-crime neighborhood, were not associated with gang membership, although it should be noted that the study did not include Los Angeles or Chicago, which are cities with a very high gang presence.

In the latest national survey of juvenile gangs, it was found that the perception of juvenile gangs as a problem had declined in the early 2000s, but has been increasing since then, although the estimates are still lower than in the mid-1990s. These statistics are from surveys of law enforcement asking them about the presence of gangs as a crime problem. It is reported that there are 27,900 gangs with 774,000 members in the United States in 2008. The number of gangs has increased by 28% since 2002 (based on the survey of law enforcement). Almost half of respondents indicated that the gang problem was getting worse in 2008.

Sources: *J. Whitehead, S. Lab, Juvenile Justice: An Introduction, LexisNexis/Matthew Bender, New Providence, NJ, 2009; A. Egley, J. Howell, J. Moore, Highlights of the 2008 National Youth Gang Survey, Office of Juvenile Justice and Delinquency Prevention, U.S. Department of Justice, Washington, DC, 2010; E. Harrell, Violence by Gang Members, 1993-2003, Bureau of Justice Statistics, U.S. Department of Justice, Washington, DC, 2005; A. Liberman, The Long View of Crime: A Synthesis of Longitudinal Research, Springer, Washington, DC, 2008.*

left axis is different for the two tables and girls' arrests are much lower in all categories.

Girls' arrest increases are evidence to some that girls are becoming more criminal. There are several problems with this thesis. The first issue is that, generally, the increases are reflected in percentage increases, which are sometimes misleading. A percentage increase (or decrease) is a statistic that shows how much of an increase or a decrease occurred over a given period. During the period when juvenile arrests increased, the percentage increase for girls was higher than for boys because their base numbers were much lower. Now, when juvenile crime is decreasing, their percentage decreases are lower than boys and some interpret this as evidence that girls are becoming as delinquent as boys. For instance, the number of girls' arrests decreased substantially between 1996 and 2005. While 445,332 girls were arrested in 1996, 381,643 were arrested

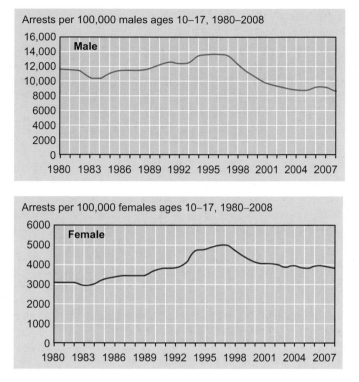

Arrests per 100,000 males ages 10–17, 1980–2008

Male

Arrests per 100,000 females ages 10–17, 1980–2008

Female

FIGURE 10.3
Juvenile arrest rates
for all crimes by sex,
1980-2008. **Source:**
*Office of Juvenile Justice
and Delinquency Prevention,
October 12, 2010, OJJDP
Statistical Briefing Book.
Available at http://ojjdp.
ncjrs.org/ojstatbb/crime/
JAR_Display.asp?ID and
http://www.ojjdp.gov/
ojstatbb/crime/JAR_Display.
asp?ID=qa05230.*

in 2005. This is a percentage decrease of 14.3% [17]. However, the percentage decrease for boys was larger, meaning that their rate declined by a greater percentage. In 2009, there were 354,012 girls arrested, which is a 13% decline from 2000 [18]. The second issue is that arrest rates reflect the actions of decision makers as well as the actions of offenders. It could be, for instance, that girls are more likely to be arrested today than in the past. For example, in 2005, there was a 59% increase in the number of girls arrested for prostitution from the previous year [19]. While that statistic seems alarming, the number of girls who were arrested is still relatively low for both years. In 2004, 420 female juveniles were detained for prostitution, and in 2005, 668 girls were arrested. Thus, while the percentage change is very high, that statistic is not meaningful on its own without knowing the real numbers of arrests that are being represented. It should also be noted that prostitution is a crime that is highly subject to enforcement policy changes. The number arrested, in fact, may have more to do with policy shifts regarding enforcement rather than a reflection of the number of juveniles involved. In 2009, there were 624 girls arrested so the trend for prostitution arrests is opposite from most crime categories, which are still declining.

🌐 **INTERNET KEY**

For tables from the Uniform Crime Reports that show 10-year arrest trends by sex and age, go to Table 33 at http://www2.fbi.gov/ucr/cius2009/data/table_33.html.

Many argue that girls are becoming more violent, pointing to an increase in the assault and aggravated assault rates of girls over the last several decades. Their rates have increased, although again, percentage increases can be high when there are low base rates. Another explanation is the "greater formalization" of the way we treat juvenile misbehavior. With "school safety officers" in schools and an increasing tendency to arrest in any domestic violence incident, it is possible that the increase in assaults by girls is reflecting a greater tendency for formal adjudication. For instance, girls have always gotten into fights, but now they are more likely to be taken into custody for it. A few girls have always hit their mothers, but now they are much more likely to be formally processed. Another point to consider is that the National Crime Victim Survey is not consistent with the increases reflected in official statistics like the Uniform Crime Reports and does not show statistically significant increases in the same periods that official statistics do show such increases. In personal violent crime, the victim would presume to know whether the attacker is male or female; therefore, the victimization statistics indicating the sex of the offender should be credible. What this means is possibly girls are not necessarily committing more violent assaults, but they are more likely to be arrested for them [20]. Ironically, the girls who are in most need of support because of dysfunctional families and victimization may be those who are most likely to be sent to secure detention [21].

There has been longstanding and consistent evidence that girls are likely to be locked up for less serious acts than boys. Throughout the 1960s and 1970s, girls were more likely to be incarcerated in secure facilities for status offenses, while boys in the same facilities were likely to have committed delinquent acts. Even today, after a concerted effort to deinstitutionalize status offenders, current research finds that girls in detention facilities are still more likely to be less serious offenders than boys. What happens today is that judges place female status offenders or less serious delinquents on probation with conditions. Then, the girl who violates a court order to not run away or skip school is found in contempt of court, which is a delinquent act and, with that finding, the girl is detained in a secure facility [22]. About 20% of girls who are locked up in secure facilities are status offenders, but only about 3% of boys locked up are there for status offenses. Twice as many girls as boys are locked up for violations of probation [23]. In many cases, these girls have babies and are mothers before their age of majority. More research is needed to understand the type of youth who receives secure detention, and what programs might be beneficial in breaking the cycle of state intervention.

Minority juvenile offenders

There are also serious concerns by observers that the juvenile justice system discriminates on the basis of race. Black and other minority youth are much more likely to be formally processed and end up in juvenile or adult facilities than whites. Poor kids are also more likely to be taken into the system. Part of this is due to lack of family support. Juveniles who have supportive families who are willing and likely to work with justice officials are more likely to be referred to community programs rather than institutionalized.

In 1997, black youth made up about 15% of the population, about 26% of juvenile arrests, about 30% of delinquency referrals, and about 40% of juveniles in long-term incarceration facilities. Minority youth are increasingly over-represented at each successive phase of the system. Further, they are more likely to be found in public facilities, while white youth are more likely to be found in private "treatment" facilities [24].

The increased punitiveness of the juvenile justice system has affected minority youth more dramatically than white youth. The violent crime rate of black young men in the mid-1980s and early 1990s provided the impetus to "toughen up" the juvenile system and de-emphasize the social work approach that had characterized juvenile corrections. Part of this get-tough movement included the increased use of the waiver to adult court. Black youth have been disproportionately subject to this option [25].

Barry Feld argues that the economic changes that took place in the 1970s, which eliminated manufacturing jobs that had been the basis of a minority middle class, created an urban underclass. The poverty and the hopelessness of inner-city minority neighborhoods were a fertile ground for the crack epidemic that swept these communities in the 1980s, and the crack trade was the primary cause of the spike in violent crime by young black men. Consequently, the changes that have taken place in the juvenile justice system have targeted minorities more than whites. Juvenile court judges are more likely to transfer minority delinquents to adult court than white delinquents, even after controlling for seriousness of crime [26].

Official statistics under-represent the divergence between minorities and whites because they do not identify ethnicity; therefore, Hispanics are combined with whites, which masks the differences between the groups. In almost every indicator, Hispanics fall somewhere between blacks and whites on such things as arrests, detentions, and victimization. In Bishop's study of minorities in the stages of the juvenile justice system, she showed that they became increasingly over-represented [27]. In Table 10.2, we see that black youth are more likely to be arrested than their population percentage would predict, and then at each stage they are more likely to be formally processed until they reach the adjudicated stage, but at this point they have already been detained.

Studies indicate that race does play a factor in judicial decisions to detain, even after controlling for legal factors of the case, such as seriousness [28]. Across offenses, for males and females, the proportion of blacks who were detained was higher than whites. This disparity is especially true for drug offenses—

Table 10.2 Minorities in the Juvenile Justice System

	White	Black	Other
Percentage of the population (10-17)	78	17	6
Percentage of total arrests	71	27	3
Percentage of arrestees that were referred to court	70	82	74
Percentage of referrals detained	19	26	22
Percentage of referrals charged	54	64	58
Percentage of charged adjudicated	70	62	74
Percentage of adjudicated placed out of home	22	27	27

Source: *Adapted from D. Bishop, Race, delinquency, and discrimination: minorities in the juvenile justice system, in: P. Benekos, A. Merlo (Eds.), Controversies in Juvenile Justice and Delinquency, second ed., LexisNexis/Matthew Bender, New Providence, NJ, 2009, p. 225.*

while 30% of black youth are detained, only 16% of whites are detained [29]. Black girls constitute about half of all youth detained in public detention centers and Latinas comprise about 13% of the detained population. While the number of black girls detained increased by 123% between 1988 and 1997, the increase for white girls was only about 41%. While seven of every 10 cases involving white girls are dismissed, only three of every 10 cases involving black girls are dismissed [30]. Black youth in the system are 2.7 times more likely than whites to end up in residential placement. They are also more likely to be waived over to adult court for prosecution and punishment [31].

What accounts for this over-representation? It is true that minority youth are more likely to commit certain crimes than white youth, but that is not the complete answer. Their arrest numbers are higher than self-report and victimization data indicate, lending support to the idea that the decision makers in the system are more likely to arrest and prosecute minorities [32]. Even controlling for crimes, minorities are more likely to be charged, processed, and detained.

THE PROCESSING OF JUVENILE OFFENDERS

Several key differences exist between the juvenile and adult justice systems in the United States. Unlike the criminal justice system, the juvenile justice system can consider extralegal factors in deciding how to handle cases. The juvenile court system can bypass all formal sanctions and judicial action, opting instead to handle matters informally [33].

The language of juvenile corrections is different from adult corrections, as shown in Table 10.3. For instance, juveniles are not *sentenced* to jail, nor are they incarcerated. Instead, juveniles are *adjudicated* with dispositions ranging

Table 10.3 Terminology Differences for Juvenile and Criminal Justice Systems

Juvenile Justice Terminology	Criminal Justice Terminology
Respondent	Defendant
Detain	Arrest
Petition	Indictment
Intake	Prosecution
Hearing	Arraignment
Adjudication hearing	Trial
Finding	Verdict
Secure detention	Pretrial detention
Disposition	Sentencing
Commitment	Imprisonment
Aftercare	Parole
Secure confinement	Imprisoned
Training school, state school, or residential placement	Jail/prison

from a variety of probations to *secure confinement* in *training schools*. Training schools are juvenile incarceration facilities that serve as a residential placement for the most serious juvenile offenders. The juveniles often live in *dorms* instead of prison *cells*, and are considered *students*, not *inmates*. These subtle differences in language may be mere euphemisms, but they reflect the historical mission of juvenile justice.

The process from offense through adjudication (conviction) for juveniles has several similarities to the adult system. First, juveniles suspected of wrongdoing come into contact with the police. During this initial contact, law enforcement officers investigate a delinquent act and decide whether to proceed with informal or formal sanctions. Just as with adult criminals, an officer's reactions are based primarily on the seriousness of the offense committed. Informal sanctions include ignoring the behavior, admonishing the juvenile and consulting his or her parents, referring the family to a social service agency, or detaining the juvenile with a "station adjustment" [34]. If the officer decides to officially respond to juvenile delinquency, the officer will detain the juvenile [35].

Arrest (intake) and interrogation

Although some states require that juveniles have counsel or parents present when being interrogated by police, other states have no such requirement, or the juvenile is allowed to waive that right. Advocates for juveniles argue that they are simply unable to protect their own interests and are vulnerable to manipulation and intimidation by police officers. The intake process is comparable to the prosecution process in the criminal justice system;

however, significant differences do exist in the juvenile system. Intake is the first step toward prosecution, but it is also a step toward returning the juvenile to the community. Once brought to a juvenile detention facility, the juvenile meets with an intake officer. These officers are typically probation officers. The probation/intake officer can decide to divert the youth from the formal juvenile justice system at any point. Frequently, an intake/probation officer can request that the case be placed on deferred prosecution or informal probation, during which time the juvenile must stay out of trouble so that all the charges will be discharged. If the case moves forward toward prosecution, the intake officer files a petition for an adjudication hearing with the juvenile court [36].

Adjudication

The adjudication hearing is the juvenile version of a trial in a criminal court. During this hearing, a judge reviews the charges and evidence, and renders a decision about the juvenile. These hearings are less formal than criminal trials and are conducted in closed courtrooms to protect the anonymity of the youthful suspect. Rarely are adjudication hearings heard by juries, because states are not required to provide jury trials for juvenile processing.

In 2007, 19% of all cases were dismissed at intake, 26% were handled informally, and 56% of cases were formally adjudicated. Of those cases (926,000), 1% were waived to adult court, 63% were adjudicated delinquent, and 36% were not adjudicated delinquent (and therefore released from the system). Of the 63% (586,200) who were adjudicated delinquent, 25% were held in secure detention, 56% were given probation, and 19% received some other form of sanction [37]. Drug courts exist in the juvenile system as well as the adult system. Several hundreds of these courts exist across the country. In these special courts, juveniles who are identified as drug abusers are provided with specialized services. Cases are assigned to a specialized caseload and juveniles may be provided with mental health counseling, as well as family counseling and other services, in addition to drug treatment [38]. In a 2000 survey, 56% of male juvenile detainees and 40% of girls tested positive for drug use at the time of their arrest [39]. There were 134,610 youth under the age of 18 arrested for drug violations in 2009 [40]. Therefore, it is clear that drug courts might be an appropriate response to a large segment of juvenile cases.

Waiver refers to when a juvenile court transfers a case over to adult court. Only four states do not have enabling statutes for waivers. The type of crime and the age of the youth eligible for waiver are set by state statute. Before waiver to adult court, juveniles must be determined to be **competent**. This legal concept means that juveniles are mature enough to know what is happening, be able to judge the consequences of the decisions they make, and be able to assist in their defense. This determination requires that juveniles understand right from wrong, but it does not require that juveniles understand why they did what they did, or that they be able to control their actions.

Judicial waivers increased 73% between 1988 and 1994, but decreased 28% between 1994 and 1997. They comprise only about 1% of all juvenile cases [41]. The Office of Juvenile Justice and Delinquency Prevention indicates that 1994 was the peak of juvenile waivers (with 12,100) and since 1994, the percentage of juvenile cases waived to adult court has declined. In 1998, there were 8100 cases waived to adult court [42]. In 2007, there were about 8500 cases waived [43].

Other information indicates that this decline in the use of waiver does not mean there are fewer juveniles in the adult system, because states are increasingly using other methods such as "direct file" and "statutory exclusion." Statutory exclusion is when a certain crime is statutorily excluded from juvenile jurisdiction, regardless of who commits the crime, so that the juvenile is automatically tried as an adult. There are 29 states that have these statutory exclusion laws. In some states, and for certain crimes, both adult and juvenile jurisdictions exist concurrently. In this situation, a prosecutor may choose to file charges on the juvenile in the adult system (**direct file**). There are 14 states that have enabling legislation for direct file by the prosecutor. It appears that the majority of cases where juveniles end up in the adult system now are not through waiver, but rather through either direct filing by the prosecutor or statutory exclusion [44].

EXERCISE: IN THE STATE OF...

The National Center for Juvenile Justice is an organization dedicated to research on the juvenile justice system. Through the Web site for this organization, you can research your own state's juvenile justice system. Go to http://70.89.227.250:8080/stateprofiles/ and find your state's description. What is the waiver policy of your state? What are the statutory exclusions, if any, to juvenile jurisdiction?

Research on youth who have been waived to adult court indicates that they are more likely to recidivate than those who were retained in juvenile court. In one study, 49% of the transferred offenders recidivated compared to 35% of those retained in the juvenile system. Reasons for the higher recidivism may include the negative effects of the greater stigma of adult punishments, a sense of injustice, learning of criminal mores and behavior from adults, or the decreased focus on rehabilitation in the adult system [45].

Sentencing

When the court finds that a juvenile committed the offense charged, the youth will appear at a disposition hearing. This disposition hearing is equivalent to a sentencing hearing in a criminal court. The key difference is that there are more options available for youthful offenders than for adults, including everything from informal sanctions to incarceration in an adult prison [46].

Figure 10.4 shows the trends in dispositions for juveniles from 1985 to 2007. As noted above, about a quarter of those youth adjudicated delinquent receive residential placement. The number of youth who are placed has been steadily declining since 2000. In 2008, there were about 81,000 delinquents sent to residential placement [47]. Table 10.4 summarizes the variety of alternatives that can be given by juvenile courts and administered in lieu of formal adjudication or as part of the sentencing disposition.

JUVENILE CORRECTIONS

Many juvenile offenders are never formally adjudicated and, therefore, are never formally disposed. Frequently, these alternative sanctions are discussed as dispositions despite the fact that there are no formal sanctions by a juvenile court. The most serious disposition is secure confinement, the juvenile version of jail or prison. Residential facilities are frequently characterized with problems such as overcrowding. Overcrowding is related to safety problems and poor service delivery. Obviously, there are some very violent juvenile offenders that need to be securely confined; however, in some cases, correctional facilities may cause juveniles to become more delinquent or exacerbate

FIGURE 10.4

Disposition of delinquency cases, 1985-2007.

Source: *Office of Juvenile Justice and Delinquency Prevention, September 8, 2006, OJJDP Statistical Briefing Book. Retrieved October 13, 2010 from http://www.ojjdp.gov/ojstatbb/court/qa06501.asp?qaDate=2007.*

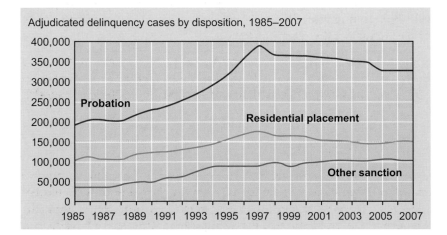

Table 10.4 Types of Dispositions for Juvenile Offenders

Disposition	Definition
Dismissal of case	The case is dismissed and the juvenile is released.
Restitution/fines	Restitution and/or damages are ordered by the court. This includes formal or informal supervision by probation officer.
Therapy	The juvenile must attend group and/or individual counseling sessions to address specific mental health concerns; formal or informal supervision by probation officer.
Mental hospitalization	The juvenile is committed to a mental health facility to treat a specific mental illness.
Group home placements	The juvenile is sent to a group home or residential treatment facility, sometimes targeted to address specific problems. Outward bound or wilderness programs or camps also are possible placements.
House arrest/electronic monitoring	The juvenile is required to be confined to home, except for school and court appearances, with or without electronic monitoring.
Probation	The juvenile is supervised in the community and required to meet set rules such as curfew, school attendance, and clean drug tests to stay out of a training school/state school facility.
Day treatment/day reporting centers	The juvenile is supervised in the community and required to attend special classes or check-ins at set times at day centers. These centers usually have mental health services, vocational training, and other services to meet the needs of the juveniles.
Secure confinement	The juvenile is sent to a placement in a state school or training school where he or she is expected to attend classes and rehabilitate. This sanction is the most serious for juvenile offenders who are not certified as adults.
Adult prison	The juvenile is certified as an adult and a trial is conducted in a criminal (not juvenile) court. The juvenile is then sentenced to serve time in a prison and/or can be sentenced to death. The juvenile may serve part of the sentence in a juvenile facility until he or she is old enough to be placed in an adult prison.

Sources: J. Austin, K.D. Johnson, R. Weitzer, Alternatives to the Secure Detention and Confinement of Juvenile Offenders, Office of Juvenile Justice and Delinquency Prevention, Washington, DC, 2005; C. Bartollas, S.J. Miller, Juvenile Justice in America, fourth ed., Pearson/Prentice Hall, Upper Saddle River, NJ, 2005; R.V. del Carmen, C.R. Trulson, Juvenile Justice: The System, Process, and Law, Thompson-Wadsworth, Belmont, CA, 2006.

psychological problems [48]. Studies consistently show that, at the very least, recidivism is often no better than it would be in a less restrictive community-based environment for the juvenile [49].

Most of the dispositions available for youth are forms of community corrections. Such sanctions can be formal, such as probation with conditions, or informal, when the judge requires that a certain set of acts be performed in order for the case to be disposed of.

Community corrections

An alternative placement to secure, institutional confinement comprises a variety of problem-oriented small residential facilities in which juveniles' specific issues are targeted in a therapeutic environment. These facilities have several different names, including group homes and residential treatment facilities, but they are usually in the juvenile's own community rather than in a rural location. Typically, each facility targets a particular issue such as substance abuse or sex offending. Mandatory completion of programs provided in these residential facilities is usually required to avoid secure confinement. The effectiveness of these programs varies according to each facility's mission. Boot camps, for example, are not particularly effective in reducing recidivism, but some sex-offender treatment facilities show success in reducing recidivism [50].

Restorative justice programs attempt to meet the needs of the community and the offender. They are typically community-based and involve the participation of the offender, the offender's family, the victim, and other community members. Restorative justice sentencing alternatives are most common for juvenile offenders. The concept of restorative justice is that it is best for the offender, victim, and community for the offender to remain in the community. Such programs, which usually include victim participation, work better with juvenile offenders who have not committed serious crimes.

One restorative justice sentencing option is family group conferencing, which began in New Zealand and Australia. In this alternative to traditional juvenile court dispositions, a group conference is held among the youth, victim, family members of both victim and offender, and other interested parties. The group determines the appropriate response to the offense and can order the youth to pay restitution, perform community service, or a range of other possibilities. In evaluations of such programs, it has been found that victims feel more satisfied after such an experience, as do the families of the offenders. However, about 26% of the youth in one such program recidivated, which was no better than a control sample who had received regular probation [51].

Probation

Probation is the oldest and most widely used model of community-based corrections. All states have had juvenile probation since the 1930s, and probation is used for all types of juvenile offenders including first-time, low-risk, and serious offenders [52]. This community-based supervision allows the juvenile to remain in a community while following a set of rules that are specifically tailored to the individual's circumstances.

Probation can be revoked if the juvenile violates the prescribed conditions, which may result in secure confinement for the juvenile offender. Probation was used in 62% of formal juvenile dispositions in 2002 and in 56% of the cases in 2007 [53].

Failure on probation is distressingly common. The factors that have been associated with failure include adjudication for a delinquent act before age 13 and several prior police contacts [54]. Intensive probation programs have been offered as a solution to the failure of regular probation to prevent juveniles from violating probation. Such programs have been evaluated and findings indicate that, similar to adult intensive probation, no significant difference exists between recidivism rates for intensive supervision caseloads and regular probation supervision [55].

Other innovations have included enriched programming, offering adjudicated youths a range of counseling and educational services. In one such integrated program in Los Angeles, program youth were exposed to self-esteem building, educational tutoring, individual and group counseling, mental health services, substance abuse education and treatment, gang prevention alternatives, crisis intervention, family preservation services, education in parenting skills, housing and financial aid information, career development planning, and employment services. In a careful quasiexperimental design, youth were assigned randomly to a treatment group or a control group who experienced regular probation. Although the treatment group performed better in school and received fewer violations, after the initial six-month reporting period there were no statistically significant differences found between the two groups [56].

Arguably, the program did not result in significant differences in outcome because both groups had fairly high success rates (about 80% in both groups did not violate their probation). Critics argue that the evaluation did not take into account the high attrition (dropout) rate, especially in the treatment group, where twice as many youth were removed to secure facilities for more intensive counseling or treatment. Those who were left, perhaps, might have performed successfully with or without such enriched services [57].

Institutionalization

The number of juveniles held in adult prisons has increased over the years. In 2005, there were 2266 inmates under age 18 in adult prisons and 6759 juveniles in jails. In 2008, the number of juveniles incarcerated in adult prisons had increased to 3670 and there were 7703 juveniles in jails. Of those, 6410 had been waived to the adult court system and 1294 were being held as juveniles [58]. A much larger number of juvenile offenders are incarcerated in training schools or youth detention facilities. In 2003, there were about 109,225 juveniles in secure placements (training schools or youth detention facilities). About two-thirds of the youth were housed in public facilities, with the remainder in private facilities. Only about 12% were status offenders. By 2008, the number had declined to 81,000. States have very different rates of imprisonment, however. For instance, in South Dakota, 513 of every 100,000 youth are placed in residential facilities, compared to 69 per 100,000 in Vermont [59].

Experts in juvenile justice agree that secure confinement in "training schools," correctional schools, or detention centers should be used only as a last resort and reserved for serious, violent offenders [60]. Juvenile secure detention and confinement institutions are overcrowded, which is not only dangerous but limits programming options [61].

These juvenile prisons and jails sometimes resemble their adult counterparts with high walls and razor wire. Most, however, have cottage-style architecture instead of cell blocks and they have enriched educational programming. Many youth facilities operate under a token or a phase system that requires juveniles to work toward release. Even in states with determinate sentencing for adults, youth offenders typically have indeterminate sentences, so that facility staff may have a great deal of input into when the juveniles are released. Youth earn points or move through phases by following rules and participating in programming.

While these facilities for juveniles generally offer more educational and vocational programming than adult institutions, there seem to be as many scandals and problems associated with their management as with the adult prisons. In 2006-2007, the Texas Youth Commission, the state agency responsible for managing the network of secure and community placements for juvenile offenders, was rocked by a scandal that eventually led to the resignation of several top administrators, the assignment of a governor-appointed special master, a threat to place the agency in receivership, and the indictments of several former staff. The scandal began with a series of news stories that detailed the investigation of supervision staff at one detention center for allegedly sexually abusing juvenile inmates of the facility. Despite a report from the Texas Rangers, and reports from the agency's own staff at the facility, no action was taken by the agency or the local prosecutor for several years. After the story broke, indictments were finally handed down for the two staff members allegedly involved, but the news stories led to a wholesale investigation of other charges and alleged cover-ups and mismanagement by agency officials. It was alleged that children in custody were held longer than their legal sentence, and that they were sexually and physically abused [62].

In Pennsylvania, a range of corruption charges were filed against two judges after it was discovered that they were taking payments from the owners of a private juvenile detention facility in return for sending juveniles who appeared in their courtrooms to the facility. The Breaking News box describes the case.

Luzerne County Judges Mark A. Ciavarella, center, and Judge Michael T. Conahan, far left, leave the William J. Nealon Federal Building and United States Courthouse in Scranton, Pennsylvania, February 12, 2009, after pleading guilty to corruption charges. *AP Photo/Times Tribune, Pamela Suchy*

BREAKING NEWS

Former Luzerne County, Pennsylvania, judges Michael Conahan and Mark Ciavarella face federal charges of racketeering, money laundering, fraud, bribery, and federal tax violations for accepting millions of dollars in return for sending juveniles who appeared before them to a private correctional facility. Conahan had earlier shut down the county-run youth corrections center so that they would have to send the kids to the private facilities. The judges conducted hearings without appointing lawyers for the juveniles and then sent them to the private facilities for minor offenses, such as fighting at school or shoplifting.

The scandal has led to overturning hundreds of juvenile convictions and releasing many of the juvenile offenders sent to the facility. No one can explain why the scheme was not exposed years ago, but red flags were raised. A newspaper had done an exposé on harsh juvenile sentencing in 2004; and a defense attorney had filed a complaint with the state judicial disciplinary board in 2006, but it failed to act until after the two judges had been indicted by the federal grand jury. The investigation began after another judge in the jurisdiction went to the Federal Bureau of Investigation with his suspicions.

Originally, both men pled guilty but when the federal judge refused to agree with the sentencing recommendation, they withdrew their guilty pleas. Michael Conahan then pled guilty in April 2010 to one count of racketeering. Ciavarella's attorney indicated that he would go to trial.

Sources: *H. Grezlak, L. Strupczewski, Pa. Judicial Corruption Probe Said To Be Eyeing Criminal Cases, Law.com, June 1, 2009. Retrieved on 4/6/2010 from http://www.law.com/jsp/law/LawArticleFriendly.jsp?id=1202431103066, 2009. T. Wilson, Ex-Judge Pleads Guilty in Luzerne "Kids-for-Cash" Scandal, Philadelphia Inquirer, April 30, 2010. Retrieved 10/13/2010 from http://www.philly.com/inquirer/local/pa/20100430_Ex-judge_pleads_guilty_in_Luzerne_kids-for-cash_html, 2010.*

Capital punishment

In 2005, the United States joined the majority of nations in banning the execution of juveniles. In *Roper v. Simmons* (May 7, 2005), the Supreme Court, in a 5-to-4 decision, held that the Eighth and the Fourteenth Amendments barred the execution of anyone who committed their crime before the age of 18. At the time, 20 states allowed the execution of offenders who committed their crimes when they were 16 or 17. In 2010, the Supreme Court decided *Graham v. Florida*, holding that juveniles could not be held under a sentence of life without parole for nonhomicide crimes. In Graham's case, he had been convicted of robbery at 16 and was found guilty of committing another at 17 and violating his probation. The majority of the court held that his sentence was a violation of the Eighth Amendment's prohibition against cruel and unusual punishment. It is not clear, however, whether the majority would uphold a life without parole sentence for other crimes committed by juveniles.[1]

Recidivism

Approximately 100,000 juvenile offenders are released each year from secure correctional placements, including state schools, residential treatment facilities, and adult jails and prisons [63]. However, once released, most juvenile offenders will recidivate. Data show that recidivism rates for juvenile offenders

---

[1]Roper v. Simmons, 543 US 551 (2005) and Graham v. Florida, 08-7412 (Decided May 17, 2010).

released from correctional facilities are 55% or higher [64]. Juvenile offenders who are released from adult facilities have equal or higher rates of recidivism as youth released from juvenile facilities.

Juvenile offenders who are confined to a secure facility are likely to function well below their age-appropriate grade level in school, and a significant proportion of these offenders are functionally illiterate. Schools are reluctant to welcome back the re-entering juveniles, and often juveniles are forced to start midyear, which puts them even further behind. As a result, many of these youths never go back to high school and have excessive free time when they return to the community [65].

In addition, many mental and physical health conditions go untreated or undertreated while juveniles are confined. Research estimates that at least one out of every five youth in the juvenile justice system has serious mental health problems [66]. Deteriorating mental health can affect a juvenile's ability to stay out of trouble. Substance abuse problems are often also left untreated while confined. Approximately half of all juvenile offenders who are confined have substance abuse problems. Yet, many of these juveniles never receive any treatment for abuse and addiction problems. Once these offenders are released, their substance abuse problems frequently lead to other acts of delinquency [67].

One example of a successful program was a specialized juvenile aftercare program in California. This 13-week course emphasized positive social skills, covered drug and alcohol abuse, education, and employment opportunities. After 90 days, the control group was twice as likely as the aftercare group to recidivate and use drugs or alcohol, and three times as likely to have returned to old peer networks. After one year, the recidivism rate of the control group was 53% compared to 32% of the treatment group [68].

In an analysis of 40 promising programs, it was found that the elements associated with successful reduction of recidivism included systematic assessment, appropriate styles of service, and treatment "fidelity," which is the extent to which the program sticks to the original program elements [69].

Finally, in one review, it was pointed out that prevention is more effective than correctional rehabilitation and prevention would include early prevention programs that target very young children. The following preventions are suggested by researchers who argue that scientific evidence supports their effectiveness:

- Early prevention (developmental and social programs that intervene during infancy and before school)
- Individual prevention (preschool enrichment, social skills training, social competence programs for high-risk children)

- Family prevention (parenting programs to teach effective discipline)
- School prevention (discipline management programs, instructional management, reorganization of grades or classes and cognitive programs to increase self control; also, after-school programs and mentor programs) [70]

CONCLUSION

The juvenile justice system began with the mission to treat juveniles differently from adult offenders and to recognize their reduced culpability and greater ability to change. With a series of court cases in the 1970s, the juvenile system lost much of its informality and juvenile offenders were granted greater due process rights. During the 1990s, a variety of legislative and procedural changes were enacted in response to a spike in juvenile offending. The consequence has been that more juveniles are processed in the adult court system.

While juvenile offense rates have decreased since the 1990s, the use of correctional institutions for youthful offenders, both secure confinement and adult prisons, continues to increase. The lack of treatment available to juveniles while they are confined is considered to be the biggest obstacle to effective reentry [71].

Serious juvenile justice debates remain unresolved, including:

- The use of adult courts to adjudicate youthful offenders
- The perceived bias of the system toward minorities
- The use of a variety of zero-tolerance measures in schools to address violence
- The identification of successful programming for juveniles

Public policy remains committed to changing the delinquent ways of juvenile offenders and preventing these youth from becoming chronic criminal offenders. Community-based programs such as probation, group homes, and day reporting centers should be utilized for all offenders who do not pose serious risks to the public because there is evidence that these are more effective at reducing recidivism and improving community adjustment than secure confinements [72].

Review Questions

1. Describe the child saver movement. When were the first juvenile courts established?
2. What are the differences between status offenders and delinquents?
3. Identify the rights established in the *Kent v. United States*, *In re Winship*, *In re Gault*, and *Roper v. Simmons* cases.

4. Describe the pattern of juvenile arrests over the last 20 years.
5. Describe the arrest pattern of female juveniles compared to male juvenile offenders.
6. Describe the evidence used to show that minority youth are incarcerated disproportionately.
7. What are the differences in the terminology between the adult and juvenile systems?
8. Describe waivers and other means by which juveniles are prosecuted in criminal court.
9. Describe some of the sanctions used for youthful offenders.
10. How many juveniles are incarcerated in adult facilities? How many in juvenile facilities? Discuss the findings regarding the recidivism of juvenile offenders.

VOCABULARY

attrition the number who drop out or quit

child saver movement involved upper-middle-class women in the late 1800s who took on as a reform project the terrible living conditions of immigrant children

competent able to understand right and wrong, understand the proceedings, and be able to assist in one's defense

delinquents those who commit an act that is defined as a crime by the penal code

direct file when the prosecutor and juvenile prosecutor both have jurisdiction to pursue a case, and the prosecutor in adult criminal court prosecutes the juvenile

parens patriae the idea that the state will take the place of the parent

restorative justice programs that are typically community based and involve the participation of the offender, offender's family, victim, and other community members

status offenders juveniles who commit behavior that is punished only because they are juveniles, such as running away, breaking curfew, or being "incorrigible"

statutory exclusion when a certain crime is statutorily excluded from juvenile jurisdiction, and the juvenile is automatically tried as an adult

waiver when a juvenile court transfers a case to be adjudicated in adult court

ENDNOTES

[1] A. Platt, The Child Savers: The Invention of Delinquency, University of Chicago Press, Chicago, 1977.

[2] A. Platt, The Child Savers: The Invention of Delinquency, University of Chicago Press, Chicago, IL, 1977.

[3] Cable News Network, Florida judge hears motions in child murder case, 2001. Retrieved 2/6/2003 from http://www.cnn.com/2001/la/02/23/child.killer.hearing.

[4] K. Zernike, Crackdown on threats in schools fails a test, New York Times, May 17, 2001. Retrieved 5/17/2001 from www.nytimes.com/2001/05/17/nyregion/17THRE.html.

[5] Federal Bureau of Investigation, Uniform Crime Reports, 1998, U.S. Department of Justice, Washington, DC, 1998.

[6] Office of Juvenile Justice and Delinquency Prevention, OJJDP Statistical Briefing Book: Law Enforcement and Juvenile Crime. Retrieved 8/7/2007 from http://ojjdp.ncjrs.org/ojstatbb/crime/JAR.asp, 2001.

[7] Bureau of Justice Statistics, Criminal Offenders, 2007. Retrieved 7/30/2007 from http://ojp. usdoj.gov/bjs.

[8] New York Times, One strike and they're out, New York Times, September 19, 2010. Retrieved 10/8/2010 from http://www.nytimes.com/2010/09/19/opinion/19sun3.html.

[9] A. Payne, Crime and education: moving school discipline from exclusion and criminal justice to restoration and social justice, Criminologist 35 (5) (2010) 1–5.

[10] E. Eckholm, Ruling limits state's power in school suspensions, New York Times, October 9, 2010. Retrieved 10/9/2010 from http://www.nytimes.com/2010/10/09/us/09suspend.html.

[11] D. Nagin, A. Piquero, E. Scott, L. Steinberg, Public preferences for rehabilitation versus incarceration of juvenile offenders: evidence from a contingent valuation survey, Criminol. Public Pol. 5(4) (2006) 627–652.

[12] Office of Juvenile Justice and Delinquency Prevention, Office of Juvenile Justice and Delinquency Prevention, OJJDP Statistical Briefing Book, 2007. Available at http://ojjdp. ncjrs.org/ojstatbb/crime/JAR_Display.asp?ID=qa05200.

[13] C. Puzzanchera, Juvenile Arrests, 2008, OJJDP, Office of Juvenile Justice and Delinquency Prevention, U.S. Department of Justice, Washington, DC, 2009, p. 4.

[14] C. Puzzanchera, Juvenile Arrests, 2008, OJJDP, U.S. Department of Justice, Washington, DC, 2009, p. 4.

[15] B. Dohrn, All Ellas: girls locked up, Feminist Stud. 30(2) (2004) 307.

[16] B. Dohrn, All Ellas: girls locked up, Feminist Stud. 30(2) (2004) 308.

[17] See the Uniform Crime Reports. Retrieved from http://www.fbi.gov/ucr/05cius/data/ table_33.html.

[18] See the Uniform Crime Reports. Retrieved from http://www2.fbi.gov/ucr/cius2009/data/ table_33.html.

[19] See the Uniform Crime Reports. Retrieved from http://www.fbi.gov/ucr/05cius/data/table_33. html.

[20] Girls Study Group, Office of Juvenile Justice and Delinquency Prevention (OJJDP), Violence by Teenage Girls: Trends and Context, OJJDP, U.S. Department of Justice, Washington, DC, 2008.

[21] M. Chesney-Lind, The Female Offender: Girls, Women, and Crime, Sage, Thousand Oaks, CA, 2006; B. Dohrn, All Ellas: girls locked up, Feminist Stud. 30(2) (2004) 313.

[22] M. Chesney-Lind, Judicial paternalism and the female status offender, Crime Delinquency 23 (1977) 121–130; M. Chesney-Lind, The Female Offender: Girls, Women, and Crime, Sage, Thousand Oaks, CA, 2006.

[23] B. Dohrn, All Ellas: girls locked up, Feminist Stud. 30(2) (2004) 311.

[24] B. Feld, The politics of race and juvenile justice: the 'due process revolution' and the conservative reaction, Justice Q. 20(4) (2003) 7.

[25] B. Feld, The politics of race and juvenile justice: the 'due process revolution' and the conservative reaction, Justice Q. 20(4) (2003) 765–800.

[26] B. Feld, The politics of race and juvenile justice: the 'due process revolution' and the conservative reaction, Justice Q. 20(4) (2003) 792.

[27] D. Bishop, Race, delinquency, and discrimination: minorities in the juvenile justice system, in: P. Benekos, A. Merlo (Eds.), Controversies in Juvenile Justice and Delinquency, second ed., LexisNexis/Matthew Bender, New Providence, NJ, 2009, pp. 223–253.

[28] M. Leiber, K. Fox, Race and the impact of detention on juvenile justice decision making, Crime Delinq. 51(4) (2005) 470–497.

[29] D. Bishop, Race, delinquency, and discrimination: minorities in the juvenile justice system, in: P. Benekos, A. Merlo (Eds.), Controversies in Juvenile Justice and Delinquency, second ed., LexisNexis/Matthew Bender, New Providence, NJ, 2009, pp. 223–253.

[30] B. Dohrn, All Ellas: girls locked up, Feminist Stud. 30(2) (2004) 309.

[31] D. Bishop, Race, delinquency, and discrimination: minorities in the juvenile justice system, in: P. Benekos, A. Merlo (Eds.), Controversies in Juvenile Justice and Delinquency, second ed., LexisNexis/Matthew Bender, New Providence, NJ, 2009, pp. 223–253.

[32] D. Bishop, Race, delinquency, and discrimination: minorities in the juvenile justice system, in: P. Benekos, A. Merlo (Eds.), Controversies in Juvenile Justice and Delinquency, second ed., LexisNexis/Matthew Bender, New Providence, NJ, 2009, 231.

[33] H. Snyder, M. Sickmund, Juvenile Offenders and Victims: 2006 National Report, Office of Juvenile Justice and Delinquency Prevention, Washington, DC, 2006.

[34] R. del Carmen, C. Trulson, Juvenile Justice: The System, Process, and Law, Thomson-Wadsworth, Belmont, CA, 2006, p. 21.

[35] R. del Carmen, C. Trulson, Juvenile Justice: The System, Process, and Law, Thomson-Wadsworth, Belmont, CA, 2006.

[36] C. Bartollas, S. Miller, Juvenile Justice in America, fourth ed., Pearson/Prentice Hall, Upper Saddle River, NJ, 2005; R. del Carmen, C. Trulson, Juvenile Justice: The System, Process, and Law, Thomson-Wadsworth, Belmont, CA, 2006.

[37] C. Knoll, M. Sickmund, Delinquency Cases in Juvenile Court, 2007, Office of Juvenile Justice and Delinquency Prevention, Department of Justice, Washington, DC, 2010, p. 3.

[38] Office of Juvenile Justice and Delinquency Prevention, Juvenile Drug Court Programs, OJJDP, Washington, DC, 2001. Retrieved from http://www.ncjrs.org/pdffiles1/ojjdp/184744.pdf.

[39] National Institute on Drug Abuse, Principles of Drug Abuse Treatment for Criminal Justice Populations: A Research-Based Guide, National Institutes of Health, Washington DC, 2006.

[40] Crime in the United States, Table 38, Arrests by Sex, 2009. Retrieved 10/12/2010 from http://www2.fbi.gov/ucr/cius2009/data/table_38.html.

[41] J. Petersilia, Reforming Probation and Parole, American Correctional Association, Lanham, MD, 2002, p. 47.

[42] C. Puzzanchera, Delinquency Cases Waived to Criminal Court, 1989-1998, Office of Juvenile Justice and Delinquency Prevention, Washington, DC, 2003. Available at www.ncjrs.gov/pdf-files1/ojjdp/fs200135.pdf.

[43] D. Bishop, Race, delinquency, and discrimination: minorities in the juvenile justice system, in: P. Benekos, A. Merlo (Eds.), Controversies in Juvenile Justice and Delinquency, second ed., LexisNexis/Matthew Bender, New Providence, NJ, 2009, pp. 223–253.

[44] G. Rainville, S. Smith, Juvenile Felony Defendants in Criminal Courts: Survey of 40 Counties, 1998, U.S. Department of Justice, Washington, DC, 2003.

[45] R. Redding, Juvenile Transfer Laws: An Effective Deterrent to Delinquency? Office of Juvenile Justice and Delinquency Prevention, U.S. Department of Justice, Washington, DC, 2010.

[46] R. del Carmen, C. Trulson, Juvenile Justice: The System, Process, and Law, Thomson-Wadsworth, Belmont, CA, 2006; C. Bartollas, S.J. Miller, Juvenile Justice in America, fourth ed., Pearson/Prentice Hall, Upper Saddle River, NJ, 2005.

[47] M. Sickmund, Juveniles in Residential Placement, 1997-2008, OJJDP, U.S. Department of Justice, Washington, DC, 2010.

[48] J. Austin, K. Johnson, R. Weitzer, Alternatives to the Secure Detention and Confinement of Juvenile Offenders, Office of Juvenile Justice and Delinquency Prevention, Washington, DC, 2005; W. Barton, Incorporating the strengths perspective into intensive juvenile aftercare,

Western Criminol. Rev. 7(2) (2006) 48–53; H. Snyder, M. Sickmund, Juvenile Offenders and Victims: 1999 National Report, Office of Juvenile Justice and Delinquency Prevention, Washington, DC, 1999, p. 98.

[49] M. Lipsey, Juvenile delinquency treatment: a meta-analytic inquiry into the variability of effects, in: T. Cook, D. Cordray, H. Hartman, L. Hedges, R. Light, T. Louis, F. Mosteller (Eds.), Meta-Analysis for Explanation: A Casebook, Russell Sage Foundation, New York, 1992, pp. 83–127.

[50] J. Austin, K. Johnson, R. Weitzer, Alternatives to the Secure Detention and Confinement of Juvenile Offenders, Office of Juvenile Justice and Delinquency Prevention, Washington, DC, 2005; H. Snyder, M. Sickmund, Juvenile Offenders and Victims: 1999 National Report, Office of Juvenile Justice and Delinquency Prevention, Washington, DC, 1999.

[51] A. Morris, G. Maxwell, Reforming juvenile justice: the New Zealand experiment, Prison J. 77(2) (1997) 125–134.

[52] H. Snyder, M. Sickmund, Juvenile Offenders and Victims: 2006 National Report, Office of Juvenile Justice and Delinquency Prevention, Washington, DC, 2006.

[53] H. Snyder, M. Sickmund, Juvenile Offenders and Victims: 2006 National Report, Office of Juvenile Justice and Delinquency Prevention, Washington, DC, 2006, p. 172; C. Knoll, M. Sickmund, Delinquency Cases in Juvenile Court, 2007, Office of Juvenile Justice and Delinquency Prevention, Department of Justice, Washington, DC, 2010, p. 3.

[54] R. Sharp, The early offender project: a community-based program for high risk youth, Juvenile Family Court J. 39(1) (1988) 13–20.

[55] W. Barton, J. Butts, Viable options: intensive supervision programs for juvenile delinquents, Crime Delinquency 36(2) (1990) 238–256.

[56] S. Zhang, L. Zhang, An experimental study of the Los Angeles county repeat offender prevention program: its implementation and evaluation, Criminol. Public Pol. 4(2) (2005) 205–236.

[57] D. Mackenzie, The importance of using scientific evidence to make decisions about correctional programming, Criminol. Public Pol. 4(2) (2005) 249–258.

[58] Bureau of Justice Statistics, Prison and Jail Inmates at Mid-Year, 2005, U.S. Department of Justice, Washington, DC, 2006; H. West, W. Sabol, Prison Inmates at Midyear 2008, Bureau of Justice Statistics, Washington, DC, 2009; T. Minton, W. Sabol, Jail Inmates at Midyear 2008, Bureau of Justice Statistics, U.S. Department of Justice, Washington, DC, 2009.

[59] M. Sigmund, Juveniles in Residential Placement, 1997-2008, Office of Juvenile Justice and Delinquency Prevention, U.S. Department of Justice, Washington, DC, 2010.

[60] L. Arthur, Ten ways to reduce detention populations, Juvenile Family Court J. 52(1) (2001) 29–36.

[61] J. Austin, K. Johnson, R. Weitzer, Alternatives to the Secure Detention and Confinement of Juvenile Offenders, Office of Juvenile Justice and Delinquency Prevention, Washington, DC, 2005.

[62] S. McGonigle, D. Swanson, Feds knew about TYC abuse cases, Dallas News, August 5, 2007. Retrieved 8/8/2007 from http://www.dallasnews.com/sharedcontent/dws/news/texassouthwest/stories/080507dnmettycabuse.389a816.html. See also N. Blakeslee, Hidden in plain sight: how did alleged abuse at a youth facility in West Texas evade detection for so long? Texas Observer, August 8, 2007. Retrieved 8/8/2007 from http://www.texasobserver.org/article.php?aid=2428.

[63] W. Barton, Incorporating the strengths perspective into intensive juvenile aftercare, Western Criminol. Rev. 7(2) (2006) 48–53.

[64] W. Barton, Incorporating the strengths perspective into intensive juvenile aftercare, Western Criminol. Rev. 7(2) (2006) 48.

[65] W. Barton, Incorporating the strengths perspective into intensive juvenile aftercare, Western Criminol. Rev. 7(2) (2006) 49.

[66] J. Cocozza, J. Shufelt, Juvenile Mental Health Courts: An Emerging Strategy, National Center for Mental Health and Juvenile Justice, Policy Research Institute, Delmar, NY, 2006. Retrieved 11/25/2006 from http://www.ncmhjj.com/pdfs/publications/JuvenileMentalHealthCourts.pdf?tr=y&auid=1879566.

[67] W. Barton, Incorporating the strengths perspective into intensive juvenile aftercare, Western Criminol. Rev. 7(2) (2006) 48–53.

[68] D. Josi, D. Seachrest, A pragmatic approach to parole aftercare: evaluation of a community reintegration program for high-risk youthful offenders, Justice Q. 16 (1999) 51–80. See also L. Goodstein, H. Sontheimer, The implementation of an intensive aftercare program for serious juvenile offenders, Crim. Justice Behav. 24 (1997) 332–359.

[69] A. Leschied, A. Cummings, L. Baker models of supervision relevant to the delivery of effective correctional service, in: American Correctional Association, What Works and Why: Effective Approaches to Reentry, American Correctional Association, Lanham, MD, 2005, pp. 35–60.

[70] B. Welsh, D. Farrington, Save children from a life of crime, Criminol. Public Pol. 6(4) (2007) 871–880.

[71] W. Barton, Incorporating the strengths perspective into intensive juvenile aftercare, Western Criminol. Rev. 7(2) (2006) 48–53.

[72] J. Howell, Guide for Implementing the Comprehensive Strategy for Serious, Violent and Chronic Juvenile Offenders, Office of Juvenile Justice and Delinquency Prevention, Washington, DC, 1995; M. Lipsey, Juvenile delinquency treatment: a meta-analytic inquiry into the variability of effects, in: D. Rosenbaum (Ed.), Community Crime Prevention: Does It Work? Russell Sage Foundation, New York, 1992.

4

Corrections as Social Control

The Function of Corrections

WHAT YOU NEED TO KNOW

- Correctional goals seem to occur in cycles and include retribution, deterrence, incapacitation, and reform/rehabilitation.
- The origin of the penitentiary was the Walnut Street Jail.
- The contributions of Maconochie, Crofton, Brockway, and Augustus led to the modern-day probation and parole systems.
- The rehabilitative era of the 1960s-1970s had ended by 1980, although its influence can still be detected in correctional programs.
- Incarceration in prison or jail is the most frequent felony sentence (69%), but the largest percentage (58%) of those under correctional supervision are on probation.
- There are over 700,000 individuals who return from prison each year to their communities.
- In 2009, about 7.2 million persons (7,225,800) were under some form of correctional supervision, or one in every 32 adults.
- Women represent about 18% of probationers, 12% of parolees, and 6.5% of prisoners.
- The three approaches to offender classification are clinical, actuarial, and risk/needs.

Criminal punishments have been around as long as there have been organized communities. Humans have been incredibly creative in inventing ways to inflict pain. At various times in history, we have employed punishments that included crucifying, drawing and quartering, boiling in oil, whipping, penal colonies, enslavement, forfeiture of all property, stocks and pillories, banishment, and many others. Historically, the goal of punishment was simply retribution, which basically means inflicting punishment proportional to the harm caused. However, deterrence has also been a goal, including specific deterrence (what is done to an individual to deter him or her from future offending) and general deterrence (what is done to an individual to discourage others from future offending). Incapacitation was added as a goal with the development of places of confinement. Incapacitation simply means to render incapable, and in corrections, it means to make the offender incapable of committing crime. Also, in more recent eras, we have added the goal of rehabilitation, which means to change the individual in terms of values, attitudes, beliefs, and behaviors. Thus, the four goals of corrections or punishment are:

- Retribution
- Deterrence
- Incapacitation
- Reform/rehabilitation

The emphasis on punishment or reform seems to occur in cycles. Today, we are in a punitive era that began in the 1980s and rehabilitation is less emphasized as a goal of the system.

THE HISTORY OF PUNISHMENT AND CORRECTIONS

In the history of punishment, we have seen two competing approaches. On the one hand, there is a tendency to employ the community to shame the offender (i.e., in the use of stocks and pillories); on the other hand, there has also been a tendency to banish the offender and remove him or her from the community. Most often, the two types of punishment response exist together in any given community or time.

Very early forms of justice, such as the Code of Hammurabi, detailed specific punishments for specific crimes and employed a harsh system of corporal and capital punishments. Early punishment systems also employed a proportional "eye for an eye" (lex talionis) form of punishment. In some societies, offenders were ordered to pay compensation, and only when they could not or would not, would corporal punishment be employed.

In medieval Europe, the term "outlaw" came to mean an offender who refused to pay the compensation ordered. When the individuals declared themselves, through their nonconformance, as "outside the law," then more serious forms of punishment were employed. Very serious crimes warranted banishment. However, most punishments were public and the community participated. Box 11.1 shows some of the types of public punishments that were used in early American colonies. If the shame of these punishments did not deter future offending, repeat offenders were banished from the colony and/or branded to

BOX 11.1 FORMS OF PUBLIC PUNISHMENT

Ducking stool: Typically for women charged with being a "common scold" or, sometimes, for those accused of witchcraft. It was a board with chair on one end, dunked in the river or other body of water.

Brank: Metal headgear, sometimes with a sharp spike that went under the tongue. Used for those accused of blasphemy or "common scolds."

Stocks: The offender's head (and sometimes hands and feet) were secured in this wooden device in the town square. The public would participate by throwing vegetables, jeering, and scolding the offender.

discourage them from living in other communities. Banishment from the colonies often meant death because it was hard to survive in the wilderness alone without the protection of the community.

The origin of the penitentiary in this country can be traced to the Walnut Street Jail and the Eastern State Penitentiary in Pennsylvania. We will discuss penitentiaries in greater detail in Chapter 13. The penitentiary was a type of banishment because penitentiaries were, by design, far away from communities. Interestingly, the offenders were banished not only to protect the community from the offender, but also to protect the offender from the community! Originators of the penitentiary believed that the community was the cause of crime. The penitentiary, with its emphasis on obedience and sobriety, was considered a utopia where the offender could contemplate his or her evil ways and perform penitence. In fact, the name *penitentiary* is derived from this function.

The rise of the use of penitentiaries and prison colonies in the late 1770s and early 1800s spurred the creation of experiments that eventually led to community correctional alternatives like probation and parole. The most important contributors to modern concepts in corrections are Alexander Maconochie's **mark system** in the Norfolk prison colony off the coast of Australia, which awarded prisoners marks or credits that earned greater liberties and Sir Walter Crofton's Irish **ticket of leave system,** which allowed prisoners who behaved well to earn early release with a "ticket to leave" a prison as long as they reported to the local constable's office in their community. These correctional experiments will be discussed more fully in later chapters. The **Progressive Movement,** from 1890 through the early 1900s, saw a great deal of activity in the growth of private charities designed to deal with the problems of the poor in Northeastern cities. Private charities and settlement houses sought to feed, clothe, and instill religious virtues in the immigrant populations. In settlement houses, such as the one run by Jane Addams, middle-class and upper-middle-class women literally moved into the ghetto and tried to recreate their middle-class community through lessons on housekeeping and etiquette in the settlement house. The other solutions to the poverty and rising crime of northeastern cities were an increasing use of prisons for adults and state care for juveniles.

Jane Addams' Hull House, now a museum at the University of Illinois at Chicago. *Courtesy en.wikipedia.org.*

The first half of the twentieth century was largely without innovation in corrections. Prisons were successful if they stayed off the front page of the newspaper. Although the legislation that created probation slowly spread across the country from its origins in Massachusetts, it wasn't until 1956 that all states finally passed enabling statutes. Between the Depression and the Vietnam War, there were no dramatic developments in correctional philosophy. All that changed in the 1960s.

The rehabilitative era

The period of the 1960s through 1974 has been called the **rehabilitative era**. Prisons were renamed correctional institutions, and guards were renamed correctional officers. Funding became available for prison treatment programs. There also developed a groundswell of support for community alternatives to prison. This period could also be referred to as the prisoner rights era. Federal courts began handing down decisions that recognized prisoners' rights to due process before further punishment, to practice religion in ways that did not threaten security, and the right to be free from cruel and unusual punishment.

The 1967 President's Commission on Law Enforcement and the Administration of Justice's report encouraged communities to develop diversion programs to keep offenders from becoming more deeply embroiled in the justice system.

One of the side effects of such programs, unfortunately, was **net-widening**. This term is used to describe how diversion programs designed for those sentenced to prison would be used for minor offenders instead. What happened, then, was not a reduction of the number of people involved in the corrections system, but an increase, because the same offenders continued to go to prison, and new offenders, who might have received only a suspended sentence before, were given the new types of sentences. Only those programs that diverted the offender *after* sentencing could be totally assured of truly diverting instead of widening the correctional population.

Part of this period can also be called the **Reintegration Era**. The term was coined to discuss the issue of inmates returning to the community and the problems they encountered. Philosophically, the approach adhered to the belief that the community was the best place to deal with most offenders and, if the offender had to be sent away to prison, then it should be for as short a time as possible. After release, the offender has trouble reintegrating into society and, in the reintegrative era, a number of programs were created to help ex-convicts in their reentry. Some of the popular programs of this era included:

- Prerelease programs
- Halfway houses to transition back into the community
- Work furloughs/release programs
- School-release programs
- Service-enriched parole

It should be noted that this period was also marked by the deinstitutionalization of other groups, such as the mentally ill and juvenile offenders. There was an emphasis on "grassroots development," community empowerment, and a belief that institutions were the least desirable societal response to social deviants [1].

Communities were enticed and encouraged to keep offenders in the community through grants and subsidies that paid counties a per diem for each offender who otherwise would have been sent to prison. Criminal Justice Partnership Acts gave financial incentives to counties to develop programs and partnerships among probation, jail, and other local agencies.

The decline of the rehabilitative ideal

By the beginning of the 1980s, the rehabilitative/reintegration era was over. States were passing determinate sentencing statutes, furloughs and work release programs were being drastically curtailed, and the incredible increase in incarceration had begun. Probation and parole continued, of course, but the philosophy shifted to surveillance rather than service.

Intensive probation programs originated in the early 1980s as a way to "beef up" this sentencing option and make it more palatable for judges who would otherwise send the offender to prison. The 1980s also saw the emergence of boot camps, created to provide tough incarceration experiences for young adults. Waivers to adult courts for juvenile offenders increased. Mandatory sentence laws for drug offenders were passed in many states. In the 1990s, three-strikes sentencing laws became more popular. By the end of the 1990s, correctional policy bore only the faintest resemblance to the rehabilitative era of the early 1970s. From the mid-1990s until today, the national crime rate has fallen dramatically while the imprisonment rate has continued to increase. A large portion of that increase has been comprised of drug offenders, spotlighted in our focus on crime box.

FOCUS ON CRIME: DRUG CRIMES

Drug crimes include simple possession, possession with intent to distribute, and drug smuggling. While other crimes, such as homicide, robbery, and assault, may be linked to drug criminals or drug abuse, these would not be considered drug crimes and will not be discussed in this summary. While some activities (smuggling, mislabeling of pharmaceuticals) are only federal crimes, there are other activities that violate both federal and state drug laws. The individual might be prosecuted in either the federal or state court system, or both! All drug crimes begin with the Uniform Controlled Substances Act, which is patterned after the federal government's Controlled Substances Act. This comprehensive code, shared by all 50 states, lists, describes, and categorizes all drugs into five "schedules" or classifications based on their medicinal value and addiction potential. Whenever a new drug is invented or is brought to the attention of authorities, it is evaluated and placed somewhere in the classification system. Schedule 1 controlled substances have no accepted medical use and have a high potential for addiction (e.g., heroin, marijuana), while Schedule 5 controlled substances have a low potential for abuse and have a currently accepted medical use (codeine cough suppressants). Any substance that is in Schedule 1 to 5 is "controlled" in its manufacture and/or distribution; however, the extent of the control is based on the factors mentioned earlier. Schedule 1 drugs are illegal to possess or distribute under federal laws. There is a current controversy over whether marijuana should be moved to Schedule 2 or lower to facilitate medically approved usage of the active ingredient in marijuana for use in antinausea or pain treatment.

The incredible rise in prison populations has been fueled to a large degree by enforcement patterns against drug offenders. In 1973, there were 328,670 arrests; by 2007, that number was 1,841,182, representing a 460% increase. In 2008, there was a 7.5% decrease in drug arrests (1,702,537), and in 2009, the number of arrests declined again to 1,663,582. On the other hand, as the following chart shows, this decline is recent and modest compared to the 30-year trend of increasing drug arrests.

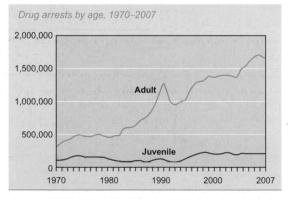

Drug arrests by age, 1970–2007

Source: *BJS, Retrieved 10/15/2010 from, http://bjs.ojp.usdoj.gov/content/glance/drug.cfm.*

FOCUS ON CRIME: DRUG CRIMES—CONT'D

As mentioned earlier, drug users may be arrested and ultimately convicted for nondrug crimes. Most research indicates that the drug-crime connection goes beyond simply arresting for drug offenses. Drug use and criminality are correlated. One source of data on drugs and criminality is the Arrestee Drug Monitoring Program (ADAM II). This federal survey obtains urine samples and interviews all arrestees on their drug use in 10 participating county jurisdictions. The ADAM program began with a 35-city sample in 2000 and has been reduced in scope and sample, but still provides interesting data on male arrestees. Findings indicate that large numbers of arrestees have some type of drug in their system. They are likely to be unemployed, uninsured, and in a transient living situation. Use figures varied from location to location and sometimes were quite different from the use percentages recorded in a general population survey (the National Survey on Drug Use and Health), the nation's primary population survey on drug use. In 2008, only 8% of male respondents 18 years or older in the general survey reported they had used marijuana in the prior 30 days, but between 34% and 52% (depending on the city) of arrestees admitted use. As for other crimes, some cities' percentages of those arrested who claimed use were roughly consistent with the national average, but other cities evidently had much higher numbers of offenders using drugs. For instance, 20% of males in the general survey reported ever having used cocaine powder and 5% to ever having used crack, but 17% (Sacramento) to 44% (Chicago) of arrestees tested positive in 2008 for cocaine in their system at the time of arrest. About 0.2% of general respondents reported ever using heroin, but from 1% to 29% of arrestees reported use. As for criminal history, about 27% of the general population sample reported any arrests, but 59% (Washington, DC) to 94% (Chicago) of arrestees reported prior arrests.

Sources: *http://drugwarfacts.org/cms/?q=node/34; http://bjs.ojp. usdoj.gov/content/glance/drug.cfm http://www.whitehousedrugpolicy. gov/publications/pdf/adam2009.pdf Obtained 10/30/2010.*

New reentry efforts

After years of dormancy, it appears that a reintegration era may have returned. Three elements can be identified as forming this new era.

First, there has been a growing uneasiness with the incredible rise of incarceration. We now incarcerate in prisons or jails 743 of every 100,000 individuals in this country [2]. We use incarceration more than any similar Western country, and only such countries as Russia and South Africa share our tendency to incarcerate so many citizens [3]. A steady and growing voice in the academic and popular press has called into question the approach of building more prisons and incarcerating more and more people. One aspect of this criticism is the "collateral" damage that imprisonment creates. Collateral damage refers to the problems of the families left behind by offenders, and to the communities who lose large numbers of their citizens to imprisonment. It also refers to the civil disabilities that prisoners experience upon release from prison.

Second, there has been recognition that the tens of thousands of people who have been incarcerated throughout the 1980s and 1990s are now being released. In states that abolished parole, the release comes with no substantive

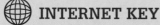

INTERNET KEY

For more information about the Second Chance Act of 2007 and reentry efforts, go to the National Reentry Resource Center at http://www. nationalreentryresourcecenter.org/about/ second-chance-act.

supervision. The statistic that has hit the news with force is that 650,000 offenders are being released into the community every year [4]. Actually, the number of prisoners exiting each year has increased to about 720,000. This has led to federal efforts to address the issue, such as the Second Chance Act of 2007. This federal legislation, signed into law in 2008, provides grants for innovative reentry programming.

The third element that might have led to this new era of community emphasis in corrections is the **restorative justice movement**. This approach to corrections recognizes that the community is essential in crime prevention and crime control. Restorative justice programs keep the offender in the community and provide a means to meet the needs of the victim, the offender, and the community. Offenders who are banished are less likely to have a stake in the community, while offenders who are embraced by the community are more likely to be reformed by the process of punishment.

In one respect, this issue of ex-inmates is no different from the situation that has always existed. Ex-prisoners have always had problems with jobs, housing, and readjustment. In another sense, however, we face a different situation today because the scope of the problem is immense. The dramatic increase in incarceration has not only created the need for more prisons, but it has also created more ex-prisoners. Further, the scourge of drug addiction qualitatively changes the reentry process from those ex-prisoners from 30 and 40 years ago. Also, in our current economic climate, with unemployment at historic levels, it is harder than ever for ex-offenders to find work. Jobs and housing were, and continue to be, identified as factors in recidivism [5].

One target of reentry efforts is to address the range of **civil disabilities**—legal barriers that remove civil rights such as voting—that accompany a felony record. In 2001, it was reported that in 46 states, felons lost their right to vote and, in 14 of these states, the loss was permanent [6]. By 2005, only three states (Florida, Kentucky, and Virginia) still retained a lifetime ban on voting rights, and in 11 other states, the offender could ask to have their voting rights restored upon successful completion of their sentence. Only two states (Maine and Vermont) had no restrictions on voting by offenders [7].

PRISON VERSUS COMMUNITY CORRECTIONS

After a conviction, criminal offenders can be given a range of different punishments, but the two used most frequently are prison and probation. One in every 32 adult residents in this country is under correctional supervision [2]. Figure 11.1 shows a breakdown of what percentage of offenders in the criminal justice system are in each kind of supervision category. In this display, we see that proba-tion holds the most offenders of any of the forms of correc-tional supervision. You might recall from Chapter 9, how-ever, that felony offenders were more likely to receive a jail or a prison sentence than a proba-tion sentence. More than 69% of all felony offenders receive a prison or jail sentence. The reasons that this table shows more individuals on proba-tion than in prison are because probation includes misde-meanants (who are likely to receive probation) and indi-viduals may spend more time on probation than they would spend in prison; therefore, the total number of offenders on probation is always larger than those in prison. One can say then that a felony offender is most likely to receive a prison or jail sentence as their pun-ishment after conviction, but most criminal offenders in the corrections system are being supervised on a probation caseload. These two statements are not contradictory.

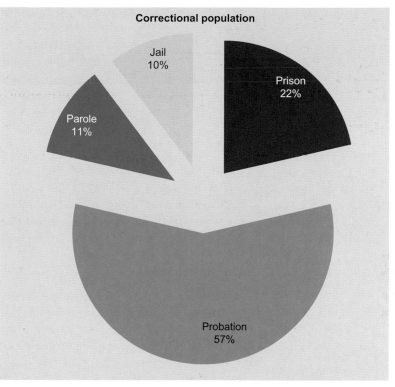

FIGURE 11.1
Correctional population.
Source: *Bureau of Justice Statistics, Total Correctional Population. Retrieved 10/13/2010 from http:// bjs.ojp.usdoj.gov/index. cfm?ty=tp&tid=11, 2010.*

COSTS OF CORRECTIONS

It is difficult to determine the true costs of corrections; however, some esti-mate that corrections consume $1 in every $15 of state funds [8]. Some esti-mates include capital construction costs for prisons, while other estimates do not. Prison costs vary tremendously from state to state, and even within a state, maximum-security institutions cost more than minimum-security, and special-needs offenders cost more to house and care for than regular inmates. Intensive probation costs much more than regular probation, and probation sentences and parole supervision that include electronic monitoring and/or GPS tracking are also more expensive. The average cost of regular probation has been reported as $2.11 a day per person and the average cost for intensive probation as $9.66 per person (using an average of 16 states) [9]. Intensive supervision, which has reduced caseloads and requires more probation

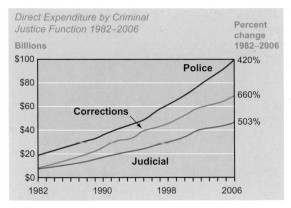

FIGURE 11.2

Direct expenditures by criminal justice function.

Source: *Bureau of Justice Statistics, 2010. Retrieved 10/27/2010 from http:// bjs.ojp.usdoj.gov/content/ glance/exptyp.cfm.*

officers, costs between $2.50 (Rhode Island) and $20 (New Jersey) a day per person. This compares to the daily cost of prison, which averages around $56.00 per day in 1999 [10]. Prison costs were also reported at $22,650 a year or $62.05 a day per prisoner in 2004 [11].

All costs associated with the criminal justice system have risen dramatically in the last 20 years. The total costs for justice expenditures between 1986 and 2006 increased by 301% from $54 billion to $214 billion. These increases are after the costs were adjusted for inflation [12]. In Figure 11.2, the increased costs show that we spend the most money on police, but that corrections costs have increased by the largest percentage in the last 20 years.

The "collateral costs" of imprisonment

While imprisonment is obviously a necessary tool in the arsenal of correctional alternatives, there is a growing belief that it is used too much, with too many offenders being sent away from their communities with consequential negative effects on the individual, the family, and the community itself. In some communities, up to a quarter of all adult men are in prison on any given day [13]. The rate of imprisonment for black men is about six times higher than that for white men, and the rate for Hispanic men is three times higher than that of whites [14].

An analysis of incarceration patterns shows that certain neighborhoods in our cities are affected most heavily by incarceration. That is, some neighborhoods have disproportionate numbers of residents either away in prison or coming back from prison. What is the effect of imprisonment on these neighborhoods? One obvious result is that there is a shortage of men, leading to single head-of-households struggling to juggle work and parenthood. Another result is that the lifetime earnings of individuals are diminished because a prison sentence will affect one's employability forever. Another effect is that children will have to deal with the experience of having a parent in prison.

It is estimated that about 1.5 million children have a parent (or parents) in prison. Children of incarcerated women are especially affected because their living situation is often disrupted and, in fact, some estimates indicate that these children are moved an average of six times during the course of their mother's imprisonment. Children of men in prison are less likely to change their custody arrangements, because about 90% of them remain with their mother; however, statistics indicate that children who have family members in prison are six times more likely to be delinquent [15]. Of course, it may be the case that the removal of a violent family member is a positive factor in a child's life, but when a prisoner comes home, reentry poses its own problems.

Researchers have found that imprisonment seemed to have some positive effects on a community, but it appears that when it reaches a certain level, there are some negative effects as well and the destabilization in families and communities may lead to more crime, not less. Some policy recommendations that have come from this research include the following:

1. Provide services to families of incarcerated offenders that include short-term financial assistance, crisis counseling, parenting classes, medical care, child care, and adult mentors for children.
2. Facilitate continued communication between the offender and his or her family that includes assistance with costs of telephoning and transportation to the prison.
3. Provide services to the children of incarcerated individuals that include counseling and assistance in maintaining contact with the incarcerated parent.
4. Provide assistance with comprehensive transition plans for release that includes job assistance, counseling, housing, and other services.
5. Reduce financial burdens of offenders that include supervision fees and court costs, at least in the short term, as well as financial restrictions that place barriers to successful reentry (such as prohibitions against felons in public housing projects).
6. Increase access to low-cost drug treatment programs.
7. Provide services at neighborhood centers that include mentoring, awareness programs, and ex-offender counseling [16].

There is a growing body of policy experts and advocates who propose a substantive change in this country's use of imprisonment. Studies show the dramatic growth in incarceration and the costs associated with the increase. Regardless of one's beliefs about what offenders deserve, it seems that the financial costs involved in our use of imprisonment are rapidly reaching a level at which even some conservatives agree that alternatives to prison must be considered.

> **⊕ INTERNET KEY**
>
> For more information about sentencing, go to the Sentencing Institute Web site at http://www.sentencingproject.org/template/index.cfm.

OFFENDERS UNDER CORRECTIONAL SUPERVISION

In 1980, there were 1,842,100 individuals under some form of correctional supervision (probation, jail, prison, or parole); by 2009 there were 7,225,800 individuals. Of course, the population has increased as well, but even the rate per 100,000, which holds the population constant, shows that the likelihood of correctional supervision has increased in dramatic ways. As mentioned previously, about one in every 32 adults was either in prison or under some other form of correctional control in 2009; this is about 3.1% of the entire population [2].

Wesley Snipes gestures as he leaves federal court after he was sentenced to three years in prison for willful failure to file a tax return on April 24, 2008 at the U.S. Federal Courthouse in Ocala, FL. Snipes was acquitted in February of five counts including felony fraud and conspiracy charges. **Source:** *AP Photo/Phil Sandlin.*

In 1980, the rate for *any form* of correctional supervision was 1132 per 100,000. By 1990, that rate had doubled to 2348 per 100,000, and by 2000, it had increased again to 3072 per 100,000 [17]. In 2005, 3150 citizens of every 100,000 were under some form of correctional supervision [18]. In effect, the rate of any form of correctional supervision has tripled in the last 25 years, although it has remained roughly steady for the last 8 years. Of the 7.2 million people under correctional supervision, more than five million were on probation or parole (5,018,900). The majority of these are on probation (4,203,967) [2].

There is also a federal correctional system that receives criminal offenders from the federal courts. In 2003, 152,459 offenders were under the jurisdiction of the Federal Bureau of Prisons; by 2009, there were 208,113 federal prisoners. About 119,493 federal offenders were under some form of community supervision [19]. In fact, declines in the state prison population have been offset by increases in the federal correctional population in recent years.

States have extremely varied supervision rates. For instance, while the state of New Hampshire has a probation supervision rate of 604 (per 100,000), Georgia has a supervision rate of 5846 (per 100,000). This means that residents are more than nine times more likely to be under probation supervision in Georgia. States also have extremely varied rates of imprisonment. The South generally has a higher incarceration rate than the north. The states with the highest rates include Louisiana (at 845 per 100,000), Mississippi (at 749), and Texas (at 668). The states with the lowest incarceration rates were Maine (at 133), Minnesota (at 191), and New Hampshire (at 213). It should be noted that the rates of incarceration are going down in many states [20].

EXERCISE: IN THE STATE OF...

Utilizing the Web site for the Bureau of Justice Statistics, go to the most recent publications showing prison and probation populations (http://bjs.ojp.usdoj.gov/index.cfm?ty=tp&tid=1), and find your state's incarceration rate and compare it to surrounding states. Look for the number of people on probation and parole as well. You can find this information by following the links to BJS publications. How does your state compare to national averages?

As you might expect, individuals on probation tend to be less serious criminals than those who are sentenced to prison. Joan Petersilia reports that in a study of criminal records and case files of 16,500 males in 17 counties in 1980, the following factors were more likely to result in a prison sentence:

- Two or more counts
- Two or more prior convictions

- Probation or parole status at time of arrest
- Drug addiction
- Use of a weapon during the crime or seriously injured victim

If an offender had three or more of these characteristics, there was an 80% probability of going to prison. Other factors that were influential were whether the offender used a private or public attorney, and whether the offender obtained pretrial release. All variables explained 75% of sentencing decisions; the remaining variance was not explained or predicted through the use of these variables [21].

Today, those factors are probably still predictive of receiving a prison sentence. We should also note that in the last five years or so, states seem to be slightly reducing their incarceration rate and increasing their probation rate, so it appears that the trend of ever-increasing imprisonment has begun to reverse itself. Table 11.1 compares those on probation, parole, and in prison by race and type of crime.

Female offenders

Women represent about 18% of the adult probation population, down from 21% in 1995. They account for about 12% of the parole population, up from about 10% in 1995. They also represent about 6.5% of the prison population, up from the 6% of 1995 [22]. The idea that women receive "chivalry" and are typically sentenced less severely than male counterparts has produced mixed findings from research studies. In general, there does seem to be a small but definite effect of gender on judicial sentencing, but it seems to be moderated by race and whether the woman has dependents [23]. It also seems to be true that women no longer benefit from chivalry in sentencing and have experienced higher percentage increases in incarceration than men over the last 25 years or so.

Table 11.1 Characteristics of Offenders under Correctional Supervision

Percentage	Probation	Prison	Parole
Race/ethnicity			
White	56	33	41
Black	29	37	38
Hispanic	13	19	19
Crime type			
Violent crime	19	50	26
Drug crime	29	20	37
Property/other crime	52	26	41

Note: Totals do not equal 100% because of other categories.
Sources: L. Glaze, T. Bonczar, Probation and Parole in the United States, 2008, Bureau of Justice Statistics, Washington, DC, 2009, p. 24; W. Sabol, H. West, M. Cooper, Prisoners in 2008, Bureau of Justice Statistics, U.S. Department of Justice, Washington, DC, 2009, p. 6.

Women, many researchers argue, follow different pathways to crime and they require **gender-specific programming**, which matches prison and community correctional programs to women's specific needs and pathways to crime. These researchers and practitioners argue that women and men are different, and that, typically, corrections systems ignore their differences or do not respond to the differences in an appropriate way. The following are some of the differences noted between male and female offenders:

- Women are more likely to be primary caregivers of young children.
- They are more likely to have experienced childhood physical and/or sexual abuse.
- They are more likely to report physical and sexual abuse victimization as adults.
- They are more likely to have drug dependency issues.
- They are less likely to be convicted of a violent crime.
- They are less likely to have any stable work history.
- They are more likely to indicate psychosocial problems.
- They are more likely to have an incarcerated parent.
- They are more likely to come from a single-parent household.
- They are more likely to suffer from serious health problems, including HIV/AIDS [24].

Prior victimization (both physical and sexual) sets women apart from their male counterparts. While both male and female offenders are more likely than the general population to have been abused as children, women are more likely to experience abuse continuing into adulthood, as seen in Table 11.2.

Researchers argue that these experiences of victimization contribute to the multiple problems female offenders have in adulthood, including an inability to cope with stress, suicide, abuse of alcohol and drugs, sensation-seeking and antisocial traits, lower levels of self-esteem, and the lack of a sense of control [25].

Researchers have found that certain factors in the lives of black women set them on a path to crime. For instance, sexual abuse in the home leads to running

Table 11.2 Female Offenders' Victimization

Percentage who have been...	Probation	Jail	Prison
Ever physically or sexually abused	41	48	57
Before age 18	16	21	12
Physically abused	15	10	18
Sexually abused	7	10	11
Both physically and sexually	18	27	28

Source: *L. Greenfield, T. Snell, Special Report: Women Offenders, Bureau of Justice Statistics, Washington, DC, 1999.*

away, which in turn leads to drug use and shoplifting. Relationships with drug-dealing male partners also lead to drug arrests for women [26]. Beth Ritchie, in particular, has detailed the way in which black women's gender and race influence the choices they make in life [27].

Critics argue that we don't know the risk factors for women in community corrections as well as we do those of men, and we miss important factors in women's lives that might lead them to crime [28]. Other authors, such as Patricia Van Voorhis, point to specific factors that have been identified in prior research with female offenders that may be risk factors for women. These are:

- Marital status
- Suicide attempts
- Family structure of childhood home
- Childhood abuse, depression, and substance abuse
- Single parenting and reliance on public assistance
- Dysfunctional relationships
- Victimization

Special needs of women may include childcare, victimization trauma counseling, self-esteem counseling, financial assistance, health care, and mental health care [29].

One major difference between female and male offenders is their relationship with children. As mentioned earlier, female offenders are more likely to be custodial parents, and the financial and emotional strain of raising young children has an impact on their ability to stay crime- or drug-free while on some form of community correction status. There have also been laws passed that have complicated the potential for success. The Personal Responsibility and Work Opportunity Reconciliation Act (PRWORA) of 1996 replaced Aid to Families with Dependent Children (AFDC) with a state block grant system that made it more difficult for single women as heads of households to receive state aid. Another section of the same Act created a lifetime ban on providing any federal assistance to those who were convicted of a state or a federal felony offense involving the use or sale of drugs. This draconian law affects only drug offenders, not those convicted of murder, robbery, or any violent crime. States may opt out of the program, but to do so means losing federal funding.

In 1996, the One Strike Initiative authorized local public housing authorities to obtain criminal conviction records of applicants from law enforcement agencies and bar those with felony drug convictions from living in public housing. Another impediment to ex-offenders was created with the Higher Education Act of 1998, which barred anyone with a drug conviction from receiving federal loan money for education. Finally, the Adoption and Safe Families Act of 1997 mandates termination of parental rights after a child has been in foster care for 15 months. This means that women serving even relatively short prison sentences may lose their parental rights and/or women who must go to residential drug programs may lose their children if they need to depend on foster care to provide a home for their children while they are in treatment. This has influenced many women to make more informal arrangements for their children's care with, perhaps, less-than-desirable family members or friends. Women would rather not depend on state assistance because they fear losing their children permanently. These programs make the transition to the community extremely difficult for many female offenders who are very likely to have drug convictions.

Barbara Bloom and Barbara Owen and others have recommended that decision makers approach the issue of correctional supervision for female offenders with the following objectives:

- Enhance supervision and treatment
- Validate assessment instruments on female samples
- Use single-gender caseloads
- Create policies and practices that acknowledge female offenders' special relationships with children, families, and significant others
- Create policies and practices that provide culturally relevant services and supervision to address substance abuse, trauma, and mental health
- Provide services appropriate to women's socioeconomic status
- Promote partnerships with other social service agencies [30]

CLASSIFICATION AND RISK ASSESSMENT

Among the most important activities of correctional professionals are classification and risk assessment. We want to know which offenders are more likely to reoffend, especially by committing violent crime. Once an offender has been sentenced, "client assessment" is concerned with two basic elements: risk and need. Prediction/assessment may be clinical, actuarial, or a combination of the two.

The **clinical approach** is when psychologists or psychiatrists employ interviews, social histories, and psychological tests to make predictions on future offending. In Box 11.2, some of the common personality characteristics associated with criminal offending are displayed.

The **actuarial approach** uses patterns of behavior and predicts risk based on prior behavior of those with similar characteristics. For instance, the U.S. Parole Commission developed the Salient Factor Score. This instrument classified parolees into high, medium, and low levels of risk of reoffending based on the following factors:

1. Prior convictions/adjudications
2. Prior commitment(s) greater than 30 days

BOX 11.2 PSYCHOLOGICAL PROFILE OF CRIMINALS

- Antisocial/antiauthority attitudes
- Procriminal associates
- Egocentric thinking
- Weak problem-solving skills
- Family conflict
- Risk-seeking
- Early misbehavior
- Below average verbal intelligence
- Poor school performance
- Troubled relationships
- Preference for unregulated activities
- Low levels of skills
- Low levels of self-respect
- Low self-control
- Drug or alcohol issues
- Impulsivity

Source: *C. Bartol, A. Bartol, Criminal Behavior: A Psychological Approach, Seventh Ed., Prentice Hall, Upper Saddle River, NJ, 2005.*

- Age at current offense
- Commitments during past three years
- Status on probation/parole
- Correctional escape
- Heroin/opiate dependence [31]

In general, actuarial approaches are better predictors of recidivism than are clinical assessments. For instance, in one study of 2850 probationers, the best predictors were found to be stability of employment, marital status, and number of past convictions [32]. Similarly, another study of 266 felony probationers found that the best predictors of recidivism were gender, employment, and prior record [33]. A study that compared the two approaches' ability to predict recidivism among sex offenders showed that the actuarial approach outperformed clinical assessments by a wide margin [34].

The most sophisticated classification and assessment assign treatment to the offender's risk and needs. As far back as the 1970s, correctional programs existed that attempted to match treatment to offenders, using a variety of personality inventories to assess the psychological profile of the individual offenders. More current classification systems also combine offenders' risk and needs to improve the ability to predict recidivism.

Risk/needs approach

The risk/need assessments approach combines the clinical and actuarial approaches. This classification uses risk instruments that are stable and don't change (e.g., demographic, file, and historical information). The classification also includes dynamic, changeable items (i.e., personality tests and clinical interviews). The types of information collected include physical health, vocational/financial situation, education, family and social relationships, residence and neighborhood, alcohol use, drug abuse, mental health, attitude, and past and current criminal behavior. This approach tracks changes in the offender during the course of the supervision period because education, mental health, attitude, and drug use will change over time, affecting the offender's risk level (likelihood of reoffending).

This approach looks at the offender's needs in areas such as medical care, mental health, education, and housing. Research continues to search for needs that are criminogenic (those that influence the offender to make criminal choices), versus those that are not. While it is a benefit to the offender if a correctional system addresses his or her needs, only criminogenic needs are high priority in a correctional program.

One of the pervasive findings of these evaluations is that intensive treatment is not recommended for all offenders. It seems to be the case that high-risk offenders are more likely to benefit than low-risk offenders when both participate in intensive treatment programs, such as halfway houses or intensive probation. In fact, correctional supervision interventions have been shown to result in *increased* recidivism among low-risk offenders as compared to control samples. In the largest study of this kind, Christopher Lowenkamp and his colleagues analyzed 97 correctional programs with 13,676 offenders involved and found that the programs that adhered to the principle of assigning services based on risk were the most successful in achieving a reduction in recidivism [35].

Proponents argue that it is important to classify and match offenders to the type of treatment they need, not only because it is a waste of resources to do otherwise, but also because the treatment program may actually influence a low-risk offender to recidivate. Why would low-risk offenders be more inclined to recidivate when exposed to a correctional intervention? It might be that low-risk offenders would have naturally avoided making any more criminal choices, but that correctional supervision brings them into contact with other criminal offenders. It could also be that being monitored identifies behaviors that are violations, but these behaviors would not have entered the radar screen of the criminal justice system except for the correctional supervision.

Researchers are also looking at the correctional program itself. The Correctional Program Assessment Inventory measures how well a program adheres to the principles of risk, need, and responsivity as described earlier. Studies have shown that higher scores for the programs are associated with better success rates for offenders in the programs [36].

Classifying female offenders

There have been few studies that attempt to validate or replicate the risk instruments described in the previous section with female offenders because there are so few women in the system. Earlier studies indicated that classification systems in use in prisons that were developed and validated with samples of male offenders "overclassified" female prisoners, meaning they indicated that women needed more secure settings than probably were necessary. Factors such as child abuse, mental health, substance abuse, and employment predicted women's institutional behavior, but age, time to serve, crime of conviction, and prior offenses were not associated with institutional behavior of women even though they were factors that were predictors for men [37].

In the few studies that have examined the predictive ability of classification instruments for female offenders, some researchers have found that these instruments effectively predict recidivism for women as well as for men [38]. However, at least one evaluation indicated that the classification instrument used was not as successful in predicting women's recidivism on parole as well as economic factors. Women who were given state support (welfare) were 83% less likely to recidivate than those who did not receive economic support [39]. These authors, as others, caution that factors such as poverty may be predictive of recidivism and, therefore, the "need" becomes a "risk" and increases an offender's risk score and that, in turn, increases the level of social control. The problem with this is that someone's status, not behavior, influences the level of punishment one endures, and second, the level of control is often related to the risk of recidivism (the more closely an offender is monitored, the more likely infractions will be found).

Current research, funded by the National Institute of Corrections, is concerned with testing whether the risk factors and needs identified above are predictive of women's future behavior, and further, whether the existing assessment tools accurately predict women's behavior. The researchers are testing certain potential risk factors for female offenders, such as self-efficacy, self-esteem, parenting, relationships, and abuse. The study is collecting information from female offenders, such as information about children, marital status, education, public assistance, and other factors [40]. With continuing study, researchers may find an appropriate adaptation of the assessment tools that were developed for male offenders.

False positives and false negatives

The difficulty inherent in any type of prediction device is the high number of **false positives** (errors involving predictions of recidivism that do not occur). There are likely many more false positives than **false negatives** (errors failing to predict recidivism that does occur), because program staff are more inclined to err on the side of caution. Some argue that our ability to predict violence will always be problematic because it is a relatively rare event [41]. Also, corrections professionals may be more concerned with *not* identifying a potentially dangerous offender than in accurately identifying someone who would not reoffend.

The level of risk willing to be taken determines the cutoff scores that are used for classification purposes. If you are worried about making false positives, then you will lower the cutoff score for high-risk offenders and assign more offenders to high-risk categories. This may make sense if one is dealing with violent offenders and makes no sense at all if one is dealing with low-level minor offenders because the cost would be greater to provide supervision than to accept a higher level of risk.

REDUCING PENAL HARM?

As mentioned previously, there has been a slowing and even reduction in the numbers sent to prison. Some observers note that it could be the beginning of reversing the penal harm approach. There are some states that are beginning to consider the cost of imprisonment when sentencing offenders (see the Breaking News box for a new approach in Missouri). There are also states that are attempting to increase evidence-based programs that are designed to reduce the numbers who return to prison as recidivists.

BREAKING NEWS: MISSOURI LOOKS AT COSTS

The Missouri Sentencing Advisory Committee, a group of lawyers, judges, and others, created a method whereby judges could obtain the cost of their sentencing decisions. Judges need only enter the offender's conviction code, criminal history, and other background information, and the computer program tells them the likelihood that Missouri criminals with similar backgrounds will recidivate and it also provides cost information on the range of sentences available. For instance, a judge may discover that a three-year sentence for someone convicted of endangering a child would cost $37,000 versus $6700 for probation; or that the bill for a murderer's 30-year sentence is $504,690. Proponents point out that the Sentencing Committee is only providing advisory information, and no judge has to take the cost of various punishments into account when sentencing. Opponents argue that cost should never be taken into account because you can't put a price on being a victim. The head of the state's District Attorneys Association is planning to push for the elimination of the Sentencing Advisory Committee during the next legislative session.

Source: *M. Davey, Missouri Tells Judges Cost of Sentences, The New York Times, September 18, 2010. Retrieved 10/8/2010 from http://www.nytimes.com/2010/09/19/us/19judges.html.*

The evidence to support the idea that we might finally, after 30 years, be cycling out of the punitive era includes findings from public opinion studies that show that even though there is widespread public support for punishment, including the death penalty (in public opinion polls close to 70% of the public favor the death penalty), these numbers are reduced when the questioning becomes more nuanced. For instance, when there is the option of life without parole, support for the death penalty decreases considerably. Those who become aware of the very real possibility of innocent people being executed as evidenced by the Innocence Project's success in exonerating more than 200 people, also show reduced support for the death penalty [42]. When real people are described, respondents are less likely to support three-strikes sentences and mandatory minimum sentences. When they are given the option of spending money on treatment or more punishment, many respondents will choose treatment. Generally, the public strongly supports rehabilitative objectives [43]. Another element that indicates that the punitive era is perhaps evolving to something else is public rejection of draconian sentences for drug offenders and reduced support for the three-strikes laws that dramatically increase the length of sentences for two-time or three-time felons. No state has passed a three-strikes law since 1995 and the states that have them have seen some taxpayer-initiated attempts to rescind them [44]. Finally, as of early 2011 there was a bill before Congress introduced by Representative William Delahunt and Senator James Webb that proposes a complete analysis of the nation's criminal justice system.

> ### 🌐 INTERNET KEY
>
> For further information about the National Criminal Justice Commission Act, go to http://www.govtrack.us/congress/bioll.xpd?bill=h111-5143.

CONCLUSION

We have seen that the history of corrections and punishment consists of cycles of retribution and reform. Other correctional goals include deterrence and incapacitation. The modern-day penitentiary began with the Walnut Street Jail in the late 1700s. Modern parole began with the efforts in the 1800s of Alexander Maconochie and Walter Crofton and, in this country, Zebulon Brockway. John Augustus is considered the father of probation with his efforts in the late 1800s. The rehabilitation era existed for only a short time in the late 1960s and 1970s.

Today, we are in an era when prison rates are very high. Incarceration is, in fact, the sentence most frequently received by felony offenders, although there are more correctional offenders on probation than in prison or on parole. Costs of corrections are extremely high and have increased by more than 500% in the last 25 years. There are 7 million people under some form of correctional supervision today.

Researchers continue to try to find ways to identify and respond to the reasons these individuals choose to commit crime. The current best practices look both at the individual offenders, using actuarial and clinical factors to determine their risk of recidivism, and the correctional program itself, measuring how well it does what it is supposed to do.

Review Questions

1. What are the goals of punishment/corrections? What were the goals of the earliest forms of punishment?
2. Discuss the origins of the penitentiary, parole, and probation.
3. Describe the rehabilitative era. When did it end?
4. Why is reentry considered an important issue today?
5. What is the most frequently given felony sentence? What type of correctional supervision has the largest number of offenders?
6. What is the typical cost of probation versus prison? What are the "collateral" costs of incarceration?
7. How many offenders are under some form of correctional supervision? What is the rate of probation supervision? What states have the highest imprisonment rates?
8. What are the differences between female and male offenders?
9. What are the three types of classification? Describe them.
10. Explain false positives and false negatives.

VOCABULARY

actuarial approach a classification system that uses patterns of behavior and predicts risk based on prior behavior of those with similar characteristics

civil disabilities legal barriers that remove civil rights such as voting that accompany a felony record

clinical approach a classification system that employs interviews, social histories, and psychological tests to make predictions about future offending

deterrence when crime has been prevented by discouraging an offender from committing further crime

false negatives errors failing to predict recidivism that does occur

false positives errors involving predictions of recidivism that do not occur

gender-specific programming matches prison and community correctional programs to women's specific needs and pathways to crime

general deterrence what is done to an individual to discourage others from future offending

incapacitation to hold incapable; in corrections, it means to make the offender incapable of committing crime

lex talionis proportional "eye for an eye" form of punishment

mark system program awarded prisoners marks or credits based on the work product of groups; marks were exchanged for greater liberties

net-widening the situation in which minor offenders are placed in new diversion programs instead of prison-bound offenders that the program was designed for

outlaw an individual who refused to abide by punishments ordered by authorities that were largely compensatory, meaning that they ordered the offender to pay back the victim

Progressive Movement from 1890 through early 1900s, private charities responded to the problems of the poor in Northeastern cities

rehabilitation to change the individual's values, attitudes, beliefs, and behavior

rehabilitative era the 1960s-1970s; prison treatment programs were expanded along with innovative community alternatives

reintegration era referred to a time when reentry programs were developed that helped inmates adjust back into the community

restorative justice movement approach that keeps the offender in the community and provides a means to meet the needs of the victim, the offender, and the community

retribution a goal of punishment that inflicts harm proportional to the harm caused

specific deterrence what is done to an individual to deter him or her from future offending

ticket of leave system early Irish system that allowed prisoners who behaved well to earn early release with a "ticket of leave" as long as they were supervised by local police

ENDNOTES

[1] R. McCorkle, J. Crank, Meet the new boss: institutional change and loose coupling in parole and probation, Am. J. Crim. Justice 21(1) (1996) 1–25.

[2] L. Glaze, Correctional Populations in the United States, 2009, Bureau of Justice Statistics, U.S. Department of Justice, Washington, DC, 2010.

[3] M. Mauer, Comparative International Rates of Incarceration: An Examination of Causes and Trends, The Sentencing Project, Washington, DC, 2003. Retrieved 9/2/2006 from http://www.sentencingproject.org/pdfs/pub9036.pdf#search=%22international%20incarceration%20rates%22.

[4] J. Austin, Prisoner reentry: current trends, practices and issues, Crime Delinq. 47(3) (2001) 314.

[5] See, for instance, J. Travis, M. Waul, Prisoners Once Removed: The Impact of Incarceration and Reentry on Children, Families and Communities, Urban Institute Press, Washington, DC, 2004.

[6] J. Travis, J. Petersilia, Reentry reconsidered: a new look at an old question, Crime Delinq. 47(3) (2001) 291–313.

[7] Re-Entry Policy Council, Voting restrictions for people with felony convictions, 2004. Retrieved 12/30/2005 from http://www.reentrypolicy.org/documents/votingrestrictions. pdf. M. Love, Relief from the Collateral Consequences of a Criminal Conviction: A State by State Resource Guide, Open Society Institute, New York, 2005. Retrieved 10/29/2010 from http://sentencingproject.org/doc/File/Collateral%20Consequences/execsumm.pdf.

[8] S. Listwan, C. Jonson, F. Cullen, E. Latessa, Cracks in the penal harm movement: evidence from the field, Criminol. Public Pol. 7(5) (2008) 423–465.

[9] G. Camp, C. Camp, Corrections Yearbook 2000, Criminal Justice Institute, South Salem, NY, 2000.

[10] C. Camp, G. Camp, The Corrections Yearbook 1999, Criminal Justice Institute, Middletown, CT, 1999, p. 39.

[11] J. Stephan, State Prison Expenditures, Bureau of Justice Statistics, Washington, DC, 2004.

[12] Bureau of Justice Statistics, Expenditures and Employment Extracts, 2010. Retrieved 10/27/2010 from http://bjs.ojp.usdoj.gov/index.cfm?ty=tp&tid=5.

[13] M. Mauer, Race to Incarcerate, The Prison Project, Washington, DC, 2000.

[14] T. Bonczar, A. Beck, Lifetime Likelihood of Going to State or Federal Prison, Bureau of Justice Statistics, Washington, DC, 1997.

[15] J. Pollock, Women, Prison, and Crime, Wadsworth Publishing, Belmont, CA, 2005.

[16] T. Clear, D. Rose, J. Ryder, Incarceration and the community: the problem of removing and returning offenders, Crime Delinq. 47(3) (2001) 335–351.

[17] L. Glaze, S. Palla, Probation and Parole in the United States, 2004, Bureau of Justice Statistics, Washington, DC, 2005.

[18] L. Glaze, T. Bonczar, Probation and Parole in the United States, 2005, Bureau of Justice Statistics, Washington, DC, 2006, p. 2. In the most recent reports, Probation and Parole in the United States, 2008 and 2009, the rate of correctional supervision was not provided.

[19] L. Glaze, Correctional Populations in the United States, 2009, Bureau of Justice Statistics, Washington, DC, 2010; L. Glaze, T. Bonczar, F. Zhang, Probation and Parole in the United States, 2009, Bureau of Justice Statistics, Washington, DC, 2010, p. 16.

[20] L. Glaze, T. Bonczar, Probation and Parole in the United States, 2008, Bureau of Justice Statistics, Washington, DC, 2009, p. 16; H. West, W. Sabol, Prison Inmates at Midyear 2008—Statistical Tables, Bureau of Justice Statistics, U.S. Department of Justice, Washington, DC, 2009, p. 11.

[21] J. Petersilia, Reforming Probation and Parole, American Correctional Association, Lanham, MD, 2002, p. 27.

[22] L. Glaze, T. Bonczar, F. Zhang, Probation and Parole in the United States, 2009, Bureau of Justice Statistics, Washington, DC, 2010; H. West, W. Sabol, S. Greenman, Prisoners in 2009, Bureau of Justice Statistics, Washington, DC, 2010.

[23] For a review, see J. Pollock, Criminal Women, Anderson Publishing, Cincinnati, OH, 1999.

[24] J. Pollock, Women, Prison and Crime, Wadsworth, Belmont, CA, 2002; B. Bloom, Women offenders in the community: the gendered impact of current policies, Community Corrections Rep. 12(1) (2004) 3–6; M. Chesney-Lind, Women and the criminal justice system: gender matters, in: Topics in Community Corrections: Responding to Women Offenders in the Community, National Institute of Corrections, Washington, DC, 2000, pp. 7–11.

[25] C. Widom, Childhood victimization and the derailment of the girls and women to the criminal justice system, in: National Institute of Justice, Research on Women and Girls in the Criminal Justice System, National Institute of Justice, Washington, DC, 2000, pp. 27–35.

[26] Z. Henriques, N. Manatu-Rupert, Living on the outside: African American women before, during, and after imprisonment, Prison J. 81(1) (2001) 6–19.

[27] B. Ritchie, Compelled to Crime: The Gender Entrapment of Battered Black Women, Routledge, New York, 1996.

[28] M. Chesney-Lind, The Female Offender, Sage, Thousand Oaks, CA, 2001; S. Funk, Risk assessment for juveniles on probation, Crim. Justice Behav. 26 (1999) 44–68; K. Holtfreter, M. Morash, The needs of women offenders: implications for correctional programming, Women Crim. Justice 13 (2003) 137–160.

[29] P. Van Voorhis, Classification of women offenders: gender-responsive approaches to risk/needs assessment, Community Corrections Rep. 12(2) (2005) 19–20.

[30] B. Bloom, Women offenders in the community: the gendered impact of current policies, Community Corrections Rep. 12(1) (2004) 3–6; B. Bloom, B. Owen, S. Covington, Gender-Responsive Strategies: Research, Practice and Guiding Principles for Women Offenders, National Institute of Corrections, Washington, DC, 2003.

[31] P. Van Voorhis, An overview of offender classification systems, in: P. Van Voorhis, M. Braswell, D. Lester (Eds.), Correctional Counseling and Rehabilitation, sixth ed., LexisNexis/Matthew Bender, Newark, NJ, 2007, p. 139.

[32] R. Sims, M. Jones, Predicting success or failure on probation: factors associated with felony probation outcomes, Crime Delinq. 43(3) (1997) 314–327.

[33] K. Morgan, Factors associated with probation outcome, J. Crim. Justice 22(4) (1994) 341–353.

[34] R. Hanson, M. Bussiere, Predicting relapse: a meta analysis of sexual offender recidivism studies, J. Consult. Clin. Psychol. 66(3) (1998) 348–362.

[35] C. Lowenkamp, E. Latessa, Increasing the effectiveness of correctional programming through the risk principle: identifying offenders for residential placement, Criminol. Public Pol. 4(2) (2005) 263–290; D. Andrews, J. Bonta, J. Wormith, The recent past and near future of risk and/or need assessment, Crime Delinq. 52(1) (2006) 7–27; C. Lowenkamp, E. Latessa, A. Holsinger, The risk principle in action: what have we learned from 13,676 offenders and 97 correctional programs, Crime Delinq. 52(1) (2006) 77–93.

[36] D. Andrews, J. Bonta, J. Wormith, The recent past and near future of risk and/or need assessment, Crime Delinq. 52(1) (2006) 7–27.

[37] P. Van Voorhis, L. Presser, Classification of Women Offenders: A National Assessment of Current Practices, National Institute of Corrections, Washington, DC, 2001.

[38] G. Coulson, G. Ilacqua, V. Nutbrown, D. Giulekas, F. Cudjoe, Predictive utility of the LSI for incarcerated female offenders, Crim. Justice Behav. 23 (1996) 427–439; .C. Lowenkamp, A. Holsinger, E. Latessa, Risk/need assessment, offender classification, and the role of childhood abuse, Crim. Justice Behav. 28(5) (2001) 543–563.

[39] K. Holtfreter, M. Reisig, M. Morash, Poverty, state capital, and recidivism among women offenders, Crime Public Pol. 3(2) (2004) 185–208.

[40] P. Van Voorhis, Classification of women offenders: gender-responsive approaches to risk/ needs assessment, Community Corrections Rep. 12(2) (2005) 19–20.

[41] K. Auerhan, Conceptual and methodological issues in the prediction of dangerous behavior, Criminol. Public Pol. 5(4) (2006) 771–778.

[42] J. Unnever, F. Cullen, Executing the innocent and support for capital punishment: implications for public policy, Criminol. Public Pol. 4(1) (2005) 3–38.

[43] S. Listwan, C. Jonson, F. Cullen, E. Latessa, Cracks in the penal harm movement: evidence from the field, Criminol. Public Pol. 7(5) (2008) 423–465.

[44] S. Listwan, C. Jonson, F. Cullen, E. Latessa, Cracks in the penal harm movement: evidence from the field, Criminol. Public Pol. 7(5) (2008) 430.

CHAPTER 12

Pretrial Diversion and Probation

WHAT YOU NEED TO KNOW

1. Pretrial release is different from pretrial diversion programs (which are also different from intermediate sanctions).
2. "Benefit of clergy" was an early form of diversion.
3. Day reporting centers, electronic monitoring, restitution, day fines, and community service can be used in both pretrial diversion programs and probation.
4. There are 4,203,967 offenders on probation; in 2009, they comprised about 58% of all those under any form of correctional supervision.
5. Rates of probation vary tremendously across the states.
6. About 55% of probationers are white, 30% are black, and 13% are Hispanic.
7. Probation began with the efforts of John Augustus in 1841.
8. Probation involves the presentence, investigative function and the postsentence, supervision function.
9. Caseloads average around 150, but vary tremendously from intensive supervision or specialized caseloads to minimum supervision caseloads.
10. About 65% of offenders successfully complete their probation sentence.

CONTENTS

Once a criminal suspect is arrested, he or she is "in the system." After arrest, the suspect is brought to the jail and "booked." He or she must see a magistrate, usually within 48 hours [1]. It is almost from this moment that a variety of opportunities for diversion may occur. Diversion from the system can occur in numerous ways. In an earlier chapter, we discussed bail and ROR programs that simply divert the defendant from spending time in jail while awaiting trial. Other forms of diversion completely replace any adjudication. **Community corrections** refer to any form of correctional alternative that does not involve incarceration in prison. The term includes pretrial, posttrial, or postprison supervision. In Box 12.1, we attempt to show the possible types of community-based correctional sentences that exist. We will discuss the pretrial diversion programs in this chapter, along with probation, the most common form of diversion from prison.

BOX 12.1 COMMUNITY CORRECTIONS IN THE CRIMINAL JUSTICE SYSTEM

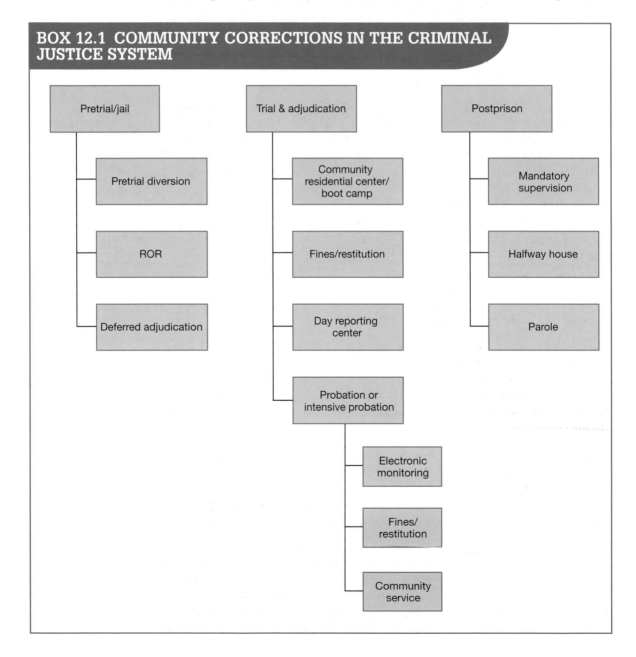

DIVERSION

The purpose of all the forms of **diversion** is to "divert" the offender from the system because of a belief that it is better for the offender and better for the system. It is better for the offender because he or she will suffer less stigma and disruption to work and family. It is better for the system because scarce resources (such as jail and prison beds) can be used for more serious offenders. Diversion is warranted when:

1. It can be done with little or no risk to the public
2. It does not offend the principles of justice

There have always been some forms of diversion from formal punishment. For instance, descriptions of The Bay of Sanctuary in Hawaiian society indicate that those accused of crimes could escape punishment by swimming across and remaining on the other side of the bay. In early Europe, the **"benefit of clergy"** was provided to those who could prove they were members of the clergy. Individuals who were facing trial and punishment in secular courts could have their cases dismissed with the expectation that ecclesiastical courts would take over and punish the clergy member. However, as time went on, the benefit became available to anyone who could read Psalm 54. It became, in effect, a type of diversion for those who, for whatever reason, the court chose to give the benefit of clergy.

TYPES OF DIVERSION PROGRAMS

We will distinguish **pretrial release programs** from deferred adjudication programs. While release on recognizance (ROR) or court surety programs are simply a means by which suspects may avoid having to pay bail before their adjudication, a pretrial diversionary program, successfully completed, takes the place of formal adjudication. The latter requires enabling legislation and usually comprises.

1. An evaluation of eligibility by pretrial services staff
2. A contract that clarifies exactly what the defendant must do for successful completion
3. A mechanism by which the defendant's case is disposed of, usually through a court order that disposes of the case without a conviction

Pretrial diversion comes before any finding of guilt. Offenders who are eligible and successfully complete a pretrial diversion program may honestly say they have never been convicted of a crime, because they haven't. Typically, once an offender is chosen for a pretrial diversion program, they may encounter one or more of the programs described, such as day reporting, community service, and electronic monitoring (EM). These programs may also be

intermediate sanctions, because they are often added to a regular probation sentence. Thus, if one of these programs is part of a deferred adjudication program, it is considered a diversion program; however, if it is added to a regular probation sentence, it is considered an intermediate sanction.

Where they exist, most pretrial diversion programs evaluate all defendants for eligibility. A sentencing statute and/or office policy usually sets eligibility. Factors that go into deciding whether an offender is eligible would include:

- Crime
- Prior record
- Drug history
- Employment
- Residential stability
- Evidence of mental illness

Martha Stewart shows off her electronic-monitoring bracelet in response to a question during a news conference as executive producer Mark Burnett, center, and president and CEO of Martha Stewart Living Omnimedia, Susan Lyne, right, look on, August 25, 2005 in New York. *AP Photo/Frank Franklin II*

Very often, offenders in pretrial diversion programs are required to pay restitution (paying back the victim or the community), perform some form of community service, and/or pay a fine and court costs. The probation department often conducts the supervision for pretrial diversion programs, although the pretrial clients may be supervised via a specialized caseload or office. In many ways, this type of supervision is virtually indistinguishable from probation. Defendants may also be placed in drug treatment programs, helped to get back into school or vocational training, or assisted with job placement.

The main difference to remember between pretrial diversion and probation is that a diversion program (and deferred adjudication) will result in no conviction if successfully completed, but a probation sentence is handed down after a finding of guilt (or a guilty plea) and conviction. Both pretrial diversion programs and probation may utilize the same variety of programs, including day reporting centers, electronic monitoring, restitution and/or fines, and community service.

Day reporting centers

Probationers or pretrial releasees may be required to "check in" to day reporting centers as a condition of their supervision. These centers offer both supervision and services; usually an array of job counseling and placement, educational, and social services are accessed at the sites. The concept was borrowed from Great Britain in the mid-1980s. The center may be publicly or privately operated, and provide services to probationers and/or pretrial diversion clients [2].

Evaluations are mixed [3]. In a survey of 54 day reporting centers, Parent found that centers reported an average "negative termination" rate of about 50%; however, the range was from 14% to 86%. Negative termination included rule violations as well as new arrests. Centers run by private agencies, those that had curfew restrictions, and those with stricter policies had more negative terminations [4]. Because the studies show such a range of outcomes, it is difficult to make generalizations about the effectiveness of such centers.

Electronic monitoring

Electronic monitoring (EM) emerged in the mid-1980s as a supplement to traditional probation or parole supervision, or house arrest. It is now used in conjunction with bail and personal recognizance release, deferred adjudication programs, as part of a suspended jail sentence, as a condition of probation, as a condition of intensive probation, or as a condition of parole release. The most recent celebrity-criminal who had to wear an electronic monitoring device was Martha Stewart, who was released from house arrest and monitoring in August 2005.

Evidently the idea came to a New Mexico judge from a "Spider Man" comic strip. The judge enlisted the aid of an engineer to design the device [5]. Florida's Palm Beach program is also cited as being one the first of this type in the country [6]. Programs now exist in virtually all U.S. states as well as several other countries. Electronic monitoring basically uses an electronic device strapped to the ankle or wrist of the offender. The monitor operates in such a way that an alarm sounds when the offender is too far away from a transmitting detector, often located in the offender's telephone. The program can be set up so that the offender can travel from home to work and back again, but an alarm sounds if he or she is not home by a certain time.

Such programs always cost less than prison or jail; however, cost savings are moderated by the fact that judges may be more likely to give longer community supervision sentences than jail sentences. Further, such cost comparisons typically do not include treatment services that seem to be an essential part of any community sanction. Even accounting for these factors, however, researchers have found that EM programs offer significant savings over incarceration. For example, Lilly et al. reported that Palm Beach County, Florida, conservatively estimated their savings at $130,000 for 26 months by using house arrest with EM and, for a 7-year period, the savings were about $600,000 [6].

Recidivism rates in EM programs have been reported as low as 8%, and as high as 70% [7]. Some researchers found that there was little difference between the recidivism rates between EM programs and a matched sample, controlled for risk level, that complete either a prison sentence, or a traditional probation sentence [8]. At least one meta-analysis found that electronic monitoring *increased* recidivism by about 5% over control groups [9]. Studies have also found that EM combined with treatment elements reduced recidivism for moderate-risk offenders but not lower-risk offenders [10]. One of the most rigorous studies to date has failed to find any evidence that EM is better than other prison diversion programs [11].

It is also important to note issues such as denial rates and completion rates. If a program has a low recidivism rate, it may be because very few are accepted into the program, or the final evaluation does not count the large number who dropped out of or were removed from the program before completion. Denial rates are often high; one study reported that only 24% of those who applied for the program were accepted [12]. Others note that the following factors are predictors of failure on EM programs: gender (male), age (younger), unemployment, criminal history, marital status (single), type of crime (drug or property), and length of time on EM (longer) [13].

The new generation of EM employs global positioning to not only monitor whether an offender returns home when he or she is supposed to, but also to track the offender's movements throughout the day. For instance, the Florida Department of Corrections in 1997 implemented EMPACT (Electronic Monitoring Protection and Crime Tracking, formerly known as CrimeTrax), an EM program that incorporates a global positioning system (GPS). The program automatically monitors the location of parolees and suspects out on bail.

Placing offenders on GPS monitoring rather than incarcerating them realizes significant savings. While one study indicated that it costs $49.75 daily to incarcerate an offender, house arrest costs only $20.33 with a satellite monitor, and $11.16 without [14]. The extra cost of GPS monitoring may be justified if the alternative is a prison sentence, but not if the alternative would be regular supervision in a diversion program or a regular probation sentence.

A trend in the use of electronic monitoring and GPS tracking devices is to use them for child sexual predators. In fact, some states have issued "lifetime" sentences to EM. Observers note that this could spell financial disaster for states because there would be ever-increasing caseloads with no end and they would need to have small caseloads, further burdening officers with non-sex offender caseloads. Another new use of EM and GPS is adjudicating family violence. When a domestic violence victim obtains a protective order, it can be accompanied with an EM that can be set to go off if the offender gets within a given distance from the victim [15].

The conclusion one reaches after reading the literature is that EM and GPS technology is expensive and should be reserved for offenders who otherwise would have received jail or prison sentences. In order for the program to address recidivism or lead to reformed behavior, there must be treatment elements included in addition to simple monitoring.

Restitution/day fines

The use of economic sanctions predates most written forms of law. Offenders may be assessed a fine, restitution, court costs, and/or probation supervision. Some jurisdictions charge offenders for services as well, including the cost of drug tests. The two types of economic sanctions we will discuss here are day fines and restitution.

Criminal fines may be set by statute, case law, or office policy but, in general, are proportional to the seriousness of the crime. Usually, fines may be used to punish property crimes and public order crimes, but not violent crimes, which are considered too serious. In Europe, even violent crimes are likely to be resolved through the use of fines. In England, 38% of all felonies and 39% of violent crimes are punished by fine. In Germany, 81% of adult crimes and 73% of violent crimes are punishable by fine [16].

The trouble with set fines is that any amount is experienced quite differently depending on one's economic situation. A fine of $1000 may be a minor nuisance to a middle-class offender but an impossible burden to a poor, unemployed offender. Therefore, **day fines** are common in Europe and are also used in some jurisdictions in the United States. Day fines are set by the amount of income the offender has—that is, if the offender is making minimum wage, his daily earnings would be about $42; therefore, a fine of 10 days would be about $420. However, a professional may earn $416 a day and his fine would be $4160. The theory is that each amount would be experienced in the same way by the two offenders. Day fine schedules sometimes also take into account number of dependents. Several jurisdictions use day fine systems. In a U.S. Department of Justice study of day fines, it was found that collection was sometimes a problem, but most professionals working in the criminal justice system liked the concept [17].

Restitution is an order by the court that requires the offender to compensate the victim for the injury or the loss suffered in the crime. It can be attached to a pretrial diversion program, included as a condition of probation, consist of a stand-alone sentence along with custody in a residential restitution center, or be added to a prison sentence. In 1984, the Victims of Crime Assistance Act and the Federal Comprehensive Crime Control Act ordered courts to consider restitution to victims as part of a criminal sentence. States followed with their own state legislation, enabling judges to set restitution amounts as part of a criminal sentence. Today, every state has enabling legislation and 29 states mandate restitution unless there are compelling reasons not to do so. However, even with these laws, it is said that restitution is imposed in only 14% of all felony cases [18].

Victim-centered restitution includes the victim in the determination of the amount to be compensated. The offender either pays the victim directly or through the court, but there is a direct link between the offender and his or her victim. The idea behind restitution is that the offender will become more responsible and law-abiding when they see the harm they caused and are successful in compensating the victim. In other forms of restitution programs, the victims are not involved in the process and/or the money is paid to a state victim compensation or restitution fund. This form of restitution may be considered not much more meaningful than a fine. It certainly does not encourage the offender to think about the victim.

One study found that restitution orders were more commonly imposed on female offenders, property offenders, those with no prior record, and white offenders [19]. Studies indicate that restitution orders are difficult to enforce. One study indicated that only about a third of the total restitution ordered in a Chicago court was ever paid over a three-year period. Enforcement practices such as registered letters or telephone solicitations threatening adverse action raised the percentage of compliance substantially, as did declaring "amnesty days," where accrued interest would be deducted from the amount owed [20].

Community service

Community service might be considered symbolic restitution. It can also be used in place of a fine, especially for those who have no financial resources to pay any type of fine, even a day fine, because they have no income. There are two basic types of community service programs and philosophies that we will call "restorative service" and "punitive service."

Restorative service programs attempt to connect the offender to the victim through some process of recognizing the harm and injury done to the specific victim and arriving at an agreement between the offender and the victim as to the appropriate action. For instance, the offender may repair the damage he caused or provide some other type of service to the victim. More often, the service is to a class of victims rather than the offender's specific victim, but it is still meaningful and related to the offense. For instance, an offender who committed fraud against an elderly victim may provide volunteer services to a nursing home. A doctor who committed Medicare fraud may be required to serve in a free or low-cost health clinic. A college student who pleads guilty to DWI may be required to assist in a high-school alcohol awareness program.

Punitive service may not be linked to the victim at all, nor have any relationship to the crime. For instance, washing police cars, picking up trash on the side of the road, and clearing vacant lots for the city are examples of community service orders, but they hold little meaning for the offender other than deterrence.

Some of the issues that have been discussed in relation to community service as a sanction include:

- ① Supervision costs
- ② Appropriate settings
- ③ Liability
- ④ Reasonableness (number of hours, types of work)

Obviously, someone has to monitor the community service order. Typically, it is the probation department that makes sure community service orders are completed. Supervision costs money—thus, some programs charge the offender for participation in the program. This presents a problem for offenders who do not have the financial resources to pay the service cost. The costs involved in supervising offenders certainly diminish the economic value of the service itself. Further, if the offender is placed in a community agency without supervision from a correctional supervisor, then the supervision costs are passed to the recipient agency.

While assisting with youth or the elderly is a more meaningful type of community service, there are serious questions as to whether these settings are appropriate for some offenders. Nursing home residents are targets for financial crime, and children are targets for sexual predators. If the community service work is done in the community, for instance, winterizing or renovating homes for the poor, then these residents are vulnerable to crimes committed by the offenders. There are also issues in how many placements can be found in any community that are relevant, meaningful, and do not subject anyone to undue risk. It may be the case that there are far fewer placements than offenders who are given a community service order.

Liability issues are raised when offenders are placed in schools, youth centers, or nursing homes. The reason so many community service hours involve picking up garbage or washing police cars is because those settings do not create undue risk or liability. If probationers identify new victims through their community service work, departments may be exposed to legal liability. If offenders are injured during their community service work, the agency may be liable if there is negligence. In many cases, such workers may access worker's compensation funds. Public and private programs may have to carry liability insurance to cover injuries experienced by offender-workers.

Another complication for low-income, employed offenders is that often community service orders dictate when an offender must put in the hours.

INTERNET KEY

To read more about community service programs, go to http://www.restorativejustice.org/university-classroom/01introduction/tutorial-introduction-to-restorative-justice/outcomes/communityserv.

In some cases, it is impossible to complete community service hours and keep one's job. Disabled offenders are at a disadvantage in those programs that only offer community service in the form of physical labor; therefore, some offenders may receive a jail or prison sentence instead of community service, simply because of their inability rather than their unwillingness to participate.

PROBATION

Probation is a Latin word meaning "period of proving" or "trial." Probation is both the sentence and a status. A criminal defendant may receive a sentence of probation, and, once on probation, it becomes a legal status of reduced liberty. Probationers are subject to a higher level of supervision than ordinary citizens and have less privacy from governmental scrutiny. The sentence of probation comes with a set of conditions that are rules for behavior. Either they specify required behaviors (like reporting once a month), or they prohibit certain behaviors (such as opening a bank account without the probation officer's approval). Typically, a probation sentence comes with the threat that, if revoked, the offender will receive a prison sentence.

Probation may be granted by a judge, jury, or as a result of plea bargaining. Most states have statutes that restrict who can be sentenced to probation. Typically, serious offenders who have committed murder or kidnapping are specifically excluded from receiving a probation sentence. Also, some states do not allow repeat offenders to receive probation. Burglary is described in the Focus on Crime box. Burglars may be eligible for probation in most states, but those who commit home invasions probably would not be.

FOCUS ON CRIME: BURGLARY AND HOME INVASION

An estimated 3.7 million burglaries occur each year. A household member was present in almost one-third (28%) of these crimes. In about 7% of cases, a household member is assaulted (266,560 burglaries). The most common crime committed against a household member was simple assault (nonsevere injury or offensive touching); however, in 1.3% of burglaries aggravated assault occurred and in 0.6% of burglaries, a rape occurred. Victims knew the offender in a third of the cases where someone was at home during the burglary, and in 65%

of the 266,560 burglaries where violence occurred, victims knew the burglar (they were twice as likely to be relatives or known acquaintances than current or former intimates).

Home invasion is a term that refers to a violent intrusion when homeowners are present with the intent of robbery and other crimes. Some states have written new laws to specifically cover this type of crime.

The number of burglaries of unoccupied households declined from 25.8 to 21.2 burglaries per 1000 between

FOCUS ON CRIME: BURGLARY AND HOME INVASION—CONT'D

2000 and 2007, while the number of burglaries where someone was at home remained at about 8.4 burglaries per 1000. The percentage that included violence increased from 6.3% to 7.7%.

Households headed by single women had the highest rate of burglary with someone present, and households with married couples experienced the least burglary victimization. Higher income households had lower burglary rates, and renters had higher rates than homeowners. In most cases, the offender gained entry through an unlocked door or window. While 30% of households that were burglarized with no one at home lost $1000 or more in goods or cash, only 17% of burglaries that took place with someone at home lost that much and in 55% of the cases where someone was at home, the burglar took nothing. In about three-quarters of all burglaries, victims report the crime to the police.

Source: *S. Catalano, Victimization during Household Burglary, Bureau of Justice Statistics, Washington, DC, 2010.*

State statutes may set the maximum length of probation. In many states, it is never more than 5 years, but in other states, such as Texas, the maximum length is set at 10 years. In most states, there is a provision for early discharge. If the probationer has successfully completed a period of supervision and met all requirements, then the probation officer has the discretion to ask the judge to grant an early discharge.

🌐 INTERNET KEY

To find out about the American Probation and Parole Officers Association, go to http://www.appa-net.org/.

About 85% of all offenders supervised in the community are on probation. In 2009, there were about 4.2 million probationers in this country and the rate of probation supervision nationwide was 1799 per 100,000 citizens. The number of people on probation varies tremendously from state to state, as does the rate per population. For instance, in 2009, Texas had 428,014 probationers, but North Dakota only had 4266. Of course, the two states' populations are very different, but even rates, which standardize by population, show extreme variations. New Hampshire supervised 434 people per 100,000 on probation, while Georgia supervised 5385 per 100,000 [21]. Determinate sentence states are more likely to use probation than states with indeterminate sentencing [22].

According to the Bureau of Justice Statistics, in 2008:

- About 24% of probationers were women.
- About 55% of probationers were white, 30% were black, and 13% were Hispanic.
- About half are on probation for felony sentences.
- Probationers are equally likely to be drug offenders (26%), or property offenders (26%), followed by violent offenders (19%), public order offenders (18%), and other crimes (10%).
- About 65% successfully complete probation (of those whose status is known) [23].

The number of adults on probation has risen more than 40% since 1990 [24]. However, felons are less likely to receive a probation sentence than a prison sentence. The Bureau of Justice Statistics reports that 31% of felony offenders receive probation and 69% receive either a sentence of prison or jail [25]. For those who do receive probation, the average sentence is about three years [26]. In 1990, about 61% of all those under some form of correctional supervision were on probation; in 2008, 58% of the total correctional population were on probation [27]. Even though probation receives less than 10% of state and local government expenditures, it deals with almost 60% of all offenders [28]. In the last several years, all correctional populations (prison, jail, parole, and probation) have grown less rapidly than in previous years. Between 2008 and 2009, the probation population decreased by 0.9%.

The Bureau of Justice Statistics reports that the per capita rate of women on probation rose 40% between 1990 and 1998. Only 9% of women on probation were convicted of violent crimes; 44% were sentenced for property crimes and 46% were sentenced for drug or alcohol crimes. Nearly two-thirds of female probationers are white, a much higher percentage than that found in jails or prisons. Only about a quarter of women on probation were married (but that was a higher percentage than those in jail or prison). About 60% had at least a high school degree. About 40% reported being physically or sexually abused [29]. Unfortunately, these data are more than 10 years old and the Bureau of Justice Statistics has not issued more recent reports on female probationers.

Research indicates that women are less likely to reoffend than men [30]. One research study of 195 female probationers found that they were less likely to return to drug dealing if they were employed, involved in a relationship, or living with their children. They were less likely to engage in other crimes if they had stable living conditions or were living with a husband or a significant other, but there was no effect on the return to drug crimes. This, the researchers note, illustrates the importance of relationships and supports prior research that found that living with a significant other in the drug trade increased a woman's likelihood of also becoming involved [31].

Minority groups are disproportionately represented in prison populations, but not as much in community corrections populations. As stated earlier, about 30% of probationers are black and about 13% are Hispanic. According to the Bureau of Justice Statistics, the percentage of minorities as a percentage of the total probation population has not increased significantly in the last 10 years. Unfortunately, not much is known about minorities on probation, unlike the substantial literature describing their experience in the nation's prisons. There are conflicting findings on whether blacks are less likely to get probation; some studies show a race effect, but other studies do not. The percentage of people on probation who are Hispanic roughly reflects their percentage of the population [32].

The history of probation

The standard history of probation begins with the work of John Augustus. He was a Boston bootmaker who was in court one day in 1841 and decided to intervene in the case of a drunk who was being sent to jail. A strong believer in the temperance movement, he decided to post bail for the man, who was charged with being a common drunk. Augustus asked the judge to defer sentencing for three weeks and release the man into his custody because he thought that he could help the man get his life in order. Evidently, his attempts were met with scorn from law enforcement, but for the next 18 years, from 1841 until his death in 1859, he bailed out more than 1800 adults and children. He selected carefully and only chose first-time offenders. Once released, he helped them find employment or a place to live and reported their progress to the court. Most of the offenders released into his custody were charged with violations of vice or temperance laws [33]. His work continued and spread after he died and, in 1878, Massachusetts hired its first probation officer. In 1901, New York passed a statute authorizing probation for adults. Volunteers or police officers supervised probationers. Early probation officers were usually retired sheriffs and policemen who worked directly for the judge.

In the early 1900s, federal judges used a form of suspended sentence to give federal offenders a second chance. In 1925, the federal government created an enabling statute for federal probation. There was a very slow increase in the number of federal probation officers, with only 62 officers in 1931. Of course, there were not that many federal criminals until the "federalization" of drug laws in the 1970s and 1980s when the number of federal drug laws that paralleled similar state laws increased exponentially.

It was not until 1956 that all states had enabling legislation that allowed for probation sentences to be handed out by judges. In Box 12.2, we see that the enabling statutes for probation continued to be created well into the middle of the twentieth century [34].

BOX 12.2 ENABLING STATUTES PASSED CREATING PROBATION

Before 1900: Massachusetts (1878), Missouri (1897), Rhode Island (1899)

1900-1905: California, Connecticut, Maine, Maryland, Michigan, New Jersey, New York, Vermont

1906-1910: Colorado, Georgia, Indiana, Kansas, Minnesota, Nebraska, Ohio, Pennsylvania, Wisconsin

1911-1915: Alabama, Arizona, Delaware, Idaho, Illinois, Montana, North Dakota, Oklahoma, Oregon, Tennessee, Washington

1916-1920: North Carolina

1921-1923: Arkansas, Utah

After 1923: Alaska, Florida, Hawaii, Iowa, Kentucky, Louisiana, Mississippi, Nevada, New Hampshire, New Mexico, South Carolina, South Dakota, Texas, West Virginia

Source: *F.R. Johnson, Probation for Juveniles and Adults, Century, New York, 1928, pp. 12-13.*

In the 1970s, probation came to the forefront of the public and policymakers' attention, and a series of reports indicated that it was not successful in its promise to reform offenders. Probation suffered the same fate as all "rehabilitative" programs in the 1980s, when politics and public sentiment moved toward a more punitive approach with offenders. Although probation never went away, the major innovation in these decades was intensive supervision, which involved more intensive supervision, not necessarily more intense programming. Interestingly, at least one writer attributed the greater enforcement/surveillance approach of probation that began in the 1980s to the influx of criminal justice majors in the field, as opposed to those who had been trained as social workers or counselors [35]. Unlike parole, however, probation was never abolished in any state and continues to absorb a large majority of offenders, either as the only correctional sentence they ever receive, or, for some, the first step on their way to prison.

Administration

There are a number of ways that probation can be administered and every state is slightly different. The most common model is that of a state executive agency that provides hiring and procedural standards. Other states have purely local executive administration. In other states, probation is administered through the judicial branch of government, either from the state level or the local level. Some states have a mixed model in which none of the categories fits exactly as a description of how probation is administered. In more than half of all states, the state provides centralized hiring, training, and standards [36]. In Box 12.3, state models are identified as they existed in 1999; there is evidently no recent information concerning the administration of probation, although a national survey in 2011 will update this information.

The major reason for the trend to centralize probation is funding. When probation is administered by a county agency, there is variation in hiring standards and pay scales. Counties vary in their ability to fund probation and so there may be wide disparities in the quality of supervision. Furthermore, procedures may be different so that offenders who move from one county to the next find a completely different probation experience. Centralized systems can standardize budgets and provide consistency in employees and procedures.

Local administration may exist with state guidelines. States provide financial assistance to counties with the expectation and requirement that they meet certain hiring and other standards. Counties may be reimbursed on a per offender basis for every offender kept in the county rather than sent to state prison. Community corrections acts provide incentives to counties to keep offenders in the community by funding local sentences (jail or probation instead of prison) [37].

BOX 12.3 PROBATION ORGANIZATION (1999)

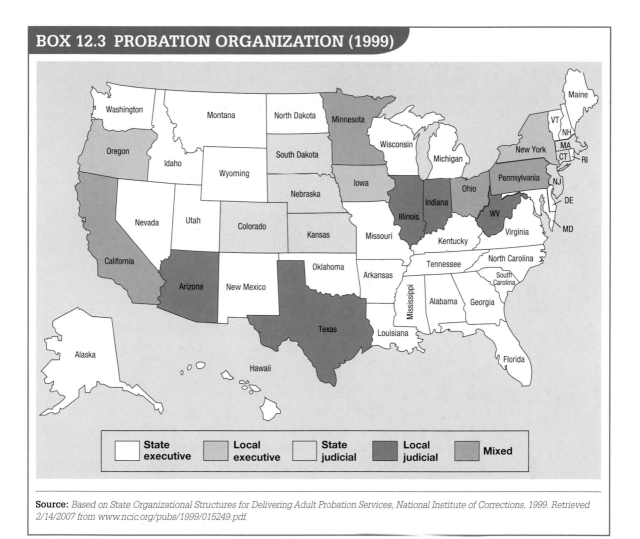

| | State executive | | Local executive | | State judicial | | Local judicial | | Mixed |

Source: *Based on State Organizational Structures for Delivering Adult Probation Services, National Institute of Corrections, 1999. Retrieved 2/14/2007 from www.ncic.org/pubs/1999/015249.pdf.*

Some states that administer probation from a centralized executive model combine probation and parole caseloads. The two supervision models are similar, of course, even though the reporting is different. While probation officers submit progress reports and violation reports to the sentencing court, parole officers submit such reports to the parole board or paroling authority. There are also those who believe that probationers and parolees are different enough to warrant different supervision styles with parolees deserving a more punitive, as opposed to service-oriented, supervision. One advantage of such a system is that it is more flexible and can more easily adapt to changing populations between the two offender groups.

The other issue in the administration of probation is whether probation is administratively under the control of the judicial branch or separate from it. While probation officers in some states are located in the courtroom and report directly to the judge, in most states the probation department is separate from judicial authority. In executive branch systems, there typically exists a close working relationship between the probation officers and the judges who sentence to probation, but the probation officer is not the employee of the court and belongs to a separate agency.

EXERCISE: IN THE STATE OF...

Using the Internet, find out whether Box 12.3 is still accurate for your state.   (Hint: Do a Google search for your state's probation department to discover what the administrative structure looks like.) Also check the most current Bureau of Justice Statistics bulletins to discover if the number of people on probation in your state is going up or down, and how the rate of sentencing to probation compares to other states.

PRESENTENCE AND SUPERVISION FUNCTIONS

Probation encompasses two major functions: presentence investigations/ recommendations and probation supervision. In larger jurisdictions, these functions are separated and assigned to different offices or divisions within the agency. In smaller jurisdictions, the same officer may perform both functions.

The presentence function includes gathering information about offenders before sentencing. This begins with an interview with the offender, often in jail, if the offender is detained. The offender answers a series of questions relating to their past and current situation and then the officer checks the facts. The probation officer writes up the finding and makes a sentencing recommendation to the court. Information in a presentence report (PSR) may include:

- Defendant's risk (typically computed through a risk score system)
- Circumstances (work, family, education)
- All sentencing options
- Recommendation

About half of all states require a presentence investigation in all felony cases. Another 16 states define the investigations as discretionary. In only two states are presentence investigations required prior to misdemeanor sentencing [38].

There is a high correlation between the recommendation in the presentence investigation and the judge's sentence. It is unclear whether the high correlation between the probation officers' recommendations and the judges' sentences is because the judge follows the officer's recommendation, or whether it is because probation officers, who are often attached to the court and spend most of every day in the judge's courtroom, become familiar with how the judge would sentence and so they recommend accordingly [39]. It should also be noted that in many jurisdictions the sentence is the result of plea bargaining. In those cases, the prosecutor and the defendant agree to a specific term and the judge either approves or disapproves. In these cases, if the presentence report is done at all, it is done before adjudication in order to help the prosecutor determine the appropriate sentence to offer or accept.

One of the legal issues that occurs with PSRs is confidentiality. In an early case, the Supreme Court held that information in the PSR could not be kept from the offender if he or she had been sentenced to death. Due process required that the offender be able to know the information in the report in order to contest it as inaccurate or misleading. It could be, for instance, that the sentencing recommendation was based on hearsay and unproven allegations by coworkers, family members, or victims. If the offender did not know what was in the report, there would be no way to defend against unfair or untruthful allegations [40]. So far, however, the Court has refused to extend this reasoning to any sentence other than death; thus, whether the report is available to the defense is based on the law and procedural rules of the jurisdiction. The Federal Rules of Criminal Procedure, for instance, require that the PSR be made available to the defendant unless it might "disrupt rehabilitation," when the information was obtained with a promise of confidentiality, or when harm may result to any person because of the disclosure [41].

The probation sentence also includes **conditions**. Conditions are the rules of probation. There are general conditions (such as to report to the probation officer), but also sometimes very specific conditions that are customized to the offender and his or her crime. Some of the possible conditions that might be attached to a probation order include standard conditions, such as reporting and notifying the probation officer of any change of address; punitive conditions, such as fines or community service; and treatment conditions, such as drug or alcohol treatment [42]. In the following Breaking News box, we see how ubiquitous drug and alcohol conditions are in deciding how best to respond to criminals—even celebrity criminals.

BREAKING NEWS

In November 2010, Charlie Sheen, actor in the hit TV series, *Two and a Half Men*, was released from unsupervised probation from his conviction for misdemeanor assault after being arrested in Aspen, Colorado, on charges of assaulting his wife. His probation conditions included a 30-day rehabilitation stay and to avoid drugs and excessive alcohol consumption. Although hotel security and police were called to his hotel room in late October after he was reported as being "emotionally disturbed," Colorado officials indicated that they had no evidence that he violated the conditions of his probation and, therefore, a judge released him from further supervision.

In a March 15, 2010 file photo, Charlie Sheen enters Pitkin County Courthouse in Aspen, Colorado to attend a hearing on domestic violence charges. His legal problems continued to escalate through 2011 and, eventually, his hit show was cancelled. *AP Photo/David Zalubowski*

While the probation officer may suggest that conditions be added to the probation order in the PSR, only judges can impose conditions and only judges can drop or change conditions. Standard conditions may be preprinted on the probation order. They are consistent for all probationers and cover fairly obvious rules, such as: "Don't commit another crime." Box 12.4 displays some common standard conditions.

It should be noted that many states have instituted fees for probation and payment of these fees is added as a condition to the probation sentence. Probationers are charged anywhere from $10 to $40 per month to be on probation. Sometimes, there is a sliding scale based on income [43]. Paying the supervision fee is one of the conditions of probation and offenders may have their probation revoked if they refuse to pay. Although the offender can be required to pay court costs, fines, restitution, and even probation fees, the court cannot revoke probation solely for an inability to pay. Of course, if the offender is deemed able to pay and refuses, it is legally acceptable to revoke the probation order and send the offender to prison [44].

Violating a condition of probation will not automatically result in a revocation and prison sentence; however, the judge has the legal authority to revoke probation if any conditions are not met. There is evidence that the number of special/punitive conditions has increased. This in itself may result in a greater likelihood of violations and increase the risk of failure because very restrictive conditions (such as never entering a bar) are difficult to live with for many years [45].

So-called **Scarlet Letter conditions** are those where the judge creates a condition designed to humiliate or call attention to the wrongdoing of the offender. Some argue that these types of conditions subject the offender and his or her family to needless humiliation; others argue that the tailored conditions mean more than

BOX 12.4 STANDARD CONDITIONS OF PROBATION

- Obey all laws
- Do not possess firearms
- Report as directed to probation officer
- Permit home visits and searches
- Avoid alcohol and illegal drug use
- Maintain suitable employment
- Notify address changes
- Do not associate with known criminals
- Pay all fines and fees

standard punishments. Some of the more unusual conditions include requiring sex offenders to post signs in their front yard warning people away, requiring DWI felons to put bumper stickers on their car identifying themselves as drunk drivers, requiring an individual to seek the forgiveness of his church, and so on [46].

Any condition of probation must have a legitimate purpose. While one might argue that conditions which humiliate the offender are designed to deter or reform, treatment deemed too humiliating may be thrown out by the court. A court in Florida agreed with an offender that his probation condition, which involved wearing a diaper in a treatment program, was not acceptable [47]. On the other hand, a Nevada court upheld a condition that required those convicted of DWI to do community service wearing a sign that identified them to passersby as "drunk drivers" [48].

Another issue that has arisen concerns the power of the probation officer to search. Typically, to search a home, a government agent must have a warrant that specifies with clarity what is being sought. Part of the probation order always requires the probationer to submit to periodic searches of one's home and/or person by the probation officer. This intrusion would never be justified toward a free person, but probationers do not have all the rights of free people. Courts have generally upheld the right of the probation officer to search without a warrant [49].

The probation officer is not legally liable for any harm that comes from the sentencing recommendation because it is considered a quasijudicial function. Thus, he or she is able to recommend probation without fear of being sued if the offender subsequently commits a crime, much in the same way that judicial immunity operates. Furthermore, the defendant cannot sue the probation officer (or court service officer) who prepares the presentence report for mistakes or false information. It should be noted that this type of immunity only applies to the quasijudicial functions of the position (decisions related to sentencing recommendations); however, how the probation officer conducts supervision can be the basis for a lawsuit. For instance, a probationer may sue under Section 1983 for alleged violations of constitutional rights by the probation officer, or third parties may sue under some cause of action such as wrongful death if the officer's gross negligence in supervision resulted in the death of someone at the hands of the probationer. These cases are rare, however, because the standard of negligence is set fairly high.

Supervision

In addition to conducting presentence investigations and writing presentence reports for the sentencing judge, the other major function of probation is supervision of probationers. Probation has followed a casework approach to service delivery. The **casework model** is typical of social work and involves the professional interacting with each "client" individually, serving as the primary and, sometimes, only service provider. This contrasts with other approaches that might have been taken, such as an investigative approach, in which officers simply perform a type of police function of tracking and patroling probationers to attempt to catch them doing something wrong and/or investigating allegations and charges. Another model might be that of a service broker, where the probation officer refers offenders to different types of professionals (similar to the primary care physician idea of HMOs). However, in the casework model, each probation officer is completely responsible for everyone on their caseload, and each offender on the caseload has a relationship with one probation officer. Interestingly, one of the complaints of probationers is that there is a great deal of turnover in probation offices, and "their officer" may change frequently.

As long ago as 1960, the federal probation system assigned probationers to supervision levels based on crime and risk level. Most were assigned a medium classification level and they were supervised in 50-person caseloads. Those who posed a minimal risk to the public were placed in caseloads of 70 to 130 cases. However, those who had higher-risk level scores were placed in intensive caseloads of only 20 offenders per officer [50]. This form of classification continues today, and probationers generally are classified as high to low risk and this classification determines the level of supervision. Typically, a probation officer has a general or a specialized caseload and may supervise anywhere from 25 (in intensive or specialized caseloads) to more than 100 offenders, with the average at about 130 [51]. There has been no definitive research indicating that there is an ideal caseload. Standards promulgated since the 1940s advocate a caseload no larger than 30, but the typical caseload has always been much higher [52].

The number of contacts made each month with probationers depends on their classification level. While intensive supervision probationers might be seen as often as nine times a month with three field contacts, regular probationers may only be seen once, and those on a "mail in" status never see a probation officer—they just mail in or call in their report [53]. Most often, probation supervision involves a contact once a month when the probationer comes into the probation office to see the officer and fill out a report, and a "field contact" once a month, where the officer meets the offender in his or her own home or workplace. In these contacts, the officer checks to see if conditions are being met, whether the offender is still employed, and whether court costs are being paid. Offenders may also be required to submit to urinanalysis and the probation officer monitors those test results as well. Probation officers also make "collateral contacts," which are meetings with family members, neighbors, and employers to gather more information about the probationer.

Periodically, the officer writes a progress report to the sentencing judge. When an offender receives probation, the judge maintains control over the offender so the progress reports go to the judge and, if there is a violation report filed, the sentencing judge might hear a motion to revoke probation filed by the prosecutor.

Models of supervision

Even though all probation officers have basically the same duties, there are differences in the way that the duties are performed. The different approaches taken may be because of individual differences among officers or because of office policies. The two most extreme roles are the "enforcer" and the "counselor" types. In one study, it was found that those who adopted a law enforcement approach to the job issued technical violation reports for 42.5% of their caseload, while those who had adopted more of a social work role only issued technical violation reports for 5.4% of their caseload [54]. This is not to say that either approach is the "right" one, merely that there are important differences in how probation officers perform their role. The different approaches may be characterized by the types found in Box 12.5.

FOCUS ON ETHICS

You are a probation officer in the town you grew up in. You have been supervising a caseload for about a year and generally enjoy your job. You are assigned a new probationer who turns out to be the former boyfriend of your older sister in high school. You felt a little strange about being his probation officer, especially because you had a kind of little sister crush on him when he was dating your sister. You asked your supervisor about whether there were any policies or procedures about knowing your probationers, and he explained to you that in a small town it was bound to happen sooner or later. He asked you if you could make objective opinions about him. You said you could, but now, six months later, you find out that he has tested positive for drugs on a random test. He explains to you that it was just one time when he was at a party and, other than that, he has been doing well on probation, has a job, is paying child support for his two kids, and it wouldn't be fair to file a violation report. You have nothing to base it on, but suspect that he has started using again. He argues that you probably wouldn't file a report for anyone else, but are considering it for him because you are afraid of being perceived of treating him with favoritism. The fact is that there is a rule in the office that dirty tests automatically require a violation report, but the general practice is to give the offender a break if the officer feels that it was an aberration. What should you do?

BOX 12.5 PROBATION OFFICER TYPOLOGY

Service Officer: This officer is more focused on the offender's needs and attempts to develop a relationship with each offender on the caseload; they may make allowances for violations of conditions based on individual circumstances.

Surveillance Officer: This officer is more focused on surveillance and monitoring the offender's performance in completing the requirements and staying out of trouble; these officers emphasize the enforcement duties of the job; they strive to see that if the probationer breaks any laws or violates any condition, he or she is off the streets quickly and efficiently.

Broker Officer: This officer balances service and surveillance, but does not attempt to provide direct counseling or service; rather, the officer uses other community resources and refers the client to the appropriate agency or service provider.

Burned-out Officer: This officer doesn't emphasize either service or surveillance and does the minimum amount of work necessary to stay out of trouble.

Source: C. Klockars, A theory of probation supervision, J. Crim. Law Criminol. Police Sci. 63(4) 1972 550-557.

Interstate Compact

After the creation of probation, it was soon apparent that probationers either would have to stay in the state they were sentenced in until they completed the probation order, or there was going to have to be some sort of shared supervision contract between the states. The **Interstate Compact** was created in September 1937 in Kansas City. All states participate and now these offenders represent about 3% of the total national probation and parole population. Each state has a state interstate compact office that accepts case transfers from other states. The offender must abide by the conditions in both states. Even if there was no supervision fee in the sentencing state, the offender may be required to pay one in the receiving state. Generally, the sending state sets the amount of time the offender is supervised, but the receiving state sets the level of supervision. In 2002, the Interstate Compact was replaced with a new compact and new organization. Today the Interstate Compact for Adult Offender Supervision is the national body that coordinates interstate agreements.

INTERNET KEY

For further information on the Interstate Compact, go to www.interstatecompact.org.

Some states may not allow certain types of offenders (i.e., sex offenders). On the other hand, some will not accept misdemeanants for supervision (evidently seeing those minor offenders as not worth the resources expended). There is no payment made to the receiving state; the idea is that as people move in and out of states, participating states will receive and send probationers in roughly equal proportions. The Parole and Probation Compact Administrators' Association meets twice a year to review standards, guidelines, and policies.

RECIDIVISM

About 65% of all probationers successfully complete their probation and are discharged from probation. The rest have their probation revoked and are sent to prison (16%), continue with new conditions, **abscond** (which means they leave supervision and cannot be located) (3%), are revoked without incarceration, or have unspecified reasons, such as death, for leaving probation supervision [55].

When a probationer violates one or more conditions, the probation officer may file a violation report and the offender's probation may be revoked by the sentencing judge and he or she is sent to prison. What due process protects the individual from governmental error in the decision to revoke? The answer was addressed by the Supreme Court about 30 years ago. The first case that arose occurred in Washington, which used deferred sentencing. In **deferred sentencing**, the decision to sentence to prison, and the length of the possible prison sentence, is not established during the sentencing hearing immediately after conviction. In *Mempa v. Rhay* [56], Jerry Mempa pled guilty to joyriding and received a two-year probation sentence with a deferred prison sentence. During the time he was on probation, he was suspected of being involved in a burglary, the prosecutor moved for revocation and the sentencing court revoked his probation, and sentenced him to 10 years in prison. Although there was a hearing, Mempa had no attorney present to help with his defense. Upon appeal, the Supreme Court held that because the state used deferred sentencing, and the decision and length of imprisonment were not set at the time of the original sentencing, the probation revocation hearing became, in essence, a sentencing hearing, and the offender deserved all the Sixth Amendment rights, including counsel.

Not surprisingly, Washington and other states stopped using deferred sentences with probation and instead began using suspended sentencing. In **suspended sentences**, the judge actually hands down a prison sentence, but then suspends it, pending successful completion of probation. If probation is revoked, the suspended sentence would be imposed. The revocation hearing in this instance is definitely not a sentencing hearing because all decisions regarding sentencing have been made.

In *Gagnon v. Scarpelli* [57], Scarpelli received a suspended sentence and probation. He committed a burglary while on probation and, without a hearing, his probation was revoked and the suspended sentence imposed. He argued that this was a violation of due process. While the Supreme Court agreed that no Sixth Amendment rights applied because the revocation hearing was not a sentencing hearing, they decided that revocation still involved a protected liberty interest and, thus, due process (coming from the Fourteenth Amendment) applied. The "process due" or the steps needed to ensure no error in the governmental deprivation of liberty were more problematic. The Supreme Court had just decided *Morrissey v. Brewer* [58], a parole revocation case, and so they used that as a guide to determine how serious the deprivation was and what process was due. Arguably, a probation revocation was more serious than a parole revocation because the probationer, unlike the parolee, had never been in prison. Thus, the due process protections required should be somewhat greater than when a person faces parole revocation.

The court held that whether the proceeding was more like an administrative hearing, or more like a judicial hearing, hinged on whether there was a factual issue of guilt. If there were questions regarding guilt or innocence, or if the offender could not understand the proceedings because of mental disability or language difficulties, then counsel might be required. However, if it was simply a matter of the offender absconding or some other clear violation of conditions, then no counsel was required. The elements of due process required for probation revocation, as specified by the court, are set out in Box 12.6.

> ### BOX 12.6 DUE PROCESS PROTECTIONS FOR PROBATION REVOCATION
>
> - Notice of alleged violations of probation and evidence
> - Opportunity to appear and to present evidence and witnesses
> - Right to confront adverse witnesses
> - Neutral decision maker
> - Written report
> - *Conditional* right to counsel

In practice, many states allow the probationer to have counsel if they request it. Remember that the right to counsel is not so much an issue of whether they have a right to be there; if an offender can afford to hire a lawyer, they are almost always allowed in a variety of proceedings. The issue concerning whether counsel is a right is important because if it is a right, then the state must provide indigent offenders with public defenders.

The Supreme Court has ruled that probationers do not have Fifth Amendment rights when being questioned by a probation officer; and probation officers do not have to give *Miranda* warnings before asking offenders about criminal activities unless the offender is already in custody [59]. Furthermore, at least one court has held that they can be punished for not responding to probation officers' questions about alleged violations, and also prosecuted or have their probation revoked if they do admit criminal activities to their probation officer [60].

If an offender violates one or more conditions of probation, the probation officer may file a violation report. The prosecutor's office may then file a motion to revoke probation or initiate the hearing before the judge that may end in a revocation of probation. This response is discretionary, however, and some probation officers may work with the offender to try to resolve the issue before filing the report. For instance, if the violation is not paying restitution and court costs, the probation officer may require the probationer to pay the arrears and monitor spending for a month. If the probationer has a "dirty" urine test, the probation officer may ask the offender to go into treatment.

However, if the probation officer learns that the probationer has been arrested for a new crime, or believes that **technical violations** (violations of rules rather than new crimes) warrant judicial intervention, then a violation report is filed. In the report, the officer presents the charges (the violations) and summarizes the proof. There is also a recommendation, much in the same way that the PSR recommends to the judge at the initial sentencing hearing.

After hearing the evidence, the judge decides whether to continue on probation, continue on probation but with modified conditions (i.e., imposing curfew, treatment, intermediate sanction, more conditions), or revoke probation and send the person to prison. In cases of new crimes, the decision is usually to send to prison. Depending on the state, the time spent on probation may not be counted at all toward the completion of the sentence. In this case, an offender may have already served four years on a probation sentence, but upon revocation, must serve the original five-year prison sentence with no credit for time served on probation. In some states, the judge has the discretion to consider time served or not.

In 1986, 74% of probationers successfully completed their term. In 1992, 67% were successful, but by 1998, only 50% successfully completed probation [61]. In 2008, about 48% of probationers were successfully discharged (but for almost a quarter of discharges the information was unknown). In Figure 12.1, the Bureau of Justice Statistics information is used to show the discharges of probationers.

One study found that most probationers failed within the first three months of probation and they failed because of technical violations, not new crimes. In this study, it was found that Michigan probationers were likely to fail because of such violations as:

- Failed drug tests
- Failure to attend or successfully complete programming
- Failure to perform community service [62]

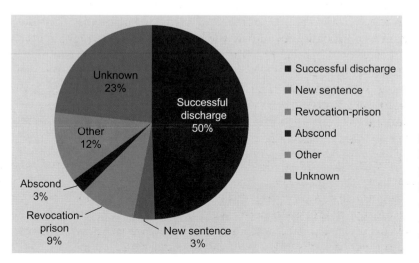

FIGURE 12.1
Discharges of probationers—2009.
Source: *L. Glaze, T.F. Zhang, Probation and Parole in the United States, 2009, Bureau of Justice Statistics, Washington, DC, 2010, p. 25.*

Factors associated with recidivism

There are obvious factors that influence whether offenders will succeed on probation or commit a new crime. If they have no job, no money, no place to live, and continue to associate with criminals, it seems fairly predictable that they will reoffend. Joan Petersilia identified the following factors as associated with recidivism:

- Type of crime (burglary and property crime have higher rates)
- Extent of prior record
- Income at arrest (high unemployment is associated with high recidivism)
- Household composition (those who live with spouse and children have lower recidivism)
- Age (younger offenders have higher recidivism rates)
- Drug use (drug users have higher recidivism rates)
- Program participation [63]

Another study reviewed the findings of prior research to conclude that the following factors may be related to failure:

- Sex (women are less likely to recidivate)
- Age (mixed findings; older offenders are more likely to be arrested for serious felonies, but in general younger offenders more likely to reoffend)
- Race (mixed findings)
- Education (higher levels are associated with success)
- Marital status (mixed, but most find marriage is related to success)
- Employment (associated with success on probation)
- Prior criminal history (associated with failure, especially property offenders) [64]

Intensive supervision programs, popularized in the 1980s, were supposed to reduce recidivism, but the results of evaluations were mixed and, after many evaluations across the country, evaluators concluded that there was little difference in the outcomes between these programs and regular probation [65].

On the other hand, there are some encouraging recent findings that indicate probation recidivism rates can be lowered. Hawaii began a probation program in 2004 called Hawaii's Opportunity Probation with Enforcement (H.O.P.E.). The program involved rapid and frequent "warning" hearings with judges when probationers were in danger of having violation reports written, and random, frequent, and unannounced drug tests. In the program, judges used short jail sentences as punishment for violations in place of revocation and prison in many instances where offenders failed. There was also drug treatment and mental health counseling for probationers who needed the services. An evaluation of the program showed that H.O.P.E. probationers spent about the same number of days in jail as a control group but in shorter and more frequent time periods. The most encouraging finding, however, was that the recidivism rate for program participants was half that of other probationers in the one year time period of the study (7% compared to 15%), and the percentage of H.O.P.E. participants who tested positive for drugs was less than one-third of other probationers (13% compared to 46%). Finally, program participants were half as likely to be rearrested (21% compared to 47%) [66].

In another study in Maryland, probation officers were trained in behavioral management techniques. The program utilized a classification system based on RNR (risk, needs, responsivity) so that the offender's readiness for change was incorporated into the determination of the type of intervention necessary. Simple techniques were taught to probation officers that encouraged them to create a social learning environment rather than a punitive, law enforcement relationship with the offender; for instance, they were trained to look the offender in the eye and shake his or her hand upon entrance and exit. The social learning model was adopted within the department itself, that is, supervisor-probation officer relationships as well as probation officer-probationer relationships were informed by the social learning approach. In an evaluation of the program, probationers in the program were slightly less likely to receive technical violations and there was no difference in the number of positive drug tests, but program participants were 42% less likely to be rearrested [67]. These programs indicate that there is a way to address the almost 40% recidivism rate that we see across the country for probationers. Because about one-third of entering prisoners are those whose probation or parole was revoked as opposed to new convictions, it is extremely important to continue to investigate what factors are necessary for a probationer to successfully complete his or her probation.

CONCLUSION

Diversion programs have the potential to keep appropriate offenders in the community and reduce total correctional costs. There are a number of programs that have diverted offenders from entering the system, such as deferred adjudication programs that use such features as restitution and electronic monitoring. For all diversion programs, the question that must be answered is whether the cost savings and benefit to the offender are worth the risk to public safety. To answer this question, prediction and classification instruments must be improved and the implementation of such programs must adhere to standards and guidelines set out by program developers.

The majority of criminal offenders have experienced probation. About 60% successfully complete their probation sentence. Although probation has the potential to be a sufficient and effective correctional sanction, there are a number of problems with the implementation of probation, which include:

1. An unclear mission
2. Overstated and/or unspecified objectives that are difficult to measure
3. Inadequate standards and training
4. Lack of substantial results
5. A history of inadequate funding
6. Isolation from the public and a lack of public awareness
7. Lack of strategic planning and effective management techniques
8. A weak constituency [68]

If probation is to be used more often for first-time and nonviolent offenders and thereby reduce the total cost of corrections, it must overcome these issues and present a more palatable sentencing alternative to decision makers.

Review Questions

1. Distinguish among pretrial release programs, pretrial diversion programs, and intermediate sanctions.
2. Discuss what benefit of clergy was and why it is called an early form of diversion.
3. Briefly describe day reporting centers, electronic monitoring, restitution, day fines, and community service.
4. How many people are on probation? What percentage of all correctional offenders are on probation? What is the percentage of felony defendants who receive a sentence of probation?
5. Describe what percentage of probationers are women and what special issues face women on probation. Describe what percentage of probationers are minorities.
6. Describe the contributions of John Augustus.
7. Describe the state, local, and mixed models of probation administration.
8. Describe the elements that comprise the presentence report, and discuss the issues of confidentiality and what conditions are placed on probation orders.
9. Describe the models of supervision.
10. Discuss the due process rights of probationers facing revocation.

VOCABULARY

abscond to leave supervision without permission

benefit of clergy early form of diversion where those who could prove they were members of the clergy (sometimes by reading Psalm 54) were released from secular adjudication

casework model involves the professional interacting with each "client" individually, serving as the primary, and sometimes only, service provider

community corrections any form of correctional alternative that does not involve incarceration in prison

conditions rules of probation

day fines fines set by the amount of income the offender has, such as the fine is three days of income, rather than a dollar amount

deferred sentencing a sentence where the decision to sentence to prison, and the length of the possible prison sentence, is not established during the sentencing hearing

intermediate sanctions more than a suspended sentence, less than a prison sentence

interstate compact agreement between states to supervise transferred probationers

pretrial release programs a means by which suspects may avoid having to pay bail to gain release before their trial

punitive service type of community service that may not be linked to the victim at all, nor have any relationship to the crime, such as washing police cars

restitution an order by the court that requires the offender to compensate the victim for the injury or loss suffered in the crime

restorative service type of community service that attempts to connect the offender to the victim through some process of recognizing the harm and injury done to the specific victim, such as providing a service to the victim or class of victims

Scarlet Letter conditions a condition designed to humiliate or call attention to the wrongdoing of the offender

suspended sentence the judge actually hands down a prison sentence, but then suspends it, pending successful completion of probation

technical violations violations of rules rather than new crimes

victim-centered restitution includes the victim in the determination of the amount to be compensated, and then the offender either pays the victim directly or through the court

ENDNOTES

[1] County of Riverside v. McLaughlin, 500 U.S. 44, 1991.

[2] D. Parent, J. Byrne, V. Tsarfaty, L. Valade, L. Esselman, Day Reporting Centers: Issues and Practices in Criminal Justice, vol. 1, National Institute of Justice, Washington DC, 1995.

[3] R. Jones, J. Lacey, Evaluation of a Day Reporting Center for Repeat DWI Offenders, National Highway Traffic Safety Administration, Washington, DC, 1999.

[4] D. Parent, Day reporting centers: an evolving intermediate sanction, Fed. Probat. 60(4): (1996) 51–54.

[5] J. Bonta, S. Wallace-Capretta, J. Rooney, Can electronic monitoring make a difference? An evaluation of three Canadian programs, Crime Delinq. 46(1) (2000) 61–75.

[6] J. Lilly, R. Ball, G. Curry, J. McMullen, Electronic monitoring of the drunk driver: a seven-year study of the home confinement alternative, Crime Delinq. 39 (1993) 462–484.

[7] A. Gibbs, D. King, The electronic ball and chain? The operation and impact of home detention with electronic monitoring in New Zealand, Aust. N. Z. J. Criminol. 36 (2003) 1–17.

[8] J. Bonta, S. Wallace-Capretta, J. Rooney, Can electronic monitoring make a difference? An evaluation of three Canadian programs, Crime Delinq. 46(1) (2000) 61–75.

[9] P. Gendreau, C. Goggin, F. Cullen, D. Andrews, The effects of community sanctions and incarceration on recidivism, Forum 12(2) (2000) 10–13.

[10] J. Bonta, S. Wallace-Capretta, J. Rooney, Can electronic monitoring make a difference? An evaluation of three Canadian programs, Crime Delinq. 46(1) (2000) 61–75.

[11] M. Renzema, E. Mayo-Wilson, Can electronic monitoring reduce crime for moderate to high-risk offenders? J. Exp. Criminol. 1 (2005) 1–23.

[12] M. Maxfield, T. Baumer, Home detention with electronic monitoring: comparing pretrial and postconviction programs, Crime Delinq. 36 (1990) 521–536.

[13] J. Lilly, R. Ball, G. Curry, J. McMullen, Electronic monitoring of the drunk driver: a seven-year study of the home confinement alternative, Crime Delinq. 39 (1993) 462–484.

[14] R. Stutzman, Ankle monitors show a higher rate of success, Orlando Sentinel, December 29, 2002 B1; R. Stutzman, State takes eyes off inmates, Orlando Sentinel, December 29, 2002 B2.

[15] R. Gable, From B.F. Skinner to Spiderman to Martha Stewart: the past, present, and future of electronic monitoring of offenders, J. Offender Rehabil. 46(3) (2008) 101–118.

[16] T. Hillsman, J. Greene, The use of fines as an intermediate sanction in: J. Byrne, A. Lurigio, J. Petersilia (Eds.), Smart Sentencing: The Emergence of Intermediate Sanctions, Sage Publications, Newbury Park, CA, 1992, pp. 123–141.

[17] Bureau of Justice Assistance, How to Use Structured Fines as an Intermediate Sanction, U.S. Department of Justice, Washington, DC, 1996.

[18] R. Ruback, G. Ruth, J. Shaffer, Assessing the impact of statutory change: a statewide multi-level analysis of restitution orders in Pennsylvania, Crime Delinq. 51(3) (2005) 319.

[19] R. Ruback, G. Ruth, J. Shaffer, Assessing the impact of statutory change: a statewide multi-level analysis of restitution orders in Pennsylvania, Crime Delinq. 51(3) (2005) 334.

[20] A. Lurigio, A. Davis, Does a threatening letter increase compliance with restitution orders? Crime Delinq. 36(4) (1984) 537–548.

[21] L. Glaze, T. Bonczar, F. Zhang, Probation and Parole in the United States, 2009, Bureau of Justice Statistics, Washington, DC, 2010, p. 25.

[22] J. Petersilia, Reforming Probation and Parole, American Correctional Association Lanham, MD, 2002, p. 49.

[23] L. Glaze, T. Bonczar, F. Zhang, Probation and Parole in the United States, 2009, Bureau of Justice Statistics, Washington, DC, 2010. See Table 3, p. 3, for completion rates; also, Table 5, p. 26.

[24] J. Petersilia, Reforming Probation and Parole, American Correctional Association, Lanham, MD, 2002, p. 3.

[25] Bureau of Justice Statistics, Felony Convictions in State Courts, 2010. Retrieved 11/1/2010 from http://bjs.ojp.usdoj.gov/content/glance/tables/felcovtab.cfm.

[26] Bureau of Justice Statistics, Criminal Sentencing Statistics. Retrieved 1/11/2005 from: http://www.ojp.usdoj.gov/bjs/sent.htm.

[27] L. Glaze, S. Palla, Probation and Parole in the United States, 2004, Bureau of Justice Statistics, Washington, DC, 2005.

[28] L. Glaze, T. Bonczar, Probation and Parole in the United States, 2005, Bureau of Justice Statistics, Washington, DC, 2006.

[29] L. Greenfield, T. Snell, Women Offenders, Bureau of Justice Statistics, Washington, DC, 1999/2000. Retrieved 2/24/2007 from http://www.ojp.usdoj.gov/bjs/abstract/wo.htm.

[30] M. Gray, M. Fields, S. Maxwell, Examining probation violations: who, what, and when, Crime Delinq. 47(4) (2001) 537–557.

[31] M. Griffin, G. Armstrong, The effect of local life circumstances on female probationers' offending, Just. Q. 20(2) (2003) 213–225.

[32] D. Steffensmeier, J. Ulmer, J. Kramer, The interaction of race, gender, and age in criminal sentencing, Criminology 36 (1998) 763–797.

[33] L. Friedman, Crime and Punishment in American History, Basic Books, New York, 1993, p. 18.

[34] L. Friedman, Crime and Punishment in American History, Basic Books, New York, 1993.

[35] J. Byrne, The social ecology of community corrections—understanding the link between individual and community change, Criminol. Publ. Policy 7(2) (2008) 263–274.

[36] J. Petersilia, Reforming Probation and Parole, American Correctional Association, Lanham, MD, 2002, p. 37.

[37] J. Petersilia, Reforming Probation and Parole, American Correctional Association, Lanham, MD, 2002, p. 38.

[38] J. Petersilia, Reforming Probation and Parole, American Correctional Association, Lanham, MD, 1998, p. 25; S. Walker, Popular Justice: A History of American Criminal Justice, second ed., New York, Oxford University Press, 2002, p. 25.

[39] J. Rosecrance, Maintaining the myth of individualized justice: probation presentence reports, Just. Q. 5(2) (1988) 235–256.

[40] Gardner v. Florida, 430 U.S. 349, 1977.

[41] Federal Rules of Procedure 32(c)(2)(A-D). See Julian v. U.S. Department of Justice, 806 F2d. 1411 (9th Cir. 1986).

[42] T. Bonczar, L. Glaze, Probation and Parole in the United States, 1998, U.S. Department of Justice, Washington DC, 1999.

[43] J. Petersilia, Reforming Probation and Parole, American Correctional Association, Lanham, MD, 2002, p. 40.

[44] Bearden v. Georgia, 461 U.S. 660, 1983.

[45] J. Petersilia, Reforming Probation and Parole, American Correctional Association, Lanham, MD, 2002, p. 31.

[46] J. Ginzberg, Compulsory contraception as a condition of probation: the use and abuse of Norplant, Brook. Law Rev. 58 (1992) 979–1019.

[47] Bienz v. State, 434 So. 2d 913 (Fla. Dist. Ct. App. 1977).

[48] Blanton et al. v. City of North Las Vegas, 489 U.S. 538 1989.

[49] Griffin v. Wisconsin, 483 U.S. 868, 1987.

[50] P. Hoffman, History of the federal parole system: part 2 (1973-1997), Fed. Probat. 61(4) (1997) 49–57.

[51] G. Camp, C. Camp, The Corrections Yearbook, Criminal Justice Institute, Inc., Middletown, CT, 2001, p. 3.

[52] G. Camp, C. Camp, The Corrections Yearbook, Criminal Justice Institute, Inc., Middletown, CT, 2000.

[53] G. Camp, C. Camp, The Corrections Yearbook, Criminal Justice Institute, Inc., Middletown, CT, 2000, p. 35.

[54] Reported in F. Taxman, No illusions: offender and organizational change in Maryland's proactive community supervision efforts, Criminol. Publ. Policy 7(2) (2008) 278.

[55] L. Glaze, T. Bonczar, F. Zhang, Probation and Parole in the United States, 2009, Bureau of Justice Statistics, Washington, DC, 2010, p. 3.

[56] 389 U.S. 128, 1967.

[57] 411 U.S. 778, 1973.

[58] 408 U.S. 471, 1972.

[59] Minnesota v. Murphy, 465 U.S. 420, 1984.

[60] United States v. Chapman, U.S. App LEXIS 12301, 2000.

[61] T. Bonczar, L. Glaze, Probation and Parole in the United States, 1998, Bureau of Justice Statistics, Washington, DC, 1999, p. 6.

[62] M. Gray, M. Fields, S. Maxwell, Examining probation violations: who, what, and when, Crime Delinq. 47(4) (2001) 537–557.

[63] J. Petersilia, Reforming Probation and Parole, American Correctional Association, Lanham, MD, 2002, p. 58.

[64] M. Gray, M. Fields, S. Maxwell, Examining probation violations: who, what, and when, Crime Delinq. 47(4) (2001) 537–557.

[65] F. Taxman, No illusions: offender and organizational change in Maryland's proactive community supervision efforts, Criminol. Publ. Policy 7(2) (2008) 279.

[66] P. Bulman, In brief: Hawaii HOPE, NIJ J. 266 (2010). Retrieved 9/14/2010 from http://www.ojp.usdoj.gov/nij/journals/266/hope.htm.

[67] F. Taxman, No illusions: offender and organizational change in Maryland's proactive community supervision efforts, Criminol. Publ. Policy 7(2) (2008) 275–302.

[68] T. Fitzharris, The federal role in probation reform, in: P. McAnany, D. Thomson, D. Fogel (Eds.), Probation and Justice, Oelgeschaler, Gunn and Hain, Cambridge, MA, 1984.

CHAPTER 13

Prisons and Jails

CONTENTS

A prison sentence is the second most severe punishment that can be inflicted upon a criminal offender. For most of us, our perceptions of prison are shaped by movies (*The Shawshank Redemption*) and television shows (*Oz*). Some of these dramatizations have been realistic, some sensationalistic, and some ridiculous. Scriptwriters may never get it right because prison is an abnormal environment that becomes normal for the persons who live and work there.

It is, at the same time, boring and terrifying; banal and soul destroying; it is a place of despair, but for some, a place of opportunity.

This country uses imprisonment as punishment more than any other Western nation. There are currently more than 2 million people incarcerated in prisons and jails. The United States' incarceration rate is the highest of the Western nations. It has not always been this way.

THE HISTORY OF PRISONS

Although the idea of solitary penitence was practiced in ecclesiastical institutions in Europe, its development as a secular punishment was purely American [1]. The **penitentiary** in America began with the **Walnut Street Jail** in Philadelphia. In 1790, the Society for Alleviating the Miseries of Public Prisons was able to get legislation passed that reformed the Walnut Street Jail. For the first time, women were segregated from men, the sick were separated from healthy prisoners, and the worst offenders were segregated from others. Food, clothing, and medical care were provided by the Society.

Most important, the mission of the institution changed from mere incapacitation to reform. Inmates were expected to contemplate their evil ways in their solitary cells and reform themselves through penitence. By the 1800s, the Walnut Street Jail was extremely overcrowded and conditions had deteriorated to the point where the Eastern State Penitentiary was built on the outskirts of Philadelphia to replace the jail. Here, the solitary system was pursued to an even greater degree, and this institution became one of the models for the penitentiary system [2]. The penitentiary was designed to isolate criminals from the contagion of the corrupt influences of the city. Prison advocates argued that prisoners would experience solitude, work, and penitence, and that this experience would transform them into good, sober citizens.

INTERNET KEY

For more information about Eastern State Penitentiary, which is now a tourist attraction, go to http://www.easternstate.org/.

Two distinct versions of the penitentiary emerged in the 1800s: the *separate* and the *congregate* systems. The **separate system** originated in Philadelphia at the Walnut Street Jail (1790) and later at the Eastern State Penitentiary (1829). This system is sometimes called the Philadelphia or **Pennsylvania system**. The regimen was one of solitary confinement and manual labor. Prisoners were kept in their cells at all times. The **congregate system** was first introduced at Auburn Prison in New York (1817), and is often called simply the **Auburn system**. Prisoners of this system slept in solitary cells, but worked and ate together. Silence was strictly enforced, however, to prevent them from being corrupted by each other. Regimentation and harsh punishment were used to control inmates, but also to reform them to become obedient and sober workers.

Separation, obedience, and labor became the "trinity" around which officials managed the penitentiary [3]. Convicts were "men of idle habits, vicious propensities, and depraved passions," who had to be taught obedience as part of their reformation [4]. The **lockstep march** was an iconic image of these prisons where prisoners shuffled together, bound by one hand on the opposite shoulder of the man in front. This was the only exercise available to inmates until the 1900s—it was eventually abolished in the first several decades of the twentieth century [5].

Advocates of the two systems argued for years about which was a better system. The similarities between the two were just as striking as the differences. Both employed a vision of the penitentiary as a place where inmates would be transformed to obedient citizens. Reformation was the dominant theme of the 1870 Prison Congress, which laid out the "principles of corrections." Interestingly, these principles were endorsed again, almost without change, in the 1970 Prison Congress now known as the American Correctional Association. The 1870 and 1970 Prison Congresses endorsed such philosophical principles as:

- Corrections must demonstrate integrity, respect, dignity, and fairness.
- Sanctions imposed by the court shall be commensurate with the seriousness of the offense.
- Offenders shall have the opportunity to engage in productive work, and participate in programs and other activities that will enhance self-worth, community integration, and economic status [6].

> 🌐 **INTERNET KEY**
>
> For more information about the American Correctional Association, go to http://www.aca.org/pastpresentfuture/.

The Auburn model became the template for other prisons, largely because it allowed factory work to partially offset the costs of imprisonment. Ironically, the separate system became a more common model for prison building in Europe.

There were few women sentenced to prison in the 1800s. Those who were confined to penitentiaries were often caged in attics, left unsupervised, and subjected to sexual abuse [7]. Early prisons also did not house many blacks, at least until after the Civil War, because they more often were punished by slave owners.

In the late 1800s, the **reformatory era** brought new ideas to the philosophies of imprisonment. Elmira Reformatory, dating from 1870, was created for young men and had a mission of reform through education and strict discipline. While reformatories for men utilized militaristic drills and staffing, reformatories for women sought to recreate home-like environments through the use of cottages. Matrons were expected to serve as role models of what women should be like [8]. Approximately 21 women's reformatories were built between 1860 and 1935. The women sent there typically were young, white women who had committed minor crimes. Even those who had committed only public order or juvenile crimes, such as running away or being promiscuous, might have been sent to a reformatory. Black women, older white women, and women who had committed serious crimes, were sent to custodial institutions. These women were housed in a wing or a building at the men's prison. Eventually, reformatory institutions lost their mission and the boundaries blurred between custodial prisons for women and reformatories. It was not until the 1970s that every state had a separate prison for women.

The *Shawshank Redemption* depicted inmate life at the fictional Shawshank Prison in the late 1940s and early 1950s. © *Bureau L.A. Collection/CORBIS*

Robert Johnson calls the maximum-security prisons of the first half of the twentieth century **big houses** [9]. In prisons of the early to mid-1900s, prisoners worked, sometimes in meaningless labor, such as the infamous rock pile. There was no purpose, and no institutional mission, other than incapacitation and punishment. The only thing that the prison did well was keep inmates behind its massive walls and out of the public's view.

Early prisons in Southern states were more likely to follow an agricultural model, rather than an industrial or a factory model. In fact, some argue that they were extensions of the slave plantation [10]. Newly emancipated blacks and others were sentenced to hard labor in the fields of landowners. These landowners leased prisoners' labor from the state prison to replace the newly freed slaves. Prisoners also labored on the infamous chain gangs. Black female prisoners were subjected to the same harsh treatment as the men, while white women were more often assigned as house servants to the wardens and other administrators [11].

Until about the 1960s, prisons were racially segregated by policy, and blacks had little power. Early sociological discussions of prisons did not mention black prisoners at all. Gresham Sykes' classic study, *The Society of Captives* (1958/1966), describes Trenton State Prison in 1950. The prison society, as Sykes described it, was a world where the strong preyed upon the weak. A few prisoners were able to obtain a range of goods, including alcohol and sex, by barter or money from the outside. Prisoners were expected to "do their own time" and ignore the victimization of their fellow inmates. In the big house prisons of the North and the Southern plantation prisons, prisoners received the minimal resources necessary to sustain life.

The **correctional institution** emerged gradually, and by the 1950s one began to see the rhetoric of reform. Gradually, prisons began to offer prisoners more privileges, such as yard and recreational privileges, more liberal mail and visitation policies, and occasional movies or concerts. The more important development, however, was the beginning of educational, vocational, and therapeutic programs. In fact, by the 1970s, there was a burst of optimism and hope that the prison could become a place of change. In some places, radical ideas were considered, such as the plan for college classes to be held on prison grounds for inmates, officers, and townspeople alike. Inmates were released through a variety of work and educational release. Some colleges even had dorms for prisoners where they would check in and out for class.

Women's correctional institutions also followed the mission of reform. Niantic prison in Connecticut, for example, was described, during this period, as "nice and cozy" where officers and inmates would meet in groups to discuss things and inmates were allowed to make their rooms more personal through pictures and possessions [12]. Some women's prisons even experimented with having apartment-like minimum-security buildings, where female inmates could go out to work in the community, returning to the prison-based apartment at night.

However, despite these examples, promises of reform did not necessarily translate into realities for most prisoners, and prisons erupted into riots, first in the 1950s, and then, 20 years later, in the 1970s. The Attica prison riot, and lesser-known riots in other prisons during the same period, have been attributed to frustrated expectations that prisons would offer meaningful programs. Another important element, however, was the greater politicization of inmates, especially minority inmates, who often had been involved in organizations such as the Black Panthers on the street. The black awareness movement of the 1960s and 1970s spurred the prisoners' rights movement, but it also may have spurred changes in the prison subculture. Prison, although becoming officially desegregated via judicial decisions, became increasingly self-segregated along racial and ethnic lines [13].

The 1970s was a time of great change for prisons. The unrest on the street seeped into prisons and led to prisoners demanding more rights; race conflict emerged and often escalated into violence; and the beginning of the scourge of drugs (which exploded in the next decade) began to affect the prison subculture and raised the stakes of the prison black market economic system. In the 1980s, the tremendous increase in the numbers of individuals being sent to prison exacerbated all these problems.

The correctional institution's rhetoric of reform gave way fairly quickly to the warehouse prison of today. Even women's prisons have changed. For example, Niantic prison, described earlier, was supplanted by York prison for women, a huge concrete-and-steel "confinement model" prison. Here, as well as all across the country, women were told they were going to be treated like inmates rather than women, and the unique characteristics of women's prisons were systematically eliminated [14].

A modern trend has been the increased use of private prisons. Although various types of private-public models have been in place since the beginning of the penitentiary, such as the lease labor system in the South, only in the last several decades have private companies been in the business of building and managing prisons under state and federal contracts. The number of prisoners in private facilities continues to grow. In 2008, there were almost 25,000 inmates in private prisons, which represented about a 15% increase since 2000 [15]. Two of the largest companies are Corrections Corporation of America and the Wackenhut Corporation. There continues to be controversy about whether private prisons are more cost effective than state-run institutions. There are many different ways of measuring costs (e.g., capital construction costs versus only using per diem costs of running an institution; average cost versus highest costs; counting public tax breaks and incentives, and so on). What is counted obviously makes a difference in the determination of whether private prisons are more cost effective than public prisons [16]. There are also vested interests involved; for instance, it is not surprising that studies funded by private companies and think tanks that support privatizing government functions show that private prisons are cost effective, whereas critics show the opposite. The most neutral evaluations have been done by the government (General Accounting Office) and show that there is very little cost savings when using private providers. Other studies have examined recidivism and discovered that there is no significant difference between the recidivism of releasees from private and public prisons [17].

The contemporary prison provides a much better life for prisoners than at earlier times in history. Prisoners get enough to eat and many probably have better medical care than they would have access to on the street. However, because of the crushing burden of numbers, reform or rehabilitation is not a central mission, which is why we call contemporary prisons **warehouse prisons** [18]. Most prisoners are simply housed and fed until release.

INCREASED IMPRISONMENT

In 2009, the total incarcerated population in America (including prisons and jails) was about 2.3 million [19]. About two-thirds (1,524,513) of this number were in prison, and the rest were incarcerated in jails. The prison population alone grew about 93.5% from 1990 to year-end 2005—from 743,382 to 1,438,701 prisoners in just 15 years [20]. In 2009, the prison population had increased to 1,524,513 persons. However, this was a decline from 1,613,656 in 2008. Interestingly, in recent years, increases in the number of federal prisoners offset declines in the number of state prisoners. In the last couple of years, state prisoner numbers have declined. It does appear as if the dramatic percentage increases in prison populations have plateaued in recent years with much smaller year-to-year increases or even declining populations in some states [21].

To better understand the increased use of imprisonment, we will examine rates per 100,000. Rates allow us to compare incarceration across different populations; therefore, we know, when comparing two different years or two different states, that the change is not due to population fluctuations. There are two different types of rates that you might see for incarceration. The first is the total incarceration rate, which includes both federal and state prisons and **jails**. The total United States rate in 2009 was 743 per 100,000. The other rate, more commonly used, is the imprisonment rate, which is just the number of people incarcerated in state or federal prisons, excluding jails, per 100,000. In 2009, this rate was 502 per 100,000 [22]. In Figure 13.1, the incarceration rates for the last 150 years are displayed, and we see that the use of prisons has increased dramatically only within the last three decades.

It is also the case that the rate of imprisonment varies tremendously among the states. In Figure 13.2, the total imprisonment rate (excluding jails) is used

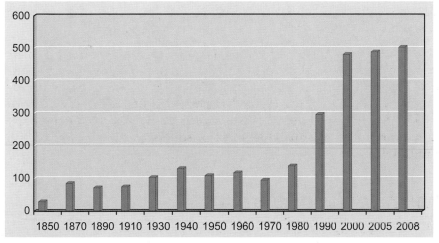

FIGURE 13.1

Incarceration rates. **Sources:** *M. Cahalan, Historical Corrections Statistics in the United States, 1850-1984, Westat, Inc., Rockville, MD, 1986; Bureau of Justice Statistics, Sourcebook of Criminal Justice Statistics, Bureau of Justice Statistics, Washington, DC, 1997; Bureau of Justice Statistics, State and Federal Prisoners, June 30, 1998, Bureau of Justice Statistics, Washington, DC, 1998; P. Harrison, J. Karberg, Prison and Jail Inmates at Midyear 2005, Bureau of Justice Statistics, Washington, DC, 2006; W. Sabol, H. West, M. Cooper, Prisoners in 2008, Bureau of Justice Statistics, Washington, DC, 2009.*

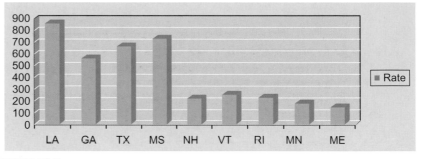

FIGURE 13.2

Prison imprisonment rate, selected states, 2008. **Sources:** *W. Sabol, H. West, M. Cooper, Prisoners in 2008, U.S. Department of Justice, Washington, DC, 2009.*

to show the variability between the states with the highest rates and the states with the lowest rates. While Louisiana incarcerates 865 per 100,000 of its citizens, Maine only incarcerates 148 per 100,000. What accounts for this difference? There is no good answer to that question, although people have explored the issue for decades.

EXERCISE: IN THE STATE OF…

Find the Web page for your state prison system. Discover how many prisons there are in your state and how many prisoners. Find out, if you can, the breakdown by race/ethnicity and gender. You might also find this information on the Bureau of Justice Statistics Web site.

🌐 INTERNET KEY

For a source that collects worldwide prison population figures, go to the International Center for Prison Studies at Kings College, London (England) and their "World Prison Population List" at http://www.kcl.ac.uk/depsta/law/research/icps/downloads/wppl-8th_41.pdf.

Rates also allow us to compare the United States to other countries. In Figure 13.3, we see that the United States uses incarceration as a punishment much more frequently than similar countries. Only a few countries have rates similar to the United States, and most of our "sister" countries, such as England, Canada, France, and Germany, have much lower incarceration rates.

The prison population of the United States contains disproportionate numbers of racial minorities relative to their proportion of the general population. The imprisonment rate for black men is an amazing 3119, which is almost six times higher than that of white men, whose rate was 487 in 2008. In Table 13.1, we can see the relative rates across race/ethnicity and gender groups.

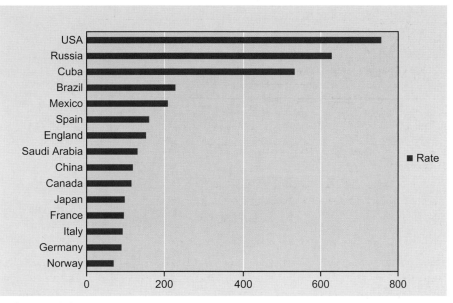

FIGURE 13.3

Imprisonment around the world. **Source:** *R. Walmsley, World Prison Population List, Eighth Ed., King's College, London, 2008. Retrieved 12/5/2010 from http://www.kcl.ac.uk/depsta/law/research/icps/downloads/wppl-8th_41.pdf.*

Table 13.1 Imprisonment Rates by Race/Ethnicity and Gender		
	Males	**Females**
Total	949	67
White	487	50
Black	3119	142
Hispanic	1193	74
Source: *H. West, W. Sabol, S. Greenman, Prisoners in 2009, Bureau of Justice Statistics, Washington, DC, 2010, p. 24.*		

Women's incarceration rates continue to rise at a faster rate than men's. Since 1995, women's annual increase has averaged 4.7%, compared to men's average of 3%. The actual number of women in prison is still low (7%), but it has been rising. In Figure 13.4, we see that the prison population is still largely male, and that, even though they comprise a very small percentage of the total population in the United States, black men represent the largest group in this country's prisons.

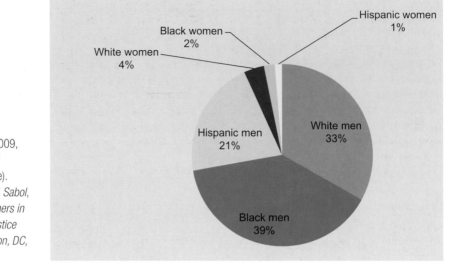

FIGURE 13.4
Prison population, 2009, by gender and race/ethnicity (percentage).
Source: *H. West, W. Sabol, S. Greenman, Prisoners in 2009, Bureau of Justice Statistics, Washington, DC, 2010, p. 25.*

PRISON LIFE

Many prisoners are young, members of a minority group, and undereducated. About half of prisoners are violent offenders. It is important to note that this is not because half of all sentenced offenders are violent; in fact, violent offenders comprise less than 30% of all sentenced felony offenders. However, because violent offenders face longer sentences and serve longer proportions of their sentence than property or public order offenders, they "stack up" in prison, which is why they represent half of all prisoners. Prisons contain "disproportionate numbers of the least mature, least stable, and most violent individuals in American society" [23]. In the prison world, the values that most of us live by are turned upside down. In prison, violence is respected and victims are despised.

A correctional officer walks past shelves holding helmets and bulletproof vests at a correctional institution on Rikers Island, Bronx, New York. © *Michael S. Yamashita/CORBIS*

Deprivation and importation

All inmates are subject to what Sykes [24] called the deprivations of prison life. They are described in Box 13.1. These deprivations are said to result in the prisoner subculture. For instance, because of the deprivation of heterosexual relationships, predatory rapists exist in prison and are not considered homosexual. Instead, negative stigma attaches to the victims and they are referred to as "punks."

BOX 13.1 SYKES' DEPRIVATIONS OF IMPRISONMENT

Liberty: Includes restrictions on the freedom of movement and deprivation of contact with family members and friends and others from the free world.

Goods and services: Inmates' inability to obtain these reduces them to an infantile state whereby they must depend on staff to provide everything from socks and underwear to shampoo and toothpaste.

Heterosexual relationships: Refers to the deprivation of "normal" sexual contact in prison settings.

Autonomy: Refers to the fact that inmates are not free to make decisions about their own lives; they are not free to do what they want, when they want, and how they want. They are told when to eat, sleep, and work by being treated like a child.

Security: Inmates are in a constant state of anxiety about their safety and there is little that they can do to avoid danger.

Source: *G. Sykes, The Society of Captives, Princeton University Press, Princeton, NJ, 1958, p. 78.*

A competing perspective on the development of a prisoner subculture explains that it does not develop from the deprivations of imprisonment, but instead is brought into or is imported to prison from the outside [25]. Researchers subscribing to the **importation hypothesis** believe that the prisoner subculture is derived from the preprison characteristics of the people coming into prisons rather than prison deprivations themselves. Research provides support for both of these explanations of the prisoner subculture.

Prisonization is the process of being socialized to the prison subculture [26]. The **"inmate code"** is described as a *sub rosa* (subcultural) set of rules by which prisoners "should" run their lives in the prison setting. Early descriptions of the inmate code portrayed a world where convicts "did their own time," shunned guards, and never lost their "cool," even in the face of extreme provocation. The prisoner who followed the code valued loyalty, autonomy, and strength. Violence is often rational, directive, and useful as it indicates toughness, strength, and the ability to "take care of business."

Group loyalty is also an important factor in the prisoner subculture. Snitching may be the most heinous prison "crime." There are a disproportionate number of names for a snitch in the prison setting, including "rat," "squealer," "snitch," "cheese-eater," and "stoolpigeon." One of the most gruesome examples of prison violence occurred during the New Mexico prison riot in 1980. Inmates took over the New Mexico Prison and eventually reached Cellblock 4, the housing area for snitches. Using acetylene torches, rioters broke into the protective custody unit and tortured, maimed, and murdered the men found there [27].

Officials and inmates alike often scorn the person identified as a snitch. Ironically, officials indicate that they could not run the prison without informers. Snitching is present in both female and male subcultures, but subcultural sanctions against this behavior were (and are) more serious in prisons for men [28].

Giallombardo [29] was one of the few researchers who made any attempt to describe the female prisoner subculture. In her study of Alderson, a federal prison for women, she found that different themes were emphasized in the female prisoners' world. She found that the principle of "do your own time" was rejected in the women's culture. Researchers continue to find that women are more likely to confide in each other and have more interactions with staff [30].

The male and female inmate codes have changed from when early researchers in the 1950s began writing about prisoner subcultures. Inmate solidarity has eroded considerably, if it ever existed at all [31]. Younger and more violent offenders entering prisons have ignored the old-timers' admonitions to stay loyal and keep a low profile. Perhaps one of the greatest change agents for the inmate subculture has been the influx of younger and more violent inmates, who appeared to take control of some prisons in the 1980s. These "low riders" or "state-raised youth" who entered prisons in the 1980s had little respect for the inmate code, were ready to use violence in any situation, on any inmate, at any time, for even the slightest provocation [32].

Today's prison subculture often forces inmates to choose between isolation or affiliation with gangs for protection. Today, race is an extremely central issue in prisons [33]. Blacks, who comprise less than 13% of the American population, have become the majority in prisons for men. In fact, it has been said that it is the one place in society where their power is clear: "I was in jail, the one place in America that black men rule" [34].

Racial gangs exist in all major prison systems in the United States. Probably the best-known gangs were formed in Illinois, California, and Texas. In Illinois and California, prison gangs were imported from the streets in the 1960s and 1970s. The formation of the Mafia and Nuestra Familia in California resulted in black inmates forming the Black Guerrilla Family and white inmates forming the Aryan Brotherhood to protect themselves [35]. In Texas, there was negligible gang activity during the same period because prisons were dominated by **building tenders** (BTs), inmates who were authorized by staff to control inmates by any means necessary [36]. After a court case forced the state to abandon the BT system, the power vacuum was filled by emerging gangs [37]. The gangs' struggle for dominance resulted in more homicides during a two year period than the previous 20 years. Gangs in Texas prisons now include the Texas Syndicate (Hispanic), the Aryan Brotherhood of Texas (white), and the Bloods and Crips (black). In a 2009 survey of prison administrators, researchers found that the majority of administrators believed that gangs had grown (75%) and were more sophisticated than in the past (61%). The same survey found that prisons varied tremendously in the percentage of the population that were gang-affiliated, ranging from zero to 39%, with a mean of 11.7% [38].

Some research indicates that gangs among female prisoners are growing, whereas others have found little evidence of this phenomenon [39]. In the 2009 survey described earlier, 44% of those surveyed believed that female gang members were increasing, but the actual percentage of female gang members in women's prisons was not presented. Perhaps the comparative lack of gang membership among female prisoners may be related to social groupings that cross racial lines and provide protection, services, and group belonging in similar ways to gang membership. It is likely that women do not form gangs because there is less need for protection.

Prisoner argot, argot roles, and prison sex

Prison slang, or argot, is the language of prisoners and thought to be an important part of the prison subculture. Ironically, correctional officers learn the prison argot and use it as adeptly as inmates [40]. Lerner [41], a college-educated middle-class man, was incarcerated in a Nevada prison and wrote a book about his experiences. Called a "lawdog" because he was someone who could assist other inmates with filing and reading court papers, Lerner encountered and described other argot terms, such as "dawg," which was slang for a friend or associate; "toads," which was a derogatory name for white inmates; and "fishcops," who were new correctional officers. "Shit," "smack," "crap," "H," and "brown" are some of the many names for heroin. Argot for marijuana may be the most numerous with traditional names from "Mary Jane," "grass," or "Aunt Mary," to less recognized names such as "lubage," and "mutha." Slang for drugs in general includes the term "junk" [42]. Argot terms for drugs are so numerous that every conceivable combination and potency of a drug may have several different names. A recent book by Erin George describes her experiences as an educated, middle-class woman entering a woman's prison [43].

Prisoner roles (or **argot roles**) serve to classify and describe inmates based on their behavior before prison, as well as what they do in prison. Gresham Sykes identified several prisoner roles in an early study, including that of rats (informers), centermen (those aligned with correctional officers), gorillas (aggressive predators), merchants (involved in the underground or black market in prison), wolves (sexual aggressors), punks (those forced into homosexual activity against their will), fags (those who engage in homosexuality voluntarily), real men (old-style convicts who do their own time), ball busters (those frequently involved in violent confrontations), toughs (affiliated with violent crime), and hipsters (drug-involved criminals) [44]. At the time, drugs were just beginning to be a factor in the subculture.

Clarence Schrag's (1944) roles have perhaps become the most well known. He described prisoner roles such as the square john, right guy, con politician, and outlaw. The "square john" was the type of inmate who did not have an extensive criminal record and identified more with prison officers than other inmates. Other inmates did not trust him. The "right guy" is characterized as the old-style convict. He was respected as a professional criminal, usually being a thief, bank robber, or a member of organized crime. He was respected as a leader in the yard and was not afraid of violence, but used it sparingly and selectively. The "con politician" was a title ascribed to inmates who held the most formal leadership roles in prison, for example, as a representative of the inmate council, and were very visible in interaction with the prison administration. The "outlaw" inmate was characterized as one who did not follow any code of behavior, even the inmate code [45].

There has not been as much research on female role types. Giallombardo described numerous social roles among female prisoners including snitchers (informers), inmate cops (affiliated with correctional officers), squares (square john equivalents), jive bitches (those who stirred up trouble), rap buddies or homies (friends), boosters (shoplifters), pinners (a trusted inmate who serves as a lookout when illicit activities are undertaken), and a number of roles associated with homosexuality—penitentiary turnouts, butches, lesbians, femmes, stud broads, tricks, commissary hustlers, chippies, kick partners, cherries, punks, and turnabouts [46].

Homosexuality in men's prisons was (and is) characterized by violent assaults and coercion where older and more experienced convicts (wolves) offer protection to younger more inexperienced inmates (punks) for sexual favors and commissary articles. Violence, intimidation, and exploitation are associated with homosexuality in prisons for men [47]. Aggressive and dominant inmates get powerful names such as "wolf" and "daddy," where submissive and weak inmates are "punks" and "fags." Only "punks" and "fags" are identified as homosexuals, and there is little distinction between those who are forced into such a role and those who were homosexual before prison.

Alternatively, homosexuality in women's prisons was (and is) more often consensual and femmes voluntarily engage in relationships with other women who assume the male role (butches). Either woman may or may not have lived a homosexual lifestyle outside of prison. Most violence in women's prisons occurs when partners become jealous and attack their partner, or the perceived "other woman." Less frequently, women manipulate others into a relationship, typically because the target has family who put money in her inmate account for the commissary [48].

Sexual victimization in prisons for both men and women came to the attention of Congress, which passed the Prison Rape Elimination Act in 2003. The Act's provisions include making the prevention of prison rape a top priority for state prison systems; developing and maintaining a national standard for the detection, prevention, reduction, and punishment of prison rape; increasing the available data and information on the incidence of prison rape through national surveys of adult and juvenile facilities; standardizing the definitions used for collecting data on the incidence of prison rape; and increasing the efficiency and effectiveness of federal expenditures through grant programs dealing with social and public health issues [49].

In the latest survey report, government researchers selected a random sample of 167 prisons and 286 jails to administer the survey to 81,566 inmates. They found that 4.4% of prison inmates and 3.1% of jail inmates reported one or more incidents of sexual victimization in the last 12 months. Of those who reported an incident in a prison, about half (2.1%) reported an inmate perpetrator and half (2.8%) reported a staff member perpetrator. About 1% of prison inmates and 0.8% of jail inmates reported they were forced or pressured to have nonconsensual sex with another inmate, with the remainder reporting abusive sexual contacts (unwanted touching of specific body parts in a sexual way). About 1.7% of prison inmates and 1.5% of jail inmates reported nonconsensual sex with a staff member, with the remainder reporting abusive sexual contacts. It was noted that while inmates in some facilities reported very few victimizations, in other institutions, up to almost 12% of inmates surveyed reported sexual victimization. Female prisoners were more than twice as likely to report sexual victimization as male inmates in prisons (4.7% compared to 1.9%) and jails (3.1% compared to 1.3%). However, male prisoners were more likely to report sexual activity with staff (2.9% compared to 2.1%). Rates of victimization were higher among white inmates, those with higher education, those with other than a heterosexual orientation, and those who had experienced sexual violence before prison [50]. The national survey is helpful in understanding the prevalence of sexual victimization in this nation's prisons. One of the important findings of the study was that sexual assault (rape) was fairly rare, but more inmates experience other forms of sexual victimization involving unwanted touching and sexual harassment. Some state systems have instituted programs to address the issue of sexual victimization in response to these findings.

While the most obvious social grouping in prisons for men is the gang, female prisoners are more likely to group in loose associations known as **pseudofamilies**. Pseudofamilies are make-believe family systems that include all the familial roles including fathers, mothers, daughters, sisters, cousins, and so on. Women relate to each other more or less consistently with their roles. Parents advise and counsel, siblings share, and husbands and wives may (but not necessarily) engage in sex [51]. These types of relationships are less frequent today than what existed in the past, perhaps because of more liberal visitation policies that allow closer contact with real families.

An increasingly common alternative to gang membership, or participation in pseudofamilies or prison homosexuality, is isolation. Some inmates have always chosen this option by avoiding the yard, staying in their cells, and developing few relationships with a few other prisoners. Barbara Owen described how many female inmates avoid going to the yard because that is where those "in the mix" hang out (referring to drugs, homosexual activity, and fighting) [52]. Both male and female inmates seek out niches and sanctuaries in prison [53].

PRISONERS' RIGHTS

What legal rights should prisoners have? Prior to the 1960s, they had very few. In fact, the **hands-off era** (1900-1960) was called that because federal and state courts rarely agreed to hear legal challenges brought forward by prisoners. In *Ruffin v. Commonwealth* [54], a Virginia court basically said that a prisoner was a "slave of the state." State and federal courts rejected prisoner appeals for the following reasons:

1. Deferral to the expertise of administrators: They believed that management of a prison should be left to the experts.
2. "Slave of the state" argument: They believed that prisoners only had privileges (that could be taken away) rather than rights.
3. Federalism: Federal courts hesitated to interfere with the business of the state prison.
4. "Opening the door": Judges didn't want to open the door to an increase in such prisoner rights litigation [55].

Actually, the feared increase is exactly what happened in the **prisoner rights era** (1960-1980). Prisoner petitions increased tremendously and several groundbreaking cases during the Warren Court era (when the chief justice was Earl Warren) advanced the legal rights of inmates. However, after 1980, the Supreme Court moved into what was called the **due deference era** (1980-today), and judges became more likely to give "due deference" to the expertise of prison administrators when faced with prisoner litigation. In 1996, Congress passed the *Prison Litigation Reform Act* (**PLRA**) [56], which significantly reduced prisoner petitions through a number of measures, including limiting attorney fees, punishing those who file "frivolous" lawsuits, and restricting federal courts from interfering with prison policies unless absolutely necessary.

Generally, prisoners' rights lawsuits allege violations of the Fifth or the Fourteenth Amendment (due process), the Eighth Amendment (cruel and unusual punishment), and the First Amendment (freedom of religion and expression).

Due process

Recall from earlier chapters that due process may apply whenever the government seeks to deprive anyone of life, liberty, or property. Although prisoners' Sixth Amendment rights to a trial, with counsel and the ability to confront and cross-examine one's accusers are over at the point of sentencing, they, along with the rest of us, still have the protection of due process whenever faced with a governmental deprivation of a protected liberty interest. Being able to have access to the courts of this nation is a fundamental element of due process. In the past, prison authorities would confiscate letters and legal documents and prevent inmates from having their grievances relayed to the courts. In a series of cases, the U.S. Supreme Court and other courts prohibited prison officials from blocking the inmates' access to the court system [57]. The Supreme Court also made it clear that inmates should have meaningful assistance to access the courts, even if it had to take the form of **jailhouse lawyers**, inmates who help other inmates file petitions for a fee, or law students [58]. The Court also held that legal mail could not be censored [59], and that prisoners should have access to either law libraries or legal services [60]. However, in more recent decisions, the United States Supreme Court has restricted the right of access to the courts and/or the ability to seek damages if the prison does not provide meaningful access by making it harder to prove that the absence of such assistance resulted in a negative impact for the inmate [61].

The **due process clauses** of the federal constitution prohibit both state and federal authorities from taking life, liberty, or property without due process of law. Prisoners challenged the adequacy of due process protections in disciplinary hearings and received the right to have at least a notice of charges and a hearing before being punished by segregation or loss of good time [62]. Later cases reduced due process rights solely to the loss of good time, and curtailed the level of proof required before punishment could be administered [63]. Prisoners never received the right to any due process protections before being transferred, even if it was to a prison far away or to a higher-security classification [64]. Prisoners also do not have the right to be incarcerated in the state in which they were convicted. Many prisoners now are housed in states far away from their home in "for-profit" prisons under contract with their sentencing state.

The Eighth Amendment: corporal punishment and the use of force

The Eighth Amendment prohibits cruel and unusual punishment and has been the basis for outlawing **corporal punishment** in prisons [65]. Later, **totality of circumstances** cases involved multiple conditions of confinement that, as a whole, constituted cruel and unusual punishment. Conditions that were cited in these cases included high levels of violence (either or both inmate-on-inmate or officer-on-inmate), lack of medical care, lack of sanitation, little or no programming, no assistance for the mentally ill or mentally retarded, and overcrowding. In some of the most egregious cases, prisoners won. As conditions improved across the country, prisoners were less likely to win such cases, although they still exist. A current case is described in the following Breaking News box.

Lack of medical care for prisoners has been defined as cruel and unusual punishment [66]. In these cases, a deliberate withholding of medical care that constitutes an unnecessary and wanton infliction of pain can be a violation of the Eighth Amendment. The key, however, is that it has to be a *deliberate* lack of care, and medical negligence does not constitute a constitutional violation. The Eighth Amendment has also been used to challenge prison treatment programs that involved the infliction of pain. Behavior modification programs must obtain free, voluntary, and knowing consent from inmates; otherwise, such pain constitutes cruel and unusual punishment [67].

BREAKING NEWS: TOO MANY INMATES?

Two cases (originating as early as 2001) dealing with medical care in California prisons have been consolidated under *Schwarzenegger v. Plata*, Docket 09-1233. California has appealed from a three-judge panel of the Ninth Circuit Court of Appeals that ruled that crowding was the cause of a violation of the Eighth Amendment in that the state's prisoners received inadequate medical care. The federal court ordered the state to release approximately 46,000 inmates to comply with an earlier court order requiring the state to either reduce its prison population or increase funding for medical care. The Supreme Court heard oral arguments in November 2010 and is expected to rule sometime in 2011 on the case. The state argues that under the Prison Litigation Reform Act, 18 U.S.C. § 3626, the federal court cannot order the state to do anything that is not "narrowly drawn, extend no further than necessary to correct the violation of the Federal right, and [is] the least intrusive means necessary to correct the ... violation" and that the court also did not give due weight to the "impact on public safety" in ordering a reduction of the prison population.

Evidence offered by the litigants supported their claims that several dozen people died in California prisons, very likely due to lack of adequate medical care. Plaintiffs alleged inadequate screening, delays of medical care, interference of custody staff in medical decisions, lack of competent medical staff, incomplete medical records, and lack of quality assurance procedures. Over the last decade, the state of California has fought with the federal court monitor about how to resolve the lack of medical care. The state's failure to meet court mandates led to the current case. The Supreme Court will now decide whether the federal circuit court went too far in ordering the release of inmates.

Source: C-Span, *Oral Arguments of* Schwarzenegger v. Plata. *Retrieved 12/10/2010 from: http://222.c-spanvideo.org/ program/Plata&showFullAbstract=1.*

First Amendment rights

The following issues derive from the First Amendment: (1) access to prisons and prisoners by the press, (2) freedom of speech and communication, (3) freedom of association and visitation, and (4) freedom of religion.

In a series of court cases in the 1970s, the Supreme Court identified prisoners' rights to have access to the press, although the press had no greater right of access to prisons than did the general public [68]. The Supreme Court also held that the prison could not stop prisoners from writing to outside citizens about prison conditions. The justices declared that restrictions on prisoners' right of correspondence must be related to a governmental interest, specifically security, order, or rehabilitation [69].

In the 1980s, courts upheld prison authorities' bans on inmate-to-inmate correspondence [70]. The Supreme Court then held that the prison can restrict such correspondence even when it is between an inmate law clerk and someone he is trying to help because the state has the right to impose "reasonable restrictions" on correspondence [71]. Other restrictions that were upheld included the publishers-only rule, where prisoners can only receive publications from official distributors. Furthermore, any publications that are deemed to be a threat to the security or order of the institution can be confiscated [72]. As would be expected, courts have never been very sympathetic to freedom of speech claims by prisoners. Prison authorities have the right to punish prisoners for angry racial comments, work stoppages, and protests.

Prisoners have virtually no rights of association. Numerous cases have categorized visitation as a *privilege* that may be curtailed or denied for just cause, not a *right*. The Supreme Court approved rigorous restrictions on visitation in a Michigan prisoner's challenge [73].

Freedom of religion is a primary constitutional right guaranteed by the First Amendment. Prisoners have the right to practice their religious beliefs as long as they do not impinge upon the state's interest in safety, security, and order. Courts use the **rational relationship test** to balance the individual's interest against the state's interest in safety and security. As long as the state's rule or procedure is rationally related to a legitimate state interest, the state will win any challenge to regulations that prohibit an inmate from practicing his or her religion [74]. Obviously, prisoners' rights are not the same as those of free people. Any right must be balanced against the state's right to run a safe and secure prison.

JAILS

Jails and prisons are often confused, but they are very different institutions. Jails are local detention facilities that house pretrial detainees and misdemeanants, as well as a variety of other detainees. Most jails are run by the county sheriff and are located in the county seat. There are also state jails that house both felons and misdemeanants and regional jails that serve several counties and are run by administrators, not sheriffs. More Americans see the inside of a jail than a prison, and the time spent in jail is, for the most part, shorter; however, the jail experience is still disruptive and traumatic to many prisoners. Suicide is a real problem in jails, as are other medical emergencies such as drug withdrawals or overdoses. The rate of suicide in jail is five to six times higher than for comparable individuals outside of jail [75]. Jail personnel must deal with all these issues, perhaps without knowing the history of the individual; thus, insulin shock may look like an alcoholic stupor, or a defendant complaining of pain may be suffering mild drug withdrawal or life threatening appendicitis. Inmates are often housed for short periods in "bullpens" or large cells. This raises the risk of victimization and creates a sanitation problem when too many people are housed in a small space, especially when some are intoxicated. Unpleasant smells, unremitting noise, and fear of the unknown characterize many individuals' first experience in jail.

Before the 1700s, jails (or gaols) were usually horrific places of confinement that housed the sick along with the healthy, women with men, and children with adults. The so-called **fee system** meant that prisoners had to pay for their room and board. Typically, stays in jails were short. The individual was held only until corporal punishment could be carried out, whether that was by whipping, the stocks or pillory, or hanging. In many cases, individuals were held for debt. In those cases, the person could be held indefinitely until he or his family could pay his debts. If they were unable, then the individual might be subject to transportation, which meant the person was sent to the colonies as an indentured servant.

Houses of corrections and bridewells sometimes took the place of the jail to confine the itinerant and poor. These institutions, such as St. Brigid's Well, first established in 1553, required inmates to earn their keep with labor [76]. The idea was that the poor, petty criminals, and orphaned children should learn a trade and become productive. Arguably, this was an improvement over the gaols. In 1777, Sheriff John Howard wrote about his findings after traveling around England visiting gaols. He recommended major reforms in the way jails were run, including classification, segregating women and children, individual cells, eliminating the fee system, and providing religious instruction [77].

In the colonies, the keeper and his wife ran the jail as a large house under the direction of the local sheriff. The fee system was also in use in this country. Like England, the imprisoned inmates were held only until they were acquitted at trial or punished. Minor offenders and debtors may have stayed longer, but the early history of the jail was simply as a temporary holding facility until punishment could be carried out.

Historical records show that there were very few women held in jails and the majority of inmates were white men. Common crimes included everything from theft to murder. While hanging was the punishment for more than

200 crimes in England, the colonies were less likely to impose capital punishment, probably because laborers were in short supply [78].

Jail populations

At midyear 2009, there were about 3365 jails in the United States, with an average daily population under supervision of 767,620. This is a decrease from the 819,434 daily population in 2005. About 9% of this population was under some form of community release from the jail (community service, work release, weekend reporting, electronic monitoring, or other programs) [79]. This does not take into account the numbers of people who have been in and out of jail during the year. There are more than 13 million separate entries and exits from jail each year [80]. About a third of all felony sentences are to local jails [81]. Since 1995, the nation's jail population has increased 31%; however, like prison populations, the increase has leveled off and, in many jurisdictions, there has been a decrease in the number of people in jail [82].

The average population in jails is about 180; however, many jails hold less than 50 inmates. On the other hand, there are extremely large jails that hold thousands of inmates. The 50 largest jails housed nearly a third of all jail inmates in 2002 [83]. Today, four states (California, Texas, Florida, and Georgia) hold a third of the nation's total population [84]. The largest jail system in the country is Los Angeles County, with a daily population average of 19,437 inmates (in 2009). New York City follows with an average population of 13,365. Following those jurisdictions in size is Harris County (Houston), Texas, with 11,361 and Cook County (Chicago), Illinois, with 9383 [85]. Jails also hold more than 24,200 individuals for the U.S. Immigration and Customs Enforcement (ICE), which is nearly double the number held in 2000 [86].

The majority of those in jail have not been convicted. About 38% of the jail population are convicted and the rest are awaiting trial or final adjudication on either a new charge or a probation or parole violation [87]. Table 13.2 shows that about 9 out of 10 jail inmates are men, although the percentage of women is increasing. As in prisons, the percentage of blacks is disproportionate to their percentage of the total population; however, the percentage of Hispanics more closely resembles their percentage of the population.

One of the major differences between prisons and jails is that jails hold a greater variety of types of prisoners, and many have not been convicted or sentenced. In Box 13.2, some of the types of individuals who are incarcerated in jails are listed.

In general, most people in jail are either misdemeanants serving sentences or pretrial detainees awaiting adjudication because they cannot make bail. It may come as a surprise to many that as many as two-thirds of jail inmates were

Table 13.2 Gender, Race, and Ethnicity, and Conviction Status of Jail Inmates

Characteristics	Percentage of Jail Inmates				
	1995	2000	2004	2005	2009
Total	100.0	100.0	100.0	100.0	100.0
Gender					
Male	89.8	88.6	87.7	87.3	87.8
Female	10.2	11.4	12.3	12.7	12.2
Race/Hispanic origin					
White	40.1	41.9	44.4	44.3	42.4
Black	43.5	41.3	38.6	38.9	39.2
Hispanic	14.7	15.1	15.2	15.0	16.2
Other	1.7	1.6	1.8	1.7	1.9
Conviction status					
Convicted	44.0	44.0	39.7	38.0	37.8
Male	39.7	39.0	34.8	33.2	33.0
Female	4.3	5.0	4.9	4.8	4.8
Unconvicted	56.0	56.0	60.3	62.0	62.2
Male	50.0	50.0	53.0	54.2	54.8
Female	6.0	6.0	7.3	7.7	7.4

Sources: *P. Harrison, A. Beck, Prison and Jail Inmates at Midyear 2005, Bureau of Justice Statistics, Washington, DC, 2006 p. 8; T. Minton, Jail Inmates at Midyear 2009, Statistical Tables, Bureau of Justice Statistics, Washington, DC, 2010, p. 10.*

BOX 13.2 JAIL INMATES

- Defendants pending arraignment, trial, or sentencing
- Probation, parole, bail-bond violators
- Absconders
- Juvenile detainees
- Mentally ill people (pending transfer to mental institution)
- Military violators (pending transfer to military facilities)
- Contempt violators
- Material witnesses
- State prisoners awaiting transfer
- Misdemeanants serving sentence

employed prior to their arrest. Unfortunately, many will lose their job before they are released. In 2009, less than 1% of jail inmates were under 18 [88]. In surveys of prisoners, about 70% used drugs regularly before incarceration and about half had used in the month prior to their arrest [89].

Between 1983 (227,541) and 2004 (784,538), the jail population increased 244% [90]. As with prison populations, the jail population has risen dramatically in the last 20 years and the rate of confinement has increased as well. In 1983, the rate of confinement to jail was 96 per 100,000 residents; by 1995 it was 193 per 100,000; and in 2009, it was 250 per 100,000 [91]. This means that, in addition to there simply being more people in jail, we also are more likely to jail those accused of crimes, or hold them longer, or be less likely to release them on pretrial alternatives.

Women have increased their percentage of the total population from less than 10% in the 1980s to about 12% today.

As Table 13.3 shows, the rate of jail incarceration for men and minorities is disproportionate to their percentage in the population. Blacks are five times as likely to be incarcerated in jail as whites and three times as likely as Hispanics.

About 13% of all black men are in prison or jail (compared to only 3.6% of Hispanics and 1.7% of white men) [92]. What this means is that in some communities, jail is not strange or unusual, it is a part of life. This does not mean that it is not damaging, however, and the thrust of diversion programs is to stop the cycle of jail to prison and back again.

As with the explosive growth of this nation's prison population, larger jail populations come at a cost. Counties that experience double-digit increases in their jail populations are unable to accommodate these numbers without cutting the budgets of other governmental services. Part of why it is difficult for jails to meet national standards is that county commissioners or other budget

Table 13.3 Jail Incarceration Rate, 2005

	Rate (per 100,000)	
	2005	**2006**
Total	252	256
Gender		
Male	447	457
Female	63	66
Race/Hispanic origin		
White	166	170
Black	800	815
Hispanic	268	283
Other	88	90

Sources: *P. Harrison, A. Beck, Prison and Jail Inmates at Midyear 2005, Bureau of Justice Statistics, Washington, DC, 2006, p. 8; W. Sabol, T. Minton, P. Harrison, Prison and Jail Inmates at Midyear 2006, Bureau of Justice Statistics, Washington, DC, 2007, p. 6. Unfortunately, this seems to be the last year that the BJS has computed rate figures by gender and race/ethnicity for jail populations.*

decision makers do not have any incentive to increase jail budgets unless there are security concerns. Jail inmates are not likely to be important constituents for politicians; they are unlikely to vote and they have no advocates in the community.

Jails can be considered, to some extent, depositories for the marginally functioning in society. It has been estimated that the percentage of jail inmates with serious mental health issues such as schizophrenia, severe depression, and mania is four times higher than the general population and the rate of substance abuse is four to seven times higher. Estimates of how many inmates have mental health issues range from 10% to 30%; one jail survey found that 20% of inmates had a mental health issue [93]. Others report that 600,000 to 700,000 individuals with mental health issues cycle through our jails every year [94].

According to the Bureau of Justice Statistics, about 64% of all jail inmates have some type of mental health problem. About 21% have been clinically diagnosed or treated within the 12 months before incarceration. Percentages of jail inmates who exhibit symptoms of mental illness diagnoses illustrate the prevalence of the problem and include mania (54%), clinical depression (30%), and psychotic disorders (24%). In this study, it was found that women, whites, and young inmates were more likely to exhibit mental health problems. About 75% of women in jails exhibited mental health problems compared to 63% of male inmates. About 71% of whites, 63% of blacks, and 51% of Hispanics were found to have a mental health problem. Jail inmates with mental health problems are more likely to have had past incarcerations, used drugs, have experienced homelessness, have experienced past physical or sexual abuse, have parents who abused drugs or alcohol, and are more likely to violate facility rules [95].

The deinstitutionalization of the mentally ill that occurred in this country in the late 1970s occurred because of court cases such as *Wyatt v. Stickney* [96]. In this case, the court held that the mentally ill could not be held indefinitely unless they could be shown to pose a danger to self or others. The original intent was that community mental health centers would be better places to serve the mentally ill than housing them in large mental hospitals. Unfortunately, that promise has not been fulfilled to the degree that many advocates had hoped; thus, many mentally ill individuals "slip through the cracks"; they are not sick enough to be institutionalized, but not well enough to fully function in today's society.

Arguably, female jail inmates have more severe problems with drugs and with mental health problems than do their male counterparts, no doubt in part due to childhood abuse [97]. Table 13.4 shows that female jail inmates are more likely than male inmates to have experienced childhood sexual and physical victimization. Even though male inmates may be under-reporting such

Table 13.4 Physical or Sexual Abuse before Current Admission (Percentage of Jail Inmates)

	Total	Male	Female
Ever	16.4	12.9	47.5
Before 18	14.3	11.9	36.6
After 18	4.7	2.3	26.7
Physically abused	13.3	10.7	37.2
Sexually abused	8.7	5.6	37.1
Raped	6.6	3.7	32.2

Source: C. Harlow, Profile of Jail Inmates 1996, Washington, DC, Bureau of Justice Statistics, 1998, p. 11 (latest year available for this data).

experiences to some extent, it is clear that women in jail are very likely to have experienced dysfunctional families and suffer from the effects of sexual victimization.

The jail experience

Coming into the jail, an inmate may spend the night in a holding cell, sometimes called a "bullpen" or "drunk tank." This one large cell may hold many offenders, and a toilet (or toilets) in the same room with no screen or privacy may be the only provision for sanitation needs. After a first appearance, the suspect may be transferred to a different section of the jail. He or she is fingerprinted, showered, and given jail-issue clothing, which is often an overall that may be several sizes too big. If the inmate is showing signs of medical distress, a quick exam by a medical professional may occur.

Most jail inmates do not stay long. The average length of stay in jail is 3 to 20 days; pretrial detainees have an average stay of three days. Those who make bail may be out in 24 hours, but those who cannot make bail or are serving a misdemeanor sentence may be there for months. Large jails such as those in Los Angeles, Chicago, and New York City bear no resemblance to the very small rural jails that still exist all across the country. The smallest jails may have less than 20 inmates in the basement of a county courthouse. A few sheriff's deputies are responsible for them and food may be catered in rather than cooked on-site. These types of jails are all but extinct in today's trend of regional jails, but they do exist. On the other side of the spectrum, counties like Los Angeles run jail systems that are larger than most state prison systems. Some large systems have state-of-the-art surveillance technology and programming that rivals what can be found in prisons. Large urban jails probably have a subculture that more closely resembles what one would find in a prison and inmates get their first sense of the inmate code in these local jails.

INTERNET KEY

For more information on the American Jail Association, go to their Web site at http://www.aja.org/.

Jails now often conform to standards promulgated by the state or the American Jail Association, and may be accredited by the American Correctional Association. Standards cover everything from sanitation to staffing to programming. The adoption of standards, however, has been slow and very few jails are accredited.

The major problem, of course, is funding. Jails are a low priority for counties when budgets are written, and because many jails are small, it is more difficult for them to meet the standards because it is more costly on a per-prisoner basis.

Because the jail is considered a temporary correctional facility, there is less emphasis on programs. Some of the larger jails may have programs such as work-release and GED tutoring. They may also have parenting classes and other life skills training. However, other jails have virtually nothing to occupy the time of the inhabitants, so inmates spend all day watching television and playing cards.

Very few jailed inmates are placed in alternative supervision. The Bureau of Justice Statistics reported that in 2009 less than 8% of jail inmates were on some form of alternative supervision. Of a total population of 837,833, only 17,738 were in some type of community service program; about 12,439 were in some form of pretrial diversion; and the rest were in electronic monitoring (11,834), weekend reporting (11,212), work release (5912), or treatment programs (2082) [98].

Jails are often understaffed and there are few career incentives to motivate workers. Often, the officers in a jail are sheriff's deputies who are waiting to get a street patrol assignment. Sometimes, sheriffs use the jail assignment as punishment or as a probation assignment for new deputies. In some jurisdictions, the position is a separate hiring line from that of deputy, but many hired as jail officers aspire to be deputies. The lesser status assigned to the jail officer is often reflected in lower pay scales. According to the Department of Labor, the average hourly wage for jail officers in 2009 was about $20.00; however, according to another source, the average starting wage in 2009 was between $9 and $13 per hour [99].

The new-generation jail and its direct supervision model, which places officers inside the living units instead of outside long tiers or pods, requires officers to interact more with inmates, which would demand a higher level of communication skill and ability on the part of officers. It is possible that eventually these demands will translate into higher wages and better status for jail officers. Early evidence indicates that these jails present better working conditions for officers, and they respond with fewer absentee days and reduced misconduct [100].

CONCLUSION

Prisons are a necessary element in society, built to house seriously violent offenders. In the United States, we may have exceeded the cost benefits of this sanction by overuse. We now incarcerate more people than any other nation. It was not always this way and the rise in incarceration rates has only occurred within the last 30 years.

The history of prisons is marked by periodic cycles of reform. The penitentiary arose with the Walnut Street Jail. The two models of the penitentiary were the separate system and the Auburn system, but it was the Auburn system that became the model for subsequent building. The reformatory era in the late 1800s and early 1900s followed the first penitentiaries. The "big house" was the type of prison that existed through the 1900s until about the 1960s. The "correctional institution" followed the "big house"; however, we now talk about the "warehouse prison" where there are few, if any, programs.

Prisoners have more freedoms, rights, and access to a few, but better programs today. Prisoners are more likely to be young, violent, drug- and gang-related; thus, the increased freedom creates more opportunity for violence. It is a world of power and violence. The prisoner subculture may be somewhat different for women. There seems to be less violence, fewer gangs, and more consensual relationships.

Prisoners in the United States are supposed to retain all the rights of free people except those that are inconsistent with institutional needs of order, security, and rehabilitation. Most prisoner lawsuits allege violations of the Fourteenth, Eighth, or First Amendments. Although prisoners won several cases in the 1970s, courts today (following the due deference approach) typically uphold the policies and procedures of the prison. Still, prisons have progressed a long way from the harshness of the big house in the early 1900s.

Jails are not prisons. There are differences in the type of people housed, their sentences, programming, and administration. Generally, jails are local, supervised by the county sheriff, and receive funding from the local jurisdiction rather than the state. Like prisons, they are much better places to be today than in the past, although there are still management problems. Dostoevsky's observation that a society can be judged by the state of its prisons is as true today as it has been throughout history.

Review Questions

1. Describe incarceration rates and compare the United States to other countries.
2. What was the origin of the penitentiary? Distinguish between the *separate* and the *congregate* systems.

3. Describe the reformatory, the "big house," the "correctional institution," and the "warehouse prison," and identify when they developed.
4. List and discuss Sykes' deprivations of imprisonment and describe the deprivation and importation theory of prisoner subcultures.
5. Compare and contrast the male and female prisoner subcultures. Describe prison argot, argot roles, homosexuality, and the inmate code.
6. Discuss how the prison subculture today is different from the 1940s through the 1960s.
7. Discuss the three eras of prisoner rights: *hands-off, prisoner rights*, and *due deference*.
8. What are some of the rights at issue under the Fourteenth Amendment? The Eighth? The First?
9. Describe some differences between jails and prisons.
10. Who is housed in jails and how are they different from those in prison?

VOCABULARY

argot the language of a subculture (in this case, prisoners)

argot roles prisoner roles; they serve to classify and describe inmates based upon their behavior before prison, as well as what they do in prison

Auburn system congregate prison system where prisoners work, eat, and exercise together but have separate cells, created in Auburn, New York, prison (1817)

"Big houses" Robert Johnson's name for prisons of the early to mid-1900s

Building tenders (BTs) Texas inmates who were authorized by staff to control inmates by any means necessary

congregate system first introduced at Auburn Prison (1817); prisoners slept in solitary cells, but worked and ate together

corporal punishment physical punishment

correctional institution prisons in the 1950s; prisoners had more privileges, such as yard and recreational privileges

due deference era (1980 to today); judges are more likely to give "due deference" to the expertise of prison administrators when faced with prisoner litigation

due process clauses in the Fifth and the Fourteenth Amendments to the Constitution; they prohibit both state and federal authorities from taking life, liberty, or property without due process of law

fee system in early jails prisoners had to pay for their room and board

hands-off era (1900-1960); referred to federal and state courts rarely accepting grievances prisoners brought to their attention

importation hypothesis theory that the prisoner subculture is derived from the preprison characteristics of the people coming into prisons rather than prison deprivations themselves

inmate code is described as a set of subcultural rules for prisoners

jailhouse lawyers inmates who help other inmates file petitions for a fee

lockstep march in congregate prison systems prisoners shuffled together, bound by one hand on the opposite shoulder of the man in front

"the mix" the subculture of women's prisons; referring to the activities associated with drugs, homosexual activity, and fighting

penitentiary began with Walnut Street Jail in 1790; prisoners were kept in single cells and expected to reform through penitence

Pennsylvania system another name for Philadelphia system or separate system; prisoners were in solitary confinement and performed manual labor in their cells

PLRA Prison Litigation Reform Act; passed in 1995, this legislation severely restricted prisoners from filing lawsuits against prison officials

prisoner rights era (1960-1980); period when prisoner petitions increased tremendously and major prisoner rights cases were decided

prisonization process of being socialized to the prison subculture

pseudofamilies make-believe family systems that include all the familial roles including fathers, mothers, daughters, sisters, cousins, and so on.

rational relationship test one of the tests used by the courts to balance the individual's interest against the state's; if the contested rule or procedure is rationally related to a legitimate state interest, the state will win the challenge

reformatory era late 1870s through early 1900s, period when reformatories, such as Elmira Reformatory, were built

separate system type of prison system that originated in Philadelphia at the Walnut Street Jail (1790) and later at Eastern State Penitentiary (1829); inmates were housed in single cells

totality of circumstances type of Eighth Amendment case that argues that multiple conditions of confinement, as a whole, constituted cruel and unusual punishment

transportation form of punishment in England where the offender was sent to the American colonies (followed by Australia after the Revolutionary War) under a form of indentured servitude

Walnut Street Jail origin of the concept of the penitentiary in the United States; built in Philadelphia in 1790, founders instituted single cells, classification, and expectation of reform through penitence

warehouse prisons a name for contemporary prisons because prisoners do not receive many programs and are simply housed and fed until release

ENDNOTES

[1] A. Hirsch, From pillory to penitentiary: the rise of criminal incarceration in early Massachusetts, in: K. Hall (Ed.), Police, Prison and Punishment: Major Historical Interpretations, Garland, New York, 1987, pp. 344–434; B. McKelvey, Penology in the Westward movement, in: K. Hall (Ed.), Police, Prison and Punishment: Major Historical Interpretations, Garland, New York, 1987, pp. 457–479.

[2] L. Zupan, Jails: Reform and the New Generation Philosophy, Anderson Publishing, Cincinnati, OH, 1991.

[3] C. Crosley, Unfolding Misconceptions: The Arkansas State Penitentiary, 1836–1986, Liberal Arts Press, Arlington, VA, 1986.

[4] D. Rothman, The Discovery of the Asylum: Social Order and Disorder in the New Republic, Little, Brown, Boston, 1971.

[5] R. Johnson, Hard Time, Wadsworth/ITP, Belmont, CA, 2002.

[6] American Correctional Association (1970/revised 2002). Retrieved 1/2/2004 from www.aca.org/pastpresentfuture/principles.asp.

[7] N.H. Rafter, Partial Justice: Women, Prisons, and Social Control, second ed. Northeastern University Press, Boston, 1990, p. xxvi.

[8] N.H. Rafter, Partial Justice: Women, Prisons, and Social Control, second ed., Northeastern University Press, Boston, 1990; E. Freedman, Their Sisters' Keepers: Women's Prison Reform in America, 1830–1930, University of Michigan Press, Ann Arbor, 1981.

[9] R. Johnson, Hard Time, Wadsworth/ITP, Belmont, CA, 2002.

[10] B. Crouch, J. Marquart, An Appeal to Justice: Litigated Reform of Texas Prisons, University of Texas Press, Austin, 1989.

[11] N.H. Rafter, Partial Justice: Women, Prisons, and Social Control, second ed., Northeastern University Press, Boston, 1990.

[12] A. Rierden, The Farm: Life Inside a Women's Prison, University of Massachusetts Press, Amherst, 1997, p. 2.

[13] L. Carroll, Hacks, Blacks and Cons: Race Relations in a Maximum Security Prison, Lexington Books, Lexington, MA, 1974.

[14] A. Rierden, The Farm: Life Inside a Women's Prison, University of Massachusetts Press, Amherst, 1997.

[15] W. Sabol, H. West, M. Cooper, Prisoners in 2008, Bureau of Justice Statistics, Washington, DC, p. 8, 2009.

[16] G. Gaes, Cost, Performance Studies Look at Prison Privatization, NIJ J. (2010), modified. Retrieved 9/14/2010 from http://www.ojp.usdoj.gov/nij/journals/259/prison-privatization.htm.

[17] W. Bales, L. Bedard, S. Quinn, D. Ensley, G. Holley, Recidivism of Public and Private State Prison Inmates in Florida, Criminol. Publ. Policy 4(1) (2005) 57–82.

[18] J. Irwin, The Warehouse Prison: Disposal of the New Dangerous Classes, Roxbury Press, Los Angeles, 2004.

[19] L. Glaze, Correctional Populations in the United States, 2009, Bureau of Justice Statistics, Washington, DC, 2010.

[20] P. Harrison, A. Beck, Prison and Jail Inmates at Midyear 2005, Bureau of Justice Statistics, Washington, DC, 2006; P. Harrison, A. Beck, Prison and Jail Inmates at Midyear 2002, Bureau of Justice Statistics, Washington, DC, 2006.

[21] H. West, W. Sabol, S. Greenman, Prisoners in 2009, Bureau of Justice Statistics, Washington, DC, 2010.

[22] W. Sabol, H. West, M. Cooper, Prisoners in 2008, Bureau of Justice Statistics, Washington, DC, 2009.

[23] J. Jacobs, The limits of racial integration in prison, Crim. Law Bull. 18 (1982) 117–153.

[24] G. Sykes, The Society of Captives, Princeton University Press, Princeton, 1958; p. 1, 2010.

[25] J. Irwin, D. Cressey, Thieves, convicts, and the inmate cultures, Soc. Probl. 10(Fall) (1962) 142–155.

[26] D. Clemmer, The Prison Community, Holt, Rinehart and Winston, New York, 1958.

[27] R. Morris, The Devil's Butcher Shop: The New Mexico Prison Uprising, University of New Mexico Press, Albuquerque, NM, 1980.

[28] B. Owen, D.L. MacKenzie, The mix: the culture of imprisoned women, in: M. Stohr, C. Hemmens (Eds.), The Inmate Prison Experience, Pearson, Upper Saddle River, NJ, 2004, pp. 152–172.

[29] R. Giallombardo, Society of Women: A Study of a Women's Prison, Wiley, New York, 1966.

[30] J. Pollock, Women, Prison, and Crime, second ed., Wadsworth, Belmont, CA, 2002; L. Girshick, No Safe Haven: Stories of Women in Prison, Northeastern University Press, Boston, MA, 1999; B. Owen, "In the Mix": Struggle and Survival in a Women's Prison, State University of Albany Press, Albany, NY, 1998.

[31] J. Irwin, Prisons in Turmoil, Little, Brown and Company, Boston, 1980; V. Hassine, Life without Parole: Living in Prison Today, Roxbury, Los Angeles, 1999.

[32] J. Irwin, Prisons in Turmoil, Little, Brown and Company, Boston, 1980.

[33] J. Jacobs, Stateville: The Penitentiary in Mass Society, University of Chicago Press, Chicago, 1977; L. Carroll, Hacks, Blacks and Cons: Race Relations in a Maximum Security Prison, Lexington Books, Lexington, MA, 1974.

[34] N. McCall, Makes Me Wanna Holler: A Young Black Man in America, Vintage, New York, 1995, p. 149.

[35] J. Irwin, Prisons in Turmoil, Little, Brown and Company, Boston, 1980.

[36] B. Crouch, J. Marquart, An Appeal to Justice: Litigated Reform of Texas Prisons, University of Texas Press, Austin, 1989.

[37] Ruiz v. Estelle, 503 F. Supp. 1265 (1980).

[38] J. Winterdyk, R. Ruddell, Managing prison gangs: results from a survey of U.S. prison systems, J. Crim. Just. 38 (2010) 730–736.

[39] S. Mahan, Imposition of despair: an ethnography of women in prison, Just. Q. 1 (1984) 357–385; K. Greer, The changing nature of interpersonal relationships in a women's prison, Prison J. 80 (2000) 442–468.

[40] J. Hargan, The psychology of prison language, J. Abnorm. Soc. Psychol. 30 (1934) 359–361; J. Lerner, You Got Nothing Coming: Notes from a Prison Fish, Broadway Books, New York, 2002; G. Sykes, S. Messinger, The inmate social system, in: R. Cloward (Ed.), Theoretical Studies in the Social Organization of the Prison, Social Science Research Council, New York, 1960, pp. 6–10.

[41] J. Lerner, You Got Nothing Coming: Notes from a Prison Fish, Broadway Books, New York, 2002.

[42] C. Trulson, The social world of the prisoner, in: J. Pollock (Ed.), Prisons Today and Tomorrow, Jones and Bartlett Publishers, Sudbury, MA, 2005, pp. 79–124.

[43] E. George, A Woman Doing Life: Notes from a Prison for Women, Oxford Publishing, Boston, MA, 2009.

[44] G. Sykes, The Society of Captives, Princeton University Press, Princeton, NJ, 1958, pp. 84–108.

[45] C. Schrag, Leadership among prison inmates, Am. Sociol. Rev. 19 (1961) 37–42.

[46] R. Giallombardo, Society of Women: A Study of a Women's Prison, Wiley, New York, 1966, pp. 105–123.

[47] R. Hanser, C. Trulson, Sexual abuse of men in prison, in: F. Reddington, B. Kreise (Eds.), Sexual Assault: The Victims, the Perpetrators, and the Criminal Justice System, Carolina Academic Press, Durham, NC, 2004.

[48] J. Pollock, Women, Prison, and Crime, second ed., Wadsworth, Belmont, CA, 2002.

[49] Prison Rape Elimination Act of 2003, Public Law (2003) 108–179.

[50] A. Beck, P. Harrison, M. Berzofsky, R. Caspar, C. Krebs, Sexual Victimization in Prisons and Jails Reported by Inmates, 2008–2009, Bureau of Justice Statistics, Washington, DC, 2010.

[51] J. Gagnon, W. Simon, The social meaning of prison homosexuality, Fed. Probat. 32 (1968) 23–29.

[52] B. Owen, "In the Mix": Struggle and Survival in a Women's Prison, State University of Albany Press, Albany, NY, 1998.

[53] R. Johnson, Hard Time, Wadsworth/ITP, Belmont, CA, 2002.

[54] 62 Va. 790 (1871).

[55] National Advisory Commission on Criminal Justice Standards and Goals Report on Corrections, U.S Government Printing Office, Washington, DC, 1973, p. 18.

[56] 42 U.S.C. § 3626.

[57] Ex parte Hull, 61 S. Ct. 640 (1941).

[58] Johnson v. Avery, 89 S. Ct. 747 (1969); Procunier v. Martinez, 94 S. Ct. 1800 (1974).

[59] Wolff v. McDonnell, 94 S. Ct. 2963 (1974).

[60] 97 S. Ct. 1491 (1977).

[61] Lewis v. Casey, 116 S. Ct. 2174 (1996), Shaw v. Murphy, 121 S. Ct. 1475 (2001).

[62] Wolff v. McDonnell, 94 S. Ct. 2963 (1974).

[63] Superintendent, Massachusetts Correctional Institution, Walpole v. Hill, 105 S. Ct. 2768 (1985), Sandin v. Conner, 115 S. Ct. 2293, 2303 (1995).

[64] Meachum v. Fano, 96 S. Ct. 2532 (1976); Olim v. Wakinekona, 103 S. Ct. 1741 (1983).

[65] Jackson v. Bishop, 404 F.2d 571 (8th Cir. 1968).

[66] Estelle v. Gamble, 97 S. Ct. 285 (1976).

[67] Knecht v. Gillman, 48 F.2d 1136 (8th Cir. 1973).

[68] Pell v. Procunier, 94 S. Ct. 2800 (1974); Saxbe v. Washington Post, 94 S. Ct. 2811 (1974).

[69] Procunier v. Martinez, 94 S. Ct. 1800 (1974); Pell v. Procunier, 94 S. Ct. 2800 (1974).

[70] Turner v. Safley, 107 S. Ct. 2254 (1987).

[71] Shaw v. Murphy, 532 U.S. 223 (2001).

[72] Thornburgh v. Abbot, 109 S. Ct. 1874 (1989).

[73] Overton v. Bazzetta, 123 S. Ct. 2162 (2003).

[74] O'Lone v. Estate of Shabazz, 107 S. Ct. 2400 (1987).

[75] L. Hayes, Suicidal signs and symptoms, Correct. Forum 14(6) (2005) 36.

[76] American Correctional Association, The American Prison: From the Beginning, ACA, Lanham, MD, 1983.

[77] N. Morris, D. Rothman, The Oxford History of the Prison, Oxford University Press, New York, 1995.

[78] J. Moynahan, E. Stewart, The American Jail: Its Development and Growth, Nelson-Hall, Chicago, 1980.

[79] P. Harrison, A. Beck, Prison and Jail Inmates at Midyear 2005, Bureau of Justice Statistics, Washington, DC, 2006; T. Minton, Jail Inmates at Midyear 2009, Statistical Tables, Bureau of Justice Statistics, Washington, DC, 2010.

[80] T. Minton, Jail Inmates at Midyear 2009, Statistical Tables, Bureau of Justice Statistics, Washington, DC, 2010, p. 2.

[81] Bureau of Justice Statistics State Court Sentencing of Convicted Felons, Statistical Tables, U.S. Department of Justice, Washington DC, 2004. Retrieved 1/11/2005 from http://www.ojp.usdoj.gov/bjs/pub/pdf/scscf02.pdf.

[82] P. Harrison, A. Beck, Prison and Jail Inmates at Midyear 2005, Bureau of Justice Statistics, Washington, DC, 2006, p. 8.

[83] P. Harrison, J. Karberg, Prison and Jail Inmates at Midyear 2002, Bureau of Justice Statistics, Washington, DC, 2003.

[84] P. Harrison, A. Beck, Prison and Jail Inmates at Midyear 2005, Bureau of Justice Statistics, Washington, DC, 2006.

[85] T. Minton, Jail Inmates at Midyear 2009, Statistical Tables, Bureau of Justice Statistics, Washington, DC, 2010, p. 12.

[86] T. Minton, Jail Inmates at Midyear 2009, Statistical Tables, Bureau of Justice Statistics, Washington, DC, 2010, p. 1.

[87] P. Harrison, A. Beck, Prison and Jail Inmates at Midyear 2005, Bureau of Justice Statistics, Washington, DC, 2005, p. 8.

[88] T. Minton, Jail Inmates at Midyear 2009, Statistical Tables, Bureau of Justice Statistics, Washington, DC, 2010, p. 9.

[89] Percent of Jail Inmates Reporting Drug Use, Sourcebook of Criminal Justice Statistics 2003, Table 6.21. Retrieved from http://www.albany.edu/sourcebook/pdf/t621.pdf; P. Harrison, A. Beck, Prison and Jail Inmates at Midyear 2004, Bureau of Justice Statistics, Washington DC, 2005.

[90] Number of Jail Inmates, Average Daily Population, and Rated Capacity, Table 6.14. Sourcebook of Criminal Justice Statistics, 2003. Retrieved 1/22/2006 from http://www.albany.edu/sourcebook/pdf/t614.pdf; P. Harrison, A. Beck, Prison and Jail Inmates at Midyear 2004, Bureau of Justice Statistics, Washington, DC, 2005.

[91] P. Harrison, A. Beck, Prison and Jail Inmates at Midyear 2004, Bureau of Justice Statistics, Washington, DC, 2005; P. Harrison, A. Beck, Prison and Jail Inmates at Midyear 2004, Bureau of Justice Statistics, Washington, DC, 2005, p. 10.

[92] P. Harrison, A. Beck, Prison and Jail Inmates at Midyear 2004, Bureau of Justice Statistics, Washington, DC, 2005.

[93] A. Bell, N. Jaquette, D. Sanner, C. Steele-Smith, H. Wald, Treatment of individuals with co-occurring disorders in county jails, Corrections Today 67(3) (2005) 86–91; L. Teplin, K. Abram, G. McClelland, Prevalence of psychiatric disorders among incarcerated women: pretrial jail detainees, Arch. Gen. Psych. 53 (1996) 505–512; P. Harrison, A. Beck, Prison and Jail Inmates at Midyear 2005, Bureau of Justice Statistics, Washington, DC, 2006, p. 8.

[94] T. White, E. Gillespie, Mental health programs: addressing the unfunded mandate, Corrections Today 67(6) (2005) 108–113.

[95] D. James, L. Glaze, Mental Health Problems of Prison and Jail Inmates, Bureau of Justice Statistics, Washington, DC, 2006.

[96] 325 F. Supp. 781 (M.D. Ala. 1971).

[97] B. Veysey, K. DeCou, L. Prescott, Effective management of female jail detainees with histories of physical and sexual abuse, Am. Jails (May/June) (1998) 50–63.

[98] T. Minton, Jail Inmates at Midyear 2009, Statistical Tables, Bureau of Justice Statistics, Washington, DC, 2010, p. 14.

[99] U.S. Department of Labor, Occupational Wages in the United States, Bureau of Labor Statistics, Washington DC, 2006. Retrieved 2/20/2007 from http://www.bls.gov/oes/current/oes_nat.htm#b33–0000. Retrieved 12/10/2010 from http://www.payscale.com/research/US/Job=Correctional_Officer_%2F_Jailer/Hourly_Rate.

[100] L. Zupan, Jails: Reform and the New Generation Philosophy, Anderson Publishing, Cincinnati, OH, 1991.

CHAPTER 14

Parole and Reentry

WHAT YOU NEED TO KNOW

- Parole is supervised release *from* prison while probation is typically supervised *release* instead of prison.
- There were 819,308 adults on parole in 2009; about 12% were women.
- The contributions of Maconochie, Crofton, and Brockway led to modern parole.
- Only 15 states still have full discretionary release parole systems.
- The rate at which eligible inmates actually receive parole varies widely from state to state, and even within a state over different periods.
- Inmates have no due process rights regarding the parole release decision, but they do have due process rights before their parole is revoked.
- About one-third of parolees are revoked, about 51% are successfully discharged.
- About 30% of all admissions to prison are of parolees who have had their parole revoked.

CONTENTS

Many people do not understand the difference between parole and probation. It used to be quite simple, in that probation was a sentence to supervision in the community *instead of* a prison sentence and parole was a supervised release *from* a prison sentence. With **split sentencing** and **shock incarceration**, the terms became less clear because those forms of sentencing involve a short period of incarceration before being supervised in the community by probation officers. The better differentiation to make today would be in the administration of the two types of correctional supervision. Recall that probation is administered by probation officers who report to the sentencing judge. While probation itself may be under the executive branch or the judicial branch, it is always the sentencing judge who determines revocation or makes changes to the conditions attached to the probation order. Parole officers, on the other hand, submit their violation reports to the paroling authority. Parole may be a division of the institutional corrections division or an independent agency. The parole board is the releasing body and also conducts violation hearings or, in larger states, delegates that function to hearing officers. The sentencing judge is not involved at all in parole decisions. One other difference between probation and parole is that while probation exists in all 50 states, some states have abolished parole.

Parole is intimately tied to the **indeterminate sentence**, where the release date is not set by the sentencing judge. The idea of indeterminate sentencing is that offenders should be rewarded for their good behavior. Once reformed, they should be released. That release is typically to parole and they are supervised in the community for the remainder of the time of their sentence. Some states, however, have abolished indeterminate sentencing, and parole along with it. Cases in which released prisoners killed their victims while on parole, such as Richard Allen Davis, who killed Polly Klaas; Jesse Timmendequas, the paroled sex offender who killed Megan Kanka; and Henry Lee Lucas, who killed several people after being paroled in Texas, have spurred some states to abolish parole entirely. The fact is that although all prisoners eventually will be released, early release to parole does carry with it some risks. However, it is estimated that parole costs about one-tenth of holding someone in prison; therefore, in some states, parole continues to be essential in the effort to keep down the cost of corrections.

CHARACTERISTICS OF THE PAROLE POPULATION

In 2009, there were 819,308 adults on parole. States with the largest parole populations were California (106,035), Texas (104,943), Pennsylvania (75,112), and New York (49,950) [1]. In 2009, the rate per 100,000 people in parole custody status for the nation was 351; however, it was only 3 in Maine because this state is largely determinative in sentencing structure, compared to 1288 per 100,000 in the District of Columbia and 761 per 100,000 in Pennsylvania [2].

According to the Bureau of Justice Statistics, at year-end 2008, more than one in every 280 people in the United States were under parole supervision. As a percentage of all releases from prison, discretionary releases to parole have declined dramatically, but have now begun to increase again. Before 1980, most releases from prison were via discretionary parole [3]. About 55% of all releases in 1980 were to discretionary parole. However, over the years, the use of discretionary releases has declined, so by 2004, only 22% of prison releases were to discretionary parole. Mandatory supervision releases increased from 19% to 39% over the same period. In 2009, the percentage of releases from prison under discretionary parole was about 27%, and 46% were released under some form of mandatory supervision. Mandatory supervision means that the offender serves a full term and then is required to be under a period of mandatory supervision in the community after release. Other forms of releases from prison, including expiration of sentence ("maxing out"), probation, and other conditional releases remained relatively stable [4].

Most parolees have served prison sentences for drug offenses (36% of all parolees). The rest of the parolee population is made up of property offenders (23%), violent offenders (27%), and all others (13%). The Bureau of Justice Statistics reports that as a percentage of the total, blacks decreased from 45% of all parolees in 1995 to 39% in 2008. Whites increased from 34% to 41% and Hispanics declined slightly from 21% to 18% [5].

Blacks are more likely to serve longer sentences before being paroled. In 1999 (the only year the data seem to be available), blacks served, on average, about 37 months before discretionary parole, while whites served 34 months and Hispanics served 33 months. Hispanics served the longest when looking specifically at drug offenses (31 months compared to 28 months for blacks and 27 months for whites) [6].

About 8% of parolees were women in 1990, about 10% were women in 1995. By 2000, the figure was 12% of the total number of parolees. Since then, their percentage has remained stable at about 12% [7]. Women on parole experience a multitude of problems. Many of them are the same problems that male parolees face, but some are different, or experienced in different ways. Women are more likely than men to have histories of drug and alcohol use, long-term unemployment, few or no skills, and a history of sexual abuse [8].

In one study of Texas releases, it was found that women were more likely than male offenders to have serious histories of drug use, but less likely to have received any treatment. About 42% reported daily cocaine use before prison, compared to only 17% of the men. More men expected to live with families than women [9]. In this same study, female parolees reported less family support and more negative family influences than did men.

One of the differences between male and female offenders is that it seems as though women's relationships with men are more central to their offending; thus, upon parole, they are less likely to stay out of trouble if they are in a relationship with a criminal partner. It is also true that women are less likely to have relationships to return to and they are wary of old partners who may be instrumental in their falling back into drug use [10].

Several research efforts have documented the difficulties of women after release. Patricia O'Brien followed 18 women after release and documented their difficulties in adjusting to life on the outside. The financial and emotional difficulties of reuniting with children comprise the most important distinguishing factor between male and female offenders. Interestingly, women seem to be more likely than men to view their parole officers as a positive force, and look to them for assistance and resource referrals [11].

Mary Dodge and Mark Pogrebin also interviewed female parolees and found that one of their greatest concerns was the difficulty of gaining custody of their children. To regain custody if the child is under state control, the female offender must show she has participated in drug treatment (if she was identified as a drug addict), maintain steady employment, and have a decent and stable home for the child. Because just meeting the requirements of daily living and the further demands of parole officers is difficult, the extra burden of children is sometimes too much for female parolees and they either cannot or do not even try to regain custody [12].

The success rate for parolees is lower than that of probationers. About 50% were successfully discharged in 2009. About 40% are returned to prison under either a new charge (9% of all parolees) or through revocation (24%). About 8% abscond, and the rest are considered either "unsuccessful," transferred, or dead [13]. States seem to vary tremendously in their patterns of success. While about 80% of Massachusetts parolees successfully complete parole, only 23% of parolees in Utah do [14]. It is important to note that more than a third of *all* prison admissions are parolees who have had their parole revoked [15]. Recidivism and the factors related to success or failure on parole will be discussed in more detail later in this chapter.

ADMINISTRATION OF PAROLE

Parole is either a division under the state's department of corrections, a separate agency, or a variation of these two models. The advantage of the parole system being part of the department of corrections is that communication is generally smoother and the paroling authority may be more responsive to prison overpopulation. On the other hand, some argue that is exactly why the paroling authority should be separate from the prison system. In some states, only the parole board is separate from the department of corrections, but parole officers and all employees related to supervision are part of the corrections department. This removes the discretionary release decision makers from the auspices of the agency, but not the supervising officers. According to the Bureau of Justice Statistics, 38 states had parole agencies attached to the department of corrections. In other states, the agency was either independent or affiliated with other agencies. In this same survey, it is reported that parole supervising agencies employed 65,000 full-time workers in 2006 (and another 2900 part-time workers) [16].

 INTERNET KEY

For an interesting interactive Web site where you can choose your state or any other state and discover key facts about its correctional system and crime rates as compared to the rest of the nation, go to the National Institute of Corrections Web site at http://nicic.gov/Features/statestats/.

THE HISTORY OF PAROLE

Parole comes from French word *parol* (*parole d'honneur*) referring to "word" as in giving one's word of honor [17]. The idea of releasing prisoners from incarceration can be traced all the way back to the punishment of **transportation**, which involved sending prisoners from England to the colonies and, after the American Revolution, to Australia. These prisoners were not paroled in the sense that we think of today, but they were released from confinement into the community, and leased to a landowner who used their labor. The last shipment of convicts to Australia was as late as 1868 [18].

Alexander Maconochie (1787-1860) developed an early form of parole on Norfolk Island. Norfolk Island was a prison colony 1000 miles off the coast of Australia where felons who committed additional crimes after being transported to Australia were sent. Maconochie's **mark system** consisted of stages of increasing responsibility. At the highest stage of responsibility, the offender could live almost independently, albeit on the island, and the final stage was a form of early release. Maconochie eliminated harsh punishments and improved the living conditions of the offenders incarcerated on Norfolk Island, but his tenure was short-lived. He held the job of prison superintendent only from 1840 until 1843, at which point he was removed because of his perceived leniency. He also tried to implement similar ideas in Birmingham Borough prison in 1849 but was dismissed two years later—again, on charges that he was too lenient [19].

Sir Walter Crofton (1815-1897) developed a concept more similar to today's parole. His **ticket of leave**, implemented around 1853, was a form of the mark system. Offenders were released early from prison upon going through graduated stages of responsibility and earning marks along the way for good behavior. When the offender had earned enough marks, he received his "ticket to leave" prison and returned to his community. The offender was required to report to police and, supposedly, a police inspector helped find the offender a job and supervised his release.

In 1870, a Prison Congress was held in Cincinnati, Ohio, which brought together many of the major prison policymakers and reformers of the era. At the Congress, Crofton's idea was disseminated and led directly to the concept of graduated liberties found in the "Declaration of Principles" from the Congress [20]. Zebulon Brockway (1827-1920), a major participant of the Prison Congress, was appointed superintendent of Elmira Reformatory in New York in 1877.

This new institution was supposed to be different from the earlier penitentiary in that it reformed young, malleable inmates through education and discipline. Although Brockway was associated with corporal punishments, he also implemented indeterminate sentences and parole release. Inmates of Elmira were young men (16 to 30) who were placed in "second grade," which was the highest form of custody. After six months of good conduct, they were promoted to "first grade." Continued good behavior would earn an early release. Offenders were released to six months of supervision, supervised by volunteer guardians. It wasn't until many years later that parole was implemented with paid employees [21].

Gradually throughout the late 1800s and early 1900s, states adopted some form of early release or parole, but it may not have included any concept of supervision, or supervision was provided haphazardly, or by volunteers. In 1907, New York became the first state to implement parole with the elements we consider associated with modern parole:

- An indeterminate sentence
- A system for granting early release
- Postrelease supervision by paid employees
- The possibility of revocation and return to prison

By 1927, only three states (Florida, Mississippi, and Virginia) did not have parole systems. By 1942, all states had a parole system, although some continued to use volunteer parole officers [22]. The federal system of parole came later than state parole, but was fully implemented by 1932. In 1973, federal parole guidelines were established that set out guidelines for sentence length based on offense severity and likelihood of recidivism [23].

It took longer for all states to establish public parole systems than it did for states to create state probation agencies. Also, unlike probation, some states have since abolished parole. In the "rehabilitative era" of the 1970s, the majority of inmates were released on parole. For instance, in 1977, 72% of all prisoners were released via parole. However, the use of parole declined dramatically in the 1980s and 1990s and, by 1997, only 28% of all prisoners were released via parole [24]. At the federal level, the Comprehensive Crime Control Act of 1984 created the U.S. Sentencing Commission, which established sentencing guidelines that specified fixed terms. Federal parole was abolished and replaced with mandatory postrelease supervision.

In the late 1970s and 1980s, parole came under criticism from both liberals and conservatives. Liberals were upset that there were no guidelines or rules in how parole boards granted parole or such guidelines were not transparent so there was no way for an offender to ensure their success or appeal the decision to refuse parole. Conservatives criticized parole for being too lenient and letting violent offenders out too early.

Joan Petersilia, an authority on probation and parole, describes the criticisms that led to the demise of parole as involving these major arguments:

- There was no perceived scientific support for rehabilitation or evidence that correct programming could ever reform criminals.

(2)■ There was a moral problem with tying release to prison behavior because one didn't necessarily predict the other.

(3)■ Not knowing one's release date was a form of cruel punishment.

(4)■ Paroling authorities had uncontrolled discretion with no guidelines [25].

Because of extreme dissatisfaction with parole and criticism of how it was implemented, Maine abolished parole in 1976 and, in 1977, California and Indiana abolished their parole release decision power and established determinate sentencing. Other states followed and, by the end of 2000, 15 states had abolished parole; 21 states allowed parole for only some types of prisoners, and just 15 states still had full parole discretion [26]. In 2008, a survey by the Association of Paroling Authorities International reported that 16 states had only determinate sentencing (with no parole), 10 states still had purely indeterminate sentencing, and the other states had a sentencing system that used a mixture [27]. Unfortunately, the survey did not list the states; therefore, it is difficult to reconcile these findings with the information presented in Box 14.1, which is from an earlier source.

During the same period when discretionary parole declined, the rate of revocations in the states that retained parole rose. Parole boards evidently became more cautious in granting parole and in leaving parolees on the street after violation reports had been filed. In 2001, 40% of prison admissions were parole revocations, compared to about half that number in 1980 [28]. As noted earlier, in 2008 about a third of all prison admissions were parolees who had their paroles revoked.

EXERCISE: IN THE STATE OF...

Find out whether your state has discretionary parole, limited discretionary parole, mandatory release, or none of the above. (Basically, confirm whether the information in Box 14.1 is correct.) How many adults are being supervised by a parole supervision authority in your state (if any)?

BOX 14.1 STATUS OF PAROLE RELEASE, 2002

Full release power: Alabama, Colorado, Idaho, Kentucky, Montana, Nevada, New Jersey, North Dakota, Oklahoma, Pennsylvania, Rhode Island, South Carolina, Utah, Vermont, Wyoming

Limited release power: Alaska, Arkansas, California, Connecticut, Florida, Georgia, Hawaii, Iowa, Louisiana, Maryland, Massachusetts, Michigan, Missouri, Nebraska, New Hampshire, New York, South Dakota, Tennessee, Texas, West Virginia, Wisconsin

No parole: Arizona, Delaware, Illinois, Indiana, Kansas, Maine, Minnesota, Mississippi, New Mexico, North Carolina, Ohio, Oregon, Virginia, Washington, federal system

Source: *J. Petersilia, Reforming Probation and Parole, American Correctional Association, Lanham, MD, 2002, p. 111.*

INTERNET KEY

For more information on parole, go to the National Parole Resource Center at http://nationalparoleresourcecenter.org/ and the Association of Paroling Authorities International at http://www.apaintl.org/.

Interestingly, several states (North Carolina, Florida, California, and Colorado) that had abolished the parole-granting authority have now reinstated it, no doubt because of prison overcrowding. Today, only Maine and Virginia have no parole or postprison supervision [29]. Other states have a form of mandatory supervision after release that is based on a percentage of time served and good time awarded. The offender is subject to revocation and return to prison until the full expiration of the original sentence.

SUPERVISION ISSUES

As explained earlier, the parole board is the paroling authority in most states (although it may be called something else). In states that have retained discretionary parole, the inmate is eligible for parole according to statute; typically when one-half or two-thirds of the sentence has been served. Just because an inmate is eligible for parole does not mean that he or she receives it. The Breaking News box shows that when one's crime is notorious, it is extremely unlikely the paroling authority will decide to release the offender. The decision to grant parole is made by the paroling authority and is based on the severity of the crime and the inmate's behavior in prison. Some states use more formal guidelines for granting parole; in others, the decision is more subjective. Even in states that have abolished parole, there may still be discretionary parole for inmates who were sentenced before the state legislature abolished discretionary parole. However, there is no doubt that fewer individuals are receiving parole today than in the past. In 1977, just 4% of prisoners **maxed out**, meaning they served their full term with no early release. By 2002, close to 20% of prisoners were "maxing out" of prison. This means that they have no conditions on their release and no supervision [30]. In 2008, 29% of releases from prison were "unconditional," meaning releases received no supervision [31].

BREAKING NEWS

In December 2010, Bobby Beausoleil, a follower of Charles Manson, was denied parole yet again, 40 years after his conviction. Even though Manson and his followers were convicted during a time when California still had discretionary parole and are technically eligible for discretionary parole, observers doubt that they will ever be released due to the horrific nature of their crimes. Susan Atkins, another follower of Manson's, had petitioned to be released due to a terminal illness but her petition was denied and she died in prison. Beausoleil is now 63 years old.

Source: *L. A. Now, Charles Manson Follower Bobby Beausoleil Denied Parole Again, December 2010, Retrieved 12/18/2010 from http://www.latimeslbogs.lattimes.com/lanow/2010/12/chares-manson-follower-denied-parole-again-in-musicians-killing-should-family-members-ever-be-freed.html.*

The rate of parole (the ratio of offenders who receive parole to those who are eligible) fluctuates widely between states and sometimes within a state over different time periods or different regions. Texas, for instance, is divided into different regions, and there is quite a wide disparity in parole approval rates. For instance, while one region approves only 38% of low-risk eligible offenders, another region in the state approves 58% of low-risk offenders. The approval rates for high-risk offenders range from 0.5% to 15% [32]. In 2005, only about half of offenders who were at the lowest risk level were approved for parole, and only about 40% of those at the second-lowest level were approved [33].

The paroling authority may be called different things in different states, but the board is typically made up of a number of individuals who have the discretion to grant parole. In many states, the board also offers recommendations to the governor on pardons. The positions are typically political appointments and consist of no more than 10 members who may come from a variety of backgrounds, including law enforcement, education, and business. The appointment is typically a term lasting from three to six years; however, in some states, the appointment is indefinite. Depending on the state, these members may have the power to grant parole, set parole decision dates, rescind parole, issue warrants and subpoenas, set conditions, restore offenders' civil rights, and grant final discharges. Some or all of these duties may be delegated.

There are about 200 individuals on state parole boards or paroling authorities across the nation. These 200 individuals are responsible for the release decisions, setting the conditions for parolees and those who are released under some form of mandatory supervision, overseeing the supervision of the more than 800,000 parolees on parole, and being responsible for revocation decisions [34]. There is a great deal of turnover on these boards and not much training. In some states, parole board members work only part-time and/or receive no compensation.

Generally, only a subset of the full board holds release hearings. Parole hearings last an average of 12 to 15 minutes. In some states, the board may not meet personally with the offender at all. The board may or may not allow the offender to appear personally and/or present witnesses and evidence in support of his or her release. The board considers a variety of factors in their release decision, including the seriousness of the offense, the amount of time served, the offender's age, juvenile history, criminal history, number of prison infractions, other arrests, participation in programs, and letters of support or protest.

The ability of parole board members to accurately judge when an offender is no longer a risk to the community has always been questionable. Studies show that board members pay most attention to the severity of the crime in making the release decision, not what the offender has done in prison. Other factors that weigh in the decision include prior criminal record, attitude toward family responsibilities, attitude toward authority, and attitude toward the victim [35]. About 96% of the states now also offer the opportunity for victims and district attorneys to provide input on the decision [36]. Recent research has found that victims can affect the decision of the parole board. In cases in which victims attend the hearing or send letters, offenders are less likely to receive parole [37].

Many states and the federal government have moved away from the idea of a **clinical assessment decision**, meaning that board members should be able to read the file and interview the inmate and predict his or her ability to be successful on release, to an **actuarial decision**, meaning that statistics are used to predict success based on demographics of those who have been successful.

Former Ohio congressman Jim Traficant, left, is released from federal prison in Rochester, MN, September 2, 2009. Democrat Traficant is ending a seven year federal prison stay for accepting bribes and other corruption charges. *AP Photo/Craig Lassig*

A prediction instrument used in a number of states is the Level of Service Inventory-Revised (LSI-R). It is one of numerous risk instruments that predicts recidivism based on a number of static and dynamic (changing) factors. Factors include criminal history, education/employment, financial history, housing, alcohol/drug problems, and attitudes and orientation, among other things. The instrument has been validated with more than 18,000 prisoners and 4000 probationers. It was developed for short-term offenders, but has also been validated with long-term offenders who have served more than 10 years. Researchers have found that, when utilizing a one year follow-up period, the LSI-R was helpful in predicting recidivism. Those who scored as high risk were five times more likely to recidivate within one year. Those who scored as moderate risk were four times as likely to recidivate. Interestingly, this study found that long-term inmates were less likely to recidivate than a general control group of prison releases (13% versus 27%) [38]. **Parole guidelines** are similar to sentencing guidelines because they give a presumptive term or guideline for how long the offender should serve in prison based on offense characteristics and characteristics of the offender. Risk factors typically include age at first admission to an incarceration facility, history of revocations, prior incarcerations, employment history, commitment offense, age, gang membership, education and/or training completions while incarcerated, disciplinary conduct, and custody level. These factors go into a risk score that is used, along with an offense severity score, to establish the guidelines.

Generally, prisoners receive parole hearings with board members. In these hearings, a future parole date is set according to a guideline system utilizing crime and offender characteristics. In subsequent hearings, the parole date may be re-evaluated. In most cases, prison violations would result in setting the date further in the future. When the presumptive date gets close, there will be a hearing at which time the parole is either granted or put off to a future tentative release date.

The Supreme Court held that parole release was not a right; therefore, states did not have to follow strict due process guidelines in parole release hearings [39]. This means that states can set up any type of procedure deemed expedient in the decision to grant parole, or eliminate the privilege entirely [40].

Parole board members are immune from liability if parolees murder or victimize others. The Supreme Court has held that officials must be immune from tort liability for their decisions [41]. This quasi-immunity is similar to that held by judges and probation officers when they are using their discretion to make sentencing recommendations on presentence reports. On the other hand, parole officers who supervise a caseload may be liable in Section 1983 actions if, acting in the course and duty of employment, they violate an offender's constitutional rights [42]. Parole officers may also be found negligent in civil actions if their carelessness or deficient performance resulted in loss or injury to a third party.

The power to parole is different from the power to **pardon** convicted offenders, which is basically a release and forgiveness of criminal culpability. This power rests in the executive power of the president and governors. Section 2 of the U.S. Constitution gives the president pardon power over federal crimes. Similar provisions exist in most state constitutions for governors to pardon state crimes. In many states, the parole board is called the board of pardons and paroles because the board makes recommendations to the governor on pardons. While a pardon is basically forgiveness and removes the conviction, a commutation is simply a reduction of sentence.

The decision to pardon can be controversial. In 1974, President Gerald Ford pardoned former president Richard Nixon. While some argued this act closed the door on a difficult time in the nation's history and began the healing process after the Watergate scandal, others argued that the nation never reached closure over the incident. In 1993, President George Bush pardoned former Defense Secretary Caspar Weinberger over the Iran-Contra affair—an act that, again, stirred controversy. The most controversial pardons, however, were made by President Clinton in 2001. He offered clemency to FALN members, a terrorist group dedicated to the freedom of Puerto Rico. He also pardoned Dan Rostenkowski for the misuse of public funds, as well as several federal prisoners who had long mandatory sentences for drug crimes. He pardoned Patricia Hearst, Roger Clinton, Susan McDougal, Henry Cisneros, and Marc Rich for wire fraud, racketeering, and tax evasion. The last pardon was heavily criticized because Rich had been a major contributor to Clinton's campaign.

There have been scandals regarding the parole process as well. In 1978, Ray Blanton, then-governor of Tennessee, and three aides were charged with accepting money in return for approving parole and pardon requests. Two were convicted and sentenced to prison. In 1991, a scandal emerged when it became known that James Granberry, an ex-parole commission member in Texas, received money from prisoners' families as a "parole advisor." Evidently, he charged between $500 and $2000 to help prisoners' quests for parole. He was indicted by a federal grand jury for lying to a federal magistrate in 1992 about what he was doing. It was later discovered that, while on the board, he voted to parole a car dealer's son in exchange for reduced lease payments on a car [43].

Caseload supervision

Generally, parole caseloads are smaller than probation caseloads. The average caseload today is about 70 and twice what some consider to be an ideal size [44]. According to a recent survey by the Association of Paroling Authorities, the average caseload size is 38, but it is unclear whether this figure utilizes all employees or only those employees who supervise caseloads [45]. Only about 14% of parolees are under some form of intensive parole. A very small number (about 3%) are under some form of specialized supervision (such as sex offenders). Intensive parole and specialized caseloads cost more than twice what regular parole costs per year [46].

Intensive parole is similar to intensive probation programs in that smaller caseloads allow officers to more intensely supervise offenders. For instance, in one state's intensive parole program, offenders who are high risk because they have committed an act of violence are supervised in caseloads of 14. Officers see the offender at least 15 times per month with at least six "face-to-face" contacts, six drivebys, and one home visitation. Offenders are on 24-hour electronic monitoring and must submit and have approved a 24-hour schedule of where they will be every hour of the day [47].

Caseloads may be assigned to officers based on geography, classification level, offender type, or random assignment. Some argue that it would be better for caseloads to be assigned geographically so that officers would be able to coordinate with community police officers and share information about parolees and their family members in a given neighborhood. In one study, it was found that in a high-crime neighborhood, 43 different probation officers supervised 218 probationers instead of concentrating all probationers under a few officers who would be better informed about the neighborhood. This same principle applies to parole as well [48]. Parolees generally are localized in a few zip codes that are also typically marked by high crime, dysfunctional families, and poverty. Furthermore, most of the neighborhoods do not have any services available in the immediate vicinity [49].

Parole conditions

Similar to probationers, all parolees are required to abide by conditions established at the time of the parole release. Generally, standard conditions are like those of probation; the offender must report monthly, notify the officer of any moves, hold a job, not commit a crime, and so on. Parolees are increasingly expected to pay supervision fees and/or victim compensation fees. Other conditions may be treatment oriented, such as participating in a treatment program or obtaining a GED; or custody oriented, such as following a curfew, or not going anywhere near children. A list of typical conditions is offered in Box 14.2.

As with probation, violating any of these conditions might result in a parole officer writing a violation report. There may also be a revocation hearing in front of the parole board or a hearing examiner. Technical violations are those that involve only breaking one or more of the conditions. Parolees are also sometimes revoked for committing new crimes, with or without formally prosecuting the new crime.

Reentry concerns

Reentry assistance has increased in recent years with support from the federal government. In his 2004 State of the Union address, President Bush made special mention of the need for reentry services and advocated a $300 million federal initiative to provide financial support for state programs to give parolees and releases a "second chance" through job training, transitional housing, and other forms of support. States were given grants to create such programs. The Second Chance Act of 2007 was a reauthorization of this earlier Act with new funding. It was passed and signed into law in April 2008 as Public Law

---

BOX 14.2 PAROLE CONDITIONS

- Pay supervision fees and restitution
- Do not use controlled substances except by prescription
- Submit to drug testing
- Remain in the state
- Find gainful employment or participate in education
- Obtain permission to change residence
- Submit to searches of home and visits to workplace
- Consent to search of person
- Obey all laws
- Cooperate in all ways with parole officer
- Do not possess any weapons

INTERNET KEY

For information about reentry, go to the National Reentry Resource Center at http://www.nationalreentryresourcecenter.org/.

110-199. Federal funding is authorized for states and local jurisdictions to try innovative programs to assist reentry efforts. Many researchers and writers are urging states to re-examine the dramatic decline of discretionary parole and the high return-to-prison rates as wasteful spending of correctional dollars [50].

There has been a great deal of press lately about the fact that more than 700,000 inmates return to the community every year. Many of these are released to parole. It bears noting that a large number of these offenders received very little assistance in prison to learn how to avoid criminal decisions, drugs, or negative lifestyles [51]. Prison treatment programs only comprise 1% to 5% of prison budgets each year [52]. The number of prisoners who participated in vocational programs dropped from 31% in 1991 to 27% in 1997; the number who had participated in education programs dropped from 43% to 35%, and the number who received any formal substance abuse treatment dropped from 25% to 10% [53].

One study points out that the prerelease programs that were more popular in past decades may have been instrumental in reducing recidivism. Researchers found that, of 3244 Massachusetts inmates released between 1973 and 1976, those who participated in both a prerelease and furlough program had a 9% recidivism rate; those who only participated in furloughs had a 17% recidivism rate; those who participated only in the prerelease program had a 26% rate; and those who participated in neither had a 29% recidivism rate (holding prisoner age and prior record constant) [54]. Even assuming that those who were allowed to participate in furloughs might have been better risks overall, this does indicate that prerelease programs should be considered essential tools in reducing recidivism.

Some argue that the problems of parolees are more serious today than they have been in the past, partly because of a lack of in-prison programming, and partly because prisoners have more barriers to overcome. In 2003, of those released from prison on parole or mandatory release, three-quarters had a history of substance abuse and one in six suffered from mental illness. However, only one-third received substance abuse or mental health treatment while in prison. The percentage of all prisoners who are participating in such programs has declined from 25% a decade ago to only 10% today. Further, 2% to 3% of releases are HIV-positive; one-third were unemployed at the time of current arrest; about 40% have no GED or high school diploma; and 11% have a learning disability [55].

In a study of releases in one state, utilizing a sample of 414 men and 262 women, it was found that 37% had no high school diploma or GED; and only half of the sample had held a job for two years or more prior to their prison term. Eighty-seven percent of this sample indicated they would need some or a lot of help in finding a job. Only 15% had a job waiting for them upon release. About 60% of this sample had not received any drug treatment, even though close to 60% reported cocaine use and a quarter reported heavy daily use. A significant percentage of this sample (almost 20%) reported mental health problems and about 30% reported a diagnosis of depression [56].

In California in 2002, there were only 200 shelter beds available for parolees, but 10,000 who had no home to be released to. Also, there were only four mental health clinics, but 18,000 who required psychiatric services, and only 750 drug treatment beds for 85,000 substance abusers [57]. Furthermore, only about 6% of releases in California participated in any kind of prerelease program [58]. On the other hand, the state of Washington has a very comprehensive prerelease system that assesses risk and need. The state also offers prerelease services in prison. Between 30% and 40% of released prisoners spend time in community residential release centers [59].

In past decades, many inmates took advantage of furloughs to help them look for a job or get reacquainted with family before release. That is no longer the case. For instance, in the 1970s, California granted 15,000 furloughs a year; however, in 2001 no furloughs were granted [60]. The "Willie Horton" incident refers to Michael Dukakis's ill-fated campaign for president that was damaged by a campaign ad in 1988 that highlighted the case of Willie Horton, a Massachusetts inmate who committed murder while on furlough. Dukakis, as governor, was not directly responsible for the decision to release Horton, but the advertisement and the voters held him accountable, and furloughs became virtually extinct [61].

About 37% of parolees have been committed for a drug offense [62], yet many received no drug treatment. In fact, it is reported that in Texas, 900 offenders were approved for parole in 2006 but remained in prison simply because the release decision included a condition of entering a drug treatment facility, and none were available [63].

Jobs are a key to success on parole, but parolees have major barriers to overcome. Many have very poor job histories and few or no skills. The stigma of being an ex-felon is a tremendous barrier to finding quality employment even if the offender has a marketable skill. Less than half of offenders have a job waiting for them upon release [64]. In fact, one study projects that ex-convicts add about 0.9% to the national unemployment rate. This number continues to grow as more and more prisoners are released and continue to have difficulty finding employment [65]. Issues that must be overcome in order to obtain decent employment in addition to lack of a job history and few skills include drug abuse, lack of transportation, restrictions imposed by parole (i.e., curfews and reporting requirements), statutory exclusions for licenses and certifications, and a lack of socialization to workplace culture. Even after a job is secured, retention is a problem.

Transitional jobs are those that the offender may obtain immediately upon release. These are important even if they provide no long-range future. Such jobs, to be adequate, must be relatively low skilled, with frequent pay periods, providing close supervision and mentoring, perhaps some subsidies to help the parolee begin life on the outside, and some training for more lucrative employment [66]. Some programs operated by community corrections departments meet most of these elements either through a partnership with a private employer or a community work project employing ex-offenders.

In many cases, families are unlikely to be of much assistance to the parolee. In a Texas study, two-thirds of the sample reported that at least one family member had been convicted of a crime. More than a third reported that a family member was currently in prison. Two-thirds reported having a family member with a serious drug or alcohol problem. Most (54%) had children under 18 years old, and 59% of these people had lived with one or more children prior to imprisonment [67].

It may be that prisoners who leave prison underestimate the difficulties they will encounter upon release. In the Texas study, almost 80% believed it would be easy to renew relationships with family, and 82% thought their family would be supportive. About 63% expected to live with family after prison, and about half (54%) expected financial support from their families. Further, 65% who did not have housing lined up thought that it would be easy or very easy to find housing, and 72% thought that it would be easy to stay out of trouble. Fully 84% thought it would be easy to stay out of prison after release, and 81% thought it would be easy to avoid any parole violations. Most also thought it was unlikely that they would commit a crime (87%) or use drugs (81%) [68]. Despite their optimism, parolees indicated they needed education (73%), job training (72%), and financial assistance (73%) [69].

Another study also documented unrealistic optimism from young offenders before release. In this study, interviews with young offenders before release were compared to interviews with young offenders who were revoked on parole. Those who were revoked exhibited a fatalism regarding their return to prison. They admitted that their expectations of release were unrealistic, and led to a letdown after release when practical matters such as jobs and housing overwhelmed them [70].

Civil disabilities refer to rights that are lost or compromised after a criminal conviction. Many disabilities exist, including rights regarding voting, employment, jury service, eligibility to hold public office, and the right to own a firearm. Many states require some criminals to register; for example, every state requires sex offenders to register [71]. Parolees may also be barred from public housing and public assistance. In most states, ex-offenders no longer have the right to vote (14 states permanently take away this right). In fact, only Maine and Vermont have no restrictions on voting by ex-felons. Ex-offenders cannot serve on juries (31 states permanently take away this right) or possess firearms (28 states permanently take away this right). In about half of all states, ex-offenders cannot hold public office, and close to half of all states allow imprisonment to be used as a reason for permanent deprivation of parental rights [72]. You might think that these deprivations are either rightfully withheld from those who broke the law, or that the offender should have thought of this result before they committed the crime, but the opposing argument is that we want the offender to become a productive, law-abiding citizen. If he or she does so, is it fair to withhold all the rights of citizenship indefinitely?

According to Joan Petersilia, the states that have the most exclusionary policies generally are in the south but also include Texas, Arizona, Kansas, and Nebraska. The most inclusive states (with the fewest civil disabilities for returning felons) are generally in the northeast, but also include Indiana, Ohio, Oregon, and Utah [73].

RECIDIVISM AND REVOCATION

Similar to probation officers, a parole officer may file a violation report when a parolee violates any of the conditions of his or her parole and/or commits a new crime. These reports go to the paroling authority, rather than the sentencing judge, and the revocation hearing will be conducted by parole board members or, in some states, hearing officers who have been given the power invested in the paroling authority. Parole board members or these hearing officers have the power to change conditions or revoke parole and send the offender back to prison. In the federal system, recall that parole has been abolished. However, there is a mandatory period of postrelease supervision, and federal offenders who violate the supervision conditions will go before their sentencing judge. In this case, it is a judicial proceeding to determine whether revocation and a return to prison are warranted.

As discussed earlier, a prison inmate has no right to parole and no rights to any particular due process elements in a parole release hearing, unless such rights are created by the state. However, once parole has been granted, the Supreme

Court has recognized it as a protected liberty interest and due process applies before parole can be revoked. In *Morrissey v. Brewer* [74], the Court held that the following elements must be granted before parole revocation:

- Bifurcated hearing (preliminary and full hearing) [75]
- Written notice of parole violation
- Disclosure to parolee of evidence against him
- Opportunity to be heard in person and to present witnesses and documentary evidence
- Conditional right to confront and cross-examine (denied if there is reason to keep identity of witnesses secret, such as police informers)
- Neutral and detached hearing body
- Written statement of fact finders as to evidence against and reasons for decision

This court decision led to a dramatic change in the way some states operated their parole system. It required parole officers to participate in revocation hearings held by parole board members or specially hired hearing officers. Generally, the preliminary hearing should take place where the parolee is located at the time of the violation. Many offenders waive the preliminary hearing, and the full revocation hearing is often located in the prison after the offender is sent back. In another case, the Supreme Court held that Oklahoma's "preparole" status was equivalent to parole and, therefore, *Morrissey v. Brewer's* due process analysis applied when the state sought to deprive the preparole participants of their liberty [76].

When an offender is revoked and sent back to prison, it used to be the case that the years spent on parole did not count as part of the sentence; therefore, an offender could have served 5 years of a 10-year term, been paroled, spent 4 years on parole and then be revoked and sent back to prison with 5 years remaining on his sentence. Now, many states have statutory restrictions on how long an offender can be returned to prison—for instance, in Georgia, the maximum amount of time is two years [77].

The parole revocation hearing is described as an administrative or a quasi-judicial hearing and, therefore, the due process protections that an individual would have in a criminal trial do not exist. As stated earlier, there is no right to counsel and the right to cross-examine is conditional. Further, some courts have held that the exclusionary rule does not apply. This means that even if evidence obtained through an illegal search could not be used to prosecute new charges, it can be used in a parole revocation hearing [78].

It is a sad fact that there is a high failure rate on parole. Revocation occurs either because of a new crime or for **technical violations** (which are not crimes but simply rule violations). According to a 2002 Bureau of Justice

Statistics study, two-thirds of parolees are rearrested within three years of release. In this study, one in three were arrested in the first six months, and 44% in the first year. This study showed that property offenders were most likely to recidivate (about three-quarters) compared to two-thirds of drug offenders and 62% of public order and violent criminals [79].

In this study, the Bureau of Justice Statistics tracked ex-prisoners in three states in 1984 for three years after their release and then did the same thing for a new sample of ex-prisoners in 1994. They found that for all crime categories, more of them were rearrested within three years of release in 1994 than in 1984. About 68% of the ex-prisoners were rearrested in 1994, an increase from the 63% in 1984. Property offenders were more likely to be rearrested than any other category of criminal, although drug and public order offenders showed the largest increases in recidivism, when comparing the 1984 and 1994 samples. Interestingly, while arrest figures had increased, reconviction numbers did not, except for drug offenders, which increased significantly. This study showed that more than half of the releasees (51.8%) were returned to prison within three years, either because of a new crime or a technical violation of parole [80].

In 2004, the Bureau of Justice Statistics analyzed nonviolent offenders who were released from prison on parole [81]. Nonviolent offenders included property, drug, and public order offenses. From their study, we learn the following:

- About three out of four inmates leaving state prisons had been convicted of a nonviolent crime. Property offenders and drug offenders each accounted for about a third of those exiting prisons.
- The single largest offense category was drug trafficking (one in five nonviolent releases).
- Nine out of 10 parolees were men.
- Two-thirds of parolees were racial minorities.
- Four in 10 had less than high school education.
- Two-thirds said they had been using illegal drugs in months leading up to prison.
- About one-quarter were alcohol dependent prior to imprisonment.
- One-third were using alcohol at the time of the offense.
- About 95% had an arrest history and 80% had at least one prior conviction.
- About one-third had been arrested for a violent offense. They had served an average of a third of their sentence.
- Sixty-four percent had committed their current offense while on parole, probation, or escape.
- Seven in 10 were rearrested within three years, half were reconvicted, and a quarter returned to prison.
- One in five was rearrested for a violent crime [82].

The results from this study suggest that the bulk of offenders released from prison will recidivate, but not all return to prison.

In 2001, about 37% of all admissions to prison nationwide were for parole revocations [83]. As mentioned earlier, about a third of new prison admissions today are parolees who have had their parole revoked. In 1997, about three out of five parolees who were revoked were sent back for technical violations, not new crimes [84]. In a study of parole releases and revocations in Tennessee, it was found that cohorts who were released between 1993 and 1999 experienced increasing likelihoods of being returned to prison on technical violations rather than new charges. About 40% of the 1993 cohort were returned to prison after two years of release and about 63% of those returns were for technical violations. The 1997 cohort had a higher percentage of revocations (about 48%) and of those, a higher percentage were revoked for technical violations (about 77%). The 1999 cohort had a lower rate of revocations (40% again), but the percentage of technical violations remained at 79% of the total who were revoked [85].

The large number of returns based on technical violations seems to indicate that the revocation process may be too harsh and intermediate community sanctions should be used because the violations are not necessarily new crimes; however, it may be the case that prosecutors are urging parole authorities to use revocations in lieu of new charges and prosecutions. If an offender is going back to prison anyway, new charges and a new sentence may be redundant. There is no way to know whether technical violations are overused, or used in lieu of new charges, without further research.

Women are less likely to fail on parole than men. In a study of Boston female parolees, community service referrals were correlated with lower recidivism. In a two year follow-up, those who completed community programs in employment, drug treatment, and other social service programs were significantly less likely to recidivate. The study found that one-third of the women did not recidivate, another third had a low violation level, and the last third had a high violation level. Those who were least likely to recidivate included older women, minorities, those with few or no children, and those who had committed a personal offense with a low number of prior arrests [86].

Some programs report recidivism of women at 3.2% to 13% after two years [87]. However, national statistics are much higher. According to the Bureau of Justice Statistics, about 45% of female parolees were returned to prison or had absconded. National statistics indicate that probably the most significant factor in recidivism is having a prior arrest history. While only 21% of the women with only one prior arrest recidivated, nearly 8 in 10 of those with 11 or more priors were rearrested. Those who had employment and stable living arrangements were more likely to succeed on parole [88].

One study reported on the types of needs identified at intake from a sample of 546 female parolees. Researchers found that if a female parolee was employed, had stable living arrangements, and was assessed as needing and receiving some type of drug and/or alcohol program intervention, she was less likely to fail on parole. The study found that many female parolees had drug and alcohol treatment needs, as well as employment, housing, and other needs that were not assessed or addressed. The authors speculate that parole is more custodial than treatment oriented, and point out that these needs are associated with failure on parole; therefore, they should be addressed [89].

Factors associated with failure

A number of studies have looked at what factors seem to be associated with recidivism while on parole or supervised release. In one study of 167 participants in a "day reporting" program, it was found that the factors associated with success were age (older offenders were more likely to be successful), family responsibilities, and no drug use history. In fact, those with a drug history were three times more likely to fail. Further, offenders with three or more criminal counts and those who received institutional detention were more likely to fail, as were repeat offenders and those with longer sentences [90]. Many studies find that failure is most likely to occur in the first three months of release; therefore, it is recommended that all services be concentrated at the front end of release, in the first three months.

Contrary to what some believe, there is good evidence that some programs can reduce recidivism by as much as 30%. Programs that use cognitive-behavioral content, address drug addiction, and provide extended support in the community have particularly positive results [91]. In a recent study of a prison drug treatment program with an aftercare component, it was found that improving services in the community led to better outcomes for ex-offenders. The researchers showed that creating a network of services for ex-offenders was associated with more successful completion of the aftercare component. They urge that the parole model be adapted to include the utilization of an aftercare plan and clinical case managers who work with parole agents to ensure that releases complete their program. In the last cohort studies, 70% of the participants successfully completed the aftercare component of the program [92].

> **INTERNET KEY**
>
> For more information on reentry and issues related to community corrections, go to the Urban Institute's Justice Policy Center at http://www.urban.org/center/jpc/index.cfm.

Intermediate sanctions are options to use for parolees who violate their parole but not seriously enough to warrant a return to prison. Such sanctions may include loss of privileges, increased reporting, drug tests, curfews, electronic monitoring, and even short stays in a community incarceration facility in some jurisdictions. Graduated sanctions have reduced the returns to prison; for instance, in Georgia, the use of such sanctions helped to increase the successful completion of parole from 61% in 1998 to 72% in 2002 [93]. Other states, such as Washington, have also attempted to reduce their rate of returns to prison by using a type of sentencing grid for parolees that provides for graduated sanctions for technical violations and petty crimes [94].

CONCLUSION

Parole has a long history and is derived from the idea that offenders should be rewarded when they reform their behavior. Unfortunately, it has always been difficult to determine whether their behavior has changed. Parole comprises one-tenth the cost of prison, so it is a cost savings as well as a reward to the offender. Despite the cost savings, however, the use of parole has declined considerably from the 1970s when the majority of inmates were released on parole. The decision to release on parole is made by a paroling authority (typically a parole board); however, only about 15 states still retain full discretionary release. About 14 states have no discretionary release (although there may be a mandatory supervision period after release), and the rest of the states have limited discretionary release (for certain crimes or offenders). Parolees have no due process rights in relation to the release decision; however, after they receive parole, there are due process rights that apply before their parole can be revoked and they can be sent back to prison.

Less than half of all parolees are successfully discharged. High failure rates are associated with parolees who have prior drug histories and criminal records. It should also be noted that it appears that parolees are more likely today to be revoked for technical violations instead of new crimes. Regardless, as long as failure rates remain high, the future of parole is uncertain.

In a national report of parole for state and federal policymakers, the authors advocated the following changes or new directions for parole:

- Reassess risk and need measures
- Enhance the offender's motivation to change through the use of positive rewards and positive interactions with parole officers
- Target the needs of the offender through the concepts of risk, need, and responsivity
- Use cognitive-behavioral programs when appropriate
- Increase the use of positive reinforcements rather than negative
- Provide prosocial supports for offenders
- Measure success and provide feedback to the decision maker [95]

Looking forward, it seems certain that the release process is an important component in reducing correctional costs while maintaining public safety. If more parolees were successfully discharged, prison populations could be reduced, freeing up more of the correctional budget for improved services. Today, the process for all too many offenders seems to be warehousing in prison, releasing, and then returning to prison for technical violations or new crimes.

Review Questions

1. What is the difference between probation and parole? What is the difference between discretionary parole and mandatory supervision?
2. How many people are on parole? What percentage are women? What is the racial/ethnic breakdown? What percentage have committed violent crimes? What percentage successfully complete parole?
3. What are the differences between female and male parolees' problems when returning to the free world?
4. What are the early forerunners of modern parole? Describe them.
5. Why was parole criticized and abandoned in some states?
6. Describe the legal rights of inmates/parolees to due process. Discuss specifically the due process elements identified in *Morrissey v. Brewer*.
7. How many people are returning to the community from prison each year? What are the problems they face?
8. How many parolees are rearrested within three years? What factors are associated with failure on parole?
9. What percentage of prison admittees are parolees who have had their parole revoked? What are intensive parole and intermediate sanctions and how might these be utilized to reduce the numbers returned to prison?
10. What are the suggestions offered to improve parole?

VOCABULARY

actuarial decision decision based on statistics

civil disabilities civil rights that are lost or compromised after a criminal conviction

clinical assessment decision prediction based on personal interview and clinical judgment

indeterminate sentence when the release date is not set by the sentencing judge

intermediate sanctions options short of a return to prison, including loss of privileges, increased reporting, drug tests, curfews, and electronic monitoring

mark system Maconochie's program of stages of increasing responsibility based on good behavior

maxed out serving the full term with no early release

pardon basically a release and forgiveness of criminal culpability

parol (*parole d'honneur*) "word" as in giving one's word of honor

parole guidelines give a presumptive term or guideline for how long the offender should serve in prison before receiving parole, based on offense characteristics and characteristics of the offender

split sentencing and shock incarceration type of sentence involving a short period of incarceration before being supervised in the community by probation officers

technical violations not crimes but simply rule violations

ticket of leave Crofton's plan of early release based on good behavior

transitional jobs those that the offender may obtain immediately upon release and involve certain characteristics, such as frequent pay

transportation punishment of being sent from England to the colonies and, after the American Revolution, to Australia

ENDNOTES

[1] L. Glaze, T. Bonczar, F. Zhang, Probation and Parole in the United States, 2009, Bureau of Justice Statistics, Washington, DC, 2010.

[2] L. Glaze, T. Bonczar, F. Zhang, Probation and Parole in the United States, 2009, Bureau of Justice Statistics, Washington, DC, 2010, p. 33, Table 12.

[3] P. Burke, M. Tonry, Successful Transition and Reentry for Safer Communities: A Call to Action for Parole, Center for Effective Public Policy, Silver Spring, MD, 2006, p. 19.

[4] L. Glaze, T. Bonczar, Probation and Parole in the United States, 2005, Bureau of Justice Statistics, Washington, DC, 2006, p. 8; L. Glaze, T. Bonczar, F. Zhang, Probation and Parole in the United States, 2009, Bureau of Justice Statistics, Washington, DC, 2010, p. 34.

[5] L. Glaze, T. Bonczar, F. Zhang, Probation and Parole in the United States, 2009, Bureau of Justice Statistics, Washington, DC, 2010, p. 36.

[6] T. Hughes, D. Wilson, A. Beck, Trends in State Parole, 1990-2000, Bureau of Justice Statistics, Washington, DC, 2001.

[7] L. Glaze, T. Bonczar, Probation and Parole in the United States, 2008, Bureau of Justice Statistics, Washington, DC, 2009.

[8] L. Greenfield, T. Snell, Women Offenders, Bureau of Justice Statistics, Washington, DC, 2000.

[9] N. LaVigne, V. Kachnowski, Texas Prisoners' Reflections on Returning Home, Urban Institute, Washington, DC, 2005.

[10] E. Ritchie, Challenges incarcerated women face as they return to their communities: findings from life history interviews, Crime Delinq. 47(3) (2001) 368–389.

[11] P. O'Brien, Making It in the "Free World": Women in Transition from Prison, SUNY Albany Press, Albany, NY, 2001.

[12] M. Dodge, M. Pogrebin, Collateral costs of imprisonment for women: complications of reintegration, Prison J. 81(1) (2001) 42–54.

[13] L. Glaze, S. Palla, Probation and Parole in the United States, 2004, Bureau of Justice Statistics, Washington, DC, 2005, p. 9; L. Glaze, T. Bonczar, F. Zhang, Probation and Parole in the United States, 2009, Bureau of Justice Statistics, Washington, DC, 2010, p. 35.

[14] T. Hughes, D. Wilson, A. Beck, Trends in State Parole, 1990-2000, Bureau of Justice Statistics, Washington, DC, 2001, p. 11; L. Glaze, T. Bonczar, Probation and Parole in the United States, 2008, Bureau of Justice Statistics, Washington, DC, 2009, p. 42.

[15] W. Sabol, H. West, M. Cooper, Prisoners in 2008, Bureau of Justice Statistics, Washington, DC, 2009, p. 34.

[16] T. Bonczar, Characteristics of State Parole Supervising Agencies, 2006, Bureau of Justice Statistics, Washington, DC, 2008.

[17] J. Petersilia, Reforming Probation and Parole, American Correctional Association, Lanham, MD, 2002, p. 129.

[18] R. Hughes, The Fatal Shore, Vintage Books, New York, 1986.

[19] H. Barnes, N. Teeters, New Horizons on Criminology, third ed., Englewood Cliffs, NJ, Prentice Hall, 1959.

[20] J. Petersilia, Reforming Probation and Parole, American Correctional Association, Lanham, MD, 2002, p. 130.

[21] D. Rothman, Conscience and Convenience, Little, Brown & Co., Boston, MA, 1980.

[22] J. Petersilia, Reforming Probation and Parole, American Correctional Association, Lanham, MD, 2002.

[23] P. Hoffman, History of the federal parole system: part 2 (1973-1997), Fed. Probat. 61(4) (1997) 49–57.

[24] J. Petersilia, Reforming Probation and Parole, American Correctional Association, Lanham, MD, 2002, p. 131.

[25] J. Petersilia, Reforming Probation and Parole, American Correctional Association, Lanham, MD, 2002, p. 135.

[26] J. Petersilia, Reforming Probation and Parole, American Correctional Association, Lanham, MD, 2002, p. 111.

[27] S. Kinney, J. Caplan, Findings from the APAI International Survey of Releasing Authorities, Center for Research on Youth and Social Policy, Philadelphia, 2008. Available through National Parole Resource Center at www.apaintl.org/documents/surveys/2008.pdf.

[28] P. Burke, M. Tonry, Successful Transition and Reentry for Safer Communities: A Call to Action for Parole, Center for Effective Public Policy, Silver Spring, MD, 2006, p. 22.

[29] J. Petersilia, Reforming Probation and Parole, American Correctional Association, Lanham, MD, 2002, p. 112.

[30] J. Petersilia, Meeting the challenges of prisoner reentry, in: American Correctional Association, What Works and Why: Effective Approaches to Reentry, American Correctional Association, Lanham, MD, 2005, p. 179.

[31] W. Sabol, H. West, M. Cooper, Prisoners in 2008, Bureau of Justice Statistics, Washington, DC, 2009, p. 34.

[32] M. Ward, Parole Rules Aren't Being Followed, Panel Says, Austin American-Statesman, 15, 2006, p. B7.

[33] M. Levin, The Role of Parole in Solving the Texas Prison Crowding Crisis, Texas Public Policy Foundation, Austin, TX, 2006, p. 3. Available at www.TexasPolicy.com 2006.

[34] P. Burke, M. Tonry, Successful Transition and Reentry for Safer Communities: A Call to Action for Parole, Center for Effective Public Policy, Silver Spring, MD, 2006, p. 25.

[35] R. Burns, P. Kinkade, M. Leone, S. Phillips, Perspectives on parole: the board members' viewpoint, Fed. Probat. 63(1) (1999) 16–22.

[36] P. Burke, M. Tonry, Successful Transition and Reentry for Safer Communities: A Call to Action for Parole, Center for Effective Public Policy, Silver Spring, MD, 2006, p. 25.

[37] K. Morgan, B. Smith, Victims, punishment and parole: the effect of victim participation on parole hearings, Criminol. Public Pol. 4(2) (2005) 333–360.

[38] S. Manchak, J. Skeem, K. Douglas, Utility of the revised level of service inventory (LSI-R) in predicting recidivism after long-term incarceration, Law Hum. Behav. 32 (2008) 477–488.

[39] Greenholtz, Chairman, Board of parole of Nebraska, et al. v. Inmates of the Nebraska Penal and Correctional Complex, 442 U.S. 1 1979.

[40] Note that states may "create" a right by statutory language, that is, in Board of Pardons et al. v. Allen et al., 482 U.S. 369 (1987), the use of the word "shall" in the enabling statute created a parole right that was then deemed to be a protected liberty interest.

[41] Martinez v. California, 444 U.S. 277 (1980).

[42] See, for example, Mee v. Ortega, 967 F.2d 423 (10th Cir. 1992).

[43] M. Jones, Community Corrections, Waveland Press, Prospect Heights, IL, 2004.

[44] J. Travis, J. Petersilia, Reentry reconsidered: a new look at an old question, Crime Delinq. 47(3) (2003) 3–15.

[45] S. Kinney, J. Caplan, Findings from the APAI International Survey of Releasing Authorities, Center for Research on Youth and Social Policy, Philadelphia, 2008, p. 2. Available through the National Parole Resource Center at www.apaintl.org/documents/surveys/2008.pdf.

[46] J. Petersilia, Reforming Probation and Parole, American Correctional Association, Lanham, MD, 2002, p. 158.

[47] Reentry Council, Report of the Re-entry Policy Council, Council of State Governments, New York, 2003, p. 362. Available at www.reentrypolicy.org.

[48] Reentry Council, Report of the Re-Entry Policy Council, Council of State Governments, New York, 2003, p. 360. Available at www.reentrypolicy.org.

[49] J. Watson, A. Solomon, N. LaVigne, J. Travis, A Portrait of Prisoner Reentry in Texas, Urban Institute, Washington, DC, 2004, p. 76.

[50] J. Austin, T. Fabelo, The Diminishing Returns of Increased Incarceration: A Blueprint to Improve Public Safety and Reduce Costs, JFA Institute, Washington, DC, 2004.

[51] J. Petersilia, Reforming Probation and Parole, American Correctional Association, Lanham, MD, 2002, p. 154.

[52] J. Petersilia, Meeting the challenges of prisoner reentry, in: American Correctional Association, What Works and Why: Effective Approaches to Reentry, American Correctional Association, Lanham, MD, 2005, p. 178.

[53] J. Watson, A. Solomon, N. LaVigne, J. Travis, A Portrait of Prisoner Reentry in Texas, Urban Institute, Washington, DC, 2004, p. 21.

[54] D. LeClair, S. Guarino-Ghezzi, Does incapacitation guarantee public safety? Lessons from the Massachusetts furlough and prerelease programs, Justice Q. 8(1) (1991) 9–36.

[55] J. Petersilia, Meeting the challenges of prisoner reentry, in: American Correctional Association, What Works and Why: Effective Approaches to Reentry, American Correctional Association, Lanham, MD, 2005, p. 176.

[56] N. LaVigne, V. Kachnowski, Texas Prisoners' Reflections on Returning Home, Urban Institute, Washington, DC, 2005.

[57] Reentry Council, Report of the Re-entry Policy Council, Council of State Governments, New York, 2003, p. 1. Available at www.reentrypolicy.org.

[58] J. Petersilia, Reforming Probation and Parole, American Correctional Association, Lanham, MD, 2002.

[59] J. Austin, Prisoner reentry: current trends, practices and issues, Crime Delinq. 47(3) (2001) 314–334.

[60] J. Petersilia, Meeting the challenges of prisoner reentry, in: American Correctional Association, What Works and Why: Effective Approaches to Reentry, American Correctional Association, Lanham, MD, 2005, p. 176.

[61] B. Feld, The politics of race and juvenile justice: the "due process revolution" and the conservative reaction, Justice Q. 20(4) (2003) p. 791.

[62] L. Glaze, T. Bonczar, Probation and Parole in the United States, 2005, Bureau of Justice Statistics, Washington, DC, 2006, p. 9.

[63] M. Ward, Parole Rules Aren't Being Followed, Panel Says, Austin American-Statesman, 15, 2006, p. B7.

[64] Reentry Council, Report of the Re-entry Policy Council, Council of State Governments, New York, 2003, p. 384. Available at www.reentrypolicy.org.

[65] J. Schmitt, K. Warner, Ex-offenders and the Labor Market, Center for Economic and Policy Research, Washington, DC, 2010.

[66] Reentry Council, Report of the Re-entry Policy Council, Council of State Governments, New York, 2003, p. 362. Available at www.reentrypolicy.org.

[67] N. LaVigne, V. Kachnowski, Texas Prisoners' Reflections on Returning Home, Urban Institute, Washington, DC, 2005.

[68] N. LaVigne, V. Kachnowski, Texas Prisoners' Reflections on Returning Home, Urban Institute, Washington, DC, 2005, p. 6.

[69] N. LaVigne, V. Kachnowski, Texas Prisoners' Reflections on Returning Home, Urban Institute, Washington, DC, 2005, p. 7.

[70] K. Hanrahan, J. Gibbs, S. Zimmerman, Parole and revocation: perspectives of young adult offenders, Prison J. 85(3) (2005) 251–269.

[71] J. Petersilia, Reforming Probation and Parole, American Correctional Association, Lanham, MD, 2002, p. 163.

[72] C. Hemmens, The collateral consequences of conviction, Perspectives 25(1) (2001) 12–13.

[73] J. Petersilia, Meeting the challenges of prisoner reentry, in: American Correctional Association, What Works and Why: Effective Approaches to Reentry, American Correctional Association, Lanham, MD, 2005, p. 182.

[74] 408 U.S. 471 (1972).

[75] While earlier analyses of this case concluded the court meant that two hearings were required, later writers and some lower court holdings have determined that there can be one hearing as long as all elements are present. See R. del Carmen, S. Ritter, B. Witt, Briefs of Leading Cases in Corrections, LexisNexis/Matthew Bender, Newark, NJ, 2005, p. 176.

[76] Young v. Harper, 520 U.S. 143 (1997).

[77] M. Jones, Community Corrections, Waveland Press, Prospect Heights, IL, 2004.

[78] Pennsylvania Board of Probation and Parole v. Scott, 524 U.S. 357 (1998).

[79] P. Langan, D. Levine, Recidivism of Prisoners Released in 1994, Bureau of Justice Statistics, Washington, DC, 2002. See also A. Solomon, V. Kachnowski, A. Bhati, Does Parole Work? Analyzing the Impact of Post-Prison Supervision and Rearrest Outcomes, Research Report, Urban Institute, Washington, DC, 2005.

[80] Bureau of Justice Statistics. Retrieved 1/10/2006 from http://www.ojp.usdoj.gov/bjs/reentry/recidivism.htm.

[81] M. Ducrose, C. Mumola, BJS Fact Sheet: Profile of Nonviolent Offenders Exiting State Prisons, U.S. Department of Justice, Washington, DC, 2004.

[82] M. Ducrose, C. Mumola, BJS Fact Sheet: Profile of Nonviolent Offenders Exiting State Prisons, U.S. Department of Justice, Washington, DC, 2004.

[83] P. Burke, M. Tonry, Successful Transition and Reentry for Safer Communities: A Call to Action for Parole, Center for Effective Public Policy, Silver Spring, MD, 2006, p. 14.

[84] Reported in Reentry Council, Report of the Re-entry Policy Council, Council of State Governments, New York, 2003, p. 391. Available at www.reentrypolicy.org.

[85] J. Wilson, Bad behavior or bad policy? An examination of Tennessee release cohorts, 1993-2001, Criminol. Public Pol. 4(3) (2005) 485–519.

[86] N. Pearl, Use of community-based social services to reduce recidivism in female parolees, Women Crim. Just. 10(1) (1998) 27–52.

[87] D. Prichard, Project reconnect responds to women offenders on a personal level, in: National Institute of Corrections, Topics in Community Corrections: Responding to Women Offenders in the Community, NIC Information Services, Longmont, CO, 2000, pp. 26–31.

[88] L. Greenfield, T. Snell, Women Offenders, Bureau of Justice Statistics, Washington, DC, 2000.

[89] P. Schram, B. Koons-Witt, F. Williams, Supervision strategies and approaches for female parolees: examining the link between unmet needs and parolee outcome, Crime Delinq. 52(3) (2006) 450–471.

[90] S. Roy, Factors related to success and recidivism in a day reporting center, Crim. Just. Stud. 17(1) (2004) 3–17.

[91] P. Burke, M. Tonry, Successful Transition and Reentry for Safer Communities: A Call to Action for Parole, Center for Effective Public Policy, Silver Spring, MD, 2006, p. 15.

[92] D. Olson, J. Rozhon, M. Powers, Enhancing prisoner reentry through access to prison-based and post-incarceration aftercare treatment: experiences from the Illinois Sheridan correctional center therapeutic community, J. Exp. Criminol. 5 (2009) 299–321.

[93] Reentry Council, Report of the Re-entry Policy Council, Council of State Governments, New York, 2003, p. 392. Available at www.reentrypolicy.org.

[94] Reentry Council, Report of the Re-entry Policy Council, Council of State Governments, New York, 2003, p. 395. Available at www.reentrypolicy.org.

[95] P. Burke, M. Tonry, Successful Transition and Reentry for Safer Communities: A Call to Action for Parole, Center for Effective Public Policy, Silver Spring, MD, 2006, pp. 17–18.

CHAPTER 15

Looking toward the Future: Criminal Justice in the Twenty-First Century

WHAT YOU NEED TO KNOW

- Crime has declined but is starting to inch upward again.
- The community has always been identified as a factor in criminal choice.
- Social disorganization theory is not unlike the Chicago or the ecological school idea that crime was localized in distressed neighborhoods.
- Restorative justice programs include victim-offender mediation, community reparation boards, family conferences, and circle sentencing.
- The Department of Homeland Security has a budget of more than $50 billion. It includes all or part of the Federal Bureau of Investigation, Customs, Border Patrol, and 19 other agencies.

CONTENTS

What is the future of criminal justice in our country? Of course, it is impossible to accurately predict what may occur in the future, but it is important to ponder the possibilities and prepare for them. In this last chapter, we will take the time to look forward. It should be clear that the criminal justice system is a massive, multifaceted, nonorganization of police, courts, and corrections across 50 states and the federal government. It affects literally millions of individuals in this country. Change is unlikely to be systemic or coordinated. On the other hand, we can identify trends and the possible directions that might be taken by the many different agencies that make up the system of criminal justice. In this final chapter, some thoughts are offered about the challenges and opportunities that lie ahead.

CHALLENGES AND OPPORTUNITIES

Crime has dramatically decreased since the early 1990s—so much so that homicide rates are at 30-year lows, and all forms of personal and property crimes have decreased to levels not seen since the 1970s. Violent crime declined from a high of 758 crimes per 100,000 in 1991 to a low of 429.4 in 2009. The violent crime rate in 2009 was about the same as reported in 1973.

Even so, it seems that citizens are not aware of this good news because media outlets tend to emphasize violent crimes disproportionately to their prevalence. Television reality "cop shows," court shows, prime-time dramas, and even the mainstream news outlets focus on violent crimes and obscure the reality that crime may not be the major social problem that people think it is.

In the last few reporting periods, we have seen a slight rise in crime, certainly in some reporting jurisdictions and for some crimes. This may be a troubling harbinger of things to come. One of the clear issues of the day is what to do about the 700,000 individuals released from prison each year, many of whom have been in prison since the early and mid-1980s. These individuals have served long periods of time, decades even, without any meaningful programs to help them conquer addictions and adapt to their freedom on the street. Due to the economic meltdown in 2007, unemployment is at a historic high of almost 10%. It is estimated that ex-felons contribute almost 1% to this unemployment rate. Difficult as it is for anyone to find a job in these trying times, the difficulty is multiplied many times over when one is an ex-offender. Perhaps crime is now beginning a slight upward trend because of the economy and unemployment. We will need to watch carefully to track whether crime rates will continue to rise.

As reported in earlier chapters of this book, crime is at a 30-year low in some categories, yet the expenditures related to criminal justice keep increasing. Today, we spend about $70 billion just for state expenditures as compared to less than $11 billion in 1982. States spend more for criminal justice than they do for education or health and human services. In fiscal year 2006, federal, state, and local governments spent about $214 billion for police protection, corrections, and judicial and legal activities. It is estimated that criminal justice functions cost every person in the United States well over $600.00 per year [1]. The current rate of increase cannot be sustained, especially as some states face billion-dollar deficits and all states are struggling with reduced budgets.

The lower crime rate offers the *opportunity* to think seriously about how to reduce criminal justice expenditures. The *challenge* is to overcome political pressure to demonize offenders as a way to attract voters or because of vested interests. It is no surprise, for instance, why the correctional officer union in California opposed legislative changes to the three-strikes bill that would reduce the number of inmates serving long sentences or, indeed, any legislation that would reduce prison populations; or why prison workers march on state capitals and call their state legislators when there is any talk of closing prisons. People need jobs, but what is important to understand is that the monies spent on bars and guards could be spent instead on education, social services, and public infrastructure like roads and bridges. These areas are losing jobs because of state budget deficits and rising costs associated with incarceration.

We have, throughout this book, concentrated primarily on domestic crime and state and local responses to it. However, since 9/11, it seems clear that the United States cannot ignore the possibility of future terrorist attacks. The response to terrorism must be a shared effort among all levels of law enforcement and public safety. Just as the first responders to the World Trade Towers tragedy were New York City police officers and firefighters, in any terrorist plot, police play an integral role in both response and prevention. The *opportunity* of new technologies aiding in such efforts is exciting—GPS, satellites, computers, and other technological advances can be and are used to track, investigate, and capture terrorists both within and outside our borders. The *challenge* is to make sure that local and federal agencies work together seamlessly to prevent future attacks. At the same time, such efforts must not violate the due process rights that are cherished as the essence of our nation's heritage.

A police officer adjusts his face mask as he walks away from debris near the site of the World Trade Center, Wednesday, September 12, 2001 in New York. Two hijacked airliners crashed into the towers on Tuesday, September 11, destroying both buildings. *AP Photo/ Richard Drew*

In thinking about the problem of crime, we are in a new era where crime is both a community issue and also occurs on a worldwide platform. It cannot be ignored that crime fighters in the United States must pay attention to criminal enterprises that go beyond our borders. In addition to Al Qaeda and other terrorist organizations that have targeted and will continue to target the United States, law enforcement in this country must deal with narcoterrorism, drug cartels, worldwide money laundering and other financial crimes, corporate criminality on a worldwide scale, and human trafficking. Each of these areas requires cooperation and involvement with Interpol and foreign law enforcement agencies. As stated before, it is also important for the law enforcement and investigative agencies in the United States to work together. It is indeed a small world and the problems of Mexico or Somalia quickly become our problems as well.

CRIME AS A COMMUNITY PROBLEM

For the last couple of decades, a more community-oriented view of the causes of crime, prevention, and enforcement has developed. Such things as community policing, community courts, reentry programs, and restorative justice all have the basic theme that crime is a community problem and any solution to it must be found in the community.

There is a long history in criminology of looking at the community as criminogenic. Recall from an earlier chapter that the ecological or Chicago school of crime theory discovered that high crime rates existed in mixed zones, which are areas of the city where the functions of retail, residential, and commerce were mixed. These researchers further discovered that the **mixed zones** also were likely to display high levels of other social ills, such as alcoholism and mental illness, in addition to crime. Further, indicators such as graffiti, abandoned houses, vandalism, and low levels of homeownership characterized the zone [2]. The Chicago school approach led to 60 years of attempting to more closely describe in what way the community and/or the residents within the community influenced the individual to commit crime.

Social disorganization theory today continues this theoretical thread, and theorists such as Robert Sampson postulate that indicators of social disorganization, such as lack of social "capital," are also indicators of high crime [3]. A strong community can prevent criminal behavior. The following quote describes this idea:

> When multiple members of a community act for each other's benefit, an overarching sense of good will and community spirit develops. When there are patterns of such reciprocity, a sense of community capital emerges, and this capital can reap strong returns in reducing crime and establishing standards of conduct among its members ... even in impoverished, inner city neighborhoods, social capital can suppress criminal activity [4].

Others, such as Robert Bursik and Harold Grasmick, also examine the informal controls on an individual that come from family, school, church, and neighborhood. They argue that formal controls, such as police, tend to undercut these more personal controls [5].

The influence of the community on crime is recognized by such efforts as community policing. The idea behind this innovation was that the community itself needed to be involved, and police officers could strengthen community resolve to conquer crime by acting as facilitators and resource mediators. Even community policing efforts become complicated, however, when attempts are made to draw the boundaries of good and bad, offender and victim, too simplistically. Some researchers note that community residents express mixed feelings toward the gang members whom the criminal justice system targets as offenders. In one sense, these youths are the problem because they create crime and scare away business development. In another sense, however, they are the community, because they are the sons and brothers of residents [6].

Criminogenic communities have more comprehensive and pervasive social problems. Typically, the communities that offenders come from and go home to are characterized by longstanding poverty from lack of jobs and business development. Schools underperform and drop-out rates are high. The residents are heavy users of government services. In fact, in a justice mapping research project in New Orleans (before Hurricane Katrina), it was found that there existed "million dollar blocks." These were areas of the city where more than a million dollars was spent incarcerating, returning, and revoking offenders from that street. Further, there is a substantial overlap between neighborhoods that are recipients of TANF (Temporary Assistance to Needy Families) and those who receive a disproportionate share of offenders (released on parole or probation) [7]. Obviously, the best approach to the "crime problem" is to deal with the community's needs as a whole. For instance, all residents could benefit from revitalization efforts, and these efforts would also provide alternatives to criminal opportunities.

More generally, research is beginning to show that the huge increase in incarceration that occurred since the 1980s has not necessarily been helpful to the communities hardest hit by crime. Todd Clear and his associates found that a **"tipping effect"** occurred at high rates of imprisonment where imprisonment seemed to result in more crime in certain communities. Positive effects of incarceration included removal of problem family members and reducing the number of dangerous individuals in the community, but negative effects also occurred. In fact, there was an apparent increase of crime in the neighborhoods that experienced high incarceration rates [8].

Further study with focus groups indicated that community members saw incarceration as both a positive force and a negative force in the community. Negative elements included the stigma attached to returning offenders for the offender and his or her family, the financial impact of imprisonment for both the offender and his or her family, and the difficulty of maintaining interpersonal relationships through a prison sentence. High levels of incarceration reduce the number of potentially positive role models for children, result in transient populations, and affect the ability of the community to control its members through informal and affective ties [9].

It appears that incarceration has mixed effects. It reduces crime by the removal of criminal offenders; on the other hand, if a community experiences high levels of incarceration, it increases social mobility and social disorganization, and weakens the ability of the community to utilize parochial methods of control [10]. The best policy recommendations based on the above research include limited incarceration and enriched services to the communities that experience moderate to high rates of incarceration. The community should be helped to reach a point where it can control its members through informal private means of control.

It cannot be ignored that prisoners almost always eventually get out and return to the community. Recently, there has been attention to the issue of the 700,000 prisoners who are released to the community each year. Community efforts are seen as essential in responding to the problem of huge numbers of prisoners being released. Because they will be returning to communities, these communities must be involved in efforts to help ex-offenders adapt and become productive citizens. Reentry efforts have included job training/placement, drug treatment, and housing assistance, as these are identified as the major problems of those released from prison.

The following quote is from the report of the Reentry Policy Council, a bipartisan agency that brings together federal, state, and local representatives, as well as representatives from institutional corrections, community corrections, and law enforcement, to address the problems of reentry for criminal offenders.

> Although the re-entry phenomenon is currently understood as a criminal justice issue, solutions to the challenges that are posed by so many people returning to their neighborhoods from prison cannot be found within the justice system alone. Instead, these solutions will require a coordinated effort among a range of actors stretching from state officials to neighborhood associations [11].

Restorative justice programs

Restorative justice programs are an example of crime being seen and dealt with as a community issue. These programs basically change the paradigm of the justice system. Instead of finding guilt or innocence and inflicting punishment, restorative justice seeks to "restore" all individuals to a state of wholeness. While this may involve restitution to the victim or some form of compensation in response to injury or loss, the approach also takes into consideration the relative needs of the victim and offender. Community members are also involved to help resolve the issues that led to the criminal event. Restorative justice efforts, in effect, reduce the need for reentry programs because, in many cases, the offender never leaves the community. Without banishment to state prison or county jail, there is no reentry difficulty.

Many different types of programs fall under the restorative justice umbrella, but they all have in common the idea of doing more than simply punishing the offender. The roots of restorative justice go back as far as Roman or Grecian law, based on repayment to the victim rather than punishment of the offender [12]. In the 1960s and 1970s, during the rehabilitative and reintegration era, restorative justice programs were popular and fit in with the community empowerment and grassroots model of President Johnson's War on Poverty. Box 15.1 presents some of the ideas of restorative justice.

BOX 15.1 RESTORATIVE JUSTICE

- The process of justice employs local leadership, is informal, and invites participation from community members.
- The goal is to repair the harm done to a community member by another community member in a way that will restore the health of the community relationship.

- The authority of the justice is through the customs and traditions accepted by all members.

Source: *F. Schweigert, Moral and Philosophical Foundations of Restorative Justice, in: J. Perry (Ed.), Repairing Communities through Restorative Justice, American Correctional Association, Lanham, MD, 2002, p. 25.*

Four types of restorative justice models related to criminal justice sentencing and corrections are:

1. *Victim-offender mediation.* This is the most common and is more than 20 years old. Some programs are called victim-offender reconciliation programs or dialog programs. There are more than 320 programs in the United States and many more in Europe. They involve the victim and offender meeting and discussing the event and coming to an agreement about restitution and reparation. The idea is to promote healing on the part of the victim and responsibility on the part of the offender. The program may be implemented as a diversion from prosecution or as a condition of probation. Research has found that victims are more satisfied when they have an opportunity to go through these programs (79% compared to 57%). Victims were also significantly less fearful of being victimized. Offenders were more likely to complete their restitution and recidivism was lower for those who went through mediation as compared to traditional sentencing.

2. *Community reparative boards.* This model has been more common in the juvenile system and has been in use since the 1920s. It re-emerged with greater popularity in the 1990s and may be called youth panels, neighborhood boards, or community diversion boards. The goals of the program are to promote citizen ownership of the sentencing process, and provide an opportunity for victims and community members to confront the offender in a constructive manner. The idea is also to reduce dependence on formal justice processing. Basically, citizens are involved in a sentencing decision and the experience is more of a dialogue between the offender and the board, who look at long-term solutions rather than retribution.

3. *Family group conferencing.* This type of program comes directly from the dispute resolution tradition of the Maori. In fact, it was adopted into national legislation in New Zealand in 1989. A similar model is taken from the Wagga Wagga people of South Australia and uses police officials to administer the conferencing. In these models, police (or another agency) set up a family

conference of the offender, victim, and the families of both, as well as others involved. The goal is to have everyone participate, to have the offender come to a greater understanding of how the crime affected others, and to allow others to help make sure that the collective decision is carried out. Participants generally report higher levels of satisfaction than those who go through traditional justice models.

4. *Circle sentencing.* This model is an updated version of tribal justice processes of North American indigenous peoples and is very similar to the models mentioned earlier. The key elements are that everyone involved with the victim and the offender participates. In this model, they sit in a circle and everyone gets an opportunity to speak. After everyone has a chance to speak, the circle decides what should be done. The goal is to promote healing, to provide the offender an opportunity to make amends, to address the underlying causes of criminal behavior, to build a sense of community, and to promote and share community values [13].

EXERCISE: IN THE STATE OF...

Do a computer search to discover if there are any restorative justice programs in your state. If they exist, where are they? Which type of program exists?

There are criticisms and potential problems with the restorative justice concept. Some argue that it is not an appropriate response for serious violent crimes. Some argue that victims may not want to participate, or that they may feel pressured to forgive the offender or feel "ganged up" on by the offender's family and friends [14]. Generally, however, research indicates that victims are more satisfied when the focus is on their needs and when the offender takes responsibility for and makes right the offense.

Although restorative justice programs received a great deal of attention and even federal funding in the mid through late 1990s, after 9/11, federal dollars were shifted to other priorities. Restorative justice programs haven't gone away, but they tend to be localized and are more common with juvenile offenders than adult offenders. Similarly, as discussed in earlier chapters, community policing has also become less emphasized across the country and federal funding has disappeared in favor of other programs. Community courts still seem to be popular and the number of drug courts, family violence courts, and even veterans' courts continues to grow. At this point, however, the role of the community in addressing crime prevention and reentry problems seems to be underutilized.

CRIME AS A WORLD PROBLEM

September 11, 2001, will take its place in United States history beside such tragedies as the bombing of Pearl Harbor. The effects of this tragedy cannot be underestimated. In addition to the loss of lives, we must also consider the psychological effects of fear, the crippling costs of military efforts in Afghanistan and Iraq, and the continuing costs of protection here at home, including costs associated with TSA and the Department of Homeland Security.

The governmental response to the threat of terrorism within the boundaries of the country has dramatically reshaped the organization and the mission of federal law enforcement. It has also created new questions for the courts to resolve and pitted federal courts against the executive branch in arguments regarding torture, renditions, executive privilege, wiretapping, civil liberties, and the security classification of government documents. Fear of crime has now been eclipsed by fear of terrorism, and new legal and ethical questions regarding the appropriate response to this threat have taken center stage in national debates.

Terrorism, whether domestic or with international elements, has been present from the beginning of this country's history, and so, too, have been government efforts to combat it. In earlier decades, communism was the enemy and the target of government investigation and suppression efforts. The first Alien and Sedition Acts were passed a mere 22 years after the birth of the United States, in 1798. The Alien Act gave the government the right to deport those thought to be a danger to the country, and the Sedition Act gave the government the right to punish those who spoke against the government's actions. These Acts were criticized by many prominent individuals as being contrary to the First Amendment and eventually disappeared; however, the Bolshevik bombings and advocacy of communism led to the Espionage Act of 1917 and the 1918 **Sedition Act**. The United States government, fearful that Russian immigrants would import their revolution as well, had thousands arrested. Under the Sedition Act, anyone who expressed support for communism could be arrested. Attorney General Palmer arrested 16,000 Soviet resident aliens in 1918 and 1919, and detained them without charges and without trial.

The government targeted emerging labor unions, especially the Industrial Workers of the World movement, as threats to the nation, and widespread violence occurred on both sides. The fear and official reaction to the Bolsheviks reached a high pitch at the anniversary of the Russian revolution on November 7, 1919. The fear that they would begin a major assault on that day never materialized [15].

The next chapter in the government's campaign against communism was carried out by Palmer's assistant, J. Edgar Hoover, who was appointed in 1924 and rose to prominence as director of the FBI. His continued investigation of communists eventually led to the McCarthy hearings (House Un-American Activities Committee) in the 1950s. Throughout the 1960s and 1970s, the FBI continued to infiltrate and investigate groups and individuals that were considered threats to the nation. At one point, Hoover had a card index of 450,000 people who were identified or suspected of having left-wing political views [16].

It should be noted that there have been violent groups that did advocate and use violence, such as the Symbionese Liberation Army, which utilized kidnapping and robberies, and the Black Panthers, who used armed robbery and hijacking to advance their cause. However, the focus of investigations carried out by the government also included those who did not pose a danger to the government, such as Martin Luther King Jr., Hollywood actors who espoused liberal views, and student and community groups that advocated nonviolent means of protest.

It was the abuses of the powers granted by antiterrorist legislation, as well as the misuse of government intelligence, by those in the Nixon administration, that led to Congress dramatically curtailing the powers of federal law enforcement in the 1970s. The Senate created the Select Committee on Intelligence in 1976 and strengthened the Freedom of Information Act. In 1978, the Foreign Intelligence Surveillance Act (FISA) was created and it mandated procedures for requesting authorization for surveillance. A secret court was created (the Foreign Intelligence Surveillance Court—FISC), which consisted of seven federal district court judges appointed by the Supreme Court's Chief Justice. Federal law enforcement officers were required to obtain permission from the court to conduct surveillance. They had to show that their target was an agent of a foreign power and information was in furtherance of counterintelligence. FISA originally approved only electronic eavesdropping and wiretapping, but was amended in 1994 to include covert physical entries, and later in 1998 to permit "pen/trap" orders and business records [17].

Typical search warrants are obtained only on a showing of probable cause that the target of the search will be found in the location specified, and that it is evidence or an instrumentality of a crime. On the other hand, FISA court approval may be obtained merely upon a showing that the target is a foreign power or agent and the search is relevant to a counterintelligence investigation. If the target is a U.S. citizen, there must be probable cause that their activities may involve espionage [18].

After the Cold War ended, the United States shifted its attention to right-wing radical groups in this country that advocated violent means to oppose the government and, to a lesser extent, international groups, such as the PLO. Hamas and Hezbollah later became targets after they claimed responsibility for violent attacks and spoke out against the United States. Through the 1980s and

1990s, the activities and the rhetoric of such groups became more and more anti-American and many analysts argued that the United States, in addition to Israel, was or would become a central target of terrorist actions.

The government did not sit idle, of course. President Reagan utilized national security decision directives rather than Congress to craft and employ a government response to the growing international threats. These directives established a hierarchy of authority regarding response to threats via aviation and kidnapping. Public laws were also passed, including:

- Act to Combat International Terrorism (1984), which sought international cooperation
- Public Law 99-83 (1985), which allowed funding to be cut off to countries that supported terrorism
- Omnibus Diplomatic Security and Antiterrorism Act (1986), which expanded the jurisdiction of the FBI to overseas when investigating acts of terrorism against U.S. citizens abroad or at home [19]

Two of the most important pre-9/11 antiterrorist laws were passed during the Clinton administration. The Omnibus Counterterrorism Act of 1995 greatly expanded the role of the federal government over local and state law enforcement in investigating and prosecuting acts of terrorism, such as bombings, within the boundaries of the United States, and also expanded the U.S. jurisdiction overseas when committed against U.S. embassies. It also criminalized fundraising for groups defined as terrorist. It expanded federal law enforcement authority to use "pen registers" and "trap-and-trace" devices, which track telephone calls. It also gave federal law enforcement the power to seek a wide range of personal and business documents with "national security letters," rather than warrants, when investigating terrorism.

This Act was replaced by the Anti-Terrorism and Effective Death Penalty Act of 1996, which incorporated most of the provisions discussed earlier, and added others, such as expanding the authority of INS to deport accused terrorists and other resident aliens, and increasing the penalties for such crimes. The other part of the Act applied to all offenders, and changed habeas corpus protections, eliminating multiple appeals and removing legal barriers to executions [20].

Prior to 9/11, few of us were aware of this nation's counterterrorism laws and few citizens gave serious thought to the threat of terrorism. There were prior events that should have alerted us to the possibility of a major attack: the 1993 bombing of the World Trade Center, the attacks on the USS *Cole* and the attacks on U.S. embassies in Africa, and the stated aim of Osama Bin Laden to "cut off the head of the snake," meaning the United States and, more specifically, U.S. economic dominance in the world. Generally, however, the FBI was largely concerned with domestic terrorism. This focus was not misplaced given the tragedy of the Oklahoma City bombing carried out by Timothy McVeigh and Terry Nichols, and the presence of other radical groups that still exist and have expressed and indicated a willingness to use violence to advance their goals.

In the aftermath of the terrorist attacks on September 11, 2001, Congress enacted the USA PATRIOT Act to combat terrorism and created the Homeland Security Council, and then later the Department of Homeland Security. These two actions have had tremendous consequences for the organization and powers of investigative and justice agencies in the United States. We will discuss the USA PATRIOT Act first and then the Department of Homeland Security.

USA PATRIOT Act

On October 11, 2001, the 107th Congress enacted Public Law 107-56, which is titled Uniting and Strengthening America by Providing Appropriate Tools Required to Intercept and Obstruct Terrorism Act. This Act is known as the **USA PATRIOT Act** of 2001. The purpose of the Act is to deter and punish terrorist acts in the United States and around the world, to enhance law enforcement investigatory tools, and for other purposes. Provisions that were expressly rejected by Congress in the earlier laws were added in the PATRIOT Act. The numerous sections of the Act are included under 10 titles as set out in Box 15.2.

BOX 15.2 USA PATRIOT ACT

Title I—Enhancing Domestic Security against Terrorism

- Amends Posse Comitatus Act
- Enhances president's power to confiscate property and assets

Title II—Enhanced Surveillance Procedures

- Eliminated restrictions on and expanded federal surveillance practices
- Eliminated barrier between domestic and international investigations
- Expanded use of pen register and trap-and-trace devices
- Relaxed rules on obtaining warrants

Title III—International Money Laundering Abatement and Antiterrorist Financing Act of 2001

- Required banks to create antilaundering procedures and audit functions
- Expanded reporting mechanisms for suspicious transactions

Title IV—Protecting the Border

- Increased the number of border security agents
- Improved monitoring capabilities

Title V—Removing Obstacles to Investigating Terrorism

- Created domestic rewards for information leading to terrorist capture
- Relaxed rules of no communication between domestic crime and international investigations of terrorism
- Relaxed requirements for obtaining National Security Letters from "specific and articulable evidence" to "relevant"
- Removed any rights of terrorists to have privacy over DNA or records

Title VI—Providing for Victims of Terrorism, Public Safety Officers, and Their Families

- Expedited processes for obtaining aid for victims and their families

BOX 15.2 USA PATRIOT ACT—CONT'D

Title VII—Increased Information Sharing for Critical Infrastructure Protection

- Increased the number of eligible participants in federal grants for information sharing

Title VIII—Strengthening the Criminal Laws against Terrorism

- Included acts of terrorism and assisting terrorists in the federal criminal code
- Made the act of providing funds to terrorist organizations a crime
- Removed statute of limitations for some crimes
- Further delineated cybercrimes

Title IX—Improved Intelligence

- Reiterated removal of the "wall" between investigations of international terrorists and domestic criminals
- Set priorities for national intelligence mission and policies

Title X—Miscellaneous

- Defined critical infrastructure components
- Addressed fraudulent charitable solicitations
- Prohibited anyone involved in money laundering from entering the country

---

Title VIII of the Patriot Act, Strengthening the Criminal Laws Against Terrorism, revised Chapter 113B, titled Terrorism in the United States Code. The earlier chapter included criminal penalties for a series of acts relating to terrorism, including: use of weapons of mass destruction, acts of terrorism transcending national boundaries, financial transactions, providing material to terrorists, and providing material support or resources to designated foreign terrorist organizations.

Title 18 U.S.C. § 2331, as it existed prior to the PATRIOT Act, defined international terrorism as activities that "involve violent acts or acts dangerous to human life that are a violation of the criminal laws of the United States or of any State, or that would be a criminal violation if committed within the jurisdiction of the United States or of any State" and that appear to be intended to do one or more of the following:

(i)   To intimidate or coerce a civilian population;
(ii)   To influence the policy of a government by intimidation or coercion; or
(iii) To affect the conduct of a government by assassination or kidnapping; and
(C)   Occur primarily outside the territorial jurisdiction of the United States, or transcend national boundaries in terms of the means by which they are accomplished, the persons they appear intended to intimidate or coerce, or the locale in which their perpetrators operate or seek asylum.

The PATRIOT Act amended § 2331 of Title 18 to include "by mass destruction, assassination or kidnapping" as one of the acts that constitutes terrorism. In addition, "domestic terrorism" was included and defined as those acts "dangerous to human life that are a violation of the criminal laws of United States or of any State and that appear to be intended to do one of the following:

(i)   To intimidate or coerce a civilian population;
(ii) To influence the policy of a government by intimidation or coercion; or
(iii) To affect the policy of a government by mass destruction, assassination, or kidnapping; and
(C)   Occur primarily within the territorial jurisdiction of the United States.

Section 2332b is titled Acts of Terrorism Transcending National Boundaries. This section expanded the concept of terrorism to include the actions of individuals who attack Americans outside of the boundaries of the United States. This expansion allowed for the prosecution of John Phillip Walker Lindh, who was charged under this Act with conspiracy to murder nationals of the United States, including American military personnel and other government employees serving in Afghanistan. He was not convicted of violating the statute, but was found guilty of other offenses [21].

Title 18 U.S.C. § 2339A, Providing Material Support to Terrorists, provides that whoever, within the United States, provides material support or resources or conceals or disguises the nature, location, source, or ownership of material support or resources, knowing or intending that they are to be used in preparation for carrying out a violation of the sections indicated, or in preparation for, or in carrying out, the concealment or escape from the commission of such violations, shall be fined under this title, imprisoned not more than 10 years, or both. This section was amended by the USA PATRIOT Act by striking out "within the United States" and by adding sections of the law covered by the Act. The effect of deleting "within the United States" makes the provisions enforceable when the acts described occur outside the United States.

Title 18 U.S.C. § 2339B, Providing Material Support or Resources to Designated Foreign Terrorist Organizations, was amended in part by the PATRIOT Act to include the idea that foreign terrorist organizations were defined by the federal government, specifically the President, and an individual who contributed money to such an organization for its charitable activities would still be guilty of violating the law and subject to a long term of imprisonment.

The other elements of the PATRIOT Act that have been controversial are those that expand federal powers of investigation. Title II, Enhanced Surveillance Procedures, substantially changed the provisions of the FISA described earlier. Specifically, the Act lowered the standard required to obtain permission to use surveillance against suspects; roving wiretaps were authorized that allowed agents to tap any phone the suspect might use; further, pen registers were allowed that followed any phone number called by the suspect. The PATRIOT Act also authorizes law enforcement agencies charged with investigating terrorism to share investigative information with domestic law enforcement investigators and vice versa.

In summary, some of the provisions that are most controversial include:

- Expanding the range of crimes trackable by electronic surveillance
- Allowing the use of roving wiretaps to track any phone a suspect might use
- Allowing the "sneak and peek" search (not notifying suspects of searches)
- Allowing federal warrants to search records with less than probable cause
- Lowering barriers of information sharing between domestic and international investigations
- Creating new tools for investigating money laundering (by requiring banks to file reports on suspicious behaviors)

On March 7, 2006, Congress approved the renewal of the USA PATRIOT Act. Most provisions of the Act were made permanent. The bill also created a national security division in the Department of Justice [22]. Three provisions of the Act were set to expire in 2010, but Congress voted to extend them and President Obama signed the bill in February 2010. The provisions were as follows:

- "Lone wolf" provision: allows federal agents to track and investigate a suspect with no discernible affiliation with known terrorist groups or foreign powers.
- "Business records": allows investigators access to suspect's records (i.e., telephone, financial) without his or her knowledge.
- "Roving wiretaps": allows agents to monitor phone lines or Internet accounts used by a suspect even if owned or also used by others (must receive FISA authorization).

Generally, the public has been supportive of the USA PATRIOT Act. In 2003, only 28% of those polled believed that it gave the government too much power over individual liberties, and 51% believed that people had to give up some individual freedom to fight terrorism [23].

The Department of Homeland Security

Nine days after 9/11, President Bush created the Homeland Security Council and a cabinet-level position was created called the Homeland Security Advisor, with Tom Ridge appointed to fill the position. Then, in March 2003, the Department of Homeland Security was created with the mission to prevent terrorist attacks within the United States and to minimize damages from any attacks. The Department of Homeland Security consolidated 22 federal agencies and more than 180,000 federal employees under one umbrella agency. It had a budget of $30 billion in 2005 and $31.4 billion in 2006 [24]. The requested budget allocation for 2011 is $56.3 billion! Funding increases are directed to initiatives such as advanced imaging technologies ($214 million), transportation security officers ($218 million), behavior detection officers ($20 million), domestic

 **INTERNET KEY**

To read about the Department of Homeland Security 2011 budget request, go to http://www.dhs.gov/ynews/releases/pr_1265049379725.shtm.

nuclear detection office systems engineering and architecture ($13 million), Secret Service information technology ($36 million), border enforcement security task forces ($10 million), intelligence analysts ($10 million), and national cyber security division ($379 million).

The major impetus for the agency was 9/11 and the finding that one of the reasons the terrorists were able to accomplish their goal was poor communication among the FBI, the Central Intelligence Agency (CIA), and the Federal Aviation Administration (FAA). For instance, while the CIA knew that two of the hijackers had attended Al Qaeda meetings in the Middle East, the FBI knew (or at least a field office knew) that several of the hijackers were acting suspiciously by taking flying lessons. Together, those bits of information might have been enough to prevent the disaster [25].

While the CIA is not one of the agencies that has been merged into the Department of Homeland Security, the idea of a national intelligence center is at the heart of the effort, and the CIA director is no longer the titular head of the U.S. intelligence function, as that role has shifted to the Department of Homeland Security. The Immigration and Naturalization Service was dismantled and the functions distributed to two agencies, U.S. Immigration and Customs Enforcement (ICE), and the U.S. Customs and Border Protection Agency, which also subsumed and redistributed the functions of the Border Patrol and U.S. Customs. The Customs and Border Protection Agency has about 40,000 employees; together, the two agencies employ 55,000 people.

We have all felt the effects of the nation's efforts to prevent terrorism. Travelers endure searches and, more recently, body scans, and a constant revision of rules concerning what can be carried onto airplanes. The national threat alert system is a routine part of news broadcasts, although whether people pay any attention to them is another matter. The vigilant efforts have met with success because there has not been a single successful terrorist incident within the borders of the country. Since 2001, nearly 200 suspected terrorists or associates have been charged with crimes and, according to authorities, 100 terrorist plots disrupted [26]. In May 2010, a potential bombing effort in Times Square was thwarted by vigilant street vendors who alerted police. In December 2010, a Somali-born U.S. citizen was caught when undercover officers posed as fellow terrorists. He thought he was going to detonate a bomb at a tree-lighting ceremony in Portland's Pioneer Courthouse Square, but the explosive was a dummy and his supposed confederates were really FBI agents. This was the second such undercover operation that same year and speaks to the ever-present reality that such bombings are a real and present danger.

Other responses to terrorism

In addition to the PATRIOT Act and the creation of the Department of Homeland Security, the United States has been involved in other actions in response to the threat of terrorism. The wars in Afghanistan and Iraq are beyond the scope of this book, but some of the controversial decisions of the Bush administration are extremely relevant to the system of criminal justice because they illustrate the centrality of law in our lives. Issues such as detaining "enemy combatants," limiting habeas corpus, the use of torture (or "extreme" interrogation techniques) during interrogation, and conducting wiretaps without court orders are legal issues, and our earlier discussion of due process is directly relevant.

For instance, in 2006, a controversy arose after it was revealed that federal officers had been using wiretaps without warrants. A presidential order signed in 2002 allowed the National Security Agency to monitor international telephone calls and international e-mail messages of thousands of people inside the United States without first obtaining a warrant. The concern expressed by opponents of the practice is that the National Security Agency has traditionally been involved in investigations external to the borders of the United States and that the FISC has hardly ever turned down a government request for a warrant when asked for one. The 1978 law that created the court has been interpreted to bar all domestic wiretapping, even for national security, unless it is sanctioned by a warrant, and the secret court was created to grant such warrants. On the other hand, the administration's position is that Congress authorized the president to take any and all steps required to combat terrorism in the wake of 9/11 [27]. Congress passed the Protect America Act of 2007, which was an amendment to the FISA. It basically removed any culpability for wiretapping that had occurred before its passage, but mandated that any future wiretapping of citizens would require authorization from the FISC. It removed the warrant requirement for noncitizens and those outside of the United States. It also protected the telecommunications companies that assisted the government in accessing private accounts from any civil liability.

Other crimes

Narcoterrorism refers to the pattern of terrorist groups to use narcotics to fund their activities. Since 9/11, several major drug raids have uncovered ties between drug dealers and terrorist groups, such as Hezbollah. Opium from Afghanistan, although condemned by the Taliban, is now believed to be one of the largest sources of funding for Al Qaeda. Reports indicate that Mexican drug cartels may be engaged in business arrangements with Islamic terrorists, sending their "soldiers" to be trained and, in return, allowing terrorists to utilize their drug smuggling routes to secretly enter the United States. Protecting our

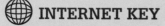

INTERNET KEY

To read about the United Nations efforts to control international drug smuggling and other crimes, go to the Web site for the United Nations Office on Drugs and Crime at http://www.unodc.org/.

borders has now become an issue, not only of drugs, but also the entry of individuals who have the sole goal of doing harm to American citizens.

Even without the threat posed by Mexican drug cartels working with terrorists, these criminal organizations have been and continue to be a problem. Mexico and the other Central and South American countries they call home have major challenges ahead in trying to fight the cartels, which have amassed great financial resources; in fact, the wealth of the cartels rivals the GNP of some small countries and their tentacles reach into the business world and governments of several countries. The cartels are not only a problem for these countries; the United States must consider them a crime problem as well. In addition to being the major provider of illegal drugs in this country, they also bring violence. Border states in the United States now are beginning to see the violence spilling over as potential victims of the cartels try to escape into the United States.

Human trafficking is another type of crime that is worldwide in its operations, but is also a problem for law enforcement in every major city in the United States. The Focus on Crime box describes this international crime in more detail.

FOCUS ON CRIME: HUMAN TRAFFICKING

It is estimated that 600,000 to 2 million people are trafficked internationally each year. In many cases, there is a "willing" person who agreed to illegally enter this country for some type of work, but once they arrive, they are held in jail-like conditions and work (typically in agriculture or food service) in various forms of debt bondage. In other trafficking cases, women are brought into the country to work as virtual sex slaves in brothels. Estimates are that 50% of trafficked persons are minors. While the victims of domestic, restaurant, and farm labor trafficking probably exceed the numbers of those trafficked in the sex industry, the most attention has been focused on this type of trafficking. The Department of State indicates that approximately 14,500 to 17,500 victims are trafficked into the United States every year, although other sources estimate that 50,000 victims are trafficked into the country each year. A recent Bureau of Justice Statistics report that presented the number of reported trafficking investigations between 2007 and 2008 in the United States indicated that 90% of the victims were women or girls. Desperately poor women, trapped in economic and social conditions that provide no means or oppor-

tunities to improve their life, are promised money, or their families are promised money for their services. Researchers note that traffickers also may promise marriage or false job opportunities. Traffickers also resort to kidnapping or actually buying the victim. The majority of victims seem to come from Southeast Asia, Central America, and Eastern Europe. If these women and girls are returned to their own countries, they are subject to shame and ridicule for returning home after their parents have obtained money for their services, and/or when they have been given away as a wife in return for a bride price. If these women or girls have been prostituted, they may not be able to return to their villages because of shame and real danger of punishment for the loss of their virginity. They face extreme challenges and hurdles in adjusting and adapting to the demands they face even if they are rescued from a trafficking situation.

Some estimates indicate that half of all trafficked victims who are brought into the United States are brought for sex trafficking. Women and girls are brought into this country illegally and then are transferred across the country to a series of brothels. The constant movement keeps them

FOCUS ON CRIME: HUMAN TRAFFICKING—CONT'D

disoriented and prevents customers from becoming curious about where a woman comes from or how she came to be in this country. The victims have no identity papers, do not speak English, and are constantly threatened with beatings, rapes, and exposure to immigration authorities who, traffickers warn, will put them in prison. Although sex trafficking has received the greatest press in recent years, it should be noted that the problem of domestic servitude and labor trafficking is also widespread and may, ultimately, involve even more victims than sex trafficking. Advocates worry that the constant attention to sex trafficking masks the problem of other forms of involuntary labor.

In 2000, Congress passed the *Victims of Trafficking and Violence Protection Act of 2000* (VTVPA), which created or revised federal crimes targeting traffickers, including "human trafficking," "sex trafficking of children," "document servitude," and "forced labor." The Act also increased the penalties associated with these crimes. The VTVPA created agencies designed to combat trafficking both internationally, by identifying problematic countries, and domestically,

by supporting task forces between federal and state agencies so that investigation and prosecution can occur more smoothly. One of the problems with state investigations of trafficking is that victims are afraid of being deported so the T-visa is used, along with other avenues, to keep the victim in this country in order to assist law enforcement and prosecution and, in some cases, the victim is granted a permanent visa in return. Trafficking is not easy to investigate or prosecute, however, and there are relatively few successful cases when compared to the scope of the problem.

Sources: *J. Pollock, V. Hollier, T visas: prosecution tool or humanitarian response? Women Crim. Just. 20(1) (2010) 127-146; S.T. Green, Protection for victims of child sex trafficking in the United States: forging the gap between U.S. immigration laws and human trafficking laws, U.C. Davis J. Juv. Law Pol. 12 (2008) 309-379; K. Hyland, Protecting human victims of trafficking: an American framework, Berkeley Women's Law J. 16 (2001) 29-70; T. Kyckelhahn, A. Beck, T. Cohen, Characteristics of Suspected Human Trafficking Incidents, 2007-2008, Bureau of Justice Statistics, U.S. Department of Justice, Washington, DC, 2009.*

Other crimes, such as money laundering, fraud, identity theft, and other financial crimes, are sometimes international in scope. Bernie Madoff's ponzi scheme, uncovered in 2008, preyed on victims in other countries as well as the United States. The federal government has investigated foreign bank involvement in income tax evasion by American citizens. Often, identity theft rings steal information in the United States to be used by criminals in Africa or Eastern Europe. Other crimes include arms smuggling, counterfeiting, cyberhacking, and corporate espionage. The Russian mafia, Japanese yakuza, as well as the drug cartels, have joined older organized crime organizations in this country, and American law enforcement agencies, especially those in large cities, must respond.

🌐 INTERNET KEY

To read an "International Crime Threat Assessment," go to http://www.fas.org/irp/threat/pub45270intro.html.

THE GLOBAL BECOMES LOCAL

Local law enforcement has obviously been greatly affected by the challenge of terrorism. As we all know, the first responders to a terrorist attack such as 9/11 are local and state public servants. Firefighters and police officers were the first to respond to the attacks on the World Trade Towers and the Oklahoma City federal building, and among those who died.

Since 9/11, more resources have been directed to **first responder training.** This type of training gives law enforcement officers the skills to approach, engage, and coordinate responses to major threats, such as terrorist actions. Local police, especially those in major metropolitan areas, must assume that they will be first responders when targets of terrorist attacks are located in their city. Bridges, buildings, schools, transportation, sports complexes, other venues where there are large crowds, and nuclear reactors and power plants are the likely targets of terrorists. Actually, there are a wide range of targets that might be vulnerable to terrorist attacks. In addition to those already mentioned, the water supplies of major cities can be contaminated with toxic agents, the banking industry can be immobilized by computers, the nation's ports can be blocked with explosions, or the nation's oil and gas supplies can be sabotaged—bringing to a standstill industry, commerce, and basic services. Federal agents are unable to protect all these targets. Police are the first line of defense, both in terms of preventive observation and surveillance, as well as response and intervention.

One of the biggest challenges has been to improve the communication between local law enforcement intelligence and federal Homeland Security personnel. Local law enforcement officials complain that the communication pattern tends to go one way only when they are expected to collect intelligence for federal agencies, but are not informed of threats in their jurisdiction. The lack of communication between the CIA and the FBI has been widely cited as one of the reasons that the 9/11 plot was not discovered and prevented, but the wider problem is the complete lack of any coordinated information sharing among the 20,000 law enforcement agencies and the Department of Homeland Security. This not only affects their ability to deal with terrorist threats, but indeed affects law enforcement response to all international crimes as well.

State and local law enforcement are now receiving more resources to address these new responsibilities. For instance, civilian analysts may be employed by state and metropolitan police agencies. These analysts track and analyze information that might lead to uncovering terrorist plots. Joint task forces between local and federal agents have also been funded. State antiterrorism agencies have also been created to coordinate local law enforcement agencies in the state.

It is clear that despite the importance of state and local law enforcement in preventing future terrorism and investigating and capturing sophisticated international criminals, at present they may not have the training or resources to be as effective as they might be. Their arsenal of weapons may not even match that of a well-armed militia group, the surveillance equipment may be inadequate to monitor suspected terrorists, and their communication networks may be deficient. Further, local officers may not be trained to investigate even domestic cybercrime, much less terrorists who use cybertactics. Further, local agencies may not have the expertise to investigate, or training to recognize, biological threats, or even forensic accountants to track international money laundering.

Local law enforcement has also been faced with difficult decisions in balancing their investigative activities against individual liberties. Federal law enforcement has sometimes taken aggressive actions in response to the threat of terrorism, especially in regard to Muslim residents and individuals of Middle Eastern descent. Immediately after 9/11, more than 5000 resident aliens were detained without charges. Many were subsequently deported for minor immigration violations. Those who were released alleged that they were subject to illegal detention and abuse during their imprisonment. The FBI also asked local law enforcement agencies to conduct surveillance and/or question Muslims and foreign residents without any reason other than their nationality or religion. The Portland, Oregon, Police Department gained notoriety when they refused the FBI's request that they conduct interviews with all foreign students in the area. Portland police supervisors thought that they had no authority to do so because the FBI did not articulate any reasonable suspicion, the questions were in areas that were constitutionally protected, such as their religion, and did not relate to criminal matters [28].

Racial profiling was held to be unconstitutional when it is used as the only element in a decision to stop a minority as a suspect in drug crimes. After 9/11, however, racial profiling of Middle Eastern-looking men was used by airline employees, federal agents, and local law enforcement officers, and continues to lead to greater scrutiny of this group of travelers. Federal guidelines clearly condemn the use of racial profiling *except* for investigations involving terrorism or national security [29].

Another area of controversy between federal and local law enforcement is the enforcement of immigration laws. Some cities and their police departments have refused to notify federal authorities when they may have reason to believe victims or witnesses of crimes are violators of immigration laws. Police departments that refuse to be the enforcers of federal laws argue that their role is domestic and involves only local security and crime fighting. These so-called sanctuary cities basically respond to crime victims or criminals, for that matter, without regard to any suspicion that the individual is an illegal alien. In the spring of 2010, Arizona passed a law that requires law enforcement officers to inquire about residency status if they have a reasonable suspicion that the individual is here illegally. Individuals are required to carry identification papers to prove their citizenship or legal residency. These provisions of the law were challenged in federal court as usurping federal powers and violating individuals' due process and equal protection rights (of Hispanic citizens who will be required to prove citizenship). The federal district court imposed an injunction against these provisions while the case is under review. The law has created a firestorm of controversy with both opponents and proponents arguing passionately about states' rights, civil liberties, and the problems illegal immigration creates, including the role it plays in other crimes. Several states are poised to pass their own laws if Arizona wins its court case.

In these examples, as well as many others, it is clear that local law enforcement is a vital element in protecting the United States against terrorism and other international crimes. The challenges faced by local and state law enforcement include attempting to respond to global threats with inadequate resources. Another challenge is to balance due process and civil liberties against security needs. Ultimately, how we balance these interests affects us all.

CONCLUSION

In this chapter, we have examined the concept of community. Criminology has long identified the community as a crucial element in crime causation. In our response to crime, we have swung back and forth between banishment and involving the community in correctional responses. Early forms of parole and probation were based on a belief that the offender should be in the community if at all possible. Older forms of justice involved the community in developing the response to offenders that would take into account the needs of the offender, the victim, and the community. Today, these programs are known as restorative justice.

There are such things as criminogenic communities—those where social capital is weak and the community is unable to utilize private and parochial controls on its members. These communities have high rates of incarceration, but also have high rates of poverty and a disproportionate use of governmental services, such as TANF. Because offenders will return to these same communities while on parole, probation, or diversion programs, it is essential to consider the community and not just the offender in any response to crime.

It is possible that the answer to international crimes like the drug cartels lies in the community as well. It is possible that prevention efforts, rather than the ever-increasing costs associated with interdiction and suppression, may be more cost effective and successful at reducing the cartel's power and bank accounts. Even conservatives are now beginning to consider the possibility that community treatment and harm reduction strategies may be more cost effective in the long run than the "war" analogy that has been used since the 1970s with little effect on the prevalence of drugs on the streets and the number of addicts in prisons. It is even possible that the community is the vehicle by which to combat terrorist threats. After all, it is important to remember that there is also the threat of domestic terrorists, and these individuals are born and raised in the communities of the South, the Northwest, and other regions of the country. They grow up and live in our communities and, for very specific reasons, decide that violence is an appropriate and acceptable response to their needs, in much the same way that an armed robber or a hired killer decides that violence is an acceptable solution. Even the Middle Eastern men who were "sleepers" and came from other countries spent years in this country, even raising families here. To what extent did the community affect them?

In this January 5, 2006, file photo, Jose Padilla, center, is escorted by federal marshals on his arrival in Miami. A federal judge rejected a motion by the alleged Al Qaeda operative to dismiss terrorism charges against him over claims that he was tortured in U.S. military custody. *AP Photo/Alan Diaz*

José Padilla, the citizen who was accused of being an enemy combatant, came from a poor Puerto Rican immigrant family. He was involved with gangs and had been in trouble with the criminal justice system since his youth. In fact, it is believed that he converted to Islam in prison. So, we come full circle. We see that the challenge of responding to the threat of terrorism is not unrelated to the challenge of responding to crime. It is not difficult to imagine that the threat of future terrorism may lie within our own cities and communities. Poor and disenfranchised citizens who do not believe that the great wealth and opportunities that exist in this country are available to them are prime subjects for indoctrination by those spouting anti-American rhetoric. An individual like José Padilla might, in a previous decade, have spent his life in and out of prison for "ordinary" crimes. Instead, he felt the need to travel to the Middle East to join a group committed to this country's destruction. How many more Padillas exist in the tenements, streets, lockups, and prisons of this country? What methods will we approve to prevent them from hurting us? Is it possible that strengthening communities, meeting the needs of victims and offenders, scrupulously adhering to the law and ideals of due process, and making it clear that everyone is a valued part of the community, regardless of what they have done, might help to prevent terrorists as well as criminals?

Review Questions

1. Discuss some of the programs or approaches that indicate the importance of community in the prevention of crime.
2. What is restorative justice and what are the principles behind it?
3. What are the four types of restorative justice sentencing programs?

4. What earlier examples of terrorism took place in this country and provide examples of the government's response?
5. What are the major controversial elements of the USA PATRIOT Act?
6. What is the FISA?
7. What major counterintelligence agency is not part of the Department of Homeland Security? What agencies do fall under DHS?
8. What are some examples of international crime?
9. What is human trafficking?
10. Why might "ordinary" crime prevention efforts also respond to the threat of terrorism?

VOCABULARY

habeas corpus an ancient due process right that protects individuals from the power of the government to hold them unlawfully or unfairly

mixed zones areas of a city where the functions of retail, residential, and commerce were mixed; these zones have high crime

Sedition Act made it illegal for anyone to express support for communism or other enemies of the country

social disorganization theory idea that indicators of social disorganization, such as lack of social "capital," are also indicators of high crime

tipping effect (of imprisonment) while some imprisonment reduces crime in a community, at a certain level, imprisonment seems to result in more crime in certain communities

USA PATRIOT Act of 2001 the purpose of the Act is "to deter and punish terrorist acts in the United States and around the world, to enhance law enforcement investigatory tools, and for other purposes"

ENDNOTES

[1] Bureau of Justice Statistics. Retrieved 9/5/2010 from ojp.usdoj.gov/bjs/glance/exptyp.htm.

[2] See, for instance, C. Shaw, H. McKay, Juvenile Delinquency and Urban Areas, University of Chicago Press, Chicago, 1942.

[3] See, for instance, R. Sampson, Local friendship ties and community attachment in mass society: a multilevel systemic model, Am. Sociol. Rev. 53 (1988) 766–779; R. Sampson, W. Groves, Community structure and crime: testing social-disorganization theory, Am. J. Sociol. 94 (1989) 774–802.

[4] M. Carey, Social learning, social capital, and correctional theories: seeking an integrated model, in: American Correctional Association, What Works and Why: Effective Approaches to Reentry, American Correctional Association, Lanham, MD, 2005, p. 9.

[5] R. Bursik, H. Grasmick, Neighborhoods and Crime: The Dimensions of Effective Community Control, Lexington Books, New York, 1993.

[6] M. Zatz, E. Portillos, Voices from the barrio: Chicano gangs, families, and communities, Criminology 38(2) (2000) 369–401.

[7] Reentry Policy Council, An explanation of justice mapping: three examples, 2005. Retrieved 12/30/2005 from www.reentrypolicy.org/report/justice-mapping.php.

[8] T. Clear, D. Rose, J. Ryder, Incarceration and the community: the problem of removing and returning offenders, Crime Delinq. 47(3) (2001) 335–351; T. Clear, D. Rose, E. Waring, K. Scully, Coercive mobility and crime: a preliminary examination of concentrated incarceration and social disorganization, Justice Q. 20(1) (2003) 33–64.

[9] T. Clear, D. Rose, J. Ryder, Incarceration and the community: the problem of removing and returning offenders, Crime Delinq. 47(3) (2001) 335–351.

[10] J. Lynch, W. Sabol, Assessing the effects of mass incarceration on informal social control in communities, Criminol. Public Pol. 3(2) (2004) 267–294.

[11] Reentry Policy Council, An explanation of justice mapping: three examples, 2005. Retrieved 12/30/2005 from www.reentrypolicy.org/report/justice-mapping.php.

[12] F. Schweigert, Moral and philosophical foundations of restorative justice, in: J. Perry (Ed.), Repairing Communities through Restorative Justice, American Correctional Association, Lanham, MD, 2002, p. 21.

[13] J. Braithwaite, Linking crime prevention to restorative justice, in: J. Perry (Ed.), Repairing Communities through Restorative Justice, American Correctional Association, Lanham, MD, 2002, pp. 55–66.

[14] J. Braithwaite, Linking crime prevention to restorative justice, in: J. Perry (Ed.), Repairing Communities through Restorative Justice, American Correctional Association, Lanham, MD, 2002, p. 85.

[15] J.A. Fagin, When Terrorism Strikes Home: Defending the United States, Allyn and Bacon, Boston, MA, 2006, p. 39.

[16] J.A. Fagin, When Terrorism Strikes Home: Defending the United States, Allyn and Bacon, Boston, MA, 2006, p. 51.

[17] D. Cole, J. Dempsey, Terrorism and the Constitution, Free Press, New York, 2002.

[18] R. Ward, K. Kiernan, D. Mabrey, Homeland Security: An Introduction, LexisNexis/Matthew Bender, Newark, NJ, 2006, p. 254.

[19] J.A. Fagin, When Terrorism Strikes Home: Defending the United States, Allyn and Bacon, Boston, MA, 2006, p. 57.

[20] J.A. Fagin, When Terrorism Strikes Home: Defending the United States, Allyn and Bacon, Boston, MA, 2006, p. 62.

[21] United States v. Lindh, 227 F. Supp. 2d 565 (E.D. Va. 2002).

[22] Cable News Network. Retrieved 7/4/2006 from www.cnn.com/2006/POLITICS/03/07/patriot.act/.

[23] Cited in J. Fagin, When Terrorism Strikes Home: Defending the United States, Allyn and Bacon, Boston, MA, 2006, p. 77.

[24] R. Ward, K. Kiernan, D. Mabrey, Homeland Security: An Introduction, LexisNexis/Matthew Bender, Newark, NJ, 2006, p. 68.

[25] R. Ward, K. Kiernan, D. Mabrey, Homeland Security: An Introduction, LexisNexis/Matthew Bender, Newark, NJ, 2006.

[26] Cited in Fagin, When Terrorism Strikes Home: Defending the United States, Allyn and Bacon, Boston, MA, 2006, p. 127.

[27] R. Ward, K. Kiernan, D. Mabrey, Homeland Security: An Introduction, LexisNexis/Matthew Bender, Newark, NJ, 2006, p. 254.

[28] Cited in J. Fagin, When Terrorism Strikes Home: Defending the United States, Allyn and Bacon, Boston, MA, 2006, p. 71.

[29] Cited in J. Fagin, When Terrorism Strikes Home: Defending the United States, Allyn and Bacon, Boston, MA, 2006, p. 305.

How to Write a Research Paper

You may be required to write a research paper; this appendix provides some guidance. Papers may range in length from 3 to 25 pages, so the comments below must be adjusted to fit the length of the paper assigned.

Choosing a topic. One of the most important steps in writing a good paper is choosing a topic. Luckily, in the field of criminal justice, there is a veritable wealth of topics to choose from that are interesting, current, and even controversial. You should try to discover a topic that is less typical; for instance, instead of the death penalty, you might do a cross-cultural comparison of the death penalty. If the paper is a small one, it is important to limit the topic. In fact, the easiest way to do that is to ask a research question: Do all states have the death penalty? Then, three to five pages will be sufficient to describe states' laws and differences between the states. You will not need to do a whole history, presentation of legal issues, and methods of execution for such a topic title.

For possible topics, you can look in your textbook table of contents, scan the book itself or even read the local newspaper for current, topical issues. Some possible topics (assuming an average length paper) are:

The extent of the use of juvenile waivers to adult court
Changes in school discipline and use of school safety officers
Television and its link to violence
Drug use among teens—is it going up or down?
Gun control research—does it reduce crime?
The CSI effect on criminal prosecution
The effectiveness of community policing
Methods to improve ethical behavior in policing
Issues in the use of tasers: legal issues, misuse, and effect on lethal force
The effectiveness of residential drug treatment versus outpatient treatment
The effectiveness of sex offender treatment

The need for gender-specific programming
Habeas corpus and recent Supreme Court decisions
USA PATRIOT Act's effect on law enforcement
Illegal aliens' involvement in crime
Issues of female police officers: performance and sexual harassment
The effect of domestic violence mandatory arrest policies
The causes of the crime decline of the 1990s
Community policing evaluations

These would all be too broad for paper lengths under 10 pages and so you would need to revise them. For instance, instead of looking at the effectiveness of drug or sex offender treatment in general, you might want to research one particular program or modality. Similarly, instead of a paper on habeas corpus in general, you may want to concentrate on two cases that deal with habeas corpus. The point is that you want to be able to present the issue or question and then comprehensively discuss it in the pages assigned.

Outline. The second step is to outline the paper, but if you don't know anything at all about your subject, you will need to do some research first. Today, the Internet makes research incredibly easy. You can use your library's online data search engine or, if you do not have access to one, you can use Google Scholar. Simply enter your topic and you will be able to access a number of academic journal articles on your subject. Remember that academic journals, not popular magazines, are usually required for research papers. Also, you may not be able to use "practitioner journals" such as *Corrections Today* or *Law Enforcement Digest.* Academic journals such as *Crime and Delinquency, Criminology, Justice Quarterly, Journal of Crime and Justice,* and *Prison Journal* are the most common sources for a research paper. Instructors seldom allow Wikipedia or other non-official Internet sources as acceptable bibliographic citations. Of course, you should also actually go to your library (remember that building?) and look for current books on your subject.

After finding several articles or books on your topic, read them and note the issues that are present in your topic. Certain themes, issues, or points, should become repetitive, and these will form the basis of your outline. Start your outline with an introduction section that explains to the reader what the paper is about and a short description of the topic. This section should be no more than one page (or paragraph for short papers) but it must be on the first page. Then, present the subtopics in some logical order. For some topics, it may be a chronology; for others, it may be that you present positive points, and then negative points. It is best to go from the general to the specific. Set your outline up in a document in a bold font and perhaps in a larger font size. The advantage of word processing is that you can cut out sections and move them around if you need to as the paper develops. At this point, it is wise to check with your instructor to make sure that the outline fits the requirements of the assignment.

Enter Notes. The next step is to enter your research notes. You should never copy from your sources! Generally, research papers are too short to include quotes anyway, so just resolve to write every word yourself. When you read the article, you should enter notes into the document under the appropriate boldface heading with a reference. See the example given later. Refrain from copying since when you begin to write, you will forget whether it is a quote or whether it is your sentence. Continue to enter in facts from the articles as you read them. Once all your references have been read and relevant facts entered, you can see where the gaps are in your outline. Then, you need to either go find that information from new sources or rearrange your outline to eliminate those topics or issues. The general rule of thumb is that you should have the ratio of one reference per page assigned, which means that for a 10-page paper you need 10 references and so forth.

Below you see an outline for a paper on probation where some beginning notes are filled in. You must have a complete reference citation for every fact entered as a note. Once your outline is filled in with notes, you can begin writing.

> The Use of Probation Today
> History
> > *John Augustus, Boston shoemaker, 1841 (reference, year)*
> Mission and Scope of Use
> Probation in State X
> > *State organization chart*
> Criticisms of Probation
> > *Slap on the wrist? (reference, year)*
> > *Percent of people who are in favor of it (reference, year, page number)*
> Future of Probation

Write the paper. If the paper is long, it is important to provide subheadings. These can be the outline headings. You should always have an introductory paragraph or page that explains what the paper is about, and a conclusion paragraph or page that basically identifies the few key points you want the reader to remember. Do not introduce new information in the conclusion.

Referencing your sources is very important, so as you take notes, make sure that you have a system for identifying where they came from. It is important to reference with an author, year, and a page number every time you use a number (i.e., the number in prison or the percentage of people who recidivate). You must also reference with a page number when you use a direct quote. For all general information, you may cite only to the author and year of the publication without a page number (but check with your instructor).

The most common reference citation style in criminal justice is the modified APA style. APA style manuals may be purchased and style sheets can be found on the Internet. Your instructor may provide a style sheet for you. Generally, the modified style puts the author's name, year, and page number (if necessary) in parentheses in the text. For instance, if I entered a fact from my note above and if I obtained the information from this textbook, it might read something like this:

> The "father" of probation was John Augustus, a Boston shoemaker. He asked the court to release an offender arrested for public drunkenness into his custody in 1841 (Pollock, 2011).

If I had used a direct quote or used a number from the source, I would need the page number as well.

> John Augustus eventually helped supervise 267 offenders (Pollock 2011, 31) [or (Pollock, 2011: 31)].

There are many ways to cite, however, so find out whether there is a particular citation style that you are required to use. Regardless of which style you use, you must be consistent throughout the paper.

Write the conclusion. The last step in writing is providing a good conclusion paragraph. Typically, you do not insert any "editorializing" in the body of the paper, but it is sometimes acceptable to insert your own opinions and conclusions in the final section of the paper. After writing your paper, it is very important to check it for grammatical errors and omissions in citations. Make sure that your references are complete and do not include any source as a reference that is not used in the text of the paper. In the checklist provided, you can see some of the most common writing problems. Make sure that you do not include them in your paper!

WRITING CHECKLIST
(These are the most common writing errors.)

1. Is there a beginning paragraph that explains what the paper is going to do and a concluding paragraph that summarizes the content?
2. Is there proper citation *in the text*? Is there a cite after the source author's name? Follow the assigned style or be consistent in your use of any standard style of citation.
3. Is there a citation for every fact that is not general knowledge? Are there citations *with page numbers* for direct quotes and any numbers or percents?
4. Are there any sentences copied from another source without quotes and/or without having a reference cited? Remember that even changing a word in a sentence is still considered plagiarism.

5. Are there any paragraphs that are longer than about a fourth of a typed page? If so, break them up into smaller paragraphs. Are paragraphs too short (less than three sentences)?

6. Are there any sentences that run on for more than three lines? If so, break up into two sentences.

7. Are there any Web pages used as references? If so, is the citation in the text the author's name (not the Web address), and does the reference at the end indicate the date you retrieved it from the Web site?

8. Are numbers spelled out in words if in single digits and displayed as numerals in double digits and above? Also, if a sentence starts out with a number, it must be spelled out.

9. Are affect (think "influence") and effect (think "consequence") used correctly?

10. Are verb "strings" correct? "They are running, walking, and singing," or "they ran, walked, and sang," NOT "they are running, walked, and sing."

11. Are verbs consistently in past tense or present tense? "He ran to the store and talked to the owner," NOT "He is running to the store and talked to the owner."

12. Are female/male (adjectives) and men/women (nouns) used correctly?

13. Is there no more than one quote per page?

14. Are any quotes that are over three lines long indented and single spaced?

15. Are all noun/verbs in agreement, depending on whether they are plural or singular?

16. Are there any "I" statements? (Typically, this is not appropriate in a research paper.)

17. Are there any conclusory or opinion statements in the text? (Typically, this is not appropriate in a research paper.)

18. Is research referred to appropriately in the text? Typically, one writes: "Smith (1987) in his research on prisoners…"; use of the title of the article or book is generally not appropriate.

19. Are law cases italicized or underlined with the citation provided?

20. If a secondary source is cited, is it appropriately referenced? An example follows: Smith, as cited in Jones, 1990: 40–41.

21. Are *were* and *where* used correctly?

Author Index

Note: Page numbers followed by *b* indicate boxes and *f* indicate figures.

423

Subject Index

Note: Page numbers followed by *b* indicate boxes; *f* indicate figures and *t* indicate tables.